*Ultim*
*DUB*
*Guide*

*This book, with 2500 entries, will entertain, inform and delight both visitor and Dublin-city dweller alike.*

It is more than a guide – it is quintessential Dublin.

All the basic information is here – on history, culture, art, music, people, parks, restaurants, places and characters.

The result of years of research, this book brings together, in a concise format, the wisdom, information and lore on every subject from A to Z relating to Dublin past and present.

*Easy to use – there are special maps for historic sites, places of entertainment, hotels, pubs, music venues and more.*

# Ultimate DUBLIN Guide

## AN A-Z *of* EVERYTHING

### BRIAN LALOR

*with illustrations by
the author*

## THE O'BRIEN PRESS
### DUBLIN

First published 1991 by The O'Brien Press, Ltd.,
20 Victoria Road, Dublin 6, Ireland.

10 9 8 7 6 5 4 3 2 1

Copyright text and illustrations © Brian Lalor
Maps © O'Brien Press, Dublin

British Library Cataloguing in Publication Data
Lalor, Brian
Ultimate Dublin Guide: an A-Z of everything
1. Dublin (Ireland)
I. Title
914.183504824
ISBN 0-86278-220-1

The O'Brien Press receives assistance from
The Arts Council/An Chomhairle Ealaíon.

Cover design: Steven Hope and Brian Lalor
Editing: Frances Power   Typesetting: The O'Brien Press
Printing: The Guernsey Press

# CONTENTS

*All entries are listed A-Z by their title*
*but major categories have been grouped*
*together on the following pages:*

## MAPS

[Words in SMALL CAPITALS in the text refer to
a separate entry for that item]

## About the Author:

Brian Lalor studied art and architecture in Ireland and England, and Classical architecture in Greece. He worked for five years on various international excavations in the Middle East and identified important elements at the Temple Mount in Jerusalem which had puzzled archaeologists for a century. His first book was a guide to Jerusalem, and later came books on Cork, Dublin and Dublin Bay, as well as a number of folios of etchings. Brian Lalor has exhibited etchings, watercolours and drawings internationally and as an author/illustrator brings an unusual combination of a documentary and aesthetic approach to bear on the subjects of his books.

# INTRODUCTORY NOTE

The geographic area covered by this guide is the urban and suburban built-up areas of contemporary Dublin, roughly corresponding to Greater Dublin. Locations of intrinsic interest outside the city, such as the Hell Fire Club in the mountains of Co. Dublin are also included, as are places further afield for the light which they shed on particular aspects of the earlier history of the area. For Georgian Dublin, with so few of its great houses accessible or furnished in the manner of the time, the mansions of the surrounding hinterland, Castletown, Carton, Newbridge and Powerscourt provide the missing ambiance as well as the contemporary landscaping, an integral part of the concept of eighteenth-century living. For the Early Christian period, of which scattered remains exist around Dublin, Glendalough provides an example of the isolation and scale of settlements in the Liffey valley. Further back into the Bronze Age and Neolithic times, the necropolis on the Boyne valley, particularly Newgrange, provides a context for the golden treasures displayed in the National Museum.

Virtually everything of interest in Dublin is well within a half hour's walking distance of College Green – the museums and art galleries, churches and historic buildings, restaurants and theatres occupy a concentrated area which allows much to be seen in a relatively short space of time. Outside the core of the city, the DART rapid transit system makes the entire circumference of Dublin Bay, with its concentrations of restaurants, nature reserves and historic sites as easily accessible as any other less distant quarter of the city.

For other parts of Dublin, not within walking distance, nor served by the DART, there is a comprehensive bus service, which outside rush hours runs smoothly and efficiently.

*For Deborah Weinstein*

**A**ARDVARK. In the company of sloths and armadillos this ant-eating creature from East Africa can be found in the NATURAL HISTORY MUSEUM where children throng on the weekends and on weekdays art students wrestle with the complexities and wonders of stuffed, skeletal and bottled examples of the entire animal world.

**ABBEY THEATRE**. See THEATRES.

**ACT OF UNION.** The Act of Union, which united Great Britain and Ireland under a single parliament based in London, was effective from 1801 to 1921 when the Irish Free State was established. Ireland had had a parliament since 1295, but its independence from London dated only from 1782. The Dublin parliament was, at best, a fairly unrepresentative assembly as elected members could be drawn only from the Protestant minority section of the population, Catholic or dissenter membership of either the British or Irish parliament being prohibited by the Penal Laws. However it was Dublin-based and the majority of its members had the welfare of the country at heart. After the rebellion of 1798 however, its loyalty to the British Crown was suspect, as was that of the evidently disaffected mass of the people, and the idea of parliamentary union was promoted by the British Government. The Act, by which the Dublin parliament – in an extraordinary act of folly – voted itself out of existence, was promoted by argument and by bribes of titles and money, a strategy which succeeded in carrying all those who wavered. The effect of the Union upon the economy of Dublin and of the country at large was to drain the country of resources and to deprive the city of the residence of those who wielded power. Conversely, the vacuum caused by the departure of the nobility and peers enabled a new and more democratic society to emerge. A more tangible effect of the Act of Union was the dramatic fall in Dublin house prices. No longer fashionable areas of the city, particularly those on the north side of the river and in the LIBERTIES, became slums and consequently developed into the wretched TENEMENTS which appalled contemporary commentators and provided rich background material for many Dublin writers.

**ADELAIDE ROAD, D2.** Nineteenth-century tree-lined street, just within the enclosure of the Grand Canal, which has an interesting mixture of late Georgian and Victorian architecture. The Donore Presbyterian Church built in 1840 forms a centrepoint to the street and a fine conclusion to EARLSFORT TERRACE, from which its elevated Ionic portico looks particularly impressive. Other religious buildings in the street are the tiny Lutheran Church of St. Finian, built 1863, where the services are held in German, and the Byzantine SYNAGOGUE of 1892. Opposite the Synagogue is a piece of Victorian extravagance, the Royal Victoria Eye and Ear Hospital, 1904, which is an amalgamation of the Ophthalmic Hospital, founded by SIR WILLIAM WILDE in 1844, with other specialist institutions. The Harcourt Street end of Adelaide Road was extensively developed during the 1970s but with the exception of St. James's House with its impressive glazed lobby, the buildings are mostly without character.

**AE, (George William Russell)** (1867-1935). The Renaissance man of the Irish Cultural Revival, AE followed a path of practical work as an agricultural economist and simultaneously occupied the role of mystic and seer, poet, painter and journalist. He edited *The Irish Homestead* from 1904 to 1923 and *The Irish Statesman* from 1923 to 1930. In his creative work he relied on a visionary approach, and in his painting he was influenced by French Symbolism, but managed to transform this decadence into an idyllic, child centred version of the CELTIC TWILIGHT. AE was a vastly influential figure between the turn of the century and the foundation of the Irish Free State. He then became disillusioned with the narrow Nationalist ethos of the country and left Dublin for London in 1933, rejecting, as he said, the 'half crazy Gaeldom growing about him'. There is a plaque on 84 MERRION SQUARE where he worked for many years, and on his home at 17 Rathgar Avenue. The NATIONAL GALLERY houses a representative selection of his paintings with such characteristic titles as 'A Spirit or Sidhe in a Landscape', and 'A Female with a Child by a Pool of Orchids'.

> I moved among men and places, and in living I learned the truth at last, I know I am a spirit, and that I went forth in old time from the self-ancestral to labours yet unaccomplished.

*(Inscription on AE's gravestone,* Mount Jerome, Dublin.)

**AGA KHAN TROPHY.** The principal show jumping award of the Dublin International Horse Show, held annually at the RDS, Ballsbridge, usually during August. In the Nation's Cup events, international teams of riders compete for this trophy presented by The Aga Khan, and made by Weirs, the Dublin silversmiths. Any team winning the event three years running can claim the trophy.

**AIDEEN'S GRAVE,** Howth Demesne. Monumental portal column in the rho-

*AE, George William Russell.*

dodendron grove of the Demesne. The capstone which has slipped from its supports weighs around 91,440 kilos (90 tons). There are approximately 1,300 Megalithic tombs in Ireland dating from around 200 BC of which AIDEEN'S GRAVE is one of the largest. Also called Fionn Mac Cumhaill quoit, the Aideen with which it is now associated died of sorrow after the death of her lover, Oscar, at the battle of Garva. SIR SAMUEL FERGUSON's poem, of the same name, is a sensitive evocation of the lives of these legendary figures.

*AJAX, HMS.* Royal Naval Guardship permanently stationed in Kingstown Harbour (now Dun Laoghaire Harbour) during the mid-nineteenth century. In February 1861 Captain John Mc Neill Boyd of the *Ajax* and three of his crew were lost while attempting to rescue the lives of seamen from the brig *Neptune* wrecked off the East Pier of Kingstown

Harbour. The Captain is commemorated by the Boyd Obelisk on the East Pier, DUN LAOGHAIRE, as well as by a statue in ST. PATRICK'S CATHEDRAL by Sir Thomas Farrell. A monument to the crew stands appropriately topped by a broken mast in Carrickbrennan Graveyard, MONKSTOWN.

**ALDBOROUGH HOUSE**, North Circular Road, D1. The designer of Aldborough House is unknown but it is in the manner of SIR WILLIAM CHAMBERS who designed the nearby CASINO at Marino for the EARL OF CHARLEMONT. Built between 1792 and 1798 at the extreme eastern limit of the Georgian city, Aldborough was the last great house of the nobility to be constructed in Dublin and in fact spent only a very few years as a residence, as its owner, Viscount Amiens Earl of Aldborough, died in 1801. Designed in the Palladian manner with three storeys and pavilions linked by curved screen walls, the house was noted for its painted interiors, but none of these survives. The orientation of the house, facing east, provides it with an unrivalled prospect of Dublin Bay and the Wicklow Mountains. By 1813 the house had become The Feinaglian Institute, a school run by Professor Gregor von Feinagle, an educational pioneer whose method of education specialised in training the memory. Aldborough House continued as a school until 1830 when it became an army barracks. Still a magnificent building, it is now owned by An Post and used as a storage depôt, but the gardens and estate which surrounded it have vanished under tarmac and housing. Bus 53 from Connolly Station.

**ALEXANDRA BASIN**, Dublin Port, East Wall Road, D1. The major mooring for large vessels in DUBLIN PORT, it was begun in the 1880s and not completed until 1931. The Basin is called after Princess Alexandra who visited Dublin in 1868, an honour it shares with Alexandra College. The two GRAVING DOCKS, where ships are repaired, open into the Basin and the older of these predates the Basin and is of considerable architectural interest. The Eucharistic Congress held in Dublin during 1932 brought some of the largest ocean-going passenger liners then afloat to Dublin Port, and these were berthed in and around the Basin – probably the greatest concentration of passenger traffic ever to disembark there in an area essentially used for freight. With the development of container traffic, the centre of the port has moved from Alexandra Basin towards the east, and major shipping now docks at Ocean Pier and at the Container Port constructed in the 1980s on reclaimed land. Access only by appointment.

**ALEXANDRA COLLEGE.** Established at EARLSFORT TERRACE in 1866 as Queen's College for the Education of Girls, it became Alexandra College in 1868 following a visit of the Princess of Wales, wife of the future King Edward VII. Demolished in 1972 when the school moved to the suburb of Milltown, the college pioneered the education of women in Dublin and campaigned for their admission to university, a goal which was achieved at TRINITY COLLEGE in 1903.

**ALL HALLOWS PRIORY.** Augustinian foundation, built in 1166 by Dermot Mc Murrough, King of Leinster, and granted to the citizens of Dublin at the suppression of the monasteries in 1534. It stood to the east of HOGGEN GREEN (now COLLEGE GREEN) and forms the site of TRINITY COLLEGE. No remnants of the Priory buildings survive.

**ALLEY, LANE, ROW AND YARD.**
While the principal streets of GEORGIAN DUBLIN reflected order in their planning and an aristocratic position in society for those after whom they were named – Dorset, Grafton, Marlborough, Molesworth and Sackville – the crooked streets and alleyways of the old Medieval part of the city reflect something altogether different. These names indicate the trades, associations and personalities of an earlier time and provide an intimate sense of the actual texture of life in those quarters of Dublin. They are of varying origin; the majority describe some activity associated with the place in question, others are corruptions. Two hundred years later, the Graftons and the Dorsets are still with us though others, such as Sackville (now O'Connell) have been changed. With the gradual replanning of the older areas, the alleys and lanes tended to disappear and their colourful names with them, but surprisingly many do remain and can be sought out in the back streets of any of the older neighbourhoods.

ALLEYS: Black Dog, Copper, Goat, Indian, Pye, Rapparee, Smock, Thundercut.
LANES: Beaux, Bumbailif, Cut Throat, Duck, Dunghill, Elbow, Fumbally, Love, Marrowbone, Mutton, Pinchgut, Rosemary, Sycamore, Tangiers.
ROWS: Cuckold, Cut Purse, Pudding, Skinners.
YARDS: Dog and Duck.

**ALLGOOD SARAH**, (1883-1950). Actress, born Dublin, she played in *Spreading the News* by Lady Gregory on the opening night of the ABBEY THEATRE 27 December 1904. Allgood acted widely abroad and toured Australia, the USA and England. She returned to the Abbey to play Juno in the first performance of SEÁN O'CASEY's *Juno and the Paycock* in 1924. SARAH PURSER's portrait of the actress hangs in the Abbey foyer.

**AMERICAN EMBASSY**, Pembroke Road, Ballsbridge, D4. Designed by John Mc L Johansen in 1964, this represents a pleasing anomaly amongst the many anonymous office buildings put up in Dublin during the past thirty years and possesses a clear and identifiable personality. It is circular in form, with an internal circular atrium which rises through the building to the roof. Externally the precast concrete screen is a modern interpretation of motifs from metalwork of the Bronze Age. A moat surrounds the Embassy, compounding the impression of a Celtic fortress rather than a contemporary consular office building. Bus 5, 7, 7A from Eden Quay, DART to Sydney Parade.

*AN TAISCE,* (The National Trust for Ireland). See *TAISCE, AN.*

**ANCIENT MONUMENTS.** Due to the intensity of occupation during historic times, nothing survives of prehistoric significance within the canals although artifacts have been excavated that indicate early occupation on the banks of the Liffey. Further from the city centre fragmentary remains exist and successful excavations have been conducted on DALKEY ISLAND and in Sutton, showing evidence of Neolithic and BRONZE AGE occupations. The probability is that the crossing point of the Liffey, which certainly had settlements around it by the Iron Age, was also occupied in earlier times. There is a number of fine portal dolmens around the outskirts of the city, in the Phoenix Park and AIDEEN'S GRAVE in Howth Demesne

**ANEMOMETER**, East Pier, Dun Laoghaire. This tiny building, probably designed by John Skipton Mulvany, represents architectural perfection in its proportions and stonework. Built in 1852 to house the mechanism invented by Professor Robinson of TRINITY COLLEGE which gauges wind speed and direction, it takes the form of an Egyptian mausoleum, reminiscent of those in MOUNT JEROME CEMETERY. Mounted on the roof is a metal pylon which bears the rotating vanes.

**ANGLING.** One of the most popular of urban leisure pastimes and still practised despite doubts about the purity of water in the Liffey and Dublin Bay. Eighteenth-century prints show anglers casting their lines along the quays, in fact few early views of Dublin are without their complement of fishermen. Angling on the river of the inner city is rare today, but upriver at Islandbridge and downriver at the Grand Canal Basin and on the BULL WALLS, or at DUN LAOGHAIRE HARBOUR anglers are to be seen at all times of day and throughout the year. Strangely, angling remains at the end of the twentieth century almost entirely a male preserve. See SPORT.

**ANGLO IRISH.** A term of considerable significance in Irish affairs from the seventeenth to twentieth centuries. Within the Anglo-Irish section of the population was to be found most of the administrative, legislative, intellectual, artistic and professional life of Dublin and the country in general. This situation was caused by the absurd prohibitions of the Penal Laws which prevented those of Catholic and, by implication, native Irish background from participation in the professions, parliament or the army. Distinct from the Anglo-Norman settlers who had no religious gulf to separate them from the native population, the Anglo Irish are essentially a Protestant people, descended from planters and adventurers of the Elizabethan and Cromwellian periods, as well as Huguenot refugees from France and Quaker refugees from England. Because preferment, landholding and education were, during the seventeenth and eighteenth centuries, largely in the hands of the Anglo Irish, virtually all the names of significance during the last three centuries in the life of Dublin, though not in the country as a whole, come from this Ascendancy stratum of society. Emasculated by the ACT OF UNION, and economically dissipated by the Land Acts of the late nineteenth century, and tragically diminished in numbers by the First World War and emigration, the Anglo Irish eschewed involvement in the politics of the emergent Nationalist state, voluntarily depriving this most vocal section of Irish life of its voice and a great deal of its power. There were of course notable exceptions to this lack of involvement, and the contribution of such as Lords Longford and Dunsany showed that taking a rigid Unionist political stance was not the only alternative. Despite reduced numbers and political invisibility, the Ascendancy contribution to Irish letters has not ceased to be of significance, providing some dissenting leaven to the more homogeneous concerns of the no longer submerged masses.

> We are one of the great stocks of Europe. We are the people of Burke; we are the people of Grattan; we are the people of Swift, the people of Emmet, the people of Parnell. We have created most of the modern literature of this country. We have created the best of its political intelligence.
> (*Senate Debate, 1925*, W.B.Yeats.)

In literary terms, Anglo Irish implies those Irish writers (the vast majority) whose mother tongue is English, as well as Irish writers of an Anglo-Irish cultural background.

*A Norman chess piece from Wood Quay.*

**ANGLO NORMANS.** A century after the Battle of Hastings at which the Norman-French barons from Normandy defeated the Anglo Saxons in 1066, their descendants, the Anglo Normans, landed at Waterford in 1168. Two years later they took the city of Dublin, until then a VIKING and briefly a Hiberno-Norse city. The first charter was granted to the city by HENRY II in 1172, prompted more by a desire to control the barons and prevent them from setting up a separate kingdom than out of any actual concern for the citizens of Dublin.

**ANNA LIVIA.** The LIFFEY, Ireland's only river to be personified as a female deity. *Abhann na Life*, the Irish name for the Liffey, was Latinised and appeared on maps into the middle of the nineteenth century as Anna Liffey. Her face may be seen among the fourteen Riverine Heads by EDWARD SMYTH at the CUSTOM HOUSE. It is in the central position on the southern façade facing the river.

**ANNA LIVIA FOUNTAIN,** O'Connell Street, D1. Erected to commemorate the DUBLIN MILLENNIUM in 1988 as a gift to the people of Dublin from the Jefferson Smurfit Group. The theme of the fountain by Eamon O'Doherty and Sean Mulcahy is the LIFFEY as personified by Anna Livia, the River of Dublin, which rises in the DUBLIN MOUNTAINS and flows down through the city to the sea. The architectural treatment of the fountain cleverly interprets the passage from mountain torrent to the wide reaches of the Bay, with the POWERSCOURT waterfall tucked into the external curve of the granite mountain. The figure of the river is a long and languid water nymph washed by the waters of the stream. This fountain has been the source of wry public comment and controversy, being dubbed by the city wits, 'The Floozy in the Jaccuzzi' and 'Anna Rexia', both extremely apt comments on this strange but successful personification of Dublin's river. See FOUNTAINS.

**ANNA LIVIA PLURABELLE.** The mother figure and personification of the Liffey in JAMES JOYCE'S *Finnegans Wake*. Joyce's archetype of the river as woman (*plurabelle-loveliest*) and generative force is characteristic of his sense of the unifying force of life and nature.

> My leaves have drifted off me. All. But one clings still. I'll bear it on me. To remind me of. Lff!

(*Finnegans Wake*, James Joyce.)

## ANNUAL EVENTS, FESTIVALS AND BANK HOLIDAYS.

JANUARY: 1 (BH), Aer Lingus Young Scientist of the Year Exhibition, RDS.

FEBRUARY: Dublin Film Festival.

MARCH: St. Patrick's Day Parade on 17 (BH), Feis Ceoil (Irish and classical music competitions), RDS; Good Friday(BH) and Easter Monday (BH), changing dates; Irish Motor Show and Irish Dog Show, RDS.

*Dublin Street carnival.*

APRIL: Dublin Grand Opera Society Spring season, Gaiety Theatre; Early Music Festival, RHK; RHA Summer Show, Ely Place.

MAY: 1(BH), Spring Show and Industries Fair, RDS.

JUNE: Music Festival of Great Irish Houses; Bloomsday (16); Dublin Street Carnival; Dublin International Organ Festival.

JULY: National Portrait Awards Exhibition, Arnotts, Henry Street; Rose Judging at St Anne's Park, Clontarf.

AUGUST: 1(BH), Dublin International Horse Show, RDS; Air Show, Baldonnel; Irish Antique Dealers Fair, Mansion House.

SEPTEMBER, Dun Laoghaire Festival; All-Ireland Hurling and Football Finals, Croke Park; The Liffey Descent (canoeing).

OCTOBER, 31 (BH), Dublin Theatre Festival; Dublin City Marathon.

NOVEMBER: Irish National Stamp Exhibition; Dublin International Indoor Horse Show, RDS.

DECEMBER: 26 (BH), Dublin Grand Opera Society Winter season, Gaiety Theatre; Tower Design Centre Art and Craft Fair, Pearse Street; Mansion House Art and Craft Fair.

**ANTIQUE SHOPS.** Individual antique shops are to be found all around the city and suburbs but the principal concentration of the trade is centred on FRANCIS STREET in the LIBERTIES. Here the complete gamut of taste, period, quality and condition can be found. At the CHRIST CHURCH end of the street is the IVEAGH MARKET, the city's only surviving flea market with a mixture of old clothes, junk and bric-a-brac, and stretching down from there to THE COOMBE the shops become more opulent and their contents more varied. One could outfit an entire period house in authentic decor from findings in this street alone, with everything from BOSSI fireplaces and family portraits for the staircase, to an eighteenth-century doll's house for the nursery. Prices range from the absurdly cheap to the vulgarly exorbitant, but the real fascination of Francis Street is the range of goods on display in some hundreds of stalls and minute shops packed into the former business premises and houses of the area. Radiating out from this street further antique shops are to be found in Christchurch Market and adjoining streets. Other centres are in POWERSCOURT TOWNHOUSE in South William Street, and across the Liffey on BACHELOR'S WALK and ORMOND QUAY.

*Just junk?*

**AOSDÁNA.** Academy of letters and the fine arts established by the government in 1981 and confined to the disciplines of literature, music and the visual arts with a maximum membership of one hundred and fifty. The initial running of Aosdána was administered by the ARTS COUNCIL, but in 1983 a sufficient number of members had been elected to the separate sections to enable the body to become self-governing, new members being elected by their peers, based on achievement and the existence of an already established reputation. Depending on members' individual circumstances, a bursary is available to run concurrently for five years. Membership of Aosdána is not confined to residence in Ireland but is restricted either to Irish birth or by contribution to the arts in Ireland. The

supreme level of the Academy, *Saoi*, was awarded to SAMUEL BECKETT and SEÁN Ó FAOLÁIN in 1986, and Patrick Collins in 1987. It is accompanied by a gold collar, the design of which is based on a Bronze Age torc.

**APOLLO.** Apollo was one of the twelve Olympian Greek gods, a symbol of masculine beauty and light, and also patron of the arts of music and medicine. Both BELVEDERE HOUSE and NEWMAN HOUSE have rooms of which a figure of Apollo forms the principal decoration, and this motif is in fact carried through in a set of bronze medallions of Apollo on the staircase handrails of Belvedere House. In the Apollo Room at Newman House a majestic figure of the god presides over the nine Muses, set in panels around the walls of the room.

**ÁRAS AN UACHTARÁIN**, Phoenix Park, D8, tel 772815. The official residence of the President of Ireland. Built in 1751 by the park ranger and amateur architect Nathaniel Clements, it became within a few years the residence of the Lord Lieutenant who acted as Viceroy. British monarchs from GEORGE IV onwards all stayed at the Viceregal Lodge, as did the three governors general of the Irish Free State, and Douglas Hyde when he became first President of the Irish Republic in 1938. The house was much altered and enlarged during the nineteenth century by FRANCIS JOHNSTON amongst others. Johnston was responsible for plastering over the brickwork façade which totally changed the external character of the house from Georgian to Regency. Áras an Uachtaráin contains some fine plasterwork on both original and additional ceilings brought from demolished buildings. No access. Bus 10 from O'Connell Street and 25, 26 from Middle Abbey Street to Phoenix Park.

**ARBOUR HILL.** Core of the old military quarter of the city. Collins Barracks, formerly the Royal Barracks, is the largest and oldest military establishment in Ireland, and one of the oldest in Europe still fulfilling its original function. Formed around a wonderful square of impassive granite buildings it was built in 1704. The Arbour Hill cemetery contains the graves of the leaders of the 1916 RISING. Bus 10 from O'Connell Street and 26 from Middle Abbey Street.

**ARCHAEOLOGY.** The principal concern of recent archaeology in Dublin has been with the considerable VIKING occupation and the remains of that civilisation which are to be found in and around the city. The mid-nineteenth-century discovery of an extensive Viking burial ground at ISLANDBRIDGE was the first important development to give substance to historical references to the Vikings other than chance finds during roadworks in the city. This find was accidentally made by workmen constructing the track for the Great Southern Railways. These burials with accompanying grave goods represent one of the largest Viking cemeteries to be discovered outside Scandinavia. Material from the Islandbridge finds is now on display in the NATIONAL MUSEUM. The absence of visible Viking remains other than burials was eclipsed by considerable architectural and documentary survivals from the Medieval period and it was not until excavations by the Board of Works in 1966 at DUBLIN CASTLE that tangible evidence began to emerge of the Viking city. Large-scale excavations, carried out by the National Museum around HIGH STREET, CHRIST CHURCH and WOOD QUAY during the early 1970s indicated that much physical information could be added to the Islandbridge finds. Sections of the tenth-century Viking city, considered by archaeologists to be the most important outside Scandinavia, were discovered. A substantial number of wattle dwellings, roadways, workshops, riverworks and quays was discovered in an excellent state of preservation and with a rich collection of domestic and craftsmen's artifacts. Regrettably, the important site of Wood Quay was earmarked by Dublin Corporation for the development of a series of Corporation offices, and due to shortsightedness on the part of the City Fathers the opportunity to preserve even a part of this remarkable site was lost. Led by Professor of Medieval History at UCD, FX Martin, with the support of scholars from Scandinavia and Europe, a campaign was launched to save Wood Quay from development. One of the largest protest marches ever held in Dublin was organised by the supporters of the archaeologists but the protests proved unsuccessful and the twin towers of the Corporation offices now stand on the site where the first Dubliners lived. A permanent exhibition of artifacts from the Viking excavations is on display at the National Museum.

**ARCHITECTS.** Despite the existence of significant monuments from the Medieval period in the form of the CATHEDRALS of CHRIST CHURCH and ST. PATRICK'S and the now vanished ecclesiastical foundations of abbeys and priories, their designers remain unknown. Shadowy figures from the Medieval period such as Nicolas of Coventry or Osbert the Quarryman are recorded but their relationship to the existing buildings is unclear. No architects of significance have come to notice prior to the seventeenth century, when with the import of Renaissance ideas of design and the stabilised political situation, a demand grew for formal new structures to be occupied by the institutions of the state. Architects trained in England or on the Continent continued to come to work in Dublin throughout the seventeenth and eighteenth centuries, and not until the establishment of the Dublin Society Schools (School of Architecture, 1765) were there any facilities for training available in Dublin. The first architect of consequence to work in Dublin was SIR WILLIAM ROBINSON, designer of the ROYAL HOSPITAL KILMAINHAM and MARSH'S LIBRARY and fast on his heels came the most important Irish-born architect of the eighteenth century, SIR EDWARD LOVETT PEARCE, whose masterpiece, the BANK OF IRELAND, is probably the single most important building in the city. JAMES GANDON followed with the major buildings of the late eighteenth century, the CUSTOM HOUSE, FOUR COURTS and KING'S INNS, and he in his turn was followed by many, perhaps the most interesting of which was FRANCIS JOHNSTON, a versatile and humorous creator of fine buildings. BENJAMIN WOODWARD was the star of the mid-nineteenth century, bringing Ruskinian Gothic to Dublin and also bringing to a close the era of dominant architectural personalities. JOHN HUNGERFORD POLLEN appeared briefly, leaving behind one eccentric masterpiece, the NEWMAN UNIVERSITY CHURCH, after which church building seemed to dominate Dublin architecture until the early twentieth century. Since the 1930s, MICHAEL SCOTT has been the most significant architect working in Dublin, and the BUSÁRAS and ABBEY THEATRE are examples of his spare Misian idiom, functional and well proportioned. Only in the 1980s has a love of materials and the use of adventurous

*Liberty Hall, the Custom House and Ha'Penny Bridge.*

shapes so prevalent in past centuries returned to Dublin's architecture, enabling a more satisfactory blending with the buildings of the past to take place.

**ARCHITECTURE.** The dominant architectural influence in Dublin today and for the last two hundred years has been the Georgian street plan and the concept of wide streets with regular rooflines and harmonious façades. This rational idea of city planning moved the city away from the old Medieval town surrounding DUBLIN CASTLE, which had lasted well into the seventeenth century, and enabled it to develop along entirely new lines on open ground. Three quarters of the city within the canals is organised along the principles established by the WIDE STREETS COMMISSIONERS and much of Victorian and post-Second World War development has followed the building lines of the Georgian architecture it replaced, allowing the spirit of the eighteenth-century city to prevail when in many cases no remnant of it actually survives. The principal set pieces of squares and public buildings are in most cases intact, but their surrounding fabric is much decayed or has altogether vanished. The nineteenth century produced no innovations to the already established Georgian concept, merely adding, extending and infilling, albeit in styles at considerable variance with the eighteenth-century idiom, but maintaining the same use of materials – brick, stone, slate and ironwork. Twentieth-century preoccupation with transport has led to an improvement in the communication arteries of the city at the expense of its architectural fabric, without a commensurate contribution to the sense of the city. The problem of how to adapt a city built for a slower pace of life to the demands of today puts continual pressure on the most vulnerable areas of the city and the Georgian character of Dublin is continually at risk. Some developments of recent years show an admirable trend towards the conservation of existing buildings of quality and the infilling of well-designed and sympathetic modern schemes. Despite the depredations of rebellions, civil war and neglect, Dublin's architectural character remains of great interest and its major buildings have admirably stood the joint tests of time and changing fashion.

**ARCHITECTURE OF THE TWENTIETH CENTURY.** The architecture of the 1890s and early twentieth century may be found under the separate headings of ART NOUVEAU, EDWARDIAN and ART DECO. The post-Second World War Modern Movement has not produced many buildings of great significance in Dublin, although from the 1960s onwards the volume of new developments has been quite considerable. Buildings which rise above the norm of the uninspired and are worthy of being considered as serious contributions to Dublin's great architectural heritage are alas very few indeed. North of the Liffey are the ABBEY THEATRE, the BUSÁRAS, the old Terminal at Dublin Airport, the FINANCIAL SERVICES CENTRE, and the PMPA Offices, Wolfe Tone Street. South of the Liffey significant buildings are the Bank of Ireland Headquarters, Baggot Street, the Berkeley Library in Trinity, Bord na Móna Headquarters, Baggot Street, the CENTRAL BANK, the RTE Radio Studios, Donnybrook, and the EBS offices on Townsend Street and Westmoreland Street. In the area of housing the number of schemes of significance is also few but some are fine contributions to the concept of inner city housing and worthy of notice. Among these in the public sector are THE COOMBE, Clanbrassil Street and Ringsend schemes and in the private sector three schemes by Dennis Anderson at Sydney Parade Avenue, Morehampton Road and Highfield Road, Rathgar, all of which show what is possible when an attempt is made to create communities rather than just build houses.

**ARDAGH HOARD**, National Museum of Ireland, Kildare Street, D2, tel 765521. The Ardagh Hoard of decorated silver and bronze objects was found during potato digging near Ardagh, Co. Limerick, in 1867, and is now in the NATIONAL MUSEUM OF IRELAND. The silver chalice (eighth century) is one of the supreme objects of Early Christian metalwork to survive and until the recent discovery of the DERRYNAFLAN chalice, it appeared to hold a unique place in the artistic remains of that period. The design is basically very simple with a large beaten silver bowl attached to a foot of a smaller diameter by an upright flange. But it is in the complex and minute decoration of the surfaces of the chalice that the remarkable nature of its craftsmanship becomes obvious, as well as the sheer abundance of materials used in its decoration. There are two principal ranges of decoration on the bowl, a band running beneath the lip and through the loops of the two handles, and below this band, four medallions. The upstanding flange is also profusely decorated. A smaller bronze bowl, similar in design, is also part of the Hoard as well as a group of brooches which suggest that the Hoard was hidden away for safety some time during the tenth century, probably as a result of the threat of Viking raids, and never recovered.

**ARDEE STREET**, The Liberties. Roque's map of 1756 gives this street as Crooked-Staff, presumably a reference in the descriptive terminology of the time to its path. It formed the south-eastern limit of the built up area of the eighteenth-century city. The Earl of Meath's town house, Ardee House, stood here at the junction with THE COOMBE. Built in 1719, it was demolished in 1943. No. 10 Ardee Street with its fine brickfront and granite archway is one of the last Georgian mansions of the area. It was the headquarters of Watkins, Jameson & Pim, whose famous brewery ranked second to Guinness in the 1880s. Though the house bears a plaque, it is threatened with demolition because of road widening plans.

**ARDILAUN, LORD, ARTHUR GUINNESS**, (1840-1915). A member of the wealthy Guinness family, owners

*The Ardagh Chalice, National Museum.*

of the brewery at St. James's Gate, and son of SIR BENJAMIN LEE GUINNESS who restored ST. PATRICK'S CATHEDRAL. Arthur continued the philanthropic work of his father and the Guinness family's remarkable contribution to the idea of responsible citizenship. Between 1874 and 1877 he virtually rebuilt The Coombe Hospital. In 1880 he donated ST. STEPHEN'S GREEN to the public, turning it into a public park. From 1815 the Green had been railed off and used as a private park by the residents of the square. Lord Ardilaun, by an Act of Parliament in 1870, had the park transferred to the Board of Works. Ten years later it was opened to the public after he had transformed it from an open field into a formal park with an ornamental lake. The statue of Lord Ardilaun by Thomas Farrell RHA, 1881, paid for by public subscription, stands on the west side of the Green. He is seated on a drawing-room chair gazing in the direction, appropriately, of St James's Gate.

**ARMS OF THE CITY OF DUBLIN,**
*Obedientia Civium Urbis Felicitas*
(Happy the city where citizens obey).
The earliest seal of the city of Dublin,
dating from the thirteenth century,
shows a miniature city under siege with
three towers being staunchly defended
by citizens armed with bows, and the
alarm being sounded by trumpeters. The
heads of decapitated enemies are shown
impaled over the main entrance – no idle
boast apparently, for this barbaric
method of dealing with malcontents was
still in use up to the seventeenth century.
The current version of the arms, which
dates from 1607, shows three gates, each
of which has turrets sprouting flames, a
reference to the continued vigilance of
the inhabitants. By this time the heads
had disappeared from the City Arms, if
not from practice. The current arms display the three gates within a crest
flanked by two gowned figures representing Justice and the Law, each bearing as well as their own particular
attributes, an olive branch, a sign perhaps of more civilised times. The City
Arms appear frequently on Dublin's
street furniture and can be seen decorating lamp posts, bollards, buildings, vehicles and in many other locations.

**ARMY HEADQUARTERS,** Black-
horse Avenue, D8, tel 771434. Designed
by JAMES GANDON in 1787 as the Royal
Military Infirmary, it became the British
Army Headquarters in 1913, and that of
the Irish Army in 1923. One of Gandon's
less known buildings, and a minor work
by comparison with the CUSTOM HOUSE
or FOUR COURTS, it is nonetheless an
attractive and finely detailed building
with a central block topped by a cupola
and pedimented side wings with all sorts
of characteristic Gandonian details. No
access.

**ARRAN QUAY,** D1. Characteristic
section of the Dublin quays, originally
laid out in 1680. These rows of brick-
faced houses, originally residences and
business premises facing the Liffey, are
an essential element in the character of
the city although some sections have
recently been demolished. ST. PAUL'S
CHURCH, 1835-7, breaks up the line of
the buildings with its dignified façade
and well proportioned cupola, a counter-
point to the more massive shallow dish
of the Four Courts' dome nearby. ED-
MUND BURKE was born in 1728 at No.
12, which like most of the historic birth
places of famous Dubliners has been
demolished.

**ART DECO.** After the political disturb-
ances of the 1920s, there was little architectural development within the city,
with the exception of the rebuilding of
O'Connell Street, but one quite remarkable example of Art Deco style which
has been well preserved is the Gas Company building in D'Olier Street. Designed by Robinson Keefe in 1927, it
remains, even at the end of the twentieth
century, one of the most distinguished
Modern Movement buildings in the city
and both within and without has fine
stylish detailing. Other examples from
the Art Deco period are the Bovril Building in Ringsend, the Carlton Cinema on
O'Connell Street and the sculptural bathing shelters on the North Bull Wall and
Clontarf Promenade. Burtons on Dame
Street, 1929, is another fine Art Deco
façade, but like the buildings on O'Connell Street detrimental changes have
been made at street level. In Rathmines
the Post Office by Howard Cooke, 1930,
is also of interest as are the Egyptian Art
Deco ESB buildings on the Fleet Street–
Bedford Row corner and the mosaic façade of the Grafton Street Bewley's.

**ART GALLERIES**. There are over fifty art galleries in Dublin, both public and private, the majority of which are located in a compact area south of the Liffey and all shades of current opinion in the visual arts find expression in their exhibitions. Historic art is shown in specialist private galleries and the principal state institutions – the CHESTER BEATTY, NATIONAL and HUGH LANE GALLERIES. With the exception of architecture and the decorative arts which thrived during the eighteenth and nineteenth centuries, the visual arts never reached the prominence which literature achieved in those times, despite the fact that there were many excellent artists working in the city. Insufficient patronage at home and the lure of Rome, London, Paris and Antwerp enticed many abroad who failed to return. Today a much healthier climate prevails and there can never have been as many artists and sculptors working in and around Dublin as at present. The bulk of what is shown in the Dublin galleries is the work of artists living and working in Ireland, both north and south. Local preoccupations and international trends mingle in the works on display and a strong tradition in landscape painting is evident as one of the more significant areas of the Irish visual art scene. Visual arts events such as ROSC, a quadrennial exhibition of the international *avant garde*, and the exhibitions at the DOUGLAS HYDE GALLERY, bring current work from Berlin, New York and Tokyo to Dublin, ensuring that the local art world remains in contact with the ideas of other countries and continents. The IRISH MUSEUM OF MODERN ART, established in 1989 at the Royal Hospital Kilmainham (RHK), will be developed as the principal national showcase of contemporary art. Admission to all galleries is free unless otherwise stated. Institutions like the National Gallery to which entrance is free, will occasionally charge admission for specific exhibitions. Virtually all Dublin art galleries are within walking distance of O'Connell Bridge, the ROYAL HOSPITAL and CHESTER BEATTY being the exceptions.

ANNABEL BOWEN GALLERY, 33 Kildare Street, D2, tel 611740. Specialists in nineteenth- and early twentieth-century Irish art, framing and restoration. Thur-Sat 12.00-1.00, 2.30-5.30.

ARNOTT'S GALLERY, Henry Street, D1. Occasional exhibitions at department store top-floor gallery. Venue in July for the annual National Portrait Awards Exhibition, an important survey of developments in the field of portrait painting in Ireland. Awards are made in various categories and the public are invited to select the most popular painting in the exhibition. Mon-Sat during shopping hours.

BERNADETTE MADDEN STUDIO, Haddington Road, D4, tel 686874. Exhibitions of batik hangings and fabric art at the artist's studio. By arrangement.

BOULEVARD GALLERY, Merrion Square, D2. Open air exhibition held on the railings of the Square opposite the National Gallery from midday every Sunday. The art ranges from the purely pretty to the accomplished and presents the viewer with a challenge in talent spotting.

CHESTER BEATTY LIBRARY AND GALLERY OF ORIENTAL ART, 20 Shrewsbury Road, D4, tel 692386. One of the world's finest collections of Oriental and European manuscripts, printed books, Japanese and Islamic art. Tue-Fri 10.00-5.00, Sat 2.00-5.00. See LIBRARIES.

CITY CENTRE, 23-25 Moss Street, D2 tel 770643. Arts centre which provides a venue for theatre, performance and exhibitions. Café overlooking the Custom House, Mon-Fri 10.30-5.30, Sat 11.00-5.00.

COMBRIDGE FINE ART, 24 Suffolk Street, D2, tel 774652. Long-established firm

*Private view.*

which shows landscape and hunting subject matter by contemporary artists. Mon-Sat 9.30-5.30.

CYNTHIA O'CONNOR GALLERY, 17 Duke Street, D2, tel 6792117. Gallery specialising in quality eighteenth- and nineteenth-century Irish art. Mon-Fri 10-5.30.

DAVIS GALLERY, 11 Capel Street, D1, tel 726969. Contemporary Irish artists and craftworkers shown in a gallery run by the artist Gerald Davis. Mon-Fri 11.00-5.00.

DOUGLAS HYDE GALLERY, Nassau Street entrance to Trinity College, tel 772941,

ext. 1116. Housed in a modern 'concrete and drain pipes' style two-storey gallery, the Douglas Hyde is the principal city centre venue in Dublin for contemporary Irish and international *avant garde*. Its programme includes visual art, lectures, performance and events. The gallery has a small art bookshop. Mon-Fri 11.00-6.00, Thur 11.00-7.00, Sat 11.00-5.00.

DUBLIN ART FOUNDRY, 3 Rostrevor Terrace, D2, tel 760690. Art foundry and exhibition of sculptors' work. By arrangement.

EUROPEAN FINE ART, 7 Lower Merrion Street, D2, tel 762506. Paintings, drawings and prints from Dutch, Flemish and Continental Old Masters as well as nineteenth- and twentieth-century Irish art. Mon-Fri 10.30-5.00.

GALLERY OF PHOTOGRAPHY, 37 Wellington Quay, D2, tel 714654. Dublin's only photograph gallery. Exhibitions of international and Irish contemporary photographers, posters and books on photography. Mon-Sat 11.00-6.00, Sun 12.00-6.00.

THE GEORGE GALLERY, 22 South Frederick Street, D2, tel 793429. Specialists in twentieth-century Irish art. Mon-Fri 10.30-5.30.

GORRY GALLERY, 20 Molesworth Street, D2, tel 6795319. Museum quality eighteenth-, nineteenth- and twentieth-century Irish artists. By appointment.

GRAPHIC STUDIO GALLERY, Cope Street, D2. tel 6798021. Attractive purpose-built gallery approached through an arch behind the Central Bank. It specialises in contemporary artists' prints and is the only gallery in Dublin with an extensive range of graphics. Mon-Sat 10.30-6.00.

*The Graphic Studio Gallery.*

GUINNESS HOP STORE, Crane Street, off Thomas Street, D8, tel 536700. Converted brewery building hosting major exhibitions of contemporary art, with adjacent GUINNESS MUSEUM. Mon-Fri 10.00-5.00, Thur 10.00-7.00. Bus 21A, 78, 78A from Fleet Street.

HQ GALLERY, Powerscourt Townhouse, South William Street, D2, tel 6797368. Highly sophisticated contemporary crafts by Irish and international artists, which include ceramics, fabrics, wood and metalwork. The Gallery is the showcase of the Crafts Council of Ireland comprising a retail outlet as well as a gallery, and runs a full programme of exhibitions throughout the year, changing every six weeks. Tue-Sat 10.00-6.00,

HUGH LANE MUNICIPAL GALLERY OF MODERN ART, Charlemont House, Parnell Square North, D1, tel 741903. Historic collection of nineteenth- and twentieth-century European art, the core of which was collected by SIR HUGH LANE and presented to the city in 1908. Originally housed in Clonmel House, 17 Harcourt Street, the collection was moved to CHARLEMONT HOUSE in 1933. Lane's intention was to establish a gallery of modern art, and the Municipal Gallery was the first institution in the British Isles established for the collection of contemporary work. Lane died in the sinking of the *Lusitania* in 1915 and thirty-nine paintings known as the 'LANE PICTURES', then in the National Gallery in London, became the cause of an ownership dispute between Dublin and London. W.B.YEATS'S poem 'The Municipal Gallery Revisited' describes portraits in the Gallery's collection, and the poet's association with their subjects, LADY GREGORY, SYNGE and other important literary figures. In the permanent collection of the Gallery, modern Irish and Continental schools are represented, to which have been added other bequests of SIR ALFRED CHESTER BEATTY, SIR ALFRED BEIT, and the Contemporary Irish Art Society. Restaurant and art shop in Gallery, also free seasonal classical music concerts, some of the best in the city, and art for children on Saturday mornings during the summer. Opening hours Tue-Sat 9.30-6.30, Sun 11.00-5.00.

IRISH LIFE EXHIBITION CENTRE, Lower Abbey Street, D1. Changing exhibitions of local and international art and graphics. The gallery space is available for hire. Mon-Sat shopping hours.

IRISH MUSEUM OF MODERN ART at the Royal Hospital Kilmainham. See MUSEUMS.

THE JAMES GALLERY, 7 Railway Road, Dalkey, Co. Dublin, tel 858703. Leading Irish artists of the present and past. Tue-Fri 300-10.00, Sat 3.00-6.00.

KELLY GREEN, 15 Heytesbury Street, South Circular Road, tel 539971. Small basement gallery devoted to Irish artist-craftworkers. Mon-Sat 10.00-6.00.

KENNEDY GALLERY, 12 Harcourt Street, D2, tel 751749. Sculpture and paintings by contemporary Irish artists displayed in the elegant first floor rooms of a Georgian building. The Kennedy Art Shop, the longest established in Dublin, has been dealing in artists' supplies for over a century. Mon-Sat 10.00-5.00.

*The Hugh Lane Gallery.*

KERLIN GALLERY, 38 Dawson Street, D2, tel 779179. *Avant garde* Irish artists, in sophisticated purpose-built gallery, the most impressive private gallery spaces in the city. Mon-Fri 10.00-6.00, Sat 10.00-5.30.

MALTON GALLERY, 23 St. Stephen's Green, D2, tel 766333. Gallery and bookshop devoted to Dublin subject matter with an attractive range of prints on local themes. A complete edition of JAMES MALTON'S eighteenth-century aquatints of Dublin is on permanent display in the Malton Room. Mon-Sat 10.00-5.30.

MILMO-PENNY FINE ART, 55 Ailesbury Road, Ballsbridge, D4, tel 693486. Specialists in Irish paintings from 1860 to 1950. Mon-Fri 11.00-7.00. Appointment advisable.

NATIONAL GALLERY, Merrion Square West, D2, tel 615133. The national collection of Irish, European and international art, representing all major schools, with particular emphasis on Dutch and French painting, and a representative sequence of rooms tracing the development of painting in Ireland from the seventeenth to the twentieth century. A single room in the Irish section is devoted to the work of JACK B. YEATS, the only artist so honoured. Outstanding masterpieces in the collection range through the whole of art history but a few are worth mentioning. Of the smaller gems, 'A Martyrdom' by Fra Angelico and Rembrandt's 'Landscape with the Rest on the Flight into Egypt' are exceptional, and portraits of 'El Conde del Tajo' by Goya, and 'Heinrich and Katherina Knoblauch' by Conrad Faber quite outstanding. The addition of the BEIT COLLECTION in 1987 has greatly increased the Gallery's holding of seventeenth- and eighteenth-century masterpieces. GEORGE BERNARD SHAW, who regarded his frequent visits to the Gallery during his youth as the basis of his education, bequeathed the Gallery one-third of his royalties, a fund which has enabled some important acquisitions to be made. A statue of Shaw by Troubetzkoy stands on the front lawn. The Gallery also promotes lecture tours and concerts and there is a restaurant and an art shop. Opening hours, Mon-Sat 10.00-6.00, Thur 10.00-9.00, Sun 2.00-5.00.

NEPTUNE GALLERY, 41 South William Street, D2, tel 715021. Eighteenth- and nineteenth-century prints and watercolours of Irish interest. Mon-Fri 10.00-6.00, Sat 10.00-1.00.

OLIVER DOWLING GALLERY, 19 Kildare Street, D2, tel 766573. Minimalist *avant garde* and conceptual artists from Ireland and abroad. Mon-Fri 10.00-5.30, Sat 10.00-1.00.

ORIEL GALLERY, 17 Clare Street, D2, tel 763410. Exhibitions of nineteenth- and early twentieth-century Irish artists – AE, Paul Henry, Jerome O'Connor, Yeats and others. Mon-Fri 10.00-6.00, Sat 10.00-1.00.

PETE HOGAN GALLERY, Molesworth Lane, off Molesworth Street, D2, tel 765288. Paintings, drawings, watercolours and prints of Dublin displayed in a miniature gallery run by an artist who specialises in line and wash, watercolours and etchings of Dublin. Mon-Sat 10.00-5.30.

PROJECT ARTS CENTRE, Essex Street East, D2, 712321. *Avant garde* painting, sculpture, theatre, music and performance in Dublin's first arts centre, set up in 1966, and for many years the only venue for the more radical trends in the visual arts. Mon-Sat 11.30-8.00.

RHA GALLAGHER GALLERY, Ely Place, D2, tel 612558. Home of the ROYAL HIBERNIAN ACADEMY, venue for the Academy's exhibitions, travelling shows and group exhibitions. The recently completed building houses the finest sequence of large-scale exhibition spaces in Dublin. Mon-Sat 10.00-5.30, Wed 10.00-9.00, Sun 2.00-5.00.

RIVERRUN, 82 Dame Street, D2, tel 6798606. Gallery of contemporary Irish art, with café and restaurant. The River-

*Project Arts Centre.*

run is the only Dublin gallery open from 10.00am to 12.00pm Mon-Sat.

ROYAL HOSPITAL KILMAINHAM (RHK), D8, tel 778526. The National Centre for Culture and the Arts and recently selected to contain the IRISH MUSEUM OF MODERN ART, (IMMA), this splendidly restored seventeenth-century building on the west side of the city can simultaneously play host to music, theatre, lectures and a number of different exhibitions in its vast array of spaces. Tue-Sun 2.00-6.00. Admission charge, free on Tuesdays. Bus 79 from Aston Quay.

RUBICON, 11 Upper Mount Street, D2, tel 762331. Basement gallery of emerging and established contemporary artists. Mon-Fri 11.00-6.00, Sat 11.00-3.00.

SOLOMON GALLERY, Powerscourt Town House, South William Street, D2, tel 794237. Gallery concentrating on the work of highly decorative contemporary Irish artists, displayed in extravagant eighteenth-century setting. The ceiling alone is worth seeing. Mon-Sat 10.00-5.30.

TAYLOR GALLERIES, 34 Kildare Street, D2, tel 766055. Exhibition on a monthly basis of leading contemporary Irish artists in the oldest established private gallery dealing in mid-twentieth century to contemporary art. The Gallery occupies a mid-eighteenth-century building converted in a curious Modernist manner. Mon-Fri 10.00-5.30, Sat 11.00-1.00.

TEMPLE BAR GALLERY, Temple Bar, D2, tel 710073. Studios and gallery of painters currently working in Dublin. Mon-Fri 11.30-5.30, Sat 12.00-4.00.

TOM CALDWELL GALLERY, 31 Upper Fitzwilliam Street, D2, tel 688629. Basement gallery dealing in contemporary Irish artists, with an emphasis on those from the North of Ireland. Tue-Fri 11.00-5.00, Sat 11.00-1.00.

UNITED ARTS CLUB, 3 Upper Fitzwilliam Street, D2, tel 762965. Exhibitions of the artist members of the club. Access by appointment.

WYVERN GALLERY, 26 Temple Lane, off Dame Street, D2, tel 6799589. First-floor gallery of established and emerging Irish contemporary art. Mon-Sat 10.00-5.00.

**ART NOUVEAU.** Dublin can never be identified with Art Nouveau in the way in which Vienna or Amsterdam are, the Classical heritage and the emergent Celtic Revival were much too strong to allow much Continental influence during the 1890s. Nonetheless, Dublin has some fine buildings of this very decorative period, which are in no way characteristic of the city and startle by their use of movement and materials. SUNLIGHT CHAMBERS on Essex Quay, Parliament Street corner, by Edward Ould, 1901, is decorated on the outside with a brightly coloured ceramic frieze displaying the history of soap, the men working and getting their clothes dirty, and the women washing them clean. Certainly a sexist view which might have perturbed a Suffragette cycling beneath, but a fascinating artistic rendering of the subject rather in the manner of Burne Jones. All the figures are organised in graceful flowing movements, carrying the eye around the building. Although much altered, the interior of BEWLEY'S Westmoreland Street premises, 1896, has features of Art Nouveau in the detailing, and its lofty ceilings and sense of space evokes the period. The now un-used and dilapidated Iveagh Baths, 1904, by NS Joseph is another important building from this period, as are the Iveagh Trust flats on Bull Alley Street.

**ARTISANS' DWELLING COMPANY.** Established in 1876 by Sir Charles Cameron, pioneering Chief Medical Officer of the city who was involved in the Dublin Sanitary Association. Extensive areas of the LIBERTIES, centred around THE COOMBE and Pimlico, were cleared of TENEMENTS and the artisans' dwellings which are now so characteristic of the area were built. Their contribution to improving the living standards and reducing the mortality rate of the population was considerable. The tenements which they replaced generally had neither running water nor sanitation, and whole families were accustomed to living in a single room. With the IVEAGH TRUST, the Company contributed substantially to the development of public housing prior to this function being taken over by the Corporation in 1921. Large parts of the Liberties were rebuilt as well as Ringsend and the North Quays.

**ARTS CENTRES.** The PROJECT ARTS CENTRE was founded in 1966 during the radicalisation of student life then an international phenomenon, and still remains the most important experimental venue in the city, with a theatre as well as exhibition and performance space. The TEMPLE BAR GALLERY is a variant on the same theme with studios and gallery in one building. DUN LAOGHAIRE ARTS CENTRE is a more recent addition to the group of artist-run facilities The arts centres provide an alternative centre of gravity to the commercial and public galleries in the city.

**ARTS COUNCIL, THE,** (An Chomhairle Ealaíon), 70 Merrion Square South, D2, tel 611840. Statutory body established by the government in 1951 to promote development in the arts. The areas in which the Arts Council is active include music, the visual arts and literature, but also encompass theatre, cinema, dance, opera and popular and traditional music. The Arts Council receives an annual budget from the state to dispense in whatever direction it thinks appropriate. These funds are used to subsidise publications, performances and exhibitions and as bursaries and grants to individuals.

*ASGARD, I* and *II. Asgard I*, a yacht belonging to ERSKINE CHILDERS, was used to bring guns into Ireland in preparation for the 1916 RISING. On 26 July 1914, 1,500 Mauser rifles as well as thousands of rounds of ammunition were unloaded at Howth, two months after the gun-running organised by EDWARD CARSON in Ulster. *Asgard I* was originally a wedding present to Erskine

Childers and his wife from his father-in-law Dr Osgood in 1904. It is now on display in the KILMAINHAM PRISON MUSEUM. *Asgard II* is a modern version of the original and is used as a sail training vessel for young people and based at Dun Laoghaire.

**ASHFORD, WILLIAM** (1746-1824). Artist, born in Birmingham, he settled in Dublin in 1764 and lived there, with the exception of a few trips abroad, for the remainder of his life, becoming a founder member and first president of the RHA in 1823. He died the following year. His house in SANDYMOUNT, recently rebuilt and now part of the Rehab complex, was designed for him by his friend, the architect JAMES GANDON. Principally remembered as a landscape painter, Ashford also painted flowerpieces and still life. He was elected president of the Irish Society of Artists in 1813. When Ashford first came to Ireland he had a sinecure in the Ordnance Department (until c.1788) which obliged him to travel widely around the country and this may have contributed to his feeling for the Irish landscape. He became the most prominent landscape painter in the country during a period when this branch of art was considered inferior to portrait and history painting; a fact which makes his appointment to the presidency of the RHA all the more remarkable. Fine examples of his work may be seen in the NATIONAL GALLERY of Ireland, including views of Dublin from Clontarf and Chapelizod and DUBLIN BAY from Clontarf.

**ASHLIN, GEORGE** (1837-1921). Architect, trained under EW Pugin, the great Gothic Revivalist, and subsequently went into partnership with him. His early work is in the French-Gothic style but he later developed into Hiberno-Romanesque under the influence of the Nationalist revival movement. John Lane's Church (AUGUSTINIAN) with Pugin, recently restored to a very high standard, is certainly Ashlin's masterpiece and the finest example of Gothic Revival in Dublin. Other buildings of interest by Ashlin are the McCabe Memorial in GLASNEVIN CEMETERY, 1887. This memorial, just inside the gates of Glasnevin, is in the architect's Hiberno-Romanesque style and shares with his Gothic buildings an intense attention to detail and decoration. Other works are a church in Inchicore, and Raheny Parish Church.

**AUDIO VISUAL ENTERTAINMENT.** Multi-media shows which provide the visitor with dramatic and wide-ranging introductions to Irish life and history have proved to be extremely popular with all sections and ages of the population. Three such shows now firmly established are the Irish Life Viking Adventure at St. Audoen's Crypt, High Street, tel 6797099, open April-Sept, which authentically presents daily life in Viking Dublin around the year AD 998; The Flame on the Hill in St. Audoen's Church, High Street, tel 6791855, next door, or rather above the Viking Adventure, is concerned with Ireland in the era of St. Patrick; and in Trinity College, The Dublin Experience tel 772941, deals with Dublin and Dubliners from King Sitric to BRENDAN BEHAN, open May-October.

BACHALL ÍOSA (Staff of Jesus). A crozier reputedly received by St. Patrick from an angel, and one of the principal relics venerated at CHRIST CHURCH CATHEDRAL from 1135 when the Anglo-Normans brought it there from Armagh. The crozier was burned by Archbishop Brown in a bonfire of relics outside the Cathedral in 1537, an event which symbolised the arrival of the REFORMATION in Dublin, but which caused the destruction of many artworks of EARLY CHRISTIAN Ireland. Curiously, the heart of SAINT LAURENCE O'TOOLE, still displayed in the Cathedral, seems to have escaped this bonfire of treasures.

**BACHELOR'S WALK.** One of the first of the Liffey quays laid out at the beginning of the eighteenth century, and a popular promenading area prior to the building of Sackville (later O'Connell) Bridge. It was the home of wealthy merchants whose ships came right up outside their hall doors. The future of this important streetscape is in jeopardy. But it is still, despite the ravages of time, a very characteristic aspect of the city. A richly evocative early painting of JACK B YEATS is entitled 'In Memory, Bachelor's Walk', and commemorates an incident which took place here during the Anglo-Irish war when the artist saw a flowergirl strewing flowers on the spot where civilians had been shot. In July 1914 soldiers of the King's Own Scottish Borders opened fire on a crowd of pedestrians on Bachelor's Walk who had jeered at them because of their failure to intervene in the HOWTH GUN RUNNING.

**BACK LANE PARLIAMENT.** Held at the TAILORS' HALL, in Back Lane off High Street, from 3-8 December 1792 by the Catholic Convention, composed of prominent supporters of the campaign for the granting of concessions to the Catholic community. Attended by the wealthy but disenfranchised Catholic merchants as well as Protestant sympathisers such as WOLFE TONE. Members were elected to present a petition to King George III which they did in the following January, 1793, demanding parliamentary representation as well as other concessions. At this time Catholics were excluded from the army, parliament, law, government service and forbidden to bear arms or to take a university degree. Partial concessions were granted by Acts of 1793 and 1795, but it was not until 1829 that CATHOLIC EMANCIPATION was achieved.

**BACK OF THE PIPES.** During the nineteenth century and earlier, the main water supply to the city came from the PODDLE river which rises in Cookstown, north-west of TALLAGHT, and flows into the Liffey on the east side of DUBLIN CASTLE. The piped water from the Poddle ran through what is now the oldest part of the GUINNESS BREWERY, south of James's Street in an area known as The Pipes.

**BAGGOT STREET,** Upper and Lower, D4 and D1. The area around Baggot Street was developed as a residential one in the late eighteenth century and the section closest to ST. STEPHEN'S GREEN with its tree-lined central division remains relatively undisturbed although no longer residential. Now the centre of a business district, the canal end of Lower Baggot Street has been substantially redeveloped by the introduction during the 1960s and 1970s of a group of modern office complexes which take their lines from the existing

Georgian houses but are otherwise unrelated to them. On the north side of the street is the bronze-clad Bank of Ireland Head Office, by Ronald Tallon, 1972-1979, on the south side is the Bord na Móna Headquarters by Sam Stephenson, 1977, which has a fine sculpture of a turfcutter by John Behan on its façade, and the Bord Fáilte building by Robin Walker, 1963. An attractive stone plaque on No.73, just to the west of Baggot Street Bridge, represents a turnstone, a naturalistic subject unusual among the Gothic and Classical stonecarvings on Dublin buildings. The upper section of the street outside the canal is Victorian. The Royal City of Dublin Hospital, 1898, by Albert Murray with its elaborate Dutch Renaissance façade of red brick and ceramic tiles is the most prominent building. Bus 10 from O'Connell Street.

**BAILE ÁTHA CLIATH.** The official name for Dublin City. Both 'Dublin' and 'Baile Átha Cliath' derive from the ancient topographical names for features on the LIFFEY estuary, current before the VIKING establishment of a city on the river. Dublin is from Dubh Linn 'the black pool' and Átha Cliath from 'hurdle ford', the crossing place on the Liffey. Átha Cliath was first used by the Annalists in 688, and Baile ('town') Átha Cliath in 1368. Eblana, a corruption of Dubh Linn, is mentioned in Ptolemy's Geography of the second century AD, and the Viking version, Dyflin, is a similar corruption. It is as Dyflin that the word first appears in print on Viking coins of King Sitric in AD 997.

**BAILY LIGHTHOUSE,** Dungriffin Promontory, Howth. Built on a promontory below the HOWTH Summit close to sea level to replace an earlier light on a higher level which was frequently obscured by fog. The summit had been the site of earlier attempts to provide a light for shipping on the northern side of DUBLIN BAY. The first light was placed in 1665 in the form of a brazier on the roof of a squat building, and was replaced in 1790 by a circular structure which functioned until 1814. George Halpin built the present lighthouse, completed in 1814, and lit first with oil and then with gas from 1865. A revolving optic which ran for seventy years was installed in 1902. This impressive example of optical engineering can be seen still rotating at the IRISH NATIONAL MARITIME MUSEUM, Haig Terrace, Dun Laoghaire, to which it was transferred when the Baily went automatic in 1972. Bus 31 from Lower Abbey Street, DART to Howth and bus to the summit.

**BAKER, HENRY AARON,** (1753-1836). Architect, pupil and successor to JAMES GANDON, he taught at the Dublin Society's Architectural School. Baker completed the KING'S INNS begun by Gandon and in 1787 designed the Rutland Fountain in MERRION SQUARE West which is Dublin's finest surviving Georgian monument, other than the Phoenix in PHOENIX PARK. Baker also restored the tower of Old St. Audoen's in High Street and laid out D'Olier Street and Westmoreland Street for the WIDE STREETS COMMISSIONERS, an early example of coordinated shops and houses.

**BALFE, MICHAEL WILLIAM,** (1808-1870). Composer and operatic singer, born in a street off Grafton Street, now re-named Balfe Street in his honour. His operas were immensely popular in Europe during the mid-nineteenth century, and *The Bohemian Girl* is still performed.

*Ballad singers.*

Balfe sang the role of Figaro in *The Barber of Seville* at Rossini's request.

**BALL OF MALT**. Dubliners' dialect for a glass of whiskey (also known as a 'half one').

**BALLADS AND BALLAD SINGERS**. Ballads about Dublin and its people composed between the eighteenth century and the present provide a rich repertoire for the contemporary ballad singer, and the traditional BALLAD form still commands great public affection. The Dublin ballad, a strictly urban form and quite different from its rural counterpart, is usually a combination of sardonic wit and a pithy and imaginative use of language. The ballad 'Molly Malone', commemorating the life and death of a street hawker, has been an anthem for the city since the eighteenth century. 'The Oul Triangle', from BRENDAN BEHAN'S play *The Quare Fellow*, and the poem 'On Raglan Road' by PATRICK KAVANAGH, are as characteristic of the sustained vigour of this type of composition as anything from previous centuries. Ballad singers perform in pubs, clubs and as BUSKERS on the streets and the more established play in theatres and the National Concert Hall where programmes of contemporary and traditional ballads continue to attract an enthusiastic audience.

> Oh! a hungry feeling, it came o're me
>   stealing,
> And the mice, they were squealing in
>   my prison cell,
> And the oul triangle, it went jingle
>   jangle,
> All along the banks of the Royal
>   Canal.

('The Oul Triangle', Brendan Behan.)

**BALLAST BOARD**. Established by an Act of Parliament in 1707, called 'An act for cleansing the Port, Harbour and River of Dublin and for erecting a Ballast Office in the said City', reconstituted in 1786 as 'The Corporation for Preserving and Improving the port of Dublin' and subsequently, 1866, as the Dublin Port and Docks Board, it is now known as the Dublin Port Authority. The Board occupied a building on the Aston Quay/Westmoreland street corner known as the Ballast Office, erected in 1802. It formed an important landmark and its clock was famed for its accuracy, being controlled by cable from DUNSINK OBSERVATORY. The Ballast Office was demolished in 1979 and replaced by an office building replica, with the clock transferred from its original position on the Westmoreland Street front to that facing the river. The functions of the Ballast Office were transferred to Port Centre in DUBLIN PORT.

**BALLOONS.** The first attempted ascent by a 'native of these islands' was made from RANELAGH GARDENS by Richard Crosbie in January 1785. LORD CHARLEMONT was amongst the ushers keeping back the crowds. A more successful attempt was made from Leinster Lawn shortly afterwards.

**BALLSBRIDGE,** D4. A substantial and elegant Victorian suburb of redbrick houses built to the east of the Georgian city from the middle of the nineteenth century, centred on the estate of the Earl of Pembroke. Ballsbridge is the epitomy of nineteenth-century Dublin and roads such as Shrewsbury and Ailesbury have some of the finest houses of the period in the city. It is now the embassy quarter, as well as the location of other important institutions and facilities – The ROYAL DUBLIN SOCIETY grounds, the CHESTER BEATTY LIBRARY, HERBERT PARK, and a number of athletic grounds, the most important of which is Lansdowne Road, headquarters of the Irish Rugby Football Union (IRFU).

**BALLYBOUGH.** Early nineteenth-century suburb north-east of the Tolka River. The first bridge over the Tolka to the north of the city was situated here on the main road from the city. During the eighteenth century the area was a notorious haven for smugglers and criminals.

**BALLYMUN.** High-rise development of sixteen-storey Corporation housing developed to the north-west of the city during the 1960s and the only quarter of its kind in Dublin. Since the building of Ballymun, high-rise local authority housing has proved unpopular with Council tenants, unlike the far superior inner city renewal schemes such as those in the LIBERTIES or at Ringsend which have been praised by tenants, architectural bodies and environ-mental groups. Bus 13 from O'Connell Street, 36, 36A from Parnell Square East.

**BALSCADDEN BAY.** Cove to the east of Howth village, a secluded stony area popular with bathers, and also for crab and lobster fishing. Bus 31 from Lower Abbey Street, DART to Howth.

**BANDS AND BANDSTANDS.** The many bandstands around the city were built during the late nineteenth century for the regimental bands stationed in Dublin and are still used for musical performances during the summer months, although these are generally performances of a civilian rather than a military nature. Bandstands are located in the following places: Blackrock Park, Blackrock; The East Pier, Moran Park and the People's Park, all in Dun Laoghaire; Herbert Park, Ballsbridge; the People's Gardens, Phoenix Park; Sorrento Park, Killiney; St. Stephen's Green.

**'BANG BANG' (THOMAS DUDLEY).** The American Western movies of the 1920s were taken to heart by this child-like Dublin street character who roamed the LIBERTIES and city centre carrying on a perpetual gun battle with the amused public. Standing on a street corner or leaping off a bus he would point his old fashioned door key at the enemy and shout 'Bang Bang, you're dead'. Many people entered into the spirit of this charade and acted out the motions of a Wild West gun battle, throwing their hands in the air or playing dead. Naturally this extraordinary behaviour in an adult made 'Bang Bang' a favourite character with children who responded with great enthusiasm to the Cowboy and Indian games amongst the passersby on streetcorners. His name is recorded, along with a host of other

*The Bank of Ireland, College Green.*

DUBLIN CHARACTERS, on the old portico of the Coombe Hospital on THE COOMBE.

**BANK HOLIDAYS**. See ANNUAL EVENTS IN DUBLIN

**BANK OF IRELAND** (The Parliament House), College Green, D2. The Bank of Ireland is the most important of a small group of significant eighteenth-century public buildings which between

them transformed the image of Dublin from an architectural backwater in the seventeenth century into one of the major cities of contemporary Europe by the end of the eighteenth. This building is all the more remarkable for being – in its present form – the work of a number of hands. The nucleus of the complex is the two-chamber Parliament House designed in 1728 by SIR EDWARD LOVETT PEARCE, and facing south onto COLLEGE GREEN with a three-sided Ionic colonnade surrounding a piazza. The area of this forecourt is half as large as that of the legislative building concealed behind it and was designed to emphasise the dignity of the institution of parliament. This majestic treatment of the entrance was reflected a century later in Robert Smirk's façade of the British Museum in London. The octagonal House of Commons was reached directly from the piazza, with the HOUSE OF LORDS' chamber set off on the eastern side of the building. In 1785 JAMES GANDON designed the Corinthian portico on the WESTMORELAND STREET side as a separate entrance for the Lords, cleverly linking this addition to Pearce's Ionic colonnade by a curved screen wall with decorative niches. This scheme enlarged the building without reducing the dominance of the original entrance. A corresponding but smaller Ionic portico was added on the western side in Foster Place by Robert Parke in 1792, linked by a curved colonnade, echoing but not copying the link used on the east. Following the ACT OF UNION in 1801, the Parliament House became redundant and the building was purchased by the Bank of Ireland in 1803. FRANCIS JOHNSTON redesigned the area of the interior which had been the Commons, totally demolishing this chamber but retaining the Lords. Externally the two curved link walls were unified in appearance to maintain the spirit of the building essentially as Pearce had designed it, but gracefully and sensitively enlarged, demonstrating the respect which each architect maintained for the work of the original designer. The House of Lords survives intact with the historic tapestries and glittering eighteenth-century glass chandelier made for it. The Lords' chamber is among the few Georgian interiors in Dublin to remain unaltered and still magnificently maintained. Currently used for board meetings and cultural events, it is open to the public. The Irish parliament met in Chichester House, College Green, from 1661 with a few interruptions until it occupied Pearce's building in 1731. The Commons had 300 members and the Lords 120. The finest period of the Dublin parliament are those years, 1782-1801, known as 'Grattan's Parliament', when after the repeal of Poynings' Law the Irish parliament had for the first time the exclusive right to legislate for Ireland. On the Bowes tomb in the crypt of CHRIST CHURCH CATHEDRAL is a model of the mace of the House of Lords, the original is in the NATIONAL MUSEUM. The Bank of Ireland retains the Commons Mace.

**BANKING HALLS.** It is probably not inappropriate that after churches the next most impressive group of post-Georgian interiors in Dublin should be the banking halls of the nineteenth century. These temples of commerce are among the finest interior spaces of any period in the city, and, like churches, their volume serves no other purpose than to impress the visitor. If, in churches, the argument for all that soaring space is that it glorifies God, what conclusion can one come to about the echoing banking halls? COLLEGE GREEN

and DAME STREET have the most interesting examples and they express clearly the confidence felt by the commercial sector in late-nineteenth-century Dublin. Below is a selection of the most interesting:

AIB, 7-12 Dame Street.
AIB, Foster Place, College Green.
AIB, College Street.
AIB, 10-11 O'Connell Street.
Bank of Ireland, 2 College Green.
Bank of Ireland, 28 Lower O'Connell Street.
National Irish Bank, 27 College Green.

**BANKS AND BANKING.** All banks maintain Monday to Friday opening with the single exception of the Bank of Ireland, at DUBLIN AIRPORT, tel 420433, which closes only on Christmas Day. Normal banking hours are 10-12.30 and 1.30 to 3.00 with late opening on Thursday until 5.00. The banks also remain closed on BANK HOLIDAYS. Between St. Stephen's Green, Grafton Street and College Green, branches of the majority of banks represented in the city both Irish and foreign, are located. The two principal banking groups, Allied Irish Bank and Bank of Ireland have branches throughout the city.

**BARNACLE, NORA,** (1884-1951). Galway-born wife and muse of JAMES JOYCE, she eloped with him from Dublin in 1904 and with the exception of a few visits remained on the Continent for the rest of her life. When Joyce met her she was working as a chambermaid in Finn's Hotel. This building at 1 South Leinster Street still stands and the ghost of the hotel sign can be seen on the gable end overlooking COLLEGE PARK. Joyce and Nora Barnacle married in London in 1931. Much of Joyce's understanding of the female archetypes in his work,

MOLLY BLOOM and ANNA LIVIA PLU-
RABELLE, is derived from his relationship with and observation of Nora.
Although lacking a formal education,
she was an astute and accomplished
woman, fluent in Italian and French and
her enormous strength of character, fortitude and humour sustained Joyce during all their wanderings and tribulations.

**BARNARDO, DR THOMAS,** (1845-
1905). Humanitarian, born 4 Dame
Street, founder of Dr Barnardo's Homes
for the care of homeless children. After
a religious conversion he went to London in 1866 and four years later opened
his first refuge for destitute and homeless children.

**BAROQUE PLASTERWORK.** The finest example of Baroque plasterwork in
Dublin is to be found in the small Church
of Ireland chapel in the ROTUNDA HOSPI-
TAL, decorated by Bartholomew Cramillion in 1759, with allegorical subjects
appropriate to the theme of childhood and
birth. This ceiling is an absolute riot of
babies, both three dimensional very realis-
tic-looking ones and the cherubic putti and
winged bodiless variety. Moulded in exceptionally high relief by the stuccodore,
the various allegorical figures represent
Biblical and New Testament verses and
the Psalms. The plasterwork of the Rotunda Chapel remains unique among Dublin
church interiors, particularly so in comparison with the restraint of the Protestant
ones. Ironically in an age so concerned
with sectarian divisions, its stylistic origins
lie in the Catholic Baroque churches of
Germany and Austria where similar swirling decoration is to be found.

**BARRACK BOARD.** 'Commissio-
ners of the barracks and Civil buildings',
a successor to the Surveyor Generals

Department which eventually developed into the Board of Works.

**BARRETT, JACKIE,** (1753-1821).
Professor of Oriental Languages at
Trinity College, scholar and eccentric.
He lived within the precincts of Trinity
for most of his life in conditions of considerable and self-imposed poverty.
Barrett's most important work was the
discovery in the Trinity Library of a
palimpsest of St Matthew's Gospel
which he edited and published.

**BARRINGTON, SIR JONAH,** (1760-
1834). Lawyer, member of parliament
and writer, he is remembered now for his
hilarious and ribald reminiscences of life
in Ireland before the ACT OF UNION, the
'*Personal Sketches of his own time*',
published in 1827 and 1832. His position on the Act of Union is ambiguous
as he appears to have both voted against
the measure and propagandised for it.
Barrington became a judge in 1797 but
was deprived of his post in 1830 after a
succession of financial scandals, involving the embezzlement of state funds.

**BARRY, JAMES,** (1741-1806). Artist,
born in Cork, he studied in Dublin, London and Rome and became the dominant
intellectual force in English painting
during the late eighteenth century. Barry
was an irascible individual and he is the
only member of the Royal Academy
ever to be expelled (1799). The NA-
TIONAL GALLERY has a representative
collection of this highly individual artist's work, two of the most interesting of
which are his 'Self Portrait as Timan-
thes', and 'Jacomo and Imogen'. Barry's
self portrait is one of the finest in the
gallery, and a powerful image of the
creative individual during the eighteenth
century.

*Killiney Beach.*

**BARRY, KEVIN**, (1902-1920). Eighteen-year-old UCD medical student, he joined the IRA when still a teenage student at BELVEDERE COLLEGE. He was involved in the ambush of British soldiers in Church Street, three of whom were killed. Barry was captured and, despite widespread appeals for clemency due to his age, was hanged for his involvement. He is commemorated in a popular ballad.

**BARTON, ROSE**, (1856-1929). Artist, watercolourist and book illustrator. She produced evocative views of Dublin at the end of the Victorian era, street life and society events. 'Going to the Levee at Dublin Castle', in the National Gallery, 1897, shows a ragged crowd watching as coaches bring guests into the Castle for a Vice Regal reception, showing clearly the gulf between the upper and lower echelons of society in the city.

**BAX, SIR ARNOLD**, (1883-1953). English composer, 'Master of the Queen's Musick'. Bax, who adopted the name of Dermot O'Byrne, was an enthusiastic supporter of Irish Nationalism and a fervent admirer of PATRICK PEARSE. One of his poems, written after the events of 1916, was banned by the British authorities as it was considered to be inflammatory.

The deuce in all his bravery,
His girth and gall grown no whit less,
He swarmed in from the fatal sea
With pomp of huge artillery
And brass and copper haughtyness.
('A Dublin Ballad – 1916', Dermot O'Byrne.)

**'BAYNO', THE**, The Iveagh Play Centre, Bull Alley Street, D8. This building which looks like the Town Hall of a thriving Victorian city borough was designed by Mc Donnell and Reid in 1915 and is an extraordinary concept for a Kindergarten built in the middle of one of the poorest area of the city. For generations, until it was closed in 1959, the children of the Liberties went to the 'Bayno' for cocoa, buns and educational activities. The colloquial name comes from 'beano', a feast, translated into the Dublin patois. The Bayno is now the Liberties Vocational School.

**BEACHES AND BATHING.** Dublin, situated on DUBLIN BAY, has beaches and seawater bathing available within minutes of the city centre. The character of the coastline on the northern and southern shores of the Bay differs considerably, the north offers the glorious expanses of Dollymount Strand, which can accommodate 10,000 people on a summer Sunday afternoon, and access further beyond the Bay to Portmarnock and Baldoyle. The Howth coastline, conversely, is rocky and mostly inaccessible. On the southern side Sandymount Strand provides a great open beach but is too close to the city for bathing purposes. Further along the coast, small coves such as Sandycove and Vico Beach and the sweeping curve of Killiney Strand are all popular summer resorts but any ray of sun brings the bathers out on to the sands at any time of year.

**BEATTY, SIR ALFRED CHESTER**, (1895-1968). Mining engineer, collector of Oriental manuscripts and philanthropist. On a visit to Cairo in 1913 he became interested in the Islamic manuscripts then available in the bazaars and this started him on a lifelong quest for the finest examples of both Oriental and European manuscripts with an emphasis on calligraphy. Forty years later he moved to Ireland (he was of Irish extraction) building a library on Shrewsbury Road, Ballsbridge, to house the collection which he presented to the Irish people. Chester Beatty was distinguished by being made the first honorary Irish citizen in 1955. He also presented a collection of nineteenth-century French paintings to the NATIONAL GALLERY and militaria to the Military College Museum at the Curragh.

**BEAU WALK.** The northern side of ST. STEPHEN'S GREEN where the SHELBOURNE HOTEL now stands. It was a popular promenading area for the young bucks of the city during the eighteenth century.

**BECKETT, SAMUEL**, (1906-1989). Playwright, novelist. Born Cooldrinagh, Foxrock, D18. He lectured in the French department in Trinity College from 1930-32 after which he left Ireland permanently. He acted as secretary to JAMES JOYCE in Paris. Beckett became involved in the French Resistance during the Second World War. After the war Beckett worked as storekeeper with the Irish Red Cross at St. Lo. His most performed play, *Waiting For Godot*, is a bleak and pessimistic view of life sustained by humour. The first Irish performance of *Godot* was at the PIKE THEATRE in 1955. In his writing Beckett is a minimalist, paring words and gestures to the bone. He won the Nobel Prize for Literature in 1969.

Make sense who may, I switch off. (Samuel Beckett.)

**BEGGARS.** Since the earliest times travellers to Dublin have remarked on the number and pathetic nature of the beggars swarming in the streets. Civic ordinances were continually being passed from the Medieval period onwards to regulate this problem. Even JAMES MALTON's celebrated series of aquatints of eighteenth-century Dublin frequently show the beggars which were a characteristic part of the street life of the Georgian city. Today begging is still commonplace in Dublin, a fact that often shocks visitors from Europe and North America. Today's beggars are mostly itinerants (colloquially, 'tinkers' or 'travellers') and the begging is done by women with babies as well as by small children from the age of six upwards. Male itinerants are rarely seen begging. Itinerant families live in caravan encampments on the outskirts of the city, often in appallingly unsanitary conditions, without electricity, running water or toilets. They are entitled to social welfare but are generally lacking in skills and education and often live a seasonally nomadic existence. Regarded by Irish society as someone else's problem it is difficult for the itinerants to remain permanently in an area due to the hostility of the settled community.

**BEGGAR'S BUSH BARRACKS**, Haddington Road, D2. Former army barracks built in 1827, it now houses the offices of the Geological Survey, the City Pound for illegally parked cars removed by the Gardai, and the Labour History Museum. On the Haddington Road front the entrance is flanked by redundant eighteenth-century cannons, set in the ground as bollards which emphasise the military nature of the premises. During the eighteenth century some prominent blackthorn bushes grew on this spot and beggars congregated in their shelter as is shown in engravings of the period, and gave that area its curious name. A contemporary play, *The Beggar's Bush*, performed in London would have given the place-name a humorous connotation in the eighteenth century. All the other army barracks are inaccessible to the public, and for security reasons their plans appear as a blank space on recent maps.

**BEGNET, SAINT**. Early Christian saint associated with the DALKEY area. Two churches are dedicated to St. Begnet, one in the village of Dalkey and the other on DALKEY ISLAND.

**BEHAN, BRENDAN**, (1923-1964). Playwright, travel writer, journalist and Dublin character, more noted for his erratic behaviour and brilliant conversation than for his considerable achievements in the field of literature. Behan spent six years in jail in Britain and Ireland for IRA activities and this experience provided the basis for his internationally successful autobio-

graphical novel *Borstal Boy*. His plays, *The Quare Fellow*, set in Mountjoy Jail, and *The Hostage*, set in a house in Eccles Street, were widely performed, and deal with themes of prison life and Irish Nationalism.

> By the moon that shines above us,
> In the misty morn and night,
> Let us cease to run ourselves down,
> But praise God that we are white,
> And better still are English,
> Tea and toast and muffin rings,
> Old ladies with stern faces,
> And the captains and the kings.

(*The Hostage*, Brendan Behan.)

**BEIT COLLECTION**, National Gallery of Ireland, Merrion Square. A collection of seventeen major masterpieces of European painting presented to the NATIONAL GALLERY by Sir Alfred Beit in 1987. The collection was largely formed by Sir Alfred's uncle, Alfred Beit, between 1895 and 1906 on the advice of the German art scholar Wilhelm von Bode. On Alfred Beit's death in 1906 the collection was inherited by his brother Otto Beit who added some further important paintings to it. Amongst the masterpieces of the collection are superb works by Constable, Gainsborough, Goya, Hobbema, Metsu, Murillo, Raeburn, van Ruisdael, Velázquez and Vermeer. Prior to the Beit Collection being presented to the gallery a small number of the most important paintings were stolen from Russborough, the Beit mansion in Co. Wicklow in 1986. So far only one of the stolen paintings has been recovered and the Gallery is in the unhappy position of owning the paintings but not as yet possessing them. Paintings by Goya, Metsu and Vermeer are still at large.

**BELFIELD, UCD.** Suburban campus of University College Dublin to which the University moved in the early 1960s from its original site at EARLSFORT TERRACE on the south of ST. STEPHEN'S GREEN. This move was at the instigation of the then Archbishop of Dublin, JOHN CHARLES MC QUAID, who wished to separate the Catholic university from the ambiance of the Protestant TRINITY COLLEGE, five minutes' walk from Earlsfort Terrace. UCD suffers the consequent social dislocation of its students being deprived of the immediate contact with the intellectual and artistic life of the city, previously on its doorstep. The masterplanner of Belfield is Andrzej Wejchert, 1964, who also designed the administration, arts and commerce buildings, 1970-73. The restaurant and industry centre are by Scott, Tallon and Walker, 1968-86. The library by Sir Basil Spence, 1972. Bus 10, 11, 11B from O'Connell Street.

**BELGRAVE SQUARE**, Rathmines, D6. The remarkably diverse nature of the houses surrounding Belgrave Square give it an attractive appearance, quite distinct from the more regular order of the other squares in the area. Ranging from grey brick of the mid-nineteenth century to the red brick of the later Victorian houses, the transitions of style through the century are emphasised by the drift from Classical to Gothic detailing. The split level central park has play areas surrounded by rambling shrubbery.

*BELL, THE*. Influential literary magazine founded in 1940 by Seán Ó Faoláin, who also edited it until 1946. It was subsequently edited by Peadar O'Donnell until it ceased publication in 1954. Many of the most important Irish writers of the period were published in *The Bell*, which carried on a vigorous editorial battle against the current CENSORSHIP laws.

**BELVEDERE COLLEGE**, 6 Great Denmark Street, D1, tel 744795. Established by the Jesuits in 1841 in the former mansion of Lord Belvedere. The house, built in 1786, occupies a commanding position looking down North Great George's Street and contains remarkable Adam plasterwork by MICHAEL STAPLETON who may also have designed the building, as well as fireplaces by BOSSI. On the first floor the rooms are decorated on the themes of Apollo, Diana and Venus. Belvedere was *alma mater* of JAMES JOYCE, HARRY CLARKE, KEVIN BARRY, and CATHAL BRUGHA among many others. Viewing only by appointment.

**BENCH MARKS**. The idea of commemorating an individual by means of a public bench is less common than other forms of memorials – plaques and statues – but there are a number of interesting seats around the city in a variety of styles from the very plain to the quite elaborate, inviting the passerby to consider the memory of the famous while resting their feet – a most practical arrangement. Commemorating two people on the same bench allows the possibility of spectral dialogues, a nice refinement of the idea. The most famous such memorial is that on the banks of the Grand Canal at Baggot Street Bridge to PATRICK KAVANAGH which has now been joined by a corresponding bench on the opposite bank for Percy French. JAMES JOYCE and his improvident father, John Stanislaus Joyce, share a bench on St. Stephen's Green South, opposite NEWMAN HOUSE where Joyce, the son, attended university. Two other pairs are located within the Green. Sharing benches are those energetic ladies, Louise Bennett and Helen Chevenix, workers for 'social justice, women's rights and world peace', and Anna Maria and Thomas Haslam, whose activity was 'public service chiefly devoted to the enfranchisement of women'.

**BERESFORD, RT. HON. JOHN,** (1738-1805). Youngest son of the Earl of Tyrone, a member of the WIDE STREETS COMMISSIONERS and also Commissioner of the Irish Revenue, he was one of the most influential men in Dublin during the eighteenth century. Beresford was responsible, with Lord Carlow, for bringing JAMES GANDON to Dublin, and Gandon's greatest works were produced under his patronage.

**BERKELEY, GEORGE,** (1685-1753). Philosopher, Bishop of Cloyne, writer and political economist. He made a valuable contribution to theories of knowledge and perception and wrote extensively on social reform in Britain and Ireland. The BERKELEY LIBRARY in TRINITY COLLEGE DUBLIN is named in his honour. He became obsessed towards the end of his life with the virtues of drinking tar water, an obsession shared by JAMES CLARENCE MANGAN. In 1735 he published anonymously *The Querist*, containing some hundreds of questions without answers on social, economic and practical issues with regard to the state of the country. Many of these questions remain as pertinent now as when they were written.

> Whether England doth not really love us and wish well to us, as bone of her bone, and flesh of her flesh? And whether it be not our part to cultivate this love and affection in all manner of ways?
> Whether, if the arts of sculpture and painting were encouraged among us, we might not furnish our houses in a much nobler manner with our own manufactures?

**BETJEMAN, SIR JOHN,** (1906-1984). Poet Laureate and propagandist for Victorian architecture, he was Press Attaché at the British Embassy in Dublin during the Second World War.

> Mr. Woilde, we 'ave come for tew take yew
> Where felons and criminals dwell:
> We must ask yew tew leave with us quoitely
> For this is the Cadogan Hotel

('The Arrest of Oscar Wilde at the Cadogan Hotel', John Betjeman.)

**BETTING SHOPS.** Also known as 'Turf Accountants', a marvellously misleading euphemism. Almost as ubiquitous as pubs and like them the activity within is screened from the street. A preserve of the male, not of course that women are excluded, but they do not form a large proportion of the permanent patrons.

**BEWLEY FAMILY.** The Bewleys were a prominent QUAKER merchant family whose founder Mungo Bewley emigrated, aged twenty-three, from England at the beginning of the eighteenth century. He left England to escape the intolerance directed at the Society of Friends. During the eighteenth century the Bewleys engaged in trade and manufacture, milling and textile importation from Europe and the Near East. By the nineteenth century they had become important in banking, insurance, brewing and mining. During the 1840s the Bewleys and other members of the Quaker community organised famine relief for the destitute, responding to the crisis of the time without the moralistic attitude of many of the religious relief organisations. Charles Bewley began to import tea from Canton in 1835, following the break in the monopoly of the East India

Company, and from this beginning evolved the Bewley tea and coffee business which in time developd into BEWLEY'S ORIENTAL CAFÉS, the hallmark of Dublin café life.

## BEWLEY'S ORIENTAL CAFÉS.

One of the essentials of Dublin's social life, the Bewley cafés have the spacious and relaxed atmosphere of Edwardian coffee houses, with customers sitting on bentwood chairs at small marble-topped tables, and in certain rooms still served by waitresses in black dresses with white lace collars. Founded nearly a century ago, the South Great George's Street premises were the first to open in 1894, followed by Westmoreland Street in 1896 and Grafton Street in 1925. The Grafton Street premises which were designed by ACC Millar have one of the most distinctive shop fronts in Dublin, a strange blending of Egyptian and Art Deco elements executed in a colourful mosaic. Inside, stained glass by HARRY CLARKE, potted palms, engraved glass, polished brass and dark wood combine to provided the background for conversation and the excellent teas and coffees that are the hallmark of the Bewley name. The Grafton Street premises contains the BEWLEY MUSEUM on the top floor, a fascinating collection of the bric-a-brac of Bewley family history, displayed between Heath Robinson style fudge machines and other antique equipment of the catering trade. The original architect's drawings and Harry Clarke's designs for his windows are among the exhibits. The Museum is open during shop hours. Of all the Bewley cafés, the one which preserves the Edwardian ambiance most successfully is the portion of the Westmoreland Street premises which is entered from Fleet Street.

*Bewley's, Westmoreland Street.*

**'BILLY IN THE BOWL'**, eighteenth century. Billy Davis, born without legs, moved around in a wooden bowl braced with iron straps, propelling himself with his hands. A character straight from a painting by Breugel, he became in his limited fashion a highway robber preying on unsuspecting victims who assumed him to be a harmless crippled beggar. He was jailed for murder and died in prison in 1786. Mentioned in the ballad 'The Twangman', which has been attributed to ZOZIMUS.

Well he took her out to Sandymount
For to see the waters roll
And he stole the heart of the twang-
man's mot,
Playing Billy in the Bowl
(*'The Twangman'*, Zozimus.)

**BINDON, FRANCIS**, (1690-1765). Painter and sometime architect, he studied in London under Kneller, the chief painter of his day. Bindon painted JONATHAN SWIFT a number of times, a version at HOWTH CASTLE commemorates the Dean's involvement in the Wood's ha'pence controversy, and that at ST. PATRICK'S DEANERY shows the Cathedral of St. Patrick before the nineteenth-century restorations. Bindon designed the eighteenth-century alterations to Howth Castle.

**BIRDS' NEST**, York Road, Dun Laoghaire. Former orphanage for boys and girls built in 1859, an impressive stone-faced building on the heights above DUBLIN BAY, with a dedicatory inscription on its façade which reads, '"Birds Nest" to the memory of Mrs Whately and Mrs George Wale, AD 1861'.

**'BLACK AND TANS'**. British recruits enrolled in the Royal Irish Constabulary during January 1920 in order to maintain order and cope with the increased IRA activity. Noted for their lawlessness, they were known as the 'Black and Tans', or more colloquially 'the Tans' because of the colours of their cap ribbons.

**BLACK DEATH, THE**. First occurred in Dublin in 1348, decimating the population, recurred continually for at least half a century.

**BLACK MONDAY**. On Easter Monday, 1209, five hundred Normans, picnicking at Cullenswood were massacred by an incursion of native tribes into THE PALE. The event was commemorated annually in Dublin up to the sixteenth century.

**BLACKPITTS**. Area in the LIBERTIES the name of which is thought to derive from the vats used by the tanners. Some of these vats remained up to recent times near Sweeny's Terrace.

**BLACKROCK**. Village and district on south shore of DUBLIN BAY, much sought after as a residential area. Features of interest are the Early Christian granite cross on the main street and the terraces of Victorian stuccoed houses facing the bay at Idrone Terrace and Maritimo Gardens. The Blackrock Shopping Centre formed around an open atrium is probably the best designed of all the recent shopping developments in or around the city. In the eighteenth century there were many aristocratic mansions in the area, remnants of which remain amongst later developments. One of the most famous of these mansions was FRESCATI, the home of LORD EDWARD FITZGERALD. DART from city centre. Bus 7, 7A, 8 from Eden Quay, 45 from Burgh Quay.

**BLACKROCK CLINIC**, Rock Road, Blackrock. Purpose-built and architecturally interesting modern medical centre and private hospital set in wooded landscape overlooking Dublin Bay. Designed in 1983 by the firm Campbell, Conroy & Hickey, the consulting rooms are arranged around a hexagonal atrium rising the full height of the building which has a bronze symbol of Asclepius, the Greek god of healing, as its finial. Bus 7, 7A, 8 from Eden Quay, 45 from Burgh Quay, DART to Blackrock.

**BLASPHEMY**. During the Medieval period persons accused and convicted of blasphemy were burned to death at HOGGEN GREEN, subsequently known as COLLEGE GREEN.

**BLIGH, CAPTAIN WILLIAM**, (1754-1817). Skipper of the *HMS Bounty* during the notorious mutiny in 1789. Bligh produced one of the most distinguished early charts of DUBLIN BAY when he was invited in 1800 to survey the harbour and make recommendations for its improvement. His chart showed that all previous soundings were inaccurate, but his proposal for channelling the Liffey by constructing a wall parallel to the Great South Wall was followed only in principle. When the North Bull Wall was being constructed it was built at an angle rather than parallel as Bligh had recommended. All Bligh's plans and reports are in the archives of the Dublin Port and Docks Board. See BULL WALLS.

**BLIND QUAY**, Exchange Street, D2. With the expansion of the Medieval city towards the river and the embankment of the channel, what had here been a quay developed into a street running along the lines of the original city wall.

**BLOODY BRIDGE**, (Rory O'More Bridge). A ferry existed at this spot in 1671 which was to be replaced by a wooden bridge then being built. A riot took place during which apprentices wrecked the wooden structure connecting Usher's Island with Oxmantown Green. In a subsequent affray three of the apprentices were killed. The rioters' objection was to the potential loss of livelihood on the part of the ferrymen. The bridge is still known locally as 'Bloody'.

**BLOODY SUNDAY**, 22 November 1920. At the order of Michael Collins, Chief of Intelligence of the IRA, fourteen suspected British Secret Service agents known as 'The Cairo Gang' were shot dead in their homes around the city in the early hours of the morning after the assassins had attended early Mass. The police retaliated by shooting dead two members of the IRA command, and the BLACK AND TANS opened fire on a crowd of spectators at a match in Croke Park, killing twelve.

**BLOOM, LEOPOLD**. Central character in JAMES JOYCE'S *Ulysses* and twentieth-century Odysseus. His day-long journey on 16 June 1904, BLOOMSDAY, charts all aspects of this Everyman's life. Much of the interest in *Ulysses* lies in the thoughts and observations of Bloom. As a Dubliner and a Jew, he is both insider and outsider to the local scene. His fictional birthplace is commemorated by a plaque on 52 Clanbrassil Street, and a sculpture trail, marked by bronze plaques designed by Robin Buick and set into the pavement, charts part of his journey between ABBEY STREET and KILDARE STREET, each plaque giving a relevant quotation from *Ulysses,* (standard corrected text).

1. Easons, 79-80 Middle Abbey Street.
2. Superrex, 49 O'Connell Street.
3. North-west corner of O'Connell Bridge.
4. Aston Quay/Westmoreland Street corner.
5. Harrison's, east side of Westmoreland Street.

6. Traffic Island, College Street, at base of Thomas Moore statue.

7. Grafton Street/Nassau Street corner.

8. Adam Court, 6-7 Grafton Street.

9. Brown Thomas, 15 Grafton Street.

10. 18 Duke Street.

11. Davy Byrne's, 21 Duke Street.

12. Aquascutum, 51 Dawson Street.

13. 10-11 Molesworth Street.

14. National Museum entrance, Kildare Street.

**BLOOM, MOLLY.** Character in *Ulysses*, wife of LEOPOLD BLOOM, lover of Blazes Boylan. Molly Bloom's soliloquy, with which *Ulysses* ends, is the most well-known single piece of Joyce's writing, with the possible exception of the short story, *The Dead*. The character and thoughts of Molly Bloom are to a considerable degree based on those of Joyce's wife, NORA BARNACLE.

**BLOOMSDAY.** 16 June 1904, the day on which the events written about by Joyce in *Ulysses* take place. He wrote in 1924, 'Will anybody remember this date?' Remarkably, the celebration in Dublin of Bloomsday has become an infatuation, and events, tours, and pilgrimages take place during the day which is indeed remembered and, like few other dates in Irish history, remembered without rancour. Cafés and restaurants host appropriate breakfasts, readings from Holy Writ and dramatisations take place both in the streets and in theatres. The pubs like Davy Byrne's, mentioned in the text, are on everybody's itinerary, with Burgundy and Gorgonzola served as they were to Bloom, and GLASNEVIN CEMETERY and the Sandycove Martello Tower, at opposite ends of the city, attract people interested in different aspects of Joyce's great celebration of Dublin. For information

*Bloom's fictional birthplace.*

on Bloomsday celebrations and all things Joycean, contact the JAMES JOYCE MUSEUM, tel 809265, and the JAMES JOYCE CULTURAL CENTRE, tel 731984.

**'BLUECOAT SCHOOL',** King's Hospital, Blackhall Place, D7. Designed by THOMAS IVORY in 1773 to replace an existing school building on the other side of the square, which was originally part of OXMANTOWN GREEN, it now forms the headquarters of the Incorporated Law Society. An attractive symmetrical composition of central block with wings attached by gently curving arcaded walls. A spire was part of the original plan but was not built due to shortage of funds. Eventually a dome was built instead. The building remained as a school until 1970 when owing to shifts in the population it was found necessary to move the school to Palmerstown in the suburbs. The Blue Coat School is one of the most attractive and least known Georgian buildings in Dublin. Bus 39, 39A, 39B from Middle Abbey Street.

**BLUESHIRTS**. Organisation formed in 1933 by the dismissed Commissioner of the Civic Guards, General Eoin O'Duffy and called the National Guard. The movement was modelled on the contemporary Fascist movements in Europe, with a raised arm salute and uniform of blue shirt and black trousers. WB YEATS wrote marching songs for the Blueshirts, a brigade of which saw active service during the Spanish Civil War on the Nationalist side.

**BOER WAR MEMORIAL**, 1907. Neo-Classical triumphal arch at the north-west corner (Grafton Street end) of St. Stephen's Green, known as the Fusilier's Arch, built to commemorate those officers and men of the Royal Dublin Fusiliers who were killed fighting on the British side during the Boer War. Another memorial to the dead of the Boer War stands in the forecourt of St. Andrew's, Suffolk Street. See WAR MEMORIALS.

**BOLANDS MILLS**, Grand Canal Basin, Ringsend Road. Flour mills on the eastern side of the GRAND CANAL Basin. The mass of brick and stone warehouses dating from the eighteenth and nineteenth centuries, which line the canal basin, are amongst the finest examples of industrial architecture in the city, more for their combination of materials and setting than for the merits of the individual buildings. An important early sugar mill building stands on the west side of the basin and now houses the TOWER DESIGN WORKSHOPS. The section of the mills on Grand Canal Street, recently rebuilt, were occupied as an outpost during the 1916 RISING. From the roofs of the mills the nearby BEGGAR'S BUSH BARRACKS could be overlooked.

**BOLTON STREET**. Called after the Earl of Bolton, Lord Lieutenant 1717-1721, this was an important residential street in the earlier part of the eighteenth century but little of distinction remains today with the exception of the adjacent HENRIETTA STREET area. Bolton Street College of Technology, designed by CJ McCarthy in 1906, an impressive brick and limestone building of the early twentieth century in a Neo-classical vein, dominates the east side of the street.

**BOND, OLIVER**, (1760-1798). Merchant and revolutionary. United Irishman, convicted of high treason but died in prison before he could be hanged. Corporation flats, Oliver Bond House on Merchant's Quay, named in his honour.

**BOOK BARROWS**. Once common on the LIFFEY QUAYS and a treasure trove for the book browser, but now to be found outside very few bookshops – George Webbs on Essex Quay, The Winding Stair Bookshop on the opposite quay and Green's Bookshop on Clare Street. Book Barrow Fairs take place at the MANSION HOUSE, Kildare Street, on the first Monday of the month.

**BOOK OF KELLS**, Trinity College Library. Described in the eleventh century by Giraldus Cambrensis as 'the chief glory of the western world' and considered today the most magnificent manuscript to have survived from the Early Middle Ages, the ninth-century AD Book of Kells has astonished viewers for a thousand years, and still continues to do so. It comprises over six hundred pages of vellum containing the four Gospels and is complete, with the exception of some pages at the beginning and end, presumably lost when the book was stolen from the monastery at Kells in the year 1006 and stripped of its decorated shrine cover. The lavishness and intricacy of the decoration on the manuscript, which is embellished on all but two of the surviving pages, certainly makes the Book of Kells one of the masterworks of the EARLY CHRISTIAN period. It is not known whether it was written in Ireland, in an Irish monastery in the north of Scotland or on the Western Isles, possibly on Iona. A subtext to the ecclesiastical function of the manuscript is the amazing bestiary which it contains, suggesting a joy in nature unrelated to the Gospels; these decorations are the contribution of the brilliant individuals who decorated the book, and a reflection of their predominantly rural lives.

**BOOKBINDING.** Important work was done in this field during the eighteenth century in Dublin. Bookbinding reached a peak in the bound sets of the parliamentary records, the principal collection of which was destroyed in the burning of the Public Records Office at the Four Courts during the Civil War in 1922. However, corresponding sets in private hands, bound for the members of parliament, have survived and they cover the development of Dublin bookbinding over its greatest period. Fine bindings can be seen at MARSH'S LIBRARY and in the CHESTER BEATTY LIBRARY.

**BOOKSHOPS.** The main concentration of bookshops in Dublin, both general and specialised, is to be found along the Nassau Street axis between

*Evangelist from The Book of Kells.*

Dame Street and Merrion Square. A further smaller number is concentrated around O'Connell Street, and a more widely dispersed selection is to be found in the suburbs, principally in the SHOPPING CENTRES.

ANTIQUARIAN AND SECONDHAND BOOKSHOPS

BYGONES, 9 Market Arcade, South Great George's Street, D2. Specialist interest, railwayana, printed ephemera, etc. Mon-Sat 10.00-6.00.

CARRAIG BOOKS, 73 Main Street, Blackrock, Co. Dublin, tel 882575. Irish interest, Catholic, religion and theology, history, biography. Mon-Sat 9.00-5.30.

CATHACH BOOKS, 10 Duke Street, D2, tel 718676. Books, maps, prints relating to Ireland. Mon-Sat 9.30-6.00.

CATHAIR BOOKS, Essex Gate, D8, tel 6792406. Irish interest, maps, prints. Mon-Sat 10.00-6.00.

EXCHANGE BOOKSHOP, 34 Castle Street, Dalkey, tel 853805. Modern second-hand paperbacks, review copies. Mon-Sat 9.15-6.00, Fri to 9.00.

FRED HANNA LTD, 27-29 Nassau Street, D2, tel 771255. Books of Irish interest. Academic and general secondhand. Mon-Sat 9.00-5.30.

GEORGE WEBB, 5-6 Crampton Quay, D2, tel 777489. Secondhand and remaindered, Irish interest. Mon-Sat 9.00-5.30.

GREEN'S BOOKSHOP, 16 Clare Street, D2, tel 762554. New and secondhand books of Irish interest, religious, novels, schoolbooks. Mon-Fri 9.00-5.30, Sat 9.00-1.00.

KEVIN CORR BOOKS, 61 Mespil Road, D4, tel 609321. Illustrated, art, English and Irish interest. Mon-Sat 10.30-6.00.

NAUGHTON'S BOOKSHOP, 8 Marine Terrace, Dun Laoghaire, tel 804392. Books, maps, prints of Irish interest. Mon-Sat 9.30-5.30.

STOKES BOOKS, 19 Market Arcade, South Great George's Street, D2, tel 538276. Irish, philosophy, theology, and general. Mon-Sat 10.00-5.30.

THE WINDING STAIR BOOKSHOP AND CAFÉ, 40 Lower Ormond Quay, D1, tel 733292. Three floors of general second-hand, poetry, Irish interest; music, coffee and views of the Liffey and Ha'penny Bridge. The most atmospheric bookshop in Dublin. Mon-Sat 10.30-6.00.

GENERAL CITY CENTRE BOOKSHOPS

ALCHEMIST'S HEAD, 56 Dame Street, D2, tel 6791306. Astrology, occult, New Age. Mon-Fri 10.00-6.00, Thur 10.00-8.00, Sat 10.30-6.00, Sun 2.00-6.00.

ASSISI BOOKSHOP, 4 Merchant's Quay, D8, tel 770890. Catholic religious interest. Mon-Sat 9.30-5.30.

AUTOMOBILE ASSOCIATION, 23 Suffolk Street, D2, tel 779481. Maps, atlases, travel guides. Mon-Fri 9.00-5.00, Sat 9.00-12.00.

BOOKS UPSTAIRS, 36 College Green, D2, tel 6796687. Small high quality bookshop dealing in drama, history, philosophy, poetry, women's studies, gay literature. Mon-Fri 10.00-8.00, Sat 10.00-7.00, Sun 2.00-6.00.

CATHEDRAL BOOKS, 4 Sackville Place, D1, tel 787372. Catholic religious, educational and counselling. Mon-Sat 9.00-5.30.

CHAPTERS BOOKSHOP, 21 Wicklow Street, D2, tel 688328. Bargain and remaindered, health and fitness, encyclopaedias, Irish interest. Chapters branches at 70 Middle Abbey Street and 1 Henry Street, also secondhand. Mon-Sat 9.30-6.30.

CHRISTIAN PUBLICATION CENTRE, 110 Middle Abbey Street, D1, tel 726754. Christian religion and theology. Mon-Sat 9.00-5.00.

CLODHANNA TEORANTA – THE CELTIC BOOKSHOP, 6 Harcourt Street, D2, tel 783814. Celtic languages. Mon-Fri 9.00-5.30, Sat 10.00-4.00.

CONNOLLY BOOKS, 43 East Essex Street, D2, tel 711943. History, politics, Marxist economics, Third World. Mon-Sat 10.00-5.45.

DUBLIN BOOKSHOP, THE, 24 Grafton Street, D2, tel 775568. General and Irish interest. Mon/Wed/Fri 10.00-7.00, Thur 10.00-8.00, Sat 9.00-6.00.

EASON & SONS, 40-42 Lower O'Connell Street, D1, tel 733811. Largest bookshop–newsagents, with stationery, records, toys, health foods. Eason branches at ILAC Centre, Irish Life Centre, and suburbs. Mon-Sat 8.30-6.15.

FRED HANNA LTD, 27-29 Nassau Street, D2, tel 771255. General, art and architecture, strong Irish interest section, separate paperback shop, second-hand, antiquarian, academic, university textbooks. Mon-Sat 9.00-5.30.

THE GALLERY SHOP, National Gallery of Ireland, Merrion 133. Art, architecture, prints, magazines, NGI publications and catalogues. Mon-Sat 10.00-6.00, Thur 10.00-9.00, Sun 2.00-5.00.

GREEN'S BOOKSHOP, 16 Clare Street, D2, tel 762554. Old and interesting long established firm with new as well as major secondhand section, schoolbooks, book barrows, post office. A browser's paradise. Mon-Fri 9.00-5.30, Sat 9.00-1.00.

HODGES FIGGIS, 57-58 Dawson Street, D2, tel 774754. Immense Irish, Celtic studies section, travel, biography, children, art, architecture, business, academic, history, politics, sociology. Spacious bookshop on three floors, admirable for browsing. Mon-Fri 9.00-8.30, Sat 9.00-6.30, Sun 11.00-6.30.

HUGHES & HUGHES, St. Stephen's Green Shopping Centre, D2, tel 782450. General hardback and paperback. Mon-Sat 9.30-6.00.

THE LIBRARY SHOP, TCD, D2, tel 772941, ex 1171. Irish interest, maps, posters, ephemera. Mon-Fri 9.45-4.45, Sat 9.45-12.00.

NATIONAL BIBLE SOCIETY OF IRELAND, 41 Dawson Street, D2, tel 773272. Religion, theology and children's books. Mon-Fri 9.00-5.00, Sat 10.00-4.00.

*The two bibliophiles.*

READER'S DIGEST BOOKSHOP, 18 Lower Liffey Street, D1, tel 730390. Reader's Digest publications and general.

ROBERTS BARGAIN BOOKS, 4 Crampton Quay, D2, tel 775618, 775549. Specialising in Irish interest, scholarly and academic. Mon-Sat 9.00-6.00, Sun 12.00-6.00.

ST. ANN'S BOOK CENTRE, St. Ann's Church, Dawson Street, D2, tel 616400. Christian religion and theology. Mon-Fri 10.00-5.00, Sat 10.00-4.00.

SINN FÉIN BOOK BUREAU, 44 Parnell Square, D1, tel 726932. Republican, revolutionary and Nationalist literature, also prison crafts from Portlaoise. Mon-Sat 11.00-5.00.

VERITAS & CO LTD, 7-8 Lower Abbey Street, D1, tel 788177. Catholic religious publications, audio and visual cassettes. Mon-Sat 9.00-5.30.

WATERSTONE'S, 7 Dawson Street, D2, tel 6791260. Attractive general bookshop, cinema, literature, excellent children's section with child-scale furniture, art and architecture, background music. Mon-Fri 8.30-9.00, Sat 9.00-7.00, Sun 12.00-7.00.

**BOOTERSTOWN MARSH**, Rock Road, Booterstown. The only bird sanctuary in south county Dublin. The 4 hectare (9.6 acre) salt marsh is confined between the DART railway line and the main coast road. A mixed freshwater-salt-water habitat. There are extensive reed-beds which provide breeding areas for a wide variety of birdlife. Easily visible from the adjacent roads. DART to Booterstown.

**BORU, BRIAN**, (941-1014). Brian Boru or Brian of the Tributes was born in Munster and succeeded to the kingship of Dal Cais and by degrees usurped the kingship of Munster, later the southern half of Ireland and ultimately the whole country, extracting tribute from the Northern Uí Néill. He married the much wedded Gormlaith, mother of Sitric, King of the Dublin Norse. Brian Boru is remembered as having driven the Norse from Ireland but in fact their power was severely diminished by the time of the BATTLE OF CLONTARF in 1014, when as High King he led the armies of various tribal or regional groups against a combined force of Leinstermen and their Norse allies from Dublin, Man and Orkney.

**BORUMBORAD, DR ACHMET**, (18th century). Patrick Joyce, a Dubliner posing as a Turkish expert on thermal bathing, introduced highly successful Turkish baths to eighteenth-century Dublin and was patronised by the aristocracy until he fell from favour after a misfortunate occasion during which a party of drunken members of parliament fell into the cold pool of the baths and had to be rescued in undignified circumstances.

**BOSSI, PETER**. Venetian by birth, worked in Dublin from 1785 to 1798. He excelled in inlaying white marble with fragments of coloured stone representing floral decorations, similar to the inlay work in eighteenth-century furniture. Bossi is particularly noted for his fireplaces which decorated many Dublin mansions. Fine examples can be seen at BELVEDERE HOUSE and the Loreto convent in North Great George's Street.

**BOSWELL, JAMES**, (1740-1795). The papers of Boswell, Samuel Johnson's biographer, were discovered at MALAHIDE CASTLE and sold to Yale University by the last Lord Talbot de Malahide who died in 1948. Boswell was a distant family connection of the Malahides and the papers had been in the house in a cabinet which came from Auchinleck, the Boswell family home in Scotland. They form the largest single collection of eighteenth-century literary manuscript material to survive. Much of this material has now been published. Neither Boswell nor Johnson ever visited Ireland despite Boswell's enthusiasm for a visit to Dublin following their Scottish tour in 1773.

> Boswell: 'Should you not like to see Dublin, Sir?'
> Johnson: 'No, Sir; Dublin is only a worse capital'

(*The Life of Samuel Johnson*, James Boswell.)

**BOTANIC GARDENS**, Glasnevin, D6, tel 374388. The National Botanic Gardens were founded in 1795 by the Dublin Society to 'increase and foster a taste for practical scientific botany'. A smaller version of the great gardens at Kew, there are over twenty thousand species growing both indoors and out, and the range of Victorian glasshouses is of particular interest. The earliest of these is the Curviliniar Range, dating from 1843. The Great Palm House was built in 1884. These glasshouses contain the Garden's collection of tropical plants and exotic species. The only portion of the gardens dating from the eighteenth-century plantings is the Great Yew Walk. Features of the Gardens are a bog garden and water garden, rose garden and rhododendron and Chinese shrubberies. Open all year round except Christmas Day. Summer, Mon-Sat 9.00-18.00, Sun 11.00-18.00. Winter, Mon-Sat 10.00-16.30, Sun 11.00-16.30. The Conservatories are open approximately the same hours as the Gardens, with a lunchtime closure 12.45-14.45. Buses 13,19,19a from O'Connell Street 34,34a, from Middle Abbey Street.

**BOTTLE TOWERS**, Whitehall Road, Churchtown-Rathfarnham. Built by the local landowner Major Hall, in 1741-42 (also known as Hall's Barn) to give work to the poor after the hard winter of that year and contemporary with the OBELISK on KILLINEY HILL constructed for the same purpose. These two stone buildings are conical in shape, the larger having an external staircase for access to the upper rooms. Not strictly follies, although belonging to that genre rather than to any other, both functioned as barns. See also the Wonderful Barn at CASTLETOWN. Bus 16, 16A, 17, 47 from O'Connell Street.

**BOUCICAULT, DIONYSIUS LARDNER (DION)**, (1820-1890). Playwright and actor, born in Dublin at 47 Lower Gardiner Street where his mother ran a boarding house. Prolific writer, his three Irish plays, *The Colleen Bawn* (1860), *Arrah na Pogue* (1864), and *The Shaughraun* (1874), were very successful in their day and are still performed. His presentation of Irish characters is variously taken as being dignified or stage-Irish caricature.

**BOWDEN, JOHN**, (d1829). Architect to the Boards of Education and First Fruits, his most important work is ST. STEPHEN'S CHURCH on an island site in Upper Mount Street, 1824, the most magnificently situated of Dublin's Georgian churches. It is affectionately known as the 'Peppercanister Church', and it ends the vista along MERRION SQUARE south with a portico and delicate lantern topped by a shallow dome.

**BOWEN, ELIZABETH**, (1899-1937). Novelist and short-story writer, born at 15 Herbert Place (plaque), off Lower BAGGOT STREET, Her impressions of her early life in Dublin are recorded in the book *Seven Winters*, 1942. Regarded equally as an English and an Irish writer, she lived the major part of her adult life in England.

**BOYLAN, BLAZES**. Character in ULYSSES, lover of MOLLY BLOOM, organiser of concerts and theatrical tours, cad.

**BOYLE, RICHARD**, Earl of Cork, (d1643). St. Patrick's Cathedral, Patrick Street, D8. The Boyle monument, erected in 1632 in ST. PATRICK'S CATHEDRAL to the Great Earl of Cork, is the finest seventeenth-century memorial in Ireland. Sixteen figures are represented on four tiers of this painted stone and stucco monument carved by Edmond Tingham, showing his wife's family, as well as all the Earl's children including, in the bottom centre, the youthful Robert Boyle, later eminent as chemist and philosopher and propounder of 'Boyle's Law'.

**BRAY**, Co. Wicklow. Victorian seaside town on to the south of Dublin Bay and dominated by the rocky outcrop of Bray Head, one of the most distinctive and geologically the oldest feature of the coastline surrounding Dublin. It is a popular summer excursion place for the residents of the inner city. The Esplanade and waterfront hotels indicate the style of the place in the nineteenth century, but the attraction today is the large number of entertainment palaces on the seafront. Bray became established as a residential area for city businessmen during the nineteenth century and flourished with the coming of the railway in the 1850s. 24km (15 miles) from the city centre. Bus 45 from Burgh Quay, 84 from College Street, DART from city centre.

**BREWERIES.** Brewing formed an important area of manufacture in Dublin from the seventeenth century to the present. At the beginning of the eighteenth century there were over fifty separate breweries in the city but these gradually amalgamated or failed, with the exception of the GUINNESS BREWERY which was established in 1759 by Arthur Guinness when he took a 9,000 year lease on the St. James's Gate premises. The Guinness Brewery has long been synonymous with Dublin and for a period at the beginning of this century was the largest brewery in the world.

**BRICKFIELD TOWN.** The name of the SANDYMOUNT area during the eighteenth century. Lord Merrion had brick

kilns here using the local clay. From 1772 the burning of brick kilns within two miles of lit streets was prohibited.

**BRICKWORK.** Although domestic architecture in the city from the seventeenth to the early twentieth centuries was almost entirely constructed of brick with the notable exception of prominent public buildings, there is little evidence of decorative brickwork before the late Victorian era. Façades were plain with scalloped gables in an Anglo-Dutch manner lasting into the early Georgian period but after that rectangular and uniform building lines predominate. Extensive brick works existed around the city perimeter and facing bricks were imported as ballast from England, in particular from Bristol. Much of the charm of the older parts of the city derives from the mellow colours of the brickwork which range from browns through reds to greys and yellows. When the brick façades of the older parts of the city catch the light of the evening sun the buildings glow in a manner that is part of the essence of the city.

**BRIDGES ON THE LIFFEY.** The first crossing of the Liffey was at the Hurdle Ford (Átha Cliath), now the position of Fr. Mathew Bridge, from which the city took one of its names in antiquity and its official name since 1922. The bridge built on this site remained the only bridge until the seventeenth century. By 1728 there were five bridges, and fourteen by 1983. Many of the bridges built in the succeeding centuries have had their names changed, giving rise to a situation where a bridge may be popularly known by more than one name. The fact that the municipality may deem a change appropriate does not guarantee that common usage will follow.

From west to east the bridges on the Liffey within the city are:

Island Bridge, Alexander Stephenson, 1794.

Sean Heuston Bridge, (King's Bridge), George Papworth, 1827.

Frank Sherwin Bridge, 1983.

Rory O'More Bridge (Bloody, Barrack Bridge), 1863.

Queen Maeve Bridge, (Queen's Bridge), Charles Vallency,1764.

Father Mathew Bridge, (Whitworth Bridge), George Knowles, 1816. On the site of the original crossing of the Liffey.

O'Donovan Rossa Bridge (Richmond Bridge), J. Savage, 1813.

Grattan Bridge (replaced Essex Bridge), 1874.

Ha'Penny Bridge (Liffey, Metal, Wellington), John Windsor, 1816.

O'Connell Bridge (Carlisle Bridge by James Gandon, widened 1890), 1791.

Butt Bridge (Congress Bridge), 1932.

Loop Line Railway Bridge, 1891.

Talbot-Memorial Bridge, 1978.

East Link Bridge, 1984.

**BROADSTONE STATION,** Phibsboro, D7. Railway terminal designed by JOHN SKIPTON MULVANY, 1846-1850, for the Midland Great Western Railway, now used as a CIE coach depot. It belongs, with HEUSTON and CONNOLLY stations, to a small but impressive group of early railway buildings in Dublin, all of which are architecturally distinguished. Built in a Neo-Egyptian style, the granite façade has an entrance pavilion with battered walls. The Ionic colonnaded cab shelter on the eastern side of the station was added by George Wilkinson in 1861. The Broadstone closed as a railway station in 1931.

*The Liffey, looking west.*

**BRODAR.** Viking chief who killed BRIAN BORU at the Battle of Clontarf. There are gruesome accounts of Brodar's death in Norse and Irish legends.

**BROIGHTER HOARD,** National Museum of Ireland, Kildare Street, D2. Hoard of gold objects which were discovered in 1896 in Co. Derry, consisting of a miniature boat, a hanging bowl, chains and a collar. The Broighter Boat is the most remarkable of these finds and it is probably a cult object used in religious rituals, although it is hard not to believe that it could be the wonderful toy of some princely child. This little craft, complete with oars, mast and benches for the absent crew, is among the greatest treasures of the Museum. Precise dating of the Hoard is difficult, but the collar which has extensive La Tène decoration may be of the first century BC, and the other objects somewhat later.

**BRONZE AGE REMAINS.** Finds have been made at various sites around the city. DALKEY ISLAND, which has been occupied since Mesolithic times, Drimnagh, PHOENIX PARK, Sutton etc. These remains are the characteristic ceramics of the Beaker Folk and personal jewellery. A cist tomb was discovered in Parliament Street with the usual grave goods, axe heads, ceramics, bronze objects.

**BROOKING, CHARLES.** Map maker. His map of Dublin, 1728, is the earliest separate map of the city to be published and has the added attraction of incorporating a set of views of the principal buildings as well as a fascinating panoramic view of the city from the north looking east across the Liffey. Only two other maps preceded it – SPEED in 1611 and Pratt in 1708. Many of the buildings depicted on Brooking's map have disappeared or been radically altered. Curiously, this map was created before the convention of having the north at the top of the sheet became generally accepted and according to modern taste it is upside down.

**BROTHELS.** The most notorious red light district in Dublin was that of

*Gold torc, from the National Museum.*

MONTO or Montgomery Street which flourished up to the emergence of the Irish Free State after which it was suppressed. Called 'Nighttown' in *Ulysses*, the brothels of the area ranged from palatial establishments reminiscent of the paintings of Toulouse Lautrec to dens of unimaginable squalidness.

**BROWN, CHRISTY**, (1932-1981). Novelist and poet, born with a severe physical disability and educated at home by his mother who taught him to write using his left foot. His autobiography *My Left Foot*, which deals with his childhood in Dublin and his struggle for a means to express himself, was the basis for a highly successful film of the same name.

come not with ornate grief

to desecrate my sleep

but a calm togetherness of hands –

('Come Softly to My Wake', Christy Brown.)

**BROWN THOMAS**, Grafton Street. 'BTs' to initiates, the smartest department store in Dublin with an impressive frontage on Grafton Street painted in black and red with gilded lettering, and like BEWLEY'S ORIENTAL CAFÉS one of the institutions of Grafton Street.

**BRUCE, KING ROBERT**, (1274-1329). Robert and Edward Bruce with 2,000 men camped at Castleknock in 1317 intending to besiege Dublin. The citizens panicked and burned the suburbs outside the walls, and demolished much of St Mary's Abbey on the northern bank of the Liffey for building materials to reinforce the city walls. The Bruces attacked Limerick instead.

**BRUGHA, CATHAL**, (1874-1922). Revolutionary and politician. He joined the VOLUNTEERS in 1913 while still a schoolboy. He was Second-in-Command of the South Dublin Union during 1916 and became Chief of Staff of the IRA in 1917. Represented Waterford as TD in the first DÁIL in 1919 but opposed the Treaty and was killed during the CIVIL WAR, fighting on the Republican side.

**BULL ISLAND**, Dollymount, D3. Five kilometre (3 miles) long, 500m (160ft) wide, artificial island running alongside the Dollymount, Raheny and Sutton coastline of DUBLIN BAY. Composed of sand dunes it was formed after the construction of the North BULL WALL in 1825 by the clockwise motion of the currents in the bay carrying sand and silt from the LIFFEY on to the northern side of the channel. The area of the island has quadrupled in the last hundred years and it is still growing to the north east towards the Sutton shore. Bull Island beach, known as DOLLYMOUNT STRAND is the finest beach close to the city centre. The Island is an important nature reserve and in 1931 it was established as the first official reserve in the country. In 1981 it

*Bull Island Interpretive Centre.*

was declared a UNESCO Biosphere Reserve, the only such reserve within the precincts of a city anywhere in the world. During the winter months Bull Island is the overwintering place for up to 3,000 Brent Geese who come there from Arctic Canada, and the lagoon behind the sand dunes frequently has as many as 30,000 birds, curlew, oystercatchers, redshank and many other waders, feeding on the mud flats. The dunes also provide a habitat for many species of plants and animals, even foxes and the Irish hare. On a hot summer Sunday the island can accommodate up to 10,000 holidaymakers. Bus 30, Lower Abbey Street.

**BULL ISLAND INTERPRETIVE CENTRE**, Dollymount, D3, tel 338341. Built by Dublin Corporation in 1985 and funded by the EC Environment Fund, following a report from An Foras Forbartha recommending its construction, and the designation of Bull Island as a Biosphere Reserve by UNESCO in 1981. Its purpose is to act as a conservation and information centre for the unique environment which the island represents as a wildlife habitat and also as a recreational area, and to balance these somewhat incompatible demands. The building, which is sensitively designed to fit into the wild grass and dune surroundings, provides a source of information for the wildlife, flora and fauna of the island, with tours, lectures, video presentations and photographic displays. Daily 10.00-4.30. DART from city centre to Raheny and ten-minute walk. Bus 30 from Lower Abbey Street.

**BULL WALLS.** The two harbour walls built to speed the flow of the LIFFEY and solve the problem of continuing silting which for centuries had made access by ships to the city extremely difficult. The Great South Wall was constructed between 1730 and the end of the eighteenth century, the POOLBEG LIGHTHOUSE, which stands at the end of the wall, was finished in 1768 and the wall then built back towards the city. The North Bull Wall was constructed between 1800 and 1825. This strategy of marine engineering largely solved the problem although some dredging is still occasionally necessary to maintain a deep channel to the port.

**BULLOCK CASTLE AND HARBOUR**, Breffni Road, Dalkey. Twelfth-century castle built by the Cistercians to fortify the small harbour which lies below it. The harbour which has finely built nineteenth-century masonry piers is now a haven for small boat owners, and fishing boats may be hired for angling along the coast. The castle with its Medieval stone-carved head on the

south-west angle of the western tower about 5m (15ft) above the ground, known as 'The Dane's Head' is now part of Our Lady's Manor Hospital.

**BURGH, COLONEL THOMAS**, (1670-1730). Architect, he was Surveyor General for twenty-eight years from 1700. Burgh designed a group of important early eighteenth-century buildings most of which survive, and Burgh Quay is called after him. His works include the Royal, now Collins's Barracks, 1706. This impressive and immense cut stone building, capable of accommodating eight regiments, presents a severe yet dignified façade to the LIFFEY, and although composed of separate blocks can be compared in scale to the ROYAL HOSPITAL. He also designed the old Custom House, 1707, TRINITY COLLEGE LIBRARY, ST. WERBURGH'S CHURCH, 1715, and DR. STEEVEN'S HOSPITAL, 1713-18.

**BURKE, EDMUND**, (1729-1797). Born Dublin, 17 Arran Quay. Parliamentarian, journalist and writer, his father was a solicitor and Burke studied law at TRINITY COLLEGE but failed to be called to the Bar. In 1759, he became the editor in London of the *Annual Register*, a precursor of the modern literary-political journal, and he continued this work for almost thirty years. As a political moderate he favoured religious toleration and belonged to the intellectual circle centred around Dr Johnson, which included his fellow Dubliner, OLIVER GOLDSMITH. His reaction to the horrors of the French Revolution provoked him to write his *Reflections on the Revolution in France* which evoked the now much more significant response from Thomas Paine, *The Rights of Man*, one of the seminal works in the definition of individual liberty. A statue of Burke stands outside the west front of Trinity College.

**'BURN ANYTHING FROM ENG-LAND'.** One of the more acerbic pronouncements of JONATHAN SWIFT, Dean of St. Patrick's Cathedral whose failure to find clerical advancement in England turned him into a reluctant patriot, campaigning vigorously against abuses of English rule in Ireland. 'Ireland would never be happy until a law were made for burning anything that came from England, except their people and their coals.'
(*A Proposal for the Universal use of Irish Manufacture*, Jonathan Swift.)

**BURTON, SIR FREDERICK WIL-LIAM,** (1816-1900). Artist, subsequently director for twenty years of the National Gallery, London. Burton was an extremely skilful draughtsman and his Irish genre and romantic subject paintings capture the popular perception of nineteenth-century rural Irish life as melancholy and dramatic. Among the NATIONAL GALLERY of Ireland's large collection of Burton's works is an ethereal drawing of the dead JAMES CLARENCE MANGAN, portraits of THOMAS DAVIS and SIR SAMUEL FERGUSON, and a great many studies for his more major works.

**BUS INFORMATION.** Dublin Bus information bureau and customer service, 59 Upper O'Connell Street, tel 734222.

**BUSÁRAS,** the Central Bus Station. Store Street, D1. Designed in 1945 by MICHAEL SCOTT but not completed until 1953. Busáras is a glass-fronted L-shaped building with the arms of the L joined by a curved scalloped roofed sec-

*Child banjo player on Grafton Street.*

tion. It was the first major modern-movement public building to be erected in central Dublin. The building has good sculptural qualities externally but is totally unrelated to its neighbour, JAMES GANDON'S CUSTOM HOUSE. The construction of the FINANCIAL SERVICES CENTRE at Custom House Dock nearby provides an appropriate twentieth-century ambiance for Busáras from which it benefits architecturally. Officially known as Áras Mhic Dhiarmada, and called after Séan Mac Diarmada, signatory of the 1916 Proclamation, Busáras houses the offices of the Department of Social Welfare. It is the terminus for the airport bus as well as all provincial bus services.

**BUSKERS.** The street musicians of Dublin contribute to making the city centre among the most musical anywhere. GRAFTON STREET is the centre of this entertainment and encompasses all known forms of music, and a wide range of talents as well. Walking from one end of the street to the other may bring the listener past the lonely and sibilant sound of a traditional tin whistle player, a bespectacled child prodigy, aged about five, performing a Mozart violin solo, an enormously vocal group of folk singers with six different instruments roaring out a ballad of Irish history, or a lone performer on the acoustic steel saw. Come back another day and the entire ensemble will have changed to perhaps a string quartet in formal attire and a virtuoso performance on the Brazilian nose flute or an emergent rock band. Henry Street is another good area for buskers – especially jazz musicians – but they may be encountered in all sorts of odd places around Dublin, under Merchant's Arch and at cinema queues. Recently the ranks of the buskers have been swelled by other forms of street entertainers, mime artists, PAVEMENT ARTISTS and pavement poets, all of whom add great interest to the street life of the city. Despite the evident enthusiasm with which buskers perform, contributions from the public are always hoped for.

**BUTT BRIDGE**. Built in 1879 as a metal swivel bridge and rebuilt and renamed in 1932 as Congress Bridge after the International Eucharistic Congress held in Dublin in that year. However, this official change of name was not publicly accepted and it is still known by its original name, commemorating ISAAC BUTT, founder of the Irish HOME RULE PARTY in 1870. A century was to

elapse before another bridge was built over the LIFFEY, Talbot Memorial Bridge in 1978 followed by the East Link Bridge in 1984.

**BUTT, ISAAC**, (1813-1879). Academic, barrister, parliamentarian. Founder of the Irish HOME RULE PARTY in 1870, which was subsequently led by PARNELL. Butt was a noted defence council for the Young Irelanders in 1848 and also for the Fenians in 1865-9.

**BUTTERY**, Trinity College, D2. Vaulted basement bar beneath the great Dining Hall on the north side of Front Square.

**BYRNE, PATRICK**, (1783-1846). Architect and Dublin's greatest church designer of the first half of the nineteenth century. Byrne studied under HENRY AARON BAKER, who was himself a student of JAMES GANDON, at the Dublin Society Schools. Byrne worked in a monumental Neo-Classic mode and the external massing of his churches makes them impressive from any angle. The façades of St. Audoen's and Rathmines churches have a lofty and uncluttered dignity which are a hallmark of Byrne's work. Examples of his work include ADAM AND EVE'S Franciscan Church, Merchant's Quay, 1829; St. Paul's, Arran Quay, 1837; St. Audoen's, High Street, 1841-6, the dome of which collapsed in 1884; OUR LADY OF REFUGE, Rathmines Road, 1850, which has the finest dome in Dublin.

CAFE, (Creative Activity For Everyone), 23-5 Moss Street, D2, tel 770330. CAFE is an all-Ireland umbrella body and information network available from a computer database of people involved in arts activities in the community. This skills resource covers a wide range of organisations and individual practitioners in everything from metalwork to mime, and arts administration to pavement artists. One of CAFE's publications is *The Funding Handbook*, a guide to funding sources in Ireland.

*The Coffee Inn.*

CAFÉS. The coffee bar in the strict sense of the word is an uncommon institution in Dublin, the term café tending to describe something which is more than a coffee bar yet less than a fully fledged restaurant. The Grafton Street and O'Connell Street areas abound in various hybrid versions of the species, most notably BEWLEY'S on Grafton Street, a perennial Dublin rendezvous, and The Coffee Inn on Duke Street, a tiny and bustling Italian café favoured by students and the Bohemian world. Pizza parlours, chip shops, hamburger joints are found the whole way from St. Stephen's Green to the Parnell Monument, and in the surrounding side streets. See RESTAURANTS.

CALDER, ALEXANDER, (1898-1976), Fellows' Square, Trinity College. The American sculptor Calder is better known for his 'Mobiles' sculptures of brightly painted sections of steel rotating on wire suspension. The example of his work in Trinity comes from a later phase in his sculpture, called 'Stabiles', static versions of his earlier pieces. This sculpture, 'Cactus', is one of the best situated examples of contemporary work in Dublin, its position on the trimmed lawns enhanced by concentric rings of granite cobbles.

CAMBRENSIS, GIRALDUS, (1146-1223). Giraldus de Barri, Welsh historian and cleric, visited Ireland in 1183 and 1185. His *History and Topography of Ireland* is an important and rather dotty account of Medieval Ireland based as much on Giraldus's vivid imagination as on his travels. Other than mentioning Dublin, it did not apparently strike him as being worth writing about.

CAMPANILE, Front Square, Trinity College. The bell tower of the Augustinian Priory of All Hallows, on the lands of which Trinity College was built, stood near the spot now occupied by the Campanile, erected in 1852-6 in a curious Victorian Baroque style. Designed by CHARLES LANYON, it replaced an eighteenth-century campanile by RICHARD CASTLE.

**CARLETON, WILLIAM,** (1794-1869). Novelist, born in Co.Tyrone but came to Dublin when he was twenty-four where he lived for the rest of his life. From his understanding of rural life, Carleton wrote the most vivid accounts of the life of Irish country people during the mid-nineteenth century. His work deals with the squalor, indignity and dissipation of all classes of society during that time – *Traits and Stories of the Irish Peasantry* (1830), *The Black Prophet* (1847). He lived in Fairview and subsequently Rathgar.

**CARSON, SIR EDWARD,** (1854-1935). Lawyer, politician, Unionist leader. Born 4 HARCOURT STREET. As a lawyer Carson successfully defended the Marquis of Queensbury during the 1895 trial in London of OSCAR WILDE (his contemporary at Trinity College) – Wilde had been charged with homosexual activities. Carson became the Chairman of the Irish Unionist Parliamentary Party in 1910 and also the founder of the Ulster Volunteers who resisted the introduction of Home Rule. He organised the arming of the VOLUNTEERS in 1914, an act which was emulated by the Republicans in the south of Ireland some months later under the leadership of ERSKINE CHILDERS, and which led indirectly to the 1916 RISING.

**CARYATIDS.** Despite an impeccable Classical provenance, caryatids are rare in the sculptural decorations of Dublin's Georgian architecture, although the examples that exist are all of considerable interest. In the NATIONAL MUSEUM is a fireplace dated 1635 from the Old Bawn House in Tallaght, with male figures bearing the entablature on either side of a panel depicting the siege of Jerusalem. Another caryatid fireplace is the fine oak carved one in the HOUSE OF LORDS, dated to 1748, though the vigorously carved male heads which flank the fireplace are more strictly terminals, lacking a body. Facing Constitution Hill, the façade of the KING'S INNS has two caryatid porches, male and female by EDWARD SMYTH, which carry the entablatures. The figures depicted are Security and Law, and Plenty and Wine. To complete the caryatid family, the NATIONAL GALLERY restaurant is graced by life-size casts of the originals from the Erechtheum in Athens.

**CASEMENT, SIR ROGER,** (1864-1916). Diplomat, humanitarian, revolutionary, he was born at 24 Lawson Terrace, Sandycove Road (plaque). Casement worked in the British Consular Service in Africa and South America and wrote reports on the exploitation of the native populations by colonial administrators. He retired from the Service to become involved in the Nationalist movement. In 1915 he travelled to Germany where he attempted unsuccessfully to form an Irish regiment in the German Army, recruited from Irish prisoners of war. Casement returned to Ireland in 1916 on a German submarine but was arrested in Co. Kerry, tried for high treason in London and executed in August 1916. His remains were repatriated in 1956 and buried with a state funeral in GLASNEVIN CEMETERY. Casement's homosexuality, revealed during his trial, contributed to the public animosity felt towards him at the time in Britain.

**CASEY, JEM.** Proletarian bard. *The Poet of the Pick*, a creation of FLANN O'BRIEN. Casey's oeuvre consists of a single much quoted poem, 'The Workman's Friend', a humorous pastiche of

*Castletown House.*

Dublin working-class culture.

> When food is scarce and your larder
> bare
> And no rashers grease your pan,
> When hunger grows as your meals
> are rare –
> A pint of plain is your only man.

(*At Swim-Two-Birds*, Flann O'Brien.)

**CASINO, THE,** Malahide Road, Clontarf, D5, tel 331618. Built for the EARL OF CHARLEMONT between 1762 and 1773 in the grounds of his country house at Marino to the design of SIR WILLIAM CHAMBERS. It is the most important and exotic example of the Palladian villa in Ireland, with remarkable stone carving by Joseph Wilton and SIMON VIERPYL. The compact arrangement of the interior makes the two-storey building appear, from the outside, to be a single storey. Sumptuously decorated, the Casino cost the extravagant sum of £20,000 to build, a prodigious amount in the eighteenth century. Recently restored by the Board of Works, the Casino glows amongst the humdrum suburbia of Fairview. It is, in a city noted for its Georgian architecture, one of the few examples of eighteenth-century palatial domestic architecture open to the public. May-Sept, Mon-Sat 10.00-7.00, Sun 2.00-4.00, Apr-Oct, Sat 10.00-4.00, Sun 2.00-4.00. Bus from city centre, 24, 27, 27A, 27B, 42, 42A, 42B, 42C, 43. Admission charge.

**CASTLE (CASSEL), RICHARD,** (1690-1751). Architect, born in Germany, came to Ireland in 1729, worked in the Palladian tradition. Better known for his country houses, he also designed some of the most notable buildings in Dublin. The delightful little Printing House, 1734, in TRINITY COLLEGE was his first building in the city. This was followed by a group of magnificent private houses for the city's leaders of fashion. CLANWILLIAM HOUSE, 1738, the Dining Hall, TRINITY COLLEGE, 1740s, TYRONE HOUSE, 1740, and LEINSTER HOUSE, 1745, the largest eighteenth-century town house in Dublin and now the seat of the DÁIL. The ROTUNDA HOSPITAL was built in 1748 as a maternity hospital and still performs that function. Castle's country houses around Dublin are Carton, Co. Kildare, 1739, NEWBRIDGE HOUSE, Co. Dublin, RUSSBOROUGH, Co. Wicklow, 1741, and POWERSCOURT, Co. Wicklow, 1741.

**CASTLETOWN HOUSE,** Celbridge, Co. Kildare, tel 288252. This splendid house, built between 1719 and 1732 by William Conolly, Speaker of the Irish House of Commons, and continued by his widow Lady Louisa Conolly, is regarded as the greatest eighteenth-century house in Ireland, and it is the prototype for many such houses as Carton and RUSSBOROUGH. Now owned by the Irish Georgian Society, it is the centre for the Music Festival of Great Irish Houses held annually in June. The house is approached from the village of CELBRIDGE, by an 800m (3/4 mile) long lime avenue and the first sight of the main façade is breathtaking. The central block, designed by ALESSANDRO GALI-LEI, is like an Italian Renaissance palazzo to which are joined the service wings, by SIR EDWARD LOVETT PEARCE. Inside, the house is richly decorated in the different tastes of the eighteenth century, with a two-storey columned entrance hall embellished with FRANCINI plasterwork. The long gallery is decorated in a Pompeian manner and the print room, which is papered with eighteenth-century prints, is unique in Ireland. The landscaping of the house is on a grand scale, although simple in treatment. Facing the garden façade is 'Conolly's Folly', a 42m (140ft) high monument designed by RICHARD CASTLE and built in 1739 as relief work for the poor. It stands, completing the vista, 1.6km (1 mile) from the house, a massive obelisk raised on a series of arches. In order to position it properly it had to be built, not on the Castletown demesne but on the adjoining estate of Carton. Also of interest is the 'WONDERFUL BARN', 1743, 1.6km (1 mile) to the east of the house, a vast folly-like conical brick structure with an external staircase, and two adjoining subsidiary barns. Lady Louisa Conolly's sister gives a contemporary reaction to the scale of living and building enterprises at Castletown.

My sister Conolly is building an Obelix to answer a Vistow at the Bake of Castletown House: it will cost her three or four hundred pounds at least, and I believe more, I don't know how she can dow so much, and live as she duse.

Opening hours, April-September, Mon-Fri 10.00-5.00, Sat 11.00-5.00, Sun 2.00-5.00. Other months, Sun only – 20.6km (13 miles) from Dublin. Admission charge. Bus 67 from Middle Abbey Street.

**CATHEDRALS.** Dublin has two Medieval cathedrals, CHRIST CHURCH, 1173, which was built within the walled city and ST. PATRICK'S, 1191, built outside the walls to the south. Christ Church or the Cathedral of the Holy Trinity is the Church of Ireland (Anglican) diocesan cathedral of Dublin and GLENDALOUGH. St. Patrick's is the National Cathedral of the Church of Ireland. There is no Catholic cathedral, although proposals have been made in the past for building one on various sites – the park of MERRION SQUARE or on Bolton Street. The PRO CATHEDRAL on Marlborough Street, 1825, functions as a Catholic cathedral but lacks this ecclesiastical status which has, since the Reformation, remained with the original foundations.

**CATHOLIC ASSOCIATION.** Organisation led by DANIEL O'CONNELL and Richard Lalor Shiel in 1823 which in the years prior to the granting of CATHOLIC EMANCIPATION continued the agitation for reform. The Association, which had a large popular following, became the first mass movement in Irish history dedicated to constitutional reform rather than force of arms. 'Simultaneous meetings' were organised throughout the country in 1828 to demand concessions from the government. The election of O'Connell as the first Catholic MP and the tide of popular support for the movement eventually convinced Sir Robert Peel, the British Prime Minister, to grant the Association's demands.

*St. Patrick's Cathedral.*

**CATHOLIC EMANCIPATION.** The repeal of the PENAL LAWS which discriminated against all religious groups other than the established church preoccupied liberal thought in both Britain and Ireland from the middle of the eighteenth century but was not achieved until 1829. Due to the intense agitation of the Repeal Association and various Catholic committees, which were staunchly supported by liberal Protestants and led by DANIEL O'CONNELL, the Westminster parliament eventually succumbed to pressure and passed the Roman Catholic Relief Act in April 1829.

**CELTIC TWILIGHT.** Generic title for all the literary and artistic movements which developed, principally in Dublin, in conjunction with the rising Irish Nationalism of the late nineteenth century. The ABBEY THEATRE was the flagship of the movement, and W.B. YEATS its capable and inspiring captain. The Celtic Twilight had strong links with visionary and occult movements in other countries, such as Madame Blavatsky's Theosophical Society in London. AE is the epitome of the Twilight visual artist, as is Yeats in his early poems, and both evoke fairies and the *sidhe* frequently in their work. The harsh realities of the 1916 RISING and CIVIL WAR made the visionary aspects of the movement untenable and most of its followers moved on to more sober realities. The last great practitioner of the Twilight school was the painter JACK B. YEATS who remarkably managed to marry Celtic themes with Continental expressionism.

**CEMETERIES.** The two principal cemeteries in Dublin, GLASNEVIN and MOUNT JEROME, were opened in the early nineteenth century in response to the inadequate space available in graveyards surrounding the existing churches.

*Central Bank from Andrew's Street.*

The then prevalent practice of body snatching from unprotected graveyards was also a strong motivating force. The 'sack-em-ups', professional body snatchers, often in league with the burial authorities, procured corpses for the dissecting rooms of the teaching hospitals. Glasnevin was opened in 1832, and Mount Jerome in 1836, and both have very interesting funerary architecture as well as being the burial places of the famous. Although Glasnevin was established as a Catholic cemetery and Mount Jerome as a Protestant one, these divisions are not rigidly adhered to. However, worthies of both communities tend to be found in their correct denominational resting places. Architecturally there is an interesting division between the two; Glasnevin favours the Nationalist imagery of Celtic crosses of which there is a superabundance, while in

Mount Jerome the imagery is strictly Neo Classical, obelisks, broken columns and splendid sarcophagi. Older cemeteries around the city, Bully's Acre, Croppies Hole and Arbour Hill, have very few monuments although these places also abound with historical associations.

**CENSORSHIP.** The new broom of the IRISH FREE STATE, wishing to protect its citizens from corruption by pernicious literature, introduced a period of state censorship which for over thirty years effectively banned many of the leading writers of the day, as well as others long dead and considered amongst the great names of world literature. The Committee on Evil Literature was set up in 1926 and the Censorship Act passed in 1929. The Censorship Board, consisting of five persons, prepared a register of banned books. This list at various times included in its ranks, Boccaccio, Balzac, and Proust, and amongst contemporary writers, BECKETT, Freud, Hemmingway, JOYCE, O'Connor, Ó Faoláin, Sartre and Shaw. The 1967 Censorship Bill introduced a more liberal attitude and although censorship still exists it is now directed against pornography rather than literature or philosophy.

**CENTRAL BANK**, Dame Street, D2. Designed by Sam Stephenson, and completed in the midst of considerable controversy in 1978. The Central Bank is unique in twentieth-century Dublin architecture for the manner in which its floors are suspended from the roof, with the structural cables clearly visible on the outside. A small piazza was created around the base of the Bank and an existing eighteenth-century building, the Commercial Buildings, 1796, by FREDERICK DARLEY was reproduced to the east of the modern block. This replica of the building which originally faced Dame Street has ingeniously been rotated so that it now opens into the Central Bank piazza. To the west of the piazza on the corner of Fownes Street is the Venetian Romanesque Revival Crown Life building by TN Deane, 1868, with a row of early eighteenth-century houses completing what must be the best newly created civic space in Dublin. Alas, the piazza always seems to be very windy.

**CHAMBERS, SIR WILLIAM,** (1723-1796). Architect, designed two Palladian masterpieces, CHARLEMONT HOUSE and the CASINO at Marino for LORD CHARLEMONT, although he never visited Ireland. Some of the furnishings of Charlemont House – cabinets for the Earl's medal collection – also designed by Chambers, have recently been identified at Elveden in Sussex, Lord Iveagh's house in England. Chambers also designed the Chapel and Theatre at Trinity College and interiors at RATHFARNHAM CASTLE. Before establishing his own practice JAMES GANDON worked in Chambers's office in London.

**CHAPTER HOUSES.** Two remain from the monastic foundations of the Medieval period, that at ST. MARY'S ABBEY off Abbey Street which is intact although submerged under later buildings, and that at CHRIST CHURCH CATHEDRAL, in a ruinous condition. The Christ Church Chapter House had a great tripartite east window, the base of which still stands.

**CHESTER BEATTY LIBRARY AND GALLERY OF ORIENTAL ART.** See LIBRARIES and ART GALLERIES.

**CHILD, ALFRED ERNEST,** (1875-1939). Stained glass artist and teacher, born in London. Child taught in the Metropolitan School of Art, Kildare Street, from 1901 and was responsible for introducing the high technical standards which became common amongst Irish stained-glass artists of the early twentieth century. He joined SARAH PURSER who had set up the stained-glass studios *AN TÚR GLOINE*, in 1903 as manager and between his work at both institutions was a guiding figure for the glass movement. Child's fine windows can be seen in the Unitarian Church, St. Stephen's Green, and the Chapel Royal, Dublin Castle. HARRY CLARKE, MICHAEL HEALY, Ethel Rhind, Beatrice Elvery and virtually every stained-glass artist of significance studied under Child's guidance.

**CHILDERS, ROBERT ERSKINE,** (1870-1922). Novelist, revolutionary, born in London. He fought in the Boer War on the British side, and in 1903 published the novel *The Riddle of the Sands*, a fictional account of a threatened German invasion of Britain. In 1914 Childers used his yacht, the *ASGARD*, to bring guns to Ireland for the Republicans in response to SIR EDWARD CARSON'S arming of the Ulster Volunteers. He then served in the Royal Navy Air Service during the First World War before becoming Director of Propaganda for the IRA, and Secretary of Treaty Negotiations in 1921. He took an anti-Treaty side in the CIVIL WAR and was shot in BEGGAR'S BUSH BARRACKS in 1922. His son Erskine H. Childers became fourth President of Ireland in 1973.

**CHILDREN OF LIR,** Garden of Remembrance, Parnell Square North, D1. Designed by Daithí Hanly and opened in 1966 on the fiftieth anniversary of the

Easter RISING, the Garden has a cross-shaped pool, decorated with a mosaic in which the ritually broken swords of Celtic warriors are depicted. The focal point of the Garden is the 8m (25 ft) high bronze group by OISIN KELLY. Representing the mythical Children of Lir, at the point of transformation from humans into swans, the sculptural group is also an interpretation of the lines 'All changed, changed utterly', from Yeats's poem 'Easter 1916'.

## CHURCHES AND PLACES OF WORSHIP. Considering the prominent place religious controversy held in Irish history, it is hardly surprising that Dublin should have a superabundance of churches and there are more than seven hundred places of worship of all denominations in the greater Dublin area, ranging from the magnificent Medieval CATHEDRALS to wayside Gospel Halls and Upper Rooms of obscure minority denominations. The places of worship include a tiny group of early Christian churches virtually all of which are in ruins, and an even smaller group of Medieval buildings which includes the two cathedrals. Little further church building took place until the late seventeenth and eighteenth centuries when a distinctive body of predominantly Anglican city churches was built. In the nineteenth century a tremendous surge of church building, in this case predominantly Catholic, occurred, followed in this century by a corresponding development. Church buildings of the late twentieth century form another small group, distinguished by a reassessment of the very nature of church building. Churches attached to institutions form a separate body, and number amongst their buildings some quite exceptional examples of ecclesiastical architecture where the em-

phasis is on the interior, unlike the usually free-standing and self-sufficient churches of all periods. The chapels of the ROYAL HOSPITAL KILMAINHAM, the ROTUNDA HOSPITAL, NEWMAN'S UNIVERSITY CHURCH, and that at DUBLIN CASTLE are examples of these institutional buildings. The work of a number of architects stand out from this mass of church building and most of the best buildings can be attributed to quite a small number of individuals. FRANCIS JOHNSTON, JOHN SEMPLE and PATRICK BYRNE between them have created more of the interesting churches of the nineteenth century than any other designers, although individual masterpieces by other architects also exist. Semple is the eccentric genius of church building in Dublin and everything he did is marked by his own peculiar and distinctive vision. Population shifts have left many of the important inner city churches without congregations, prey to decay and vandalism, and the new uses to which a deconsecrated church may be put – as stores, offices and showrooms – often seem unfitting and wasteful of fine architectural space. As well as the predominantly Christian denominations, Jewish synagogues, a mosque and places of meeting for followers of oriental religions add to the variety of Dublin's ecclesiastical buildings, and make them – after the architecture of the Georgian period – probably the most interesting group of buildings in Dublin. The churches listed below, a small proportion of the total number, are chosen for their historic, architectural, or individual merit.

ABBEY PRESBYTERIAN CHURCH, Parnell Square, D1. Known as Findlater's Church because the costs of the building were borne by Alexander Findlater of the merchant family whose opulent food shops were a characteristic element of the city from the nineteenth century down to the 1950s. This Gothic Revival building is a startling intrusion into the Georgian architecture of Parnell Square and it replaced Bective House, one of the mansions of Palace Row, as the northern side of the square was known. Abbey Church, designed by Andrew Heiton in 1864, is one of the outstanding examples of Gothic Revival in Dublin. The abbey of the title refers to ST. MARY'S ABBEY in Meeting House Lane, where the congregation originally met.

ADAM & EVE'S CHURCH, (RC, The Immaculate Conception), Merchant's Quay, D2. Franciscan church built in 1829 by PATRICK BYRNE and identified by its green copper dome, the rest of the church being largely hidden by the Franciscan Friary buildings on the quay, although visible from behind on Cook Street. The curious name by which the church is popularly known comes from a Catholic mass house which originally stood here. This was reached through an inn called The Adam and Eve. The strictures of the PENAL LAWS necessitated that Catholic and Dissenter worship should be carried on in unobtrusive locations, and the concealed position of the earlier chapel on Merchant's Quay is an indication of the difficulties experienced by worshippers during the seventeenth and eighteenth centuries.

ADELAIDE ROAD PRESBYTERIAN CHURCH, D2. Plain Classical building of the mid-nineteenth century with an Ionic portico on a high podium which ends the vista of Earlsfort Terrace admirably.

BLACK CHURCH, THE, (St. Mary's Chapel of Ease), Granby Row, off Parnell Square, D1. Severe Gothic Revival church by JOHN SEMPLE, the architect of the Board of First Fruits, and the most

*Interior of the Black Church.*

original church builder in Dublin during the nineteenth century. This building is entirely characteristic of his work, with a deeply recessed narrow doorway and the pronounced emphasis of abundant pinnacles. The construction of the interior is quite remarkable, walls and roof being united in a single parabolic arch which leans inward over the viewer in a rather intimidating manner. While this novel solution is structurally ingenious, visually it is rather confusing as the inclining vault is decoratively treated as though it were a drunken wall. The popular name of the church aptly describes its appearance as it is built of black calp, the local limestone, which darkens after rain. Local lore states that 'if you go twice around the Black Church you will see the Devil'. With the decrease in its congregation the church was deconsecrated in 1962. No access.

CHAPEL ROYAL, THE, (RC, Church of the Most Holy Trinity), Dublin Castle, D2. Official chapel of the Viceroy, whose arms adorn the front of the gallery in this richly decorated example of early Gothic Revival. Designed by FRANCIS JOHNSTON, architect to the Board of Works in 1807, it has one of the last completed examples in Dublin of the extravagant plasterwork ceilings which had been such a characteristic of the decoration of all types of building. Here, the fan vaulting is particularly fine, as are the figures in high relief placed at the springing of the arches. The severe whiteness of the interior plasterwork contrasts admirably with the dark bog oak carving of the woodwork, and there is some early continental glass in the window of the nave that is unique to this Dublin church. Externally there are many carved stone heads of historic and legendary persons. The plasterwork is by George Stapleton and the stonecarvings are the work of EDWARD SMYTH and his son John. Built as an Anglican church, it was converted to Catholic worship in 1943, with some alterations to the interior, such as the removal of the finely carved pulpit which may be seen in ST. WERBURGH'S.

CHRIST CHURCH CATHEDRAL (Cof I), Christchurch Place, D2. Of the two Medieval cathedrals, Christ Church and ST. PATRICK'S, the former is the senior in both age and authority, and unlike St. Patrick's, it stood within the walls of the city. Founded in 1038 by Sitric, King of VIKING Dublin, none of this original wooden structure has survived. The present building, begun in 1172 by the Norman earl Richard Le Clare known as STRONGBOW, was in the Romanesque style, but of this building only the north and south apses can be considered to remain substantially of the period. The Hiberno-Romanesque doorway, now set into the outside wall of the southern apse facing the remains of the Chapter House, was removed from its original position on the north side during the nineteenth-century re-construction. Christ Church was finished in 1234 in the Norman Gothic style. The church today is largely a restoration by George Edmund Street who between 1871 and 1878 demolished and rebuilt much of the Cathedral which had long been in a semi-derelict condition. This tidying up exercise has unfortunately left Christ Church looking more Gothic Revival than Gothic. The crypt of the Cathedral, dating from the twelfth century, is unique in Irish church architecture, and contains some interesting relics, the seventeenth-century stocks, and other memorials. On the other side of St. Michael's Hill, Street added the Synod Hall to the existing Medieval tower of St. Michael's parish church, and linked it to the Cathedral by St. Michael's Arch. Christ Church is the diocesan cathedral of the Church of Ireland for Dublin and Glendalough. May-Sept, Mon-Sat 9.30-5.00, Admission donation. Bus 21A, 78, 78A from Fleet Street.

CILL MACNESSAN, Ireland's Eye, Howth. Ruined church of the Early Christian period, heavily restored in the nineteenth century. On the arch over the east window is the remains of a miniature round tower, like that on St. Kevin's Kitchen in Glendalough.

DUBLIN MOSQUE, THE, South Circular Road, D8. Formerly the Donore Avenue Presbyterian Church, converted to a Mosque in 1985, and now the centre of a growing Muslim community in the streets around the South Circular Road.

HOLY TRINITY (Cof I), Church Avenue, Rathmines, D6. Placed on an island site like the BLACK CHURCH, this church is best viewed from the Upper Rathmines Road from which its façade makes a pleasing conclusion to the street. Designed by JOHN SEMPLE in 1833, it has all the hallmarks of the architect – entrance doorway like a deeply recessed lancet window, sharp pinnacles, and an equally needle-like spire. The interior of Holy Trinity was roofed by a parabolic vault like that of the Black Church, but this was removed when the church was later enlarged.

HOWTH ABBEY, Abbey Street, Howth Village. Founded by Sitric, Viking king of Dublin in 1042, nothing of this early period is now visible. The present building is of many phases, but substantially fourteenth-century with fifteenth-century additions. The bell tower on the western gable dates from the seventeenth century, but a set of Medieval bells from the Abbey may be seen on the terrace of HOWTH CASTLE. The finest Medieval tomb in the Dublin area is preserved inside the Abbey. This is the recumbent double figure of Christopher St. Lawrence and his wife, Anna Plunkett of Ratoath, dated 1462. Key of church from Mrs McBride, 20 Church Street.

KILLINEY CHURCH, Marino Avenue West, Killiney Hill Road. Eleventh-century church with many interesting details, and some later additions. It has suffered comparatively little rebuilding. The churchyard which surrounds it has a somewhat circular form and this probably represents the line of the earthen embankment which originally enclosed the church.

MARY IMMACULATE REFUGE OF SINNERS (RC), Rathmines Road, D6. By PATRICK BYRNE, 1854, externally one of the finest nineteenth-century churches in Dublin. Built in a Classical Revival style, the massive green copper dome, with strong echoes of Rome, is a landmark in the area, and the most substantial dome on any building in the city. Facing on to Lower Rathmines Road, the church has a massive Corinthian portico and at the sides and rear, like St. Audoen's, another of Byrne's churches, the vast expanse of undecorated stone is patterned into a sculptural composition, with shallow recesses and string courses, making it an interesting building from any angle. A particularly fine view of the dome can be had from Mount Pleasant Square in RANELAGH.

MONKSTOWN CHURCH (C of I), Monkstown, Co. Dublin. JOHN SEMPLE'S eccentric masterpiece, perfectly sited at the junction of Monkstown Crescent and Carrickbrennan Road, and facing down the main road towards Blackrock. Opened in 1831, this extraordinary and imaginative exercise in the Gothic idiom looks on the outside like a fairytale fortress, with castellations, turrets and heavily moulded windows and entrance way. Inside, the character is quite different, and the ceiling is a riot of swirling fan vaults on a massive scale.

OUR LADY OF LOURDES (RC), Seán McDermott Street, D1. Neo-Romanesque basilica on a windswept site in the most depressed area of the inner city. The chief feature of interest in the church, opened in 1954 to replace an earlier temporary building, is the tomb of the ascetic labourer, MATT TALBOT, of whom a limestone figure embracing a baulk of timber stands on Talbot Memorial Bridge.

PRO CATHEDRAL (RC), Metropolitan Church of St. Mary, Marlborough Street, D1. Greek Revival Doric temple, built between 1815 and 1825, and one of the most architecturally distinguished buildings in Dublin, the merits of which are wasted on a cramped corner site. The designer of the Pro Cathedral is not known and it has in consequence been attributed to many different hands. The cathedral was originally intended to occupy the site where the GENERAL POST OFFICE (GPO) now stands on O'Connell Street, but it was felt at the time that this might represent too public a profile for the Catholic community, then emerging from the strictures of the PENAL LAWS. Both the building and the ironwork surrounding it have a severe and heavy detailing which contributes to the impressiveness of the composition, the absolute antithesis of the movement and grace of churches in the Gothic Revival manner of roughly the same period. There are several interesting monuments within the cathedral. The Palestrina Choir, founded by EDWARD MARTYN, performs at an 11.00am Latin mass on Sundays.

QUAKER MEETING HOUSE, Eustace Street, D2. Seventeenth-century building with some nineteenth-century additions, now used as the theatre of the Irish Film Institute.

ROTUNDA HOSPITAL CHAPEL, (Cof I), Parnell Square, D1. Baroque chapel in the ROTUNDA HOSPITAL, designed in 1748 by RICHARD CASTLE. The exuberant plasterwork in the Chapel is the only Baroque church interior in Dublin, and is the work of Barthelemy Cramillion. Large-scale allegorical figures form the centrepieces of the wall decoration above the cornice, and these are united by curving forms festooned with cherubs and putti. The centre of the ceiling was intended to have a painting of the Nativity by Cipriani, but due to the death of Dr Bartholomew Mosse, the philanthropic founder of the Hospital, the scheme was not carried to completion.

ROYAL HOSPITAL CHAPEL, Kilmainham, D8. In the north-west corner of the great courtyard of the Royal Hospital, the Chapel forms part of the range occupied by the Dining Hall and Master's quarters. Begun in 1680, the style of the building reflects the taste of the period prior to the erection of all the major buildings of the Georgian era. The Chapel is remarkable for its ceiling, the decoration of which is predominantly floral and executed in exceptionally high relief. The original ceiling, which was in a state of decay by the end of the nineteenth century, was replaced by a papier-maché replica in 1902. James Tarbary, a noted Huguenot wood carver of the period, was responsible for the oak decorations and carved altar in the chapel.

ST. ANDREW'S (RC), Westland Row, D2. Fine Greek Revival church by James Bolger, 1832. The Doric portico of the street façade is flanked by two brick terrace buildings which accommodate a school and the presbytery, nicely blending the church into the architecture of the street. The most interesting feature of the interior is the beautifully observed Farrell Memorial relief by JOHN HOGAN, appropriately executed in the manner of a Classical Greek funerary monument.

ST. ANN'S, Dawson Street, D2. Eighteenth-century church disguised by Victorian Romanesque façade. The original building of 1720 by Isaac Wills was intended to have a Classical façade with a spire, but this was never completed. When Sir Thomas Deane reconstructed the church in 1868, his scheme included a spire, but this attempt also failed to reach completion. Inside, much of the eighteenth-century furnishings remain and of particular interest is the shelving, dated 1723, where loaves of bread were displayed before being presented to the poor of the parish as a bequest from The Right Hon. Theophilus Lord Newton.

ST. AUDOEN'S (C of I), Commarket, off High Street, D8. The only surviving Medieval parish church in Dublin, the west doorway dates from 1190, and the nave from the thirteenth century. To the south, Lord Portlester's Chapel is fifteenth century, but this section of the building is roofless. In the seventeenth-century tower hangs a fifteenth-century peal of bells. The location of the church inside St. Audoen's Arch and approached by a winding and narrow alleyway is the closest one can get in Dublin to the atmosphere of the Medieval city. St. Audoen's is named after St. Ouen of Rouen. An Early Christian gravestone, *circa* eighth century, which is displayed in the porch is known as the 'Lucky Stone'. To touch it was believed to bring luck. The stone's existence suggests there may be Early Christian foundations at the site.

ST. AUDOEN'S (RC), High Street, D8. By PATRICK BYRNE, 1841-6. With a commanding presence from whatever angle it is viewed, the sheer dark stone walls which rise up over the City Wall at Cook Street were originally topped by a dome, but this collapsed in 1880. The Corinthian portico was added by STEPHEN ASHLIN in 1898. Today the crypt of the church is used for a theatrical presentation of Viking Dublin, and an audio visual presentation about St. Patrick is shown in the nave.

ST. BEGNET'S, Castle Street, Dalkey Village, Co. Dublin. Dedicated to the same saint as the church on Dalkey Island, its foundation probably dates from the same period, but the present remains are largely fifteenth century with some evidence of an earlier structure. A grave slab of the tenth century is displayed on the south wall and this indicates the

*The two St. Audoens.*

probable existence of an ecclesiastical enclosure from the Viking period. The church was in use up to the seventeenth century after which Dalkey declined in prosperity.

ST. BEGNET'S, Dalkey Island, Dalkey, Co. Dublin. Well preserved Early Christian church with later modifications. The straight lintel and slightly battered sides of the main doorway and the projecting side walls are typical of churches of the ninth century AD. On the bedrock facing the west door are two Early Christian Greek crosses carved in low relief.

ST. CATHERINE'S, Thomas Street, D8. Coming up Bridgefoot Street from the Liffey, through the decrepit blocks of flats, the sight of the Roman Doric façade of St. Catherine's is impressive in the extreme, rather like chancing upon the ruins of a Classical building in the slums of Rome. Built in 1769 and designed by John Smith, it is externally the finest of the eighteenth-century churches in the city, but like many others, its spire was never completed. Inside, the arrangements are mainly of the eighteenth century, with little alteration, and the organ is particularly fine. The church was deconsecrated in 1966, and now belonging to Dublin Corporation, it is occasionally used for concerts. In the railed area in front of St. Catherine's is a memorial to ROBERT EMMET who was hanged here in 1803. No access.

ST. DOULAGH'S (Cof I), Balgriffin, Malahide, Co. Dublin. Early Medieval church which is remarkably still in use. The stone roof of this building indicates the survival of a system of building which had been common some centuries before, of which an intact example can be seen in Glendalough. The tower contains what are thought to be anchorite or hermit's cells. An extension was sensitively added in 1863, designed by W.H. Lynn, maintaining the steep pitch of the original roof and generally harmonising with the Medieval structure.

ST. FINTAN'S, Carrickbrack Road, Shielmartin, Sutton, Co. Dublin. Miniscule Early Christian church, with Medieval additions. More like a toy than a real building, it ranks as one of the smallest churches in Ireland.

ST. FRANCIS XAVIER (RC), Upper Gardiner Street, D1. Jesuit church by JB Keane, 1829, and like ST. ANDREW'S, Westland Row, it is fitted into a street of terraced houses, with the adjoining buildings forming part of the church complex. The powerful Ionic entrance portico leads one into a vast columnless vaulted interior with heavy coffered ceiling, with the obvious intention of reflecting a Roman sense of dignity. On the north side of the church is a spacious corridor with shrines and ante rooms attached.

*St. Fintan's, Sutton.*

ST. GEORGE'S, Hardwicke Place, Temple Street, D1. By FRANCIS JOHNSTON, 1802, and it bears comparison with his Gothic CHAPEL ROYAL of some five years later, as an indication of this architect's impressive versatility. St. George's is the only Dublin church in the manner of Wren's London city churches, and unlike many others in Dublin, complete with spire it is the most handsome church building of the late Georgian period. The Greek Revival Ionic portico is topped by the 60m (180ft) high spire, rising in richly moulded stages which are Baroque in character. The interior has fine woodwork and panelling. St. George's has been converted into a conference centre.

ST. MAELRUAIN'S (Cof I), Tallaght Village, Co. Dublin. Small church by JOHN SEMPLE, 1829, attached to the Medieval bell tower of an earlier building. The bell tower was preserved when the earlier church was demolished to make way for the present one.

ST. MARY'S, Anglesea Road, Donny-brook, D4. At the junction of Simons-court Road and Anglesea Road, now spireless, but still characteristically a JOHN SEMPLE building of 1827.

ST. MARY'S, Mary Street, D1. Attributed to Thomas Burgh, 1697, and the only free-standing seventeenth-century church in Dublin. The exterior is undistinguished, but internally there are many fine features, particularly the Renatus Harris organ. The choir and side galleries are carried on plain wooden pillars, from which fluted Ionic pillars carry the roof. It is to open in 1991 as an enterprise co-operative.

ST. MARY'S ABBEY, Meetinghouse Lane, Upper Abbey Street, D1. Cistercian Abbey founded in 1156 on the north bank of the Liffey on what was then open land opposite the walled city of Dublin. The extensive lands of the Abbey included the manor farm of MONKSTOWN and the fisheries of BUL-LOCK HARBOUR. The only fragment of the considerable buildings of the Abbey to survive is the historic CHAPTER HOUSE which is now buried beneath an eighteenth-century warehouse in Meeting-house Lane. The building is associated with Lord THOMAS FITZGERALD, known as Silken Thomas, who began his revolt against the British Crown here. Abbey Street, and consequently the ABBEY THEATRE, takes its name from St. Mary's Abbey. A small historic exhibition is displayed in the Chapter House. Mon-Fri 10.00-5.30.

ST. MICHAEL & ST. JOHN (RC), Blind Quay, D2. Plain Gothic church of 1815 by J. Taylor, built on the site of Smock Alley Theatre and now visible from Merchant's Quay, but originally concealed from the river by buildings. It has an uncluttered interior with fine fan vaulting springing from slender pillars. The phenomena which afflicted the Protestant churches earlier in the century, of dwindling or vanishing congregations, is now being experienced by the inner city Catholic churches, and this church closed in 1990.

ST. MICHAN'S (Cof I), Church Street, D7. Medieval church of which only the tower now survives. The only parish church on the north bank of the Liffey to survive from its Viking foundation in 1095. The seventeenth-century vaults contain remarkably well preserved or mummified corpses displayed in open coffins. In the church is some particularly fine seventeenth-century woodcarving and an organ which Handel is reputed to have played, but the main body of the church was reconstructed in the last century.

ST. NICHOLAS OF MYRA (RC), Francis Street, D8. By John Leeson 1829, with portico by PATRICK BYRNE, 1860. This Classical church, set back from the street by a deep courtyard, is crowned by a lantern with a small dome. The pietà over the altar and attendant angels are by JOHN HOGAN.

ST. PATRICK'S CATHEDRAL (Cof I), Patrick Street, D8. The most impressive church building in Dublin, its splendid spire is probably the city's most distinctive landmark, and it is the hub of the LIBERTIES which surround the Cathedral. Founded in 1191 by the Norman Archbishop, John Comyn, St. Patrick's was not raised to cathedral status until 1213. The tower, built by Archbishop Minot in 1370, has, of any part of the building, suffered the least alteration or restoration, although the spire – the tallest in

Ireland – was not added until 1749 by
GEORGE SEMPLE. CHRIST CHURCH Cathedral already existed within the walls of
Dublin when Comyn built St. Patrick's
on open land to the south of the city
outside the jurisdiction of the City Provost. This led to Dublin having two
buildings of cathedral status, an anomaly which was not resolved until the
nineteenth century. St. Patrick's was declared the National Cathedral of the
Church of Ireland in 1872. The present
building is in the Early English style,
with extensive rebuilding during the late
nineteenth century when the fabric was
found to be much decayed. Apart from
the lofty simplicity of the nave, the most
impressive feature in the Cathedral is the
collection of monuments and memorials
which crowd the side aisles, and the
battle-tattered flags of Irish regiments
and banners of the Order of St. Patrick
which hang in the Choir and Transepts.
JONATHAN SWIFT was Dean of St. Patrick's from 1713 to 1745, and is buried
here. Swift's death mask, chair, pulpit
and other memorabilia are displayed in
the Swift Corner. The fabric of the Cathedral is now threatened by road-wide-
ning proposals which will affect its west
façade.

ST. PAUL'S (RC), Arran Quay, D1. By
PATRICK BYRNE, 1837, after the FOUR
COURTS, the most important building on
the north quays between HEUSTON and
O'CONNELL BRIDGES. The fine Ionic river
façade is topped by a bell tower with an
egg-shaped bronze dome, a marked contrast to the saucer dome of its neighbour,
the Four Courts. The plain interior is
relieved by a painted reredos of The
Conversion of St. Paul

ST. STEPHEN'S (Cof I), Upper Mount
Street, D2. By John Bowden 1824, and
known as 'The Peppercanister Church',

*Coffins in the Crypt, St. Michan's.*

because of the form of the cupola which tops the bell tower. Viewed along the southern side of Merrion Square, this is the epitomy of GEORGIAN DUBLIN, with long regular lines of brick terrace houses leading the eye to a pleasing Classical conclusion. The Greek Revival design is suggestive of a tiny temple, with a single massive doorway recessed behind a screen of columns. Internally, the church is plain, with galleries carried on columns around three sides. Although still used for services, the church is also the venue for classical music concerts and poetry readings.

ST. TERESA'S (RC), Clarendon Street, D2. Carmelite church, begun in 1793, and continuously enlarged till it reached its present form in 1876. This was the first post-PENAL LAW church to be legally and openly erected in Dublin following the Catholic Relief Act of 1793, although an unobtrusive siting – an alleyway off Grafton Street – was still chosen for the building. JOHN HOGAN'S rather chilling 'Dead Christ', 1829, is displayed beneath the altar. This naturalistic sculpture is among the most famous work by any Irish artist of the nineteenth century and it established Hogan's reputation as one of the leading Neo-Classical sculptors of the day.

ST. WERBURGH'S (Cof I), Werburgh Street, D2. Designed by Thomas Burgh in 1715, but of this building little but the rather hacked Baroque façade remains. A fire in 1754 destroyed much of the interior but, rebuilt by 1768, it had by then a tower and spire. In the panic following the Emmet rebellion of 1803, the spire was removed as it overlooked Dublin Castle and the authorities had visions of rebels taking pot shots at them from this vantage point. St. Werburgh's has the best-preserved eighteenth-century interior in Dublin, with box pews, galleries, and a splendidly ornamented pulpit and organ.

SACRED HEART ORATORY, Dominican Convent, George's Street, Dun Laoghaire. The Celtic Revival movement of the late nineteenth century continued into the early years of the following century and this tiny oratory is one of its last achievements. A member of the Dominican order, Sister Concepta Lynch, decorated the interior of the building between 1919 and 1936 in her own personal combination of Celtic and Art Nouveau styles. Internally the oratory measures 5.58m x 3.60m (16'7" x 10'8"), a very small space indeed, yet by entirely covering the walls and ceiling with an intricate interlace of patterns in glowing colours, the overall effect is of an overpowering richness of colour and intensity of feeling, creating a totally unexpected sense of grandeur. Access by appointment.

SAINTS AUGUSTINE & JOHN, Thomas Street, D8. Popularly known as John's Lane Church from the surviving remains of the Abbey of St. John where the Augustinians established themselves in the mid-eighteenth century. The present church, the finest example of Gothic Revival in Dublin, is the work of E.W. Pugin and George Ashlin and was built between 1860 and 1890, its elaborate granite and red sandstone spire forming one of the most dominant elements in the city's skyline. Within, the richness of the high Victorian decoration has not been swept away by modern church practices and the surfaces are as encrusted with ornamentation as a Gothic reliquary.

SYNAGOGUE, Adelaide Road, D2. By JJ O'Callaghan, 1892, plain brick building in a somewhat Byzantine Romanesque style. There was an extensive Jewish community in the area during the nineteenth century.

SYNAGOGUE, Rathfarnham Road, Terenure, D6. Modern synagogue designed in 1952 by Wilfred Cantwell, following the gradual migration of the Jewish community from the city centre to the suburbs.

SYNAGOGUE, Walworth Road, D8. Now the Irish-Jewish Museum, it formed the centre of what was, at the turn of the century, a thriving Jewish community. See MUSEUMS.

TRINITY COLLEGE CHAPEL (Cof I), TCD, D2. One of a pair of buildings with Corinthian porticos flanking the Front Square and designed by SIR WILLIAM CHAMBERS in 1774.

UNIVERSITY CHURCH (RC), St. Stephen's Green, D2. Byzanto-Romanesque curiosity by JOHN HUNGERFORD POLLEN, 1855, and the most individual church building in Dublin.

WHITECHURCH (Cof I), Rathfarnham, Co. Dublin. A simple JOHN SEMPLE church of 1825, with – for an architect with an enthusiasm for needle-like spires – an exceptionally dart-like one.

WHITEFRIARS CHURCH (RC), Aungier Street, D8. Carmelite Friary on the site of the pre-Reformation foundation. The original building, 1827, by George Papworth, has been vastly enlarged and an entire block of residential buildings added. The fifteenth-century black oak Madonna, OUR LADY OF DUBLIN, is particularly fine, and a unique survival of Medieval religious art in Dublin. The church also contains the remains of the celebrated St. Valentine of Valentine's Day fame.

CHURCH SERVICES. Catholic masses celebrated daily in most churches at differ-

ing hours, on Saturdays 5.00-7.00pm and on Sundays 8.00-1.00am and 5.00-7.00pm. Local details from the daily papers. Protestant services are mostly on Sunday except in areas of substantial Protestant populations (Dundrum, Malahide), and in the two cathedrals. Details of Greek Orthodox, Jewish, Muslim, Quaker meetings and other services from the daily papers.

CINEMAS (See MAP). The majority of Dublin's cinemas are concentrated in the O'Connell Street area and show English-language first-run general release films. Most of these cinemas have a number of screens, showing up to five films simultaneously. Arthouse cinema is very poorly represented in Dublin, with the Lighthouse in Middle Abbey Street the only permanent venue at present, and to a lesser extent, the Screen at College Street. See daily papers for listings. For Irish Film Institute see IRISH FILM CENTRE.

CITY CENTRE CINEMAS

ADELPHI, Middle Abbey Street, D1, tel 730433.

CAMEO, Middle Abbey Street, D1 730249.

CARLTON, 52 Upper O'Connell Street, tel 731609.

CURZON, Middle Abbey Street, tel 730438.

GERMAN FILM CLUB, Goethe Institute, Merrion Square East, D2, tel 611155.

IRISH FILM CENTRE & IRISH FILM INSTITUTE, Eustace Street, off Dame Street, tel 6795744.

LIGHTHOUSE, Middle Abbey Street, D1, tel 730438.

SAVOY, Upper O'Connell Street, D1, tel 748487.

SCREEN, College Street, D2, tel 714988.

SCREEN, O'Connell Bridge, D1, tel 744611.

**CIRCULAR BUILDINGS.** Circular buildings were not uncommon in Dublin in the past but few examples now remain and fewer still are of recent origin. The AMERICAN EMBASSY, Ballsbridge, a vaneless WINDMILL at the Guinness Brewery on Thomas Street, the Round Room of the MANSION HOUSE and in the Rotunda, the assembly room from which the hospital takes its name, are all that exist now, although each of these is of considerable interest. Vanished are the INKBOTTLE SCHOOL in Glasnevin, the Temple Church on Suffolk Street and many glass houses, shot towers and windmills. Terenure was once known as Roundtown because of the circular arrangement of its buildings.

**CIRCULAR ROADS.** The North Circular and South Circular Roads (NCR and SCR) were constructed by order of an act of parliament during the eighteenth century to give vehicular access to the city, following the route of the canals. Interesting nineteenth-century artisan suburbs developed around both arteries which now form some of the most attractive residential areas of the inner city.

**CITY ARCHIVES**, City Hall, Dame Street, D2, tel 796111. Dublin Corporation archives are housed in the City Hall and contain a wealth of documents relating to the development of Dublin, including all the Charters issued by British monarchs from Henry II in 1172 to George II in 1727. The archives also hold records of the Urban District Councils such as Rathmines and Ballsbridge which were amalgamated into Dublin, the WIDE STREETS COMMISSIONERS, lists of Free Citizens dating from 1468 and important early manuscript volumes, *The White Book of Dublin* and the *Chain Book of Dublin*. Mon-Fri 10.00-1.00,
2.15-5.00. An advance appointment is desirable.

**CITY ARMS HOTEL**, 54 Prussia Street, D7. Fine eighteenth-century mansion with interesting interiors in a quarter of the city characteristic of Dublin's appearance prior to the great planned developments of the latter half of that century.

**CITY HALL**, Dame Street, D2, tel 796111. Now the headquarters of Dublin Corporation, the City Hall was designed by THOMAS COOLEY and built by the Dublin Guild of Merchants in 1769 as the Royal Exchange, a place where the merchants of the city could transact business. The carving on the City Hall is by SIMON VIERPYL whose major work is the CASINO at Marino. Although smaller than some of the more prominent Georgian public buildings, the Exchange was designed to represent the wealth and importance of the merchants and decorated accordingly, with a Corinthian portico facing Parliament Street and another opening on to Cork Hill. Bills of exchange were bought and sold in the central rotunda and the upstairs room which is now the Council Chamber was the coffee room. The Rotunda is the most impressive space in the building and it now contains a number of important monuments to DANIEL O'CONNELL, THOMAS DAVIS and others. Since 1852 the building has been known as the City Hall, and now houses the offices of the City Manager, the Finance and Treasurer's Department and is the venue for meetings of the Corporation. The City Archives and Theatre Archives are kept at the City Hall. Mon-Fri 10.00-1.00, 2.15-5.00, for visits to the Rotunda. The archives by appointment.

**CITY WALLS.** After the establishment of the first VIKING settlement in AD 841 an area of the Hill of Dublin was surrounded with an earthen rampart topped by a wattle stockade. From this rudimentary beginning the size of the enclosed area spread and by 1170 the Hiberno-Norse had replaced the original stockade by a stone wall. Later the ANGLO NORMANS extended this fortification and built DUBLIN CASTLE in 1204. Between the twelfth and seventeenth centuries the wall was gradually strengthened and augmented with gates and towers and it is shown in an aerial projection on SPEED'S map of 1610 as being walled from the river quays all around to the Castle. Fragments of this wall have survived, principally around the Castle but also along High Street and in the excavations at WOOD QUAY. A few substantial fragments of the city wall can be seen and with one gate as well as a number of towers, give a sense of the scale of the Medieval city. On Cook Street is St Audoen's Arch with surrounding portions of the wall and a postern gate. This section was heavily restored during the nineteenth century. On the south side of Dublin Castle in Ship Street and within the Castle Gates a section of the wall with massive towers remains, incorporated into the eighteenth-century buildings. The towers are, looking east from the corner of Ship Street, Stanihurst's Tower, Bermingham Tower and the Record Tower, this last the most intact and better seen from inside Lower Castle Yard.

**CIVIC OFFICES**, Fishamble Street, D2, tel 796111. Two-tower offices of Dublin Corporation, designed in 1968 by Sam Stephenson and completed in 1986 with plans for two more towers, as yet unbuilt. The offices occupy the site

*City Hall from Parliament Street.*

of the Wood Quay excavations of the tenth-century Viking city of *Dyflin*. Considerable public controversy surrounded the construction of these buildings as Wood Quay was considered by archaeologists and historians from many countries as the finest Viking site in Europe, the quality and quantity of the archaeological remains warranting their preservation on the site. It was proposed that the corporation offices should be sited elsewhere but this objective was not achieved. These offices are designed in an uncompromisingly severe modern idiom at variance with the variety and delicacy of CHRIST CHURCH Cathedral and lack the civic presence which their position warranted. Beneath Block 2 the tenth-century Dublin CITY WALL can be seen skulking unhappily. Departments of the Corporation are located in different areas of the city, with a concentration at the Civic Offices of Engineering,

Housing, Inner City Development, Public Relations, Roads and Traffic.

**CLARINDA PARK**, Dun Laoghaire. Mid-nineteenth-century stucco-fronted houses with bay windows arranged around three sides of an open park. The fourth side is occupied by Stoneview House, a granite mansion built by the contractor engaged in the construction of Dun Laoghaire harbour. Clarinda Park is the epitomy of Victorian Dun Laoghaire, climbing up the hill in an attractive pattern of grey and cream coloured buildings, still maintaining some of the spirit of affluence of the age in which it was built.

**CLARKE, AUSTIN**, (1896-1974). Poet, dramatist, broadcaster, he lectured in English at UCD and previously lived in England (1921-37), where he was assistant editor of the London literary magazine *Argosy*. Clarke founded the Dublin Verse Speaking Society and produced his own and others' verse plays. He became President of the Irish Academy of Letters in 1952. Clarke, more than any other twentieth-century Irish poet, identified with Dublin, and his subject matter and sympathies are often drawn from the life of its citizens. See AUSTIN CLARKE POETRY LIBRARY.

The tolling from St. Patrick's
Cathedral was brangled, repeating
Itself in top-back room
And alley of the Coombe,

('Burial of an Irish President', Austin Clarke.)

**CLARKE, HARRY**, (1889-1931). Stained-glass artist and book illustrator. Clarke is among a small group of significant figures to come out of the stained-glass revival which occurred in Dublin in the early years of the twentieth century, and his colourful and finely drawn windows can be seen in churches throughout Ireland as well as in England and the United States. His work shows an amalgam of the influences of French Symbolism, the English Pre-Raphaelite Movement and, in his draughtsmanship, the manner of Aubrey Beardsley, yet he managed to create out of these beginnings an exceptionally individual style, coupled with masterful technical execution. He inherited a familiarity with the medium of stained glass from his father who ran a church decoration business in Dublin, and he later studied under AE CHILD at the Metropolitan School of Art. While most of Clarke's commissions were ecclesiastical, he also did secular works and it is in this area that his finest pieces were accomplished. Clarke's masterpiece, the window for the League of Nations in Geneva which the Irish government refused to present to that institution, is now in the United States, but a similar window, the Eve of Saint Agnes, based on a poem by Keats, is in the HUGH LANE GALLERY. Not many of Clark's windows are to be seen in Dublin as his work is widely scattered. BEWLEY'S ORIENTAL CAFÉ on Grafton Street, has a set of decorative architectural windows in which brimming plates of cakes are carried on columns of the four Classical orders. Suburban parish churches also have examples of his work: at Balbriggan, RC; Castleknock, Cof I; Clontarf, Pres; Donabate, RC; Donnybrook, RC; Killiney, Cof I; Lusk, RC; Phibsboro, RC; Raheny, RC; Ranelagh, Cof I and Terenure, RC. Clarke's macabre taste in art made him eminently suitable as an interpreter of the works of Edgar Allan Poe and Algernon Charles Swinburne, something he did with great power. In the pavilions of the ISLAND-BRIDGE WAR MEMORIAL are volumes recording the names of all the soldiers of Irish regiments who died in the First World War. These books were embellished by Clarke with marginal decorations, much of them derived from imagery of the horrific trench warfare of the period. The books are also on display in the north apse of ST. PATRICK'S CATHEDRAL.

**CLONDALKIN**. The best-preserved ROUND TOWER of the three in Dublin is on the Main Street of Clondalkin. It is the only one in the country to have an external flight of steps to the entrance, and this is apparently early although not contemporary with the building of the tower. The tower, 28m (84 ft) high and probably of the eighth century, retains its distinctive conical cap and is one of the narrowest of those surviving. There are the remains of a Medieval church in the graveyard on the opposite side of the road as well as two Early Christian stone crosses. Tully's Castle, a sixteenth-century tower house is at the eastern end of the town. Bus 51, 51B, 68, 69 from Fleet Street.

**CLONTARF, BATTLE OF**. Took place on Good Friday, 23 April 1014, on the north side of the LIFFEY between the VIKINGS of Dublin, Man and Orkney and their allies the Leinstermen, against an Irish force led by BRIAN BORU. The exact site of the battle has not been established. The significance of the Battle is not, as was generally believed, that it drove out the Vikings, but that it ended their already diminished supremacy.

**CLONTARF CASTLE**. Built in 1835 by WILLIAM VITRUVIUS MORRISON on the site of a Norman fortification, it is now a hotel and concert venue.

**CLUBS**. The most well known Gentlemen's Club in Dublin was the KILDARE STREET CLUB, an Establishment enclave amidst turbulent tides, whose monumental premises, designed by Dean and WOODWARD, overlooks College Park. It has now merged with the United Services Club. On the north side of St. Stephen's Green are four surviving clubs, all in important Georgian and Victorian mansions: No. 8, the Hibernian United Services Club; No. 9, the St. Stephen's Green Club; No. 17, the University Club; No. 22, the Friendly Brothers. These clubs are private institutions, with membership by nomination only.

**COINAGE**. Ireland was late among European nations in minting its own coinage. Not having been colonised by the Romans, it was not until the Viking invasion and the establishment of Dublin that coins of Sitric were minted in AD 997. In subsequent centuries, coinage followed the English pattern although Ireland did not have a permanent mint and depended largely on the circulation of English and Continental currency, often at inflated values. JONATHAN SWIFT'S involvement in foiling the attempt to introduce brass halfpennies during the eighteenth century by writing the *DRAPIER'S LETTERS* highlights the absence of local control. Bishop BERKELEY devoted a large proportion of the *QUERIST* to the subject of the absence of an Irish bank, which he saw as the root of most of the nation's ills. From 1775 currency was standardised to coinage circulating in Great Britain, and in 1825 the Irish currency was amalgamated into sterling. After 1922 an Irish Coinage Committee was established with WB YEATS as its chairman and was responsible for introducing the new Irish coinage. Designed by Percy Metcalfe in 1928, the new coinage abandoned the traditional symbols of Irishness – round towers and shamrocks – which had been current throughout the eighteenth and nineteenth centuries, in favour of animal motifs which are still in circulation. Yeats described the national coinage as 'the silent ambassadors on national taste'.

**COLIEMORE HARBOUR.** Small boat and fishing harbour on the south coast of Dublin Bay, near Dalkey village. The embarkation point for trips to Dalkey Island. DART to Dalkey.

*Viking coinage, AD 997.*

**COLLEGE GREEN.** Formerly HOG-GEN GREEN, from the Scandinavian, *hogges* – a mound. A VIKING cemetery is believed to have been in the area. Now the hub of the city, and architecturally most interesting for the variety and excellence of its eighteenth- and nineteenth-century buildings and monuments. The west front of Trinity College and the façade of Parliament House, now the BANK OF IRELAND, are amongst Dublin's most impressive examples of monumental Georgian architecture. Facing them across the Green, now a somewhat hazardous busy street crossing, are ornate Victorian banks and the statues of HENRY GRATTAN, OLIVER GOLDSMITH, EDMUND BURKE and THOMAS DAVIS. College Green develops into DAME STREET and LORD EDWARD STREET. The buildings of College Green are – starting from the west front of TRINITY COLLEGE, 1752 – on the north side, Parliament House, 1729 and later, now the Bank of Ireland; No. 3, Daly's Club, by Richard Johnston, 1788; No. 9, by Horace Porter, 1909; the rebuilt Commercial Buildings by Edward Parke, 1796 and 1967. On the

south side of College Green on the Trinity Street corner are Nos. 12-14, 'Pen Corner', the former Star Insurance Building by A. Blomfield Jackson, 1890; Nos. 20-22, AIB, former Royal Bank by WH Lynn, 1893; on the Church lane corner the National Irish Bank, former Hibernian Bank by WG Murray, 1862; No. 33, the Ulster Bank, by Sir Thomas Drew, 1891; No. 34, The Bank of Ireland, former National Bank by Barnes and Farrell, 1842; Hewett's Travel Agency and Fox's Cigar Shop by TN Deane, 1881, lie on the southern corner facing Trinity.

**COMHALTAS CEOLTÓIRÍ ÉIREANN**, Belgrave Square, Monkstown, tel 800295. Comhaltas, as the organisation is known, was founded in 1951 to promote the traditional music, song, dance and language of Ireland both in Ireland and abroad. Music sessions are held nightly throughout the summer months and at weekends during the rest of the year at Belgrave Square which acts as a general cultural centre for anything to do with traditional music. See MUSIC. DART to Monkstown.

**COMMEMORATIVE PLAQUES ON BUILDINGS.** See PLAQUES.

**CONNOLLY, JAMES,** (1868-1916). Socialist, journalist and trade union leader, born in Scotland. He was involved in the Labour movement for many years in Ireland from 1896 and subsequently in the United States and was among the founders of the Wobblies, (Industrial Workers of the World), an important development in US labour history. He returned to Dublin in 1910 and, with JIM LARKIN organised the workers during the lockout strike of 1913. Connolly was in command of the Irish Citizen Army during the 1916 RISING and was executed at KILMAINHAM JAIL.

**CONNOLLY STATION,** Amiens Street, D1, tel 366222. Designed by William Dean Butler for the Dublin and Drogheda Railway in 1844, and linked in 1891 to the southern rail system by the Loop Line Bridge. Both lines were elevated in order to pass over the existing roads and canals in the city. Connolly, or Amiens Street as it is still known, is designed in an elaborate Italianate manner with the vista from Abbey Street dominated by its central tower. The name of the station was changed to Connolly in 1966 to commemorate JAMES CONNOLLY, one of the 1916 leaders. Now the principal station on the DART for the O'Connell Street area, and also for mainline CIE trains to the North.

**CONNOR, JEROME,** (1876-1943). Sculptor, spent much of his life in the United States, but returned to Dublin in 1925. A cast of his statue of ROBERT EMMET, 1917, which is in the Smithsonian Institution, Washington DC, stands on St. Stephen's Green West, opposite the site of the house in which Emmet was born. Two other pieces of Connor's work are in Merrion Square – a bust of AE, 1927, and a recent cast of the Kerry Poets' Memorial, called Éire, 1930, which was not erected in his lifetime.

**COOLEY, THOMAS,** (1740-1784). Architect, born in England. Designed the Royal Exchange, a commission which he won by competition, now the City Hall, Dame Street, and the west wing of the Four Courts, subsequently absorbed into JAMES GANDON'S building.

**COOMBE, THE.** The heart of the Earl of Meath's Liberty, it runs east-west along the valley of the Poddle river. The Coombe is both a street and a district. The Coombe Lying-In Hospital stood here but now only the portico remains as a foil to the new Corporation housing – some of the best urban renewal to be seen in Dublin – where considerable care has been taken to preserve indigenous communities and streetscapes.

**CROKE PARK.** Headquarters of the Gaelic Athletic Association (GAA), called after Archbishop Croke, one of its founders. The All-Ireland Football and Hurling Finals as well as other fixtures are held here. See SPORT.

**CROMWELL, OLIVER,** (1599-1658). General and Lord Protector, he arrived in Ireland in August 1649 and was welcomed by the beleaguered inhabitants of Dublin. Cromwell can claim to be one of the city's least benevolently remembered visitors, although he did not wreak his wrath in the city as he did in Drogheda and elsewhere.

**CROMWELL'S QUARTERS,** Mount Brown, D8. Flight of forty steps

*James Gandon's Custom House.*

which link Mount Brown with Bow Lane West. The Cromwell is not Oliver Cromwell but his son Henry, Governor General of Ireland from 1655 to 1659.

**CROSTWAITHE PARK**, Dun Laoghaire. Two- and three-storied stucco-fronted houses of the mid-nineteenth century, arranged around two sides of a park with mature trees. This is one of the most attractive Victorian squares in Dublin.

**CROWN JEWELS**. The Irish Crown Jewels were stolen from the Genealogical Office in Dublin Castle in 1907 a few days prior to the visit of King Edward VIII. A reward of £1,000 was offered for their recovery by the Dublin Metropolitan Police, but the money was never claimed. The jewels consisted of the gold and silver regalia of the Knights of St. Patrick, stars, badges, collars, brooches and rings, richly set with diamonds, rubies and other precious stones. The Metropolitan Police regarded the theft as an 'inside job', but nobody was charged, and the jewels have never been traced.

**CÚCHULAINN**, GPO, O'Connell Street, D1. In the centre of the open space in the public office of the GPO is Oliver Sheppard's splendid bronze of the dying Cúchulainn lashed to a stake, with a raven perched on his shoulder. Erected in 1936 as a memorial to those killed here during the RISING of 1916, the choice of a hero from the Red Branch Knights to symbolise the deeds of the twentieth-century revolutionaries was a carefully considered gesture designed to link the Ireland of the early Free State years with the Ireland of remote and heroic antiquity. Like the statue of St. Peter in the Vatican, the foot of which has been rubbed smooth by pilgrims, the bare foot of Cúchulainn has been polished by people touching it as a talisman.

**CUSTOM HOUSE**, Custom House Quay, D1. JAMES GANDON's masterpiece and probably the most perfect building of the eighteenth century in Dublin. Situated on the edge of the Liffey, the magnificent view of the building from the southern bank shows off the purity and grace of the Custom House to great advantage and the twentieth-century buildings which now surround it, LIBERTY HALL, BUSÁRAS, and the FINANCIAL SERVICES CENTRE enhance rather than diminish the fine proportions and glowing stonework of the Custom House. The only blot is the Loop Line railway bridge which cuts off the view from the west, a crime which may not be laid at the door of contemporary architecture. The Custom House was begun in

1781 on land reclaimed from the Liffey, replacing THOMAS BURGH'S Custom House upstream at Essex Quay, and effectively shifting the axis of the city to the east. The south front which faces the river has a central Corinthian portico, with graceful arcades on either side linking the wings, each with a recessed columnular entrance. The roofline is broken by the Royal Arms, sculpted by EDWARD SMYTH, whose massive figure of Commerce tops the dome. Smyth's fourteen RIVERINE HEADS over the doors and windows, personifications of the rivers of Ireland, are some of the finest examples of this sculptor's work. The north front of the building faces up the once magnificent but now dilapidated Georgian 1.6km (0.5 mile) of Gardiner Street. During the Civil War of 1922 the building was destroyed by arsonists, but it has undergone a number of phases of restoration, culminating in the recent six-year conservation project and the cleaning of the façade which is of a startlingly bright Portland stone. The drum of the dome, restored after 1922 with Ardbraccan stone rather than Portland stone, has unfortunately a grey colour which is out of sympathy with the rest of the building. Had Gandon designed nothing else of merit, the Custom House alone would have assured him a place in the history of architecture.

**D**ÁIL ÉIREANN, Kildare Street, D2, tel 789911. Two-chamber parliamentary assembly, the structure of which roughly parallels that of the original Irish parliament disbanded in 1801, with a lower house of 166 members – the Dáil – voted for by the general electorate and an upper house of sixty members – the Seanad (Senate) – representing sectional interests, economic, academic, social and intellectual. (The eighteenth-century parliament had roughly 300 members in the Commons and 120 in the Lords.) The first Dáil was composed of seventy-three Sinn Féin MPs elected to Westminster in 1918 who chose not to attend the London parliament but to sit in Dublin instead. They met first in the MANSION HOUSE on 21 January 1919, when the Irish Republic, proclaimed in 1916, was ratified. Following the establishment of the Irish Free State in 1922 an assembly was set up consisting of Dáil and Seanad. With some modifications this arrangement has continued to govern the Republic of Ireland to the present time. The Dáil may be visited when the House is in session (Tue, Wed, Thur), by obtaining an admission card from the Superintendent of the Houses, or by application to an individual member. During non-sitting days visits can be arranged by application to the Kildare Street entrance. See LEINSTER HOUSE for the history of the building occupied by the Dáil.

**DALKEY HILL.** Rugged high land above DALKEY VILLAGE connected by a saddle of parkland to KILLINEY HILL PARK. The superb granite from which DUN LAOGHAIRE Harbour was built was quarried here, and the immense bite it took out of the side of the hill can be seen from many miles away. A funicular railway for bringing down the cut blocks from the quarry ran along the hillside

*Martello tower on Dalkey Island.*

and sections of this, known as 'the Metals', can still be seen at Dalkey Avenue. Today the quarry is used by the local rock climbing clubs for training purposes. Dalkey Hill is crowned by an old telegraph tower from which it derives the name by which it was previously known, Telegraph Hill. From the summit of the Hill stunning views may be had of the city and of DUBLIN BAY. Bus 8, DART to Dalkey.

**DALKEY ISLAND.** Rocky windswept island of 6.8 hectares (17 acres) 400m (quarter-of-a-mile) offshore from SORRENTO POINT, the southern tip of Dublin Bay, and separated from the mainland by St. Begnet's or Dalkey Sound. Excavations during the 1950s showed that the island had been occupied during the Mesolithic, Neolithic and Bronze Age periods but no contemporary structures were found. On the island are three buildings, all of interest. An Early Christian church dedicated to St. Begnet stands at the western end, which despite modifications to accommodate masons working on the MARTELLO TOWER and battery during the nineteenth century is in an excellent state of preservation. Carved on the bedrock facing the doorway of the church are two Early Christian crosses. There is also a Holy Well associated with St. Begnet on the island. Further to the east stand a martello tower, 1804, and a gun battery from the Napoleonic period. Dalkey Sound was used as a safe mooring for ships throughout the Medieval period and was even considered as a possible site for the proposed harbour later built in Dun Laoghaire. Access to the island is by small boat from COLIEMORE HARBOUR, a journey of a few minutes. The only inhabitants of the island are a herd of wild goats, other than the ubiquitous rabbits and sea birds. Bus 8, DART to Dalkey.

**DALKEY, KING OF.** From 1779 to 1797, in the spirit of a popular lampoon on the monarchy, a King of Dalkey was annually elected. The celebration of the occasion was generally an excuse for picnics and parties on Dalkey Island. The last King, a Dublin bookseller who reigned in 1797, was grandly styled, 'His facecious Majesty, Stephen the First, King of Dalkey, Emperor of the Muglins, prince of the Holy land of Magee, and Elector of Lambay and Ireland's Eye, defender of his own Faith, and respecter of all others, Soverign of the illustrious order of the Lobster and Periwinkle.' The ceremony was abandoned in the growing unrest of 1797 but has recently been revived and takes place in August.

**DALKEY VILLAGE.** Village on southern shore of DUBLIN BAY, now the centre of an affluent suburban area. The main street still maintains the typical linear quality of Irish country villages with a single street of shops. Dalkey is unusual in having two Medieval towers, Archbold's Castle, now the Town Hall, and Goat Castle, as well as the Medieval St. Begnet's Church on the main street. These represent the remains of a walled town with many towers used as a staging post by the traders of Dublin up to the sixteenth century. Some of the finest areas of the built up coastline of Dublin Bay are around Dalkey with many interesting nineteenth-century houses. GEORGE BERNARD SHAW lived as a child at Torca Cottage in Dalkey (plaque) from 1866 to 1874. Bus 8, DART to Dalkey.

**DAME STREET**, D2. The name derives from the Medieval church of St. Mary del Dam which stood near the site of the CITY HALL. Dame Street was the principal street of the city outside the walls during the early eighteenth century, connecting the pillars of the establishment, DUBLIN CASTLE at the west end with the Parliament House and TRINITY COLLEGE at the east end. Today it is a noble street of banks and finance companies, concealing behind their façades, on the northern side of the street, Dublin's Left Bank area, TEMPLE BAR, which stretches from the Central Bank to the Liffey. Dame Street develops from COLLEGE GREEN and leads into LORD EDWARD STREET and displays a characteristic cross section of all the relevant periods of Dublin's architectural history, from the eleventh to the twentieth century with notable eighteenth-century monumental buildings and the finest Victorian commercial architecture in Dublin. Buildings of significance on Dame Street are, on the north side coming from College Green, the CENTRAL

BANK by Sam Stephenson, 1978; the Crown Life building by T.N. Deane, 1868; the Olympia Theatre by J.J. O'Callaghan, 1878; the Riverrun Gallery, 1850. On the south side of the street the Millennium Gardens contain three statues of the Crafts from the 1865 Dublin Exhibition; Nos. 7-12 AIB are by T.N. Deane, 1872; Nos. 13-16 by J.J. O'Callaghan, 1879; Burton's, an Art Deco building of 1929 stands on the corner of South Great George's Street; further east at No. 31, is the Caledonian Insurance Company by James E. Rogers, 1865; and Trinity Bank, 1864, by David Bryce stands on the corner of Trinity Street.

**DANBY, FRANCIS**, (1793-1861). One of the greatest apocalyptic painters of the nineteenth century, Danby studied at the Dublin Society Schools, but his career was spent abroad, in England and the Continent. His vast canvases depicting Biblical subjects swirl with the violence of nature and are peopled with tiny figures, dwarfed by the majesty of Creation. Danby's major work in the NATIONAL GALLERY, 'The Opening of the Sixth Seal' is a terrifying vision of darkness, illuminated by a searing flash of lightning.

**DARGAN, WILLIAM**, (1799-1867). Railway developer and contractor, his statue now stands on the lawn of the NATIONAL GALLERY and a wing of the building is named after him for the contribution he made to establishing a national collection of art. Dargan built the DUBLIN TO KINGSTOWN RAILWAY, in 1834, the first railway in Ireland and he became the principal builder of railways in the country. He organised and very heavily subsidised the Dublin Industrial Exhibition of 1853 which was contained

in a Crystal Palace-like cast iron and glass building on LEINSTER LAWN but this venture was a financial failure. Although one of the wealthiest men in mid-nineteenth-century Dublin, he died in poverty. The collection of paintings displayed during the exhibition eventually became the nucleus of the National Gallery.

**DARLEY, FREDERICK**, (1800s). Architect. He came of a prominent family of architects and builders. Among his Dublin buildings are New Square, TRINITY COLLEGE, Trinity Church, 50 Gardiner Street, 1838, now the Labour Exchange, the BOTANIC GARDEN's Palm House, Merchant's Hall on Merchant's Quay and the KING'S INNS Library, Henrietta Street.

**DART**, (Dublin Area Rapid Transit). The old CIE railway line from HOWTH to BRAY was electrified between 1980 and 1984, providing the coastal region of Dublin with the only first-class transport in the city. These high-speed electric trains, which were built in Germany, travel around the entire span of DUBLIN BAY. On the south side the track runs along some of the most splendid coastline in the Dublin area, culminating in the sweep of KILLINEY BAY. The DART runs from 6.00am-11.30pm, and a single fare will take the passenger to the end of the line. Starting from Howth on the northside, there are DART stations at Sutton, Bayside, Howth Junction, Kilbarrack, Raheny, Harmonstown and Killester. The next station is CONNOLLY, the stopping point for O'CONNELL STREET and mainline terminus for trains to the north and west of Ireland. Crossing the Liffey, Tara Street and Pearse Street are the stations for the GRAFTON STREET and MERRION SQUARE area. The southern coast DART stations are, Lansdowne Road, SANDYMOUNT, Sydney Parade, Booterstown, BLACKROCK, MONKSTOWN-Seapoint, Salthill, DUN LAOGHAIRE, SANDYCOVE, Glenageary, DALKEY, KILLINEY, Shankill and BRAY.

**DARTMOUTH SQUARE**, Ranelagh, D6. Oblong square surrounded by uniform terraces of 1880s brick houses with Moorish-arched doorways over granite basements. The well-planted park has a recently constructed pergola.

**DAVITT, MICHAEL**, (1846-1906). Journalist, parliamentarian, social reformer. Davitt was the founder, with CHARLES STUART PARNELL, of the Land League in 1897. As a child he lost an arm working in a Lancashire mill, an experience which gave him an acute awareness of the plight of the disadvantaged. He served seven years imprisonment for his involvement in the Fenian movement.

**DAY TRIPS**. Organised from the city centre to areas of natural beauty or historic interest in the surrounding city and counties. Bus Éireann and Dublin Bus, Upper O'Connell Street, D1, tel 366111. Grayline Tours, 3 Clanwilliam Terrace, Grand Canal Quay, D2, tel 619666.
Boat trips around Dublin Bay are available during the summer season from Sir John Rogerson's Quay, D2, and The East Pier, Dun Laoghaire Harbour.
COLIEMORE HARBOUR for Dalkey Island, and Howth Harbour for Ireland's Eye. Detailed information may be had from Dublin Tourism.

**DE VALERA, EAMON**, (1882-1975). Revolutionary, academic, politician, born New York of Irish extraction. Returned to Ireland when a child to Co. Limerick. De Valera became involved in the Nationalist movement from 1908, and joined the VOLUNTEERS in 1913. He took part in the *ASGARD* gun running in 1914 and commanded BOLANDS MILLS during the RISING of 1916. Elected MP for Clare in 1917, he devoted the rest of his long life to Irish affairs, founding Fianna Fáil in 1926 and becoming Taoiseach on three occasions, 1932, 1951 and 1957, holding this office for twenty-one years in all. He was elected President of Ireland in 1959 and re-elected in 1966. De Valera exerted an enormous influence on the development of the IRISH FREE STATE and subsequent IRISH REPUBLIC as an independent state, and was instrumental in the maintenance of Irish neutrality during the Second World War. However his clear concept of Ireland as an independent and non-aligned nation was confused with a desire to recreate a Gaelic Nirvana, 'a land whose countryside would be bright with cosy homesteads... with the romping of sturdy children... and the laughter of comely maidens', a concept which might have made some sense in 1903 but hardly in 1943, the year of this statement. De Valera's outlook had little relevance to the needs of the agricultural poor and unemployed who continued to emigrate in substantial numbers throughout the period of his leadership of the country. With an academic interest in mathematics and the sciences, he was responsible for the establishment of the DUBLIN INSTITUTE FOR ADVANCED STUDIES in 1940.

**DEANE, SIR THOMAS NEWENHAM**, (1828-1899). Architect and first Inspector of National Monuments, he designed many fine buildings in Dublin, the most prominent of which are the NATIONAL LIBRARY and NATIONAL MUSEUM, Kildare Street, 1884-90, constructed in a Classical style, but his Gothic Revival buildings, mostly of a commercial nature, form a more individual contribution to the architecture of the city. With BENJAMIN WOODWARD he collaborated on the TRINITY MUSEUM, 1852-57, alterations to the Library at Trinity, 1856-61 and the KILDARE STREET CLUB, 1858-61. After Woodward's death in 1861, Deane continued to design in an Italian Gothic manner and there are a number of interesting buildings of his on Dame Street, the Crown Life Building, 1868; No. 7-12 AIB, 1872; and on the Grafton Street/College Green corner Fox's Cigar Shop, 1881. In Trinity he designed the Graduates' Memorial Building, 1891, in a more conventionally Gothic Revival manner.

**DEANERY, THE,** Kevin Street, D8. The Deanery of ST. PATRICK'S CATHEDRAL which is associated with JONATHAN SWIFT was destroyed by fire during the late eighteenth century. The present building, erected in 1783, occupies the same position on Kevin Street. Amongst the fine collection of portraits and busts in the Deanery is FRANCIS BINDON'S portrait of Swift in a remarkable carved oak frame by John Houghton.

**DEDALUS, STEPHEN.** Alter ego used by JAMES JOYCE in *A Portrait of The Artist as a Young Man* and *ULYSSES*, a name which he derived from that of the Athenian artist-craftsman of Greek mythology. Dedalus, mentioned by Homer, Pausanias, Ovid and other Classical writers, is credited with the invention of flight. He manufactured wings in order to escape from the maze he had constructed at Knossos for King Minos, and is an artistic father figure. Stephen Dedalus ends the *Portrait* with an appeal to his namesake, 'Old father,

old artificer, stand me now and ever in good stead'.

**DEGENERATE ART.** See NOLDE, EMIL.

**DELANEY, MARY,** (1700-1788). Amateur artist and voluminous correspondent. She married Dr Delaney, the friend of JONATHAN SWIFT and lived at Deville, Glasnevin. Her letters give a lively picture of life in Georgian Dublin. In her eighties, Mrs Delaney started to make botanical paper collages, which are extraordinarily modern in conception, and skilful 'portraits' of plants. Her plant collages are now in the British Museum.

**DEPARTMENT STORES.** Like much else in Dublin, the department stores are gathered around the two most important shopping areas north and south of O'Connell Bridge, HENRY STREET and GRAFTON STREET, the former tending towards good value and economy, the latter towards the expensive and exclusive.

**DICEY REILLY.** Popular and very characteristic Dublin song concerned with a city 'character' and like most Irish folk songs, both urban and rural, the mythic quality invested in the landscape is celebrated in the listing of placenames.

She will walk along Fitzgibbon Street
    with an independent air
And then it's down by Summerhill,
    and at the people stare
She'll say 'It's nearly half past one,
    time I went in for another little one'
But the heart of the rowl is Dicey
    Reilly.

**DISCOS/NIGHTCLUBS.** Basement clubs in and around the Leeson Street area are the centre of Dublin's nightlife, with venues opening to fanfares and disappearing overnight, victims of changes in fashion.

*Bindon Blood Stoney's Diving Bell.*

**DIVING BELL** (opposite the Gasometer), Sir John Rogerson's Quay, D2. Mid-nineteenth-century diving bell designed by the chief engineer of the Port and Docks Board, Bindon Blood Stoney. It was used in the preparation of the river bed for the construction of the quays which surround ALEXANDRA BASIN. The Diving Bell is an important, and in Dublin unique, survival of the engineering skills of the great age of steam, and it belongs with the HA'PENNY BRIDGE and the Curvilinear Glasshouses at the BOTANIC GARDENS as an important link with the Industrial Revolution. It is a simple iron box, 6.6m x 3.00m (20sqft x 6ft 6in) in height with an access funnel on top. The upper part of the funnel

remained above the water level, and between the funnel and the chamber was an air lock. The men who worked in the Diving Bell did so without any breathing equipment, air pressure was maintained to expel the water, operated from a barge supporting the Bell. There is a contemporary model of both barge and Bell in the TRINITY MUSEUM.

**DOCKS.** The dockland area of DUBLIN PORT has been steadily moving east since the eighteenth century, and now with the construction of the East Link Tollbridge, which connects the Pigeon House Road to the East Wall Road, the effective navigable area of the Liffey for shipping is restricted to the seaward side of this bridge although the bridge can be raised for upriver traffic. However, new areas of the Bay have been reclaimed and the docking facilities of the port considerably extended out into deeper waters where the B&I terminal and container docks now lie.

**DODDER, THE.** Rising in the DUBLIN MOUNTAINS not far from the source of the LIFFEY, the Dodder is the principal southern tributary of the Liffey and it joins the river at the GRAND CANAL Docks, Ringsend. A linear park is being developed along the valley of the Dodder. The earliest surviving bridge in Dublin – a narrow Medieval twin-arched stone bridge just wide enough for horse-and-cart traffic – is at Milltown on the Dodder.

**DOLMENS.** The earliest visible monumental remains of human occupation in the Dublin area are the portal dolmens – groups of boulders placed over the grave of some notable person – dating from the Neolithic period (2,500-2,000 BC). Excellent examples are dotted around the outskirts of the city, the most spectacular being that in Howth Demesne, about which SIR SAMUEL FERGUSON wrote a long poem, '*AIDEEN'S GRAVE*', evoking the life of the ancient inhabitants of Howth. Dolmens are also situated at Ballybrack, Shanganagh Road and Phoenix Park, near Knockmary Lodge in the Fifteen Acres.

**DONNELLY, DAN**, (d1820). Prizefighter, born in RINGSEND, his open-air fights were attended by enormous crowds and the scene of his 1815 match in the Curragh is known as 'Dan Donnelly's Hollow'. Donnelly fought many matches in England before retiring to run a pub in Chancery Street, Dublin. The pugilist's arm is preserved in The Hide Out bar in Kilcullen, Co. Wicklow.

**DONNYBROOK**. The notorious Donnybrook Fair, a riotous and bacchanalian affair was held here until it was supressed during the mid-nineteenth century. Donnybrook is now the home of RTE, the radio and television broadcasting station.

> Oh Donnybrook, jewel! full of mirth
>    is your quiver,
> Where all flock from Dublin to gape
>    and to stare
> At two elegant bridges, without e'er a
>    river:
> So, success to the humours of Donny-
>    brook fair!

('Donnybrook Fair', nineteenth-century Dublin ballad.)

**DOORS**. The front doors of eighteenth-century Dublin houses are their most evident external point of decoration, and the variety and individuality of the doorcases, fanlights, wrought ironwork, foot scrapers, steps and decorative manhole covers, in contrast to the uniformity of the brick façades, is worthy of note, particularly when seen *en masse* as in Merrion or Fitzwilliam and Parnell Squares. Harcourt, Henrietta, Molesworth, and many other streets also contain interesting examples, and this tradition was extended into the suburbs during the Victorian era after which it seems to have evaporated. The doorcases of earlier Georgian houses, heavily carved in stone, often have a sculptural quality which as the century develops progresses into more refined detail. All of a more or less Classical idiom, culminating in the same forms decorated in Ruskinian Gothic and Hiberno Romanesque manner by the late nineteenth century. Some doors of particular interest are, 86 St. Stephen's Green; 35-38 Merrion Square East; 37/8, 51/2, 69-71 Merrion Square South; 15/16 and 20 Molesworth Street; 46 Fitzwilliam Square; 9-11 Hume Street; 19 Dawson Street; 38 North Great George's Street; 9 Henrietta Street; 62-67 Harcourt Street; 10a/11, Parnell Square; in the suburbs, Orwell Road and Kenilworth Square contain some fine late examples of the Dublin door, richly embellished with carved decoration.

**DORSET STREET**, D1. Important residential street on the north side of the city during the eighteenth century but now much decayed, it was called after the Lord Lieutenant, the Earl of Dorset. RICHARD BRINSLEY SHERIDAN was born at No. 12, now demolished. During the early eighteenth century Dorset Street was the principal thoroughfare of Dublin north of the Liffey, running into Bolton and Capel Streets before crossing the river at what is now Grattan Bridge. The building of Sackville, later O'Connell Bridge completely altered the axis of the city and Dorset Street ceased to have importance as a focal point on the north side of the Liffey.

**DOWLAND, JOHN**, (1562-1626).
Composer and musician. He is reputed
to have been born in DALKEY, Co. Dublin. Dowland was the most celebrated
lute player of his day and made a considerable contribution to sixteenth-century
music. The current Early Music Revival
has brought back much of Dowland's
music to public attention after a long
period of neglect. There is a memorial
plaque, now much damaged, to Dowland in SORRENTO PARK, Dalkey, designed by SARAH PURSER, and executed
*in opus sectile* (glass mosaic) by H V
McGoldrick in 1937.

**DRACULA.** Novel of vampirism written by Dublin novelist BRAM STOKER in
1897, probably the least acclaimed best
seller of Irish literature. Dracula may be
encountered in the flesh, so to speak, in
the NATIONAL WAX MUSEUM.

*DRAPIER'S LETTERS, THE.* JONA-
THAN SWIFT'S most effective adventure
into the area of public affairs. A patent
had been issued for the introduction of
copper coinage into Ireland and purchased by a speculator, William Wood,
a Wolverhampton ironmonger. This patent allowed Wood to coin £100,000 of
copper, with a metallic value of £30,000.
Swift wrote a series of five pamphlets in
1724, under the name of M.B. Drapier
(draper), heaping ridicule on the administration and arousing public passions
against the project which was then abandoned. Although it was well known that
Swift was the author of the letters and
the government offered a reward for the
identification of the Drapier, no one was
prepared to testify to Swift's involvement. However the printer of the *Drapier's Letters* was arrested and died
while in prison. Swift was immensely
proud of his role as a champion of jus-

tice and referred to his success as the
spurious Drapier in his autobiographical
poems.
  Must we the Drapier then forget?
  Is not our Nation in his debt?
('The Life and Character of Dean Swift',
Jonathan Swift.)

**DRIMNAGH CASTLE**, Long Mile
Road, Drimnagh, D12. Moated thirteenth-century castle with sixteenth-
century tower and later buildings
currently in the process of restoration
under the auspices of AN TAISCE.

**DUBLIN.** Capital of the Irish Republic,
Cathedral and University City, seat of
Government and the largest centre of
population in Ireland. The Vikings
founded a settlement here in 841 which
they called *Dyflin*, a corruption of the
Irish, *Dubh Linn* (black pool), and the
city which resulted remained an outpost
of colonial administration for most of its
history, only gradually extending its influence over the whole country. Dublin
exerted a cultural influence outside Ireland during the tenth century when it
was a Viking kingdom, the eighteenth
century when its street planning and
architecture were in advance of much of
northern Europe, and in the early years
of the twentieth century during the Irish
Literary Revival. Dublin has moved a
long way from the place encapsulated in
the poet Louis MacNeice's resonant
phrase, 'Fort of the Dane, Garrison of the
Saxon, Augustan capital, Of a Gaelic
nation', and has become culturally inte-
grated into both its own rural hinterland
and also into Europe in a way which was
glimpsed during the eighteenth century,
but remained unrealised until the mid-
twentieth century.

DUBLIN IN 1248.

'And about the same time, the citie of Dublin was defaced by fire, and the steeple of Christs church utterlie destroied. The citizens before they went about to repare their owne privat buildings, agreed together to make a collection for reparing the ruines of that ancient building first begun by the Danes, and continued by Citrius prince of Dublin at the instance of Donat sometime bishop of that citie, and dedicated to the blessed trinitie.'

(*The Description of Ireland*, Richard Stanyhurst.)

DUBLIN IN 1577.

'This citie, as it is not in antiquitie inferiour to anie citie in Ireland, so in pleasant situation, in gorgious buildings, in the multitude of people, in martiall chivalrie, in obedience and loialtie, in the abundance of wealth, in largness of hospitalitie, in manners and civilitie, it is superiour to all other cities and townes in that realme.'

(*Hollinshed's Chronicles*, Richard Stanyhurst.)

DUBLIN IN 1771.

'Ireland is itself a poor country, and Dublin a magnificent city; but the appearances of general extreme poverty among the lower people are amazing. They live in wretched hovels of mud and straw, are clothed in rags, and subsist chiefly on potatoes. Our New England farmers, of the poorest sort, in regard to the enjoyment of all the comforts of life are princes when compared to them.'

(Benjamin Franklin.)

DUBLIN IN 1804.

'The city of Quang-tcheu is much celebrated amongst the Quang-tongese for its size and magnificence, and is sup-posed to contain 400,000 souls, but this cannot be; for, in that case, 200,000 of them must, of necessity, be hurdled together in extreme filth and misery, which, in such a polished and charitable age and nation, it is absurd to suppose.'

(John Wilson Croker.)

**DUBLIN ARGOT.** The subtle distinction between a native of the city and an interloper are defined in 'Dublinman' and 'Dubliner', the former implying someone bred within the canals, an authentic native, while the latter encompasses those who have a more tenuous claim to citizenship – suburbanites and people of country descent. The bench on St. Stephen's Green opposite Newman House where JAMES JOYCE studied bears a plaque commemorating the writer and his father, respectively referred to as Dubliner and Corkonian. Joyce was not a 'Dublinman' and probably no true son of the city could have distanced himself sufficiently from it to be able to render Joyce's exacting portrait of his birthplace.

**DUBLIN BAY.** Dublin is singularly lucky in having on its doorstep some of the loveliest countryside on the east coast of Ireland, in particular the coastline of Dublin Bay, no part of which is more than a half-hour journey from the city centre. This remarkable mixture of natural beauty, interesting suburbs and villages extends from Howth on the north to Killiney on the south, incorporating in its coastline two important nature reserves – BULL ISLAND and BOOTERSTOWN MARSH – beaches for bathing, walking or solitude, and all manner of facilities for water sports, with clubs catering for everything from canoeing to the most ambitious of yacht racing. With the largest man-made har-

*Dublin Bay from Howth Summit.*

bour of the Victorian world at DUN LAOGHAIRE, which acts as a centre for yachting, and the diverse interests of the IRISH NATIONAL MARITIME MUSEUM and the JAMES JOYCE MUSEUM nearby, this section of the southern coast of Dublin Bay can claim to be one of the most fascinating areas of Dublin outside the centre. On the north side of the Bay the sweep of BULL ISLAND has both extensive strands and the primary migrant bird reserve in Ireland, and further out at HOWTH the Demesne of HOWTH CASTLE vies in attraction with the bare Summit of Howth, one a lush area of cultivated parkland, the other a windswept height of gorse and heather with views across to the Wicklow Hills. In all the residential quarters around the Bay it is easy to forget that the turmoil of the city is nearby, so much does the marine atmosphere dominate.

    And up the back garden
    The sound comes to me
    Of the lapsing, unsoilable,
    Whispering sea.
('Ringsend', Oliver St. John Gogarty.)

**DUBLIN CASTLE**, Cork Hill, Dame Street. D2. The Castle of Dublin has been synonymous with civil authority in Ireland for almost eight hundred years, and closely identified with British rule since the sixteenth century. So great a

symbol of British power was it, that the term 'the Castle' was laden with associations of both oppression and opportunity up to the emergence of an independent Ireland. Some of these associations it still maintains as the base of the detective force. The Castle was founded by the mandate of King John in 1204, some thirty years after the ANGLO NORMANS arrived in Ireland. For strategic reasons it was built on the high ground on the south bank of the Liffey where the river PODDLE entered a pool (the Dubh Linn or dark pool from which the city derives its name) opening into the Liffey. The Poddle formed a partial moat on the south, east and north of the Castle. With circular towers at the four corners of a rectangular courtyard the shape of the Castle was established at its inception and although it has expanded both to the east and west the original form and indeed some of the walls and towers can still be seen under a gloss of Georgian administrative and Viceregal buildings. As the residence of the Viceroy (the representative of the British monarch in Ireland), Ascendancy social life centred around receptions at the Castle during the 'Castle Season' which ran from February to St. Patrick's Day, and power and patronage emanated from within its walls. An important objective of the rebellions of 1534, 1646, 1798,

1803 and 1916 was the seizure of the Castle, but this was never achieved and it was handed over to the local administration on 17 August 1922. Within the Castle walls, the State Apartments are housed on the south side of Upper Castle Yard in a range of buildings that run along the lines of the ancient southern fortifications and incorporate some of the remaining twelfth-century Castle

*The Upper Yard, Dublin Castle.*

into their plan. In these rooms all the social and official functions of the Castle were held during the era of the Viceroys and they are still used for important State functions. Upper Castle Yard which resembles a university quadrangle of brick and stone-dressed Georgian buildings does not prepare the viewer for the opulence of the State Apartments, a succession of ornately decorated rooms, circular, scalloped, pillared and painted in Georgian, Victorian and modern styles and lavishly maintained for current post-Viceregal entertaining and, more recently, for meetings of EC leaders. Abutting the Records Tower, the only one of the Anglo-Norman towers substantially intact, is the Church of The Most Holy Trinity, formerly the CHAPEL ROYAL, the official chapel of the Viceroys. This charming little Gothic building, designed by FRANCIS JOHNSTON, opened for worship in 1814. Richly decorated within and without, it contains the arms of every Viceroy since 1172, as well as fantastical plasterwork by George Stapleton and wood carving by Richard Stewart. On the exterior are stone heads of over a hundred historical and legendary characters carved by EDWARD SMYTH and his son. Facing the State Apartments across Upper Castle Yard is the Genealogical Office, a small eighteenth-century building flanked by two Baroque archways, and capped by the Bedford Tower, which forms the centrepiece of the Castle Yard. The Bedford Tower stands on the stump of one of the original towers which flanked the drawbridge to the Anglo-Norman Castle. In the UNDERCROFT excavations in the lower Castle yard the base of the Powder Tower at the north-east corner of the Castle has been revealed as well as a portion of the moat, postern gate, city wall and a Viking embankment. The

Castle Yards are generally open during normal office hours as well as at weekends. The State Apartments, Chapel Royal and Undercroft Mon-Fri 10-12.15, 2.00-5.00, Sun 2.00-5.00. Admission charge.

**DUBLIN CHARACTERS.** In the heart of the LIBERTIES on THE COOMBE, the old portico of the Coombe Lying-In Hospital has been preserved, and on a flight of steps at the back of this architectural relic are inscribed the names of the eccentric flotsam of street people whose peculiarities endeared them to generations of Dubliners. Here are remembered the lost and the deranged, the war–damaged and the merely comic misfits who performed their curious rituals on street corners for so many years that they seemed to have always been part of the life of the inner city. The names by which these characters became known derive from their occupation, from the strange things they said, or from reasons that have become lost in time, but as the children play around the steps, chanting skipping rhymes, there seems to be a fellowship between the the language of children's games and the names of these vanished eccentrics. Those remembered in the inscription are:
BANG BANG, Bugler Dunne, Damn The Weather, Dunlavin, The Earl of Dalcashin, The Grindstone Man, Hairy Yank, Hamlet, Houdini, Jembo No Toes, JOHNNY FORTY COATS, Johnny Wet Bread, Lady Hogan, Love Joy and Peace, The Magic Soap Man, Michael Bruen, Nancy Needle Balls, The Prince of Denmark, Rags Bottles and Bones, Shell Shock Joe, Soodlum, Stab The Rasher, The Tuggers, The Umbrella Man, Windy Mills.

**DUBLIN CIVIC SWORDS.** Dublin has two civic swords in the city's Regalia, the Great Sword and the King's or City Sword, which are used during ceremonial occasions. The Great Sword was presented to the city by King Henry VI in 1403 and is a rare and important example of late Medieval personal armour. Engraved with the personal insignia of the King, the iron sword, sheathed in silver-gilt, was carried in processions as a symbol of royal authority. The King's Sword is probably seventeenth century and was used during the ceremony of RIDING THE FRANCHISES, during which the city council and guilds traversed the borders of their area of authority.

**DUBLIN CORPORATION**, City Hall, Dame Street, D2, tel 776811. The Corporation meets on the first Monday of the month at 7.30pm, and the public can attend, but a ticket is required, available from your local representative or by application to the City Hall. For the functions of the Corporation, see CIVIC OFFICES.

**DUBLIN INSTITUTE FOR ADVANCED STUDIES** (DIAS). Established by the Irish Government in 1940, with two constituent departments, The School of Celtic Studies and The School of Theoretical Physics. DUNSINK OBSERVATORY was incorporated into the Institute in 1947 as the School of Cosmic Physics.

**DUBLIN LITERARY WORLD.** 'As warm and friendly as an alligator pool,' Cyril Connolly.

*DUBLIN PENNY JOURNAL.* In 1832 The Society for the Diffusion of Useful Knowledge in London published *The*

*Penny Magazine,* a journal which as the name of its publisher implies, might legitimately be interested in anything. In the same year Dublin saw a similar periodical, profusely illustrated and taking the same extensive brief. Edited and founded by P. Dixon Hardy, *The Dublin Penny Journal* ran from 1832 to 1835 and was an important influence on popularising interest in the antiquarian and natural aspects of the environment as well as publishing important contemporary writers such as WILLIAM CARLETON.

**DUBLIN PORT.** East Wall Road, D1, tel 722777. The premier Port Authority in Ireland, dealing in cargo and passenger traffic with a twice daily B&I car ferry service to Holyhead and direct cargo sailings to Great Britain, Europe, North and South America, West Africa and the Middle East. The Port had existed on the Liffey quays in the middle of the city from at least the tenth century up to the building of JAMES GANDON'S CUSTOM HOUSE in 1781, but from that point onwards it developed outside the urban area of Dublin. Gradual expansion over the succeeding two hundred years has led to the present form of the Port, which now extends to the east on reclaimed land into the deep waters of DUBLIN BAY. The Dublin Port Estate currently occupies an area of 350 hectares and has 9 kilometres of berthage servicing 3,500 ships a year.

**DUBLIN STOCK EXCHANGE,** 28 Anglesea Street, D2, tel 778808. The Dublin Exchange has never been very large due to the proximity of a major financial centre in London's City. Trading may be observed from the visitor's gallery, Mon-Fri 9.30-10.00, 2.15-3.00, a ticket is required.

**DUBLIN TO KINGSTOWN RAILWAY.** Made its maiden voyage on 17 December 1834. So great was public curiosity about the first railway in Ireland that in the first two days of business it carried 18,000 passengers. By 1838 the weekly passenger load was 20,000 per week. As in the case of the innovative new CUSTOM HOUSE designed by JAMES GANDON in the previous century, the proposers of the railway met with fierce opposition from many quarters. This was eventually overcome by the railway company making substantial concessions and payments to those landowners who opposed its crossing their land. Lord Cloncurry and Sir Harcourt Lees in BLACKROCK were firm opponents of the railway's path along the seaward side of their marine villas and footbridges as well as a tunnel had to be provided to appease them. The citizens of Kingstown (Dun Laoghaire) were even more adamant in opposing this threat, and initially the company was not able to run the track through the town. The Kingstown residents considered the proposed railway to be a 'vulgar and democratic mode of conveyance'. They were right of course, but hardly in the negative manner in which they regarded it.

**DUBLIN TOURISM,** 14 Upper O'Connell Street, D1, tel 747733. The principal, and most conveniently located, tourist information office in Dublin. Open, Jan-Mar, Mon-Fri 9.00-17.00, Sat 9.00-13.00. Mar-Oct, Mon-Sat 9.00-17.00, Nov-Dec, Mon-Fri 9.00-17.00, Sat 9.00-13.00. Other tourism offices are Baggot Street Bridge, D2, tel 765871, and St. Michael's Wharf, Dun Laoghaire, tel 806984. The main office on O'Connell Street caters for general tourist enquiries, car hire, bureau de change, hotel, bed & breakfast and farmhouse accommodation, coach tours and just about anything else one might need to know.

**DUBLIN TRADES.** Many of Dublin's trades were in the past concentrated in specific streets or quarters, such as the Weavers in the LIBERTIES, or shipbuilders in Ringsend. This popular song from the eighteenth century gives a particular trade to each street.

> And in Temple Bar I've dressed old hats
> And in Thomas Street a sawer,
> And in Pill Lane I've sold a plate
> In Green Street an honest lawyer,
> In Plunkett Street I sold cast clothes
> In Bride's Alley a broker,
> In Charles' Street I had a shop
> Sold shovel, tongs and poker.

('The Dublin Jack of All Trades'.)

**DUBLIN'S ORIGINS.** In order to appreciate exactly why the tenth-century Viking city was situated where it was on the Liffey, take a walk along High Street, the main thoroughfare of the Viking settlement. From this ridge of land the terrain falls away in every direction, yet the river is very close at hand. With outstandingly clear views of the approaches to the city and a safe harbour for their ships, the site was the most satisfactory on the whole of DUBLIN BAY. In the period of the city's foundation, the Liffey was twice as wide as it is now, so that the distance to the riverbank would have been even less than it appears at present.

**DUN LAOGHAIRE.** The Township of Dun Laoghaire developed from the small eighteenth-century fishing village of Dunleary into the most vigorous Victorian commercial and residential region in the country. This growth was due to the advances which were being achieved in mechanics and engineering during the early nineteenth century, and also the need to find a safe and accessible mailboat harbour for rapid communications with Britain. The magnificent 'Asylum Harbour', designed by John Rennie and built between 1817 and 1842, was the primary factor in the town's remarkable growth, but the development of the first railway in Ireland in 1834, the Dublin to Kingstown, established the town as being within easy access of the centre of Dublin. From this date the population grew rapidly and speculative developments of fine villas were built in large numbers on the hills above the harbour, of which Clarinda Park, 1850, and Crostwaithe Park, 1860, are well preserved examples. The name was changed from Dunleary to Kingstown in 1821 after the visit to Dublin of GEORGE IV, and it was as Kingstown that the character of the town was firmly established when it became a fashionable residential area for merchants and professional people working in Dublin. After 1922, the town was renamed Dun Laoghaire, in reference to the Iron Age Fort of King Laoghaire situated in the area between De Vesci Gardens and the harbour, but removed during construction of the railway. Today the Sealink Ferry docks in Dun Laoghaire harbour, and it is the yachting centre of the east coast, with four yacht clubs on the harbour – The Royal St. George, the Royal Irish, the National, and the Motor Yacht Club. There are few more popular or more exhilarating places in the environs of Dublin for walking than on the piers of Dun Laoghaire harbour and throughout the year and all day long walkers stride out into the bracing winds of the Bay, and admire the splendid masonry with which the piers are constructed. Dun Laoghaire has very strong literary associations, the most well known being the brief residence of James Joyce in the Sandycove Martello in 1904 now the JAMES JOYCE MUSEUM, J.M. SYNGE, DENIS JOHNSTON, Padraic Colum, L.A.G. Strong, OLIVER ST. JOHN GOGARTY, Lennox Robinson, and Peadar O'Donnell have all lived in the borough.

**DUNSINK OBSERVATORY**, Castleknock, Co. Dublin, tel 387911. Established by TRINITY COLLEGE in 1783, it was taken over by the Irish government in 1946 and provided with modern equipment for astronomical research. Many distinguished names in the world of mathematics have been connected with Dunsink, and SIR WILLIAM ROWAN HAMILTON was director for most of his life. One of the principal functions of the observatory was the regulation of the public 'slave' clocks in Dublin – at the BALLAST OFFICE, GENERAL POST OFFICE and TRINITY COLLEGE – which were linked by cable to Dunsink and maintained a margin of error of a fraction of a second per day. Among the important early optical equipment is a 12 inch refractor telescope, built in Dublin in 1863 and still in use. The observatory holds open nights and application for tickets may be made by post to the Secretary. See IRISH ASTRONOMICAL SOCIETY.

**DÜRER, ALBRECHT**, (1471-1528). German painter and graphic artist, the CHESTER BEATTY LIBRARY contains a remarkable collection of Dürer's graphic work, but because the Library is associated with Oriental and European manuscript material, artworks of other periods and cultures have tended to get overlooked. Although the Dürer prints were purchased by SIR ALFRED CHESTER BEATTY around the turn of the century, the engravings, etchings and woodcuts

*'Dutch Billies' in Chambers Street.*

were not catalogued until the 1980s. Almost half of Dürer's entire output of prints is represented, including a complete set of the 'Apocalypse' (1498).

**'DUTCH BILLIES'.** Dublin colloquial term for the characteristic gabled houses associated with the HUGUENOTS of the LIBERTIES, and called after William of Orange, but in fact the style of architecture which they represented was also found in the south of England and may have been imported from there. The house type – with a gable end facing the street – had been common throughout the city since the sixteenth century as can be seen in early illustrations of Dublin, giving a sawtooth roofline to the streets. More elaborate houses in an Anglo-Dutch style with scalloped gables, more properly called Dutch Billies, were to be found all over the Liberties but no examples survived later than the 1930s with the exception of a single house on Kevin Street. Similar, but later, gables can still be seen today in Molesworth Street.

**EARLSFORT TERRACE**, D2. Avenue leading from the south-west corner of St. Stephen's Green to ADELAIDE ROAD. The University College building which contains the NATIONAL CONCERT HALL as well as the UCD faculties of Architecture, Engineering and Medicine is the most significant building, while behind it lie the almost unknown IVEAGH GARDENS. Beside the Hotel Conrad is the newly laid out Earlsfort Piazza in which a fountain sculpture represents a theme from W.B. YEATS's poem 'The Lake Isle of Innisfree'.

**EARLY CHRISTIAN PERIOD.** Monastic settlements developed in the Liffey valley from the sixth century AD at Clondalkin, Finglas, Glasnevin, Kilmainham and other locations and, at the site of the present city, two community clusters were located from which Dublin's present names originate. Átha Cliath was on the southern river bank at the crossing point, and Dubhlinn to the south of the present-day Castle Gardens. The great roads of pre Christian Ireland, the Slige Dala and Slige Chualann on the south and the Slige Midluachra from the north met at the Liffey river crossing, now the site of Father Mathew Bridge. This established the early importance of the area as a trading location prior to the arrival of the VIKINGS in AD 841. See BAILE ÁTHA CLIATH.

**EAST WALL ROAD**, D1. Originally the eastern limit of the lands reclaimed from the river during the eighteenth century, now the connecting road between the East Link Toll Bridge and the northern shore of Dublin Bay. The entrance to DUBLIN PORT and the B&I FERRY TERMINAL is from East Wall Road, and the POINT DEPOT, a venue for international music and ballet, is at the Liffey end of the road.

*Early Christian tombstone, St. Patrick's Cathedral.*

**EASTER RISING.** At noon on Easter Monday, 24 April 1916, the IRISH VOLUNTEERS led by PATRICK PEARSE, and the IRISH CITIZEN ARMY led by JAMES CONNOLLY, seized the GENERAL POST OFFICE in O'Connell Street, the Royal College of Surgeons, the FOUR COURTS, BOLANDS MILLS, the Mendicity Institute and other prominent buildings throughout the city, proclaiming the foundation of an Irish Republic. With a total force of around eighteen hundred men and armed with guns brought into Dublin during the HOWTH GUN RUNNING, the revolutionaries could not have hoped to achieve anything more than a symbolic assault upon British rule in Ireland. An attempt to seize the Castle, a prime objective of every Irish rebellion, was no more successful than on previous occasions. After fierce fighting, during which over four hundred people were killed, many more wounded and a substantial portion of the city centre destroyed, the leaders of the rebellion capitulated unconditionally on 29 April. By 12 May, fifteen of them had been tried for treason and executed by firing squad. Public reaction to the revolutionaries was initially one of dismay and criticism because of the damage to the city. However, the execution of the leaders caused a wave of sympathy for their cause and had the radical effect of reversing public opinion. The dramatic swing towards the Sinn Féin candidates in the 1919 Westminster elections indicated a rallying of support towards the aspirations of the insurgents of 1916. One of the first acts of the First DÁIL, which was established as a result of the 1919 elections by MPs who refused to go to Westminster, was to ratify the Proclamation of 1916. During the shelling of O'Connell Street virtually the whole east side of the street between the bridge and North Earl Street was destroyed, as was a block on either side of the GPO. British soldiers killed during the 1916 Rising are buried in Bully's Acre, the Irish dead are in AR-BOUR HILL and GLASNEVIN.

Was it needless death after all?

For England may keep faith

For all that is done and said.

We know their dream enough

To know they dreamed and are dead;

('Easter 1916', W. B. Yeats.)

**ECCLES STREET**, D1. Eighteenth-century residential street of which now only the western side remains, it is famous as the residence of LEOPOLD BLOOM who, in Joyce's imagination, lived at No. 7 on the eastern side, now demolished. The front door to this house is in the BAILEY Pub in Duke Street. Actual residents of Eccles Street were ISAAC BUTT, Cardinal Cullen, SIR BOYLE ROCHE and FRANCIS JOHNSTON, whose house is decorated on the outside with Classical medallions. The top of the street is dominated by the Mater Misericordiae Hospital, known as the Mater and built in the 1850s as a fever hospital. It is still functioning as a general hospital.

**EDICT OF NANTES.** This edict guaranteed freedom of conscience to French religious minorities. It was the revoking of this law in 1685 which forced the Protestant HUGUENOTS to emigrate from France and led to the establishment of an important Huguenot community in Dublin during the late seventeenth century.

**EDWARDIAN DUBLIN.** Between the death of Queen Victoria in 1901 and the beginning of the First World War in 1914 was a strangely enigmatic period, and its architecture belongs to no one era, simultaneously harking backwards and forwards. The heritage of design in Dublin was a strongly Classical one with a Gothic interlude. The four major buildings erected during the Edwardian era all have Classical overtones, but the breath of the Modern Movement has blown away much of the detail, and they are rather unsatisfactory. GOVERNMENT BUILDINGS, 1904, by Aston Webb and T.M. Deane, the Bolton Street College of Technology, 1906, by C. J. McCarthy, the UNIVERSITY COLLEGE building on EARLSFORT TERRACE, 1912, by R.M.Butler and the BAYNO, the Iveagh Play Centre by Mc Donnell and Reid, 1915, are all monumental compositions of which the earliest, Government Buildings, is the most interesting.

**EDWARDS, HILTON,** (1903-1982). Theatre director and actor, he came to Ireland in 1928 to tour with Anew Mac Master and during this tour he met Mí-CHÁEL MAC LIAMMÓIR with whom he formed a lifelong theatrical partnership. Edwards co-founded the GATE THEATRE in 1928 with Mac Liammóir and introduced European ideas of lighting and direction to Dublin. During fifty years of work with the Gate he directed most of the international classics of the modern theatre.

**ÉIRE, ÉIREANN.** One of the ancient names by which the island of Ireland was known, and which was adopted as the official name for the Irish Free State (1921-1949 when Ireland was declared a republic). It is the name which still appears on both postage stamps and COINAGE, but has no popular currency, its use being considered a solecism.

**ELECTRIC LIGHTING.** Since the sixteenth century some form of street lighting has been in existence in Dublin and householders have been obliged to maintain lights on their houses. Originally lights were attached by brackets to individual houses, but later on developed as free-standing lamp posts. It was customary up to the nineteenth century for people not to go abroad at night in the city unaccompanied, so poor was the lighting and in consequence so considerable the possibility of being assaulted. Fish oil and paraffin oil were the principal fuels used until the advent of gas lighting in 1825. The lamplighter was in the past as much an institution as the postman is today. Electricity was introduced in 1880, and the Pigeon House Power Station, built in 1903, made electric street lighting possible throughout the city. Poolbeg Power Sta-

*Megaloceros Giganteus.*

tion, 1971-1979, with its twin tall stacks, runs on gas from the Kinsale Natural Gas fields which is piped to Dublin.

**ELK, THE,** Natural History Museum, D2, tel 765521. The extinct Giant Irish Deer or Elk, *Megaloceros Giganteus*, was the largest of the deer species in the world and inhabited open areas of the Irish countryside in the Pleistocene Age, around 10,000 BC. Examples of its extraordinary skeleton can be seen in the Natural History Museum, and also in Trinity Museum. In common with the beasts of more prehistoric ages it looks quite improbable with its absurd antler span – the elk stood at six feet to the shoulder, and ten to the top of the antler tines. The antlers, which were generally ten feet wide, could span twelve feet in an exceptionally large male. Estimates suggest that the elk could have weighed up to one thousand pounds. The elk, as a symbol of Ireland's primeval past, has been the inspiration for a particularly fine series of paintings by the contemporary artist Barrie Cook.

**ELY HOUSE,** 8 Ely Place, D2, tel 761835. Late eighteenth-century town mansion, built for Henry Loftus, Marquess of Ely in 1771, whose home was at RATHFARNHAM CASTLE. Ely House is now the headquarters of the Knights of Columbanus. The seven-bay brick façade faces into Hume Street and inside the house is richly decorated with plasterwork by MICHAEL STAPLETON. The most remarkable feature of the house is the life-size statue of Hercules at the base of the main stairway, and the low-relief gilded wooden panels depicting five of the twelve Labours of Hercules set into the balustrade. These panels represent the Erymanthian Boar, the Nemean Lion, the Cretan Bull, the Arcadian Stag and Cerberus, with eagles at the turn of the stairs. Upstairs, on the first floor, there is a marble mantelpiece that continues the Hercules theme, showing the god asleep, resting after his activities below stairs. Open by appointment.

**ELY PLACE,** D2. Quiet Georgian cul-de-sac off Merrion Row. The principal buildings of interest today are ELY HOUSE and the ROYAL HIBERNIAN ACADEMY'S Gallagher Gallery. The Gallery is built where the house of OLIVER ST. JOHN GOGARTY once stood, and also on gardens belonging to GEORGE MOORE, who lived on the other side of the street at No. 4. There is some very fine Georgian ironwork on the east side of the street.

**EMERGENCY, THE.** Irish euphemism for the 1939-1945 war, during which Ireland remained neutral, maintaining diplo-

*Ely House from Hume Street.*

matic relations with both sides although tacitly supporting the Allies.

**EMMET, ROBERT,** (1778-1803). Member of UNITED IRISHMEN and revolutionary leader, born at 124 St. Stephen's Green (now demolished), opposite which stands a fine statue of Emmet by JEROME CONNOR. As a student activist in TRINITY COLLEGE he came under government scrutiny and had to leave without taking a degree. He subsequently went to France where he attempted, unsuccessfully, to interest Napoleon in an Irish invasion. With a band of ill-trained followers Emmet launched an abortive attack on DUBLIN CASTLE in 1803, after which he went into hiding. Eventually captured, he was tried for treason and hanged outside ST. CATHERINE'S CHURCH, Thomas Street. He was then twenty-five years old. Emmet is the subject of a number of romantic ballads and remains a popular figure in the mythology of Irish Republicanism.

> Oh in Green Street courthouse in
> eighteen and three
> Stood young Emmet the hero true
> and brave,
> For fighting the tyrant, his country to
> free
> And to tear from her brow the name
> of slave.

('Young Emmet', nineteenth-century Dublin ballad.)

**ENGRAVERS.** The principal contribution to the art of engraving and printmaking by Dubliners was made during the eighteenth century when an active school of mezzotinters developed. This form of engraving, which was particularly suitable for rendering the qualities of portraits in oils, took many of these engravers to London in pursuit of opportunity where they became known as 'The Dublin Scrapers'.

**ENSOR, JOHN,** (Flourished 1750-70). Architect, he was assistant to RICHARD CASTLE on the ROTUNDA Hospital and took over from him after Castle's death. Ensor designed the Rotunda rooms from which the hospital now takes its name.

**ENTERTAINMENT.** The wide range of entertainment available in the city falls into two categories, the occasional and the permanent. Occasional are the festivals and events of limited duration which will be found under ANNUAL EVENTS AND FESTIVALS IN DUBLIN. Of the year-round activities, ART GALLERIES, CINEMAS, DISCOS, MUSEUMS, MUSIC, NIGHTCLUBS, RESTAURANTS and THEATRE will all be found under those separate headings.

**ESSENTIALS.** The essential Dublin can be many things to many different people, but the essence of the city must be on some level tangible and identifiable. Certain quarters of the city and the work of particular individuals, writers and artists, as well as a manner of life and the nature of the people clearly contribute to the essential picture. On a physical level the rays of the setting sun illuminating the glowing façades of the Georgian streets is something indubitably of Dublin. Another essence is the sight of the Dublin Mountains at the end of every south-facing street. This proximity of wild fastnesses to urban order is part of the magic of the place. DUBLIN BAY must also rank high on the phenomena of Dublin, allowing the city to spread, yet maintaining another kind of wildness, the violence of the sea, within easy reach of the very centre. Conversation, a remark overheard in the streets, a street trader's witticism, the pungent, satirical humour of everyday encounters – is certainly an engaging aspect of life in Dublin, and the city would be unimaginable without it. The Liffey, centre of the city, running under a dozen looping bridges between the reedy banks of Islandbridge and the sea, passed over and passed again by a million people every day seems to hold everything which is essential to Dublin; coming from the mountains and heading for the Bay, it is as unavoidable as it is ubiquitous. See also WONDERS.

**EUROPA NOSTRA AWARD.** Awarded to the Royal Hospital Kilmainham restoration in 1985 for making a 'distinguished contribution to the conservation of Europe's architectural heritage'. The TOWER DESIGN CENTRE on Pearse Street also received a Europa Nostra award in 1983.

**EUROPEAN CITY OF CULTURE.** Following Glasgow in 1990, Dublin became the 1991 holder of this title. In 1985 the European Community instituted this rotating honour by choosing Athens as the first official Cultural Capital of the Community for a year. Florence, Amsterdam, Berlin and Paris followed Athens, in different ways taking the opportunity to promote the arts of the separate regions of Europe. In Dublin the year was marked by significant additions to the cultural institutions of the city, for the visual arts and literature the opening of the IRISH MUSEUM OF MODERN ART and the DUBLIN WRITERS' MUSEUM, and in the area of architecture and the applied arts the restored eighteenth-century CUSTOM HOUSE and NEWMAN HOUSE, the ESB GEORGIAN MUSEUM and Government Buildings.

FARRELL, SIR THOMAS, (1827-1900). Sculptor, he is the most well-known member of a sculpting family which produced seven sculptors in two generations. There are more monuments by Farrell in Dublin than by any other artist, but unfortunately his figures are rather uninspired, or perhaps his subjects were too worthy to be inspiring! The Boyd Memorial in ST. PATRICK'S CATHEDRAL and the frieze around the drum of the Cullen Memorial in the PRO CATHEDRAL show his work in a more interesting light. Both Sir John Grey and William Smith O'Brien on O'Connell Street are by Farrell, as is the William Dargan statue on the lawn of the National Gallery.

**FASHION HOUSES.** Irish fashion designers, using a combination of native fabrics and techniques such as tweeds, linen, lace and knitting combined with internationally recognised materials, have since the late 1940s established Dublin on the Haute Couture circuit. A small number of designers with their own shops in Dublin or selling through some of the smarter stores such as BROWN THOMAS have brought Irish fashion into a position of international prominence. Design faculties at the Art Colleges, in particular the NATIONAL COLLEGE OF ART AND DESIGN, have begun to produce a generation of highly skilled fashion designers whose contribution to the vitality of the fashion industry is already being felt. See SHOPPING.

**FEIS CEOIL.** Founded in 1897 in order to raise the standard of vocal and instrumental music, with an emphasis on the Irish tradition, the annual Feis is held in March with graded competitions for children and adults. JAMES JOYCE and JOHN MCCORMACK both competed on the same platform in the 1904 Feis. The operatic singer Margaret Burke-Sheridan also came to notice performing in the Feis.

**FENIAN BROTHERHOOD.** James Stephens, a patriarchal figure in Irish Nationalist circles, founded the Fenian Brotherhood in Dublin on 17 March 1858. The organisation developed into the Irish Revolutionary Brotherhood (IRB), and launched an unsuccessful rebellion in Dublin and Munster in 1867, the leaders of which were transported.

**FERGUSON, SIR SAMUEL,** (1810-1886). Poet, antiquarian, barrister. He became in 1867 the first Deputy Keeper of Public Records of Ireland. Many of Ferguson's translations and versions of Irish poetry have been anthologised. He founded the Protestant Repeal Association, and supported the Young Ireland movement, but later abandoned politics and devoted his life to literature and scholarship. He became President of the Royal Irish Academy in 1881. Two remarkably contrasting poems by Ferguson, 'AIDEEN'S GRAVE' about the Cromlech of HOWTH, and 'At the Polo Ground' concerning the PHOENIX PARK MURDERS, show the wide range of his sympathies and understanding of vastly different aspects of Irish life, both historic and contemporary.

**FERRIES.** Both B&I Line, tel 724711, and Sealink, tel 808844, operate daily ferry services out of Dublin to Britain, and seasonal ones to the Continent, B&I from Dublin Port to Liverpool and Holyhead, and Sealink from Dun Laoghaire to Holyhead. Offices of both ferry services are in Westmoreland Street, D2. Irish Continental Lines, 19 Aston Quay, tel 774331, operate Rosslare to Le Havre and Cherbourg. DART to Dun Laoghaire for Sealink; Bus 53 from Connolly Station to Dublin port for B&I.

**FESTIVALS.** See ANNUAL EVENTS IN DUBLIN.

**FIELD, JOHN,** (1782-1837). Composer and pianist, born at 8 Golden Lane, in the LIBERTIES. He was performing by the age of twelve in London, demonstrating pianos for Clementi, under whom he studied. Field lived most of his life as a teacher and concert pianist in Europe, principally in Russia and he died in Moscow. He is credited with the invention of the piano nocturne, made famous by Chopin.

**FINANCIAL SERVICES CENTRE,** Custom House Docks, D1. In 1985 the Irish government decided to establish a centre for international banking and financial services in Dublin. The site chosen was the redundant western end of DUBLIN PORT, facing onto the Liffey and adjoining the CUSTOM HOUSE, BUSÁRAS and DART and mainline services at CONNOLLY STATION. The area of this development, 11 hectares (27 acres), is larger than that of St. Stephen's Green, and it represents not only the most important urban renewal project to take place in Dublin in the twentieth century, but also the largest single project to be carried out in the inner city since the eighteenth century. As well as the Financial Services Centre, the site will contain a major hotel, cultural complex, housing sited around the eighteenth-century dock basins and extensive office accommodation, much of which is currently in the course of construction or actually completed. The scheme, designed by Benjamin Thompson and Burke, Kennedy, Doyle, is a combination of sophisticated glass-walled office buildings balanced by the retention of some important nineteenth-century warehouse buildings.

*FINNEGANS WAKE.* James Joyce's last major work, an immense 'novel' in which the whole content is a layering of multiple meanings to which many scholars, but few of the general reading public, have devoted their lives in efforts of elucidation. The only recording of Joyce reading his own writing is one in which he reads passages from *Finnegans Wake*, and in this the intensely musical quality of the language is evident. *The Wake* was published in two parts, *Anna Livia Plurabelle* 1930, and *Haveth Childers Everywhere* 1931. The entire book, an interlocking Chinese puzzle of language, allusion and abstruse information was published in 1939. It contains many intensely lyrical passages, especially those describing the journey of the Liffey to the sea.

> Annushka Lutetiavitch Pufflovah, and the lellipos cream to her lippe--eens and the pick of the paintbox for her pommettes, from strawbirry reds to extra violates.

(*Finnegans Wake*, James Joyce.)

**FISHAMBLE STREET,** D2. The site of the old fish shambles or markets, the street runs directly up the hill from WOOD QUAY on the Liffey to Christchurch Place on the summit, and excavations have shown that its contours follow the line of the tenth-century street. Now the site of Dublin Corporation's CIVIC OFFICES, Fishamble Street was, during the eighteenth century, the location of Neal's Music Hall in which HANDEL's *Messiah Oratorio* was first performed. The site of the Music Hall is now occupied by Kennan's Ironworks.

**FITZGERALD, LORD EDWARD,**
(1763-1798). Younger son of the Duke
of Leinster, he was born in LEINSTER
HOUSE, the family town house, now the
home of the DÁIL. Fitzgerald lived in
France and had a military career in North
America prior to returning to Ireland and
entering Parliament, where he was the

*Neal's Music Hall, Fishamble Street*

Member for Athy. In France he had
become friendly with Thomas Paine,
author of *The Rights of Man*, and espoused the principles of the French Revolution. After his return to Ireland he
lived at FRESCATI LODGE in BLACKROCK,
the home of his mother, the Duchess of
Leinster. Fitzgerald joined the UNITED
IRISHMEN and planned a revolt for May
1798 but Dublin Castle authorities had
infiltrated the rebel organisation and the
rebellion was thwarted in Dublin. He
fled but was captured and died in prison
from wounds received in the struggle.
Fitzgerald's French wife, Pamela, and

their three small children were deported
by the Castle authorities. There is a fine
portrait by MALLARY of PAMELA FITZ-
GERALD with one of their daughters in
the NATIONAL GALLERY. Fitzgerald's involvement in the rebellion, as a member
of the most powerful aristocratic family
in the country, did nothing to appease
British government suspicions as to the
loyalty of the Irish nobility.

**FITZGERALD, LORD THOMAS,**
(1513-1537). Known as Silken Thomas,
son of the Ninth Earl of Kildare, and
grandson of the 'Great Earl', he was
Deputy Governor of Ireland during his
father's absence in London in 1534. In
June of that year he heard false rumours
that his father had been executed in London, and being an impetuous young
man, took the initiative by renouncing
his allegiance to the English Crown before the Council in the Chapter House of
ST. MARY'S ABBEY. The following month
he launched an unsuccessful attack on
DUBLIN CASTLE and remained in revolt
until 1535 when he went to London to
seek the King's pardon. He was hanged
at Tyburn in 1537, aged twenty-five, in
the company of his five uncles.

**FITZMAURICE,    COLONEL
JAMES,** (1898-1965). Aviator, born at
35 Cowley Place. In the *Bremen*, a 300
HP Junker Monoplane, he made the historic first east-west transatlantic flight
with Captain Herman Kohl and Baron
von Hunefeld, the owner of the plane.
They flew from Baldonnel Aerodrome
in Co. Dublin to Greely Island, New-
foundland on 28 April 1928, in a 37-
hour flight of 2,300 miles. Fitzmaurice,
who was commanding officer of the
Irish Air Corps, had made a previous
attempt in 1927 from which he had to
turn back. The three aviators were made

FREEMEN OF THE CITY in recognition of their achievement.

**FITZWILLIAM SQUARE.** The last of the great Georgian squares to be developed in Dublin, it is also the smallest. Developed during the 1820s, the houses are substantially the same as those of earlier periods although the doorcases are less sculptural and more lightly detailed. The park remains private, the only city-centre one to do so.

**FIVE LAMPS, THE,** North Strand Road, D1. Ornate Victorian five-branched street light on a traffic island, erected in 1870 to commemorate General Henry Hall of the Indian Army.

**FLORA AND FAUNA.** Within the greater Dublin area there are over a hundred parks, two important nature reserves (BULL ISLAND and BOOTERSTOWN MARSH) and 30 kms (18.6 miles) of sea coast in DUBLIN BAY. These areas form the habitat for both indigenous and migratory birds, as well as plants and animals of an abundance remarkable for any built-up urban area. PHOENIX PARK with its herds of fallow deer, wild goats on DALKEY ISLAND, seals playing off DUN LAOGHAIRE Harbour, a gannetry on IRELAND'S EYE, and many species of exotic plants on HOWTH, present the city dweller with the wildness and beauty of nature.

**FOLEY, JOHN HENRY,** (1818-1874). Sculptor, born in 6 Montgomery Street. He studied at the Dublin Society Schools and later in London where he lived for the rest of his life. During his career, Foley received many important commissions in Dublin, including the statues of EDMUND BURKE, OLIVER GOLDSMITH and HENRY GRATTAN in College Green, of which contemporary wits claimed that he cast all the legs from the same moulds. Foley's major work in Dublin is the O'CONNELL MONUMENT in O'Connell Street, on which he was working when he died. The naturalism of his studies of groups of figures, as in this case those around the drum of the O'Connell Monument, or the figure of Asia on the Albert Memorial in London show Foley at his best. Other works by him in Dublin are, Prince Albert on Leinster Lawn, Sir Benjamin Lee Guinness at ST. PATRICK'S CATHEDRAL, and Ino and Bacchus in the ROYAL DUBLIN SOCIETY.

**'FORTY COATS'.** A character of the LIBERTIES who begged in the Thomas Street area dressed in voluminous rags and layers of coats. He has been the subject of a popular children's TV series. With other eccentrics he is commemorated on the Coombe Hospital portico. See DUBLIN CHARACTERS.

**FORTY STEPS.** Flight of winding steps which descends from High Street past ST. AUDOEN'S CHURCH and into a almost subterranean passageway which leads to St. Audoen's Arch on Cook Street. This alley is known as the 'Forty Steps', and another similar forty steps exists at Mount Brown, known as CROMWELL'S QUARTERS.

**FORTYFOOT GENTLEMEN'S BATHING PLACE,** Sandycove, Co. Dublin. Traditionally, this nude bathing area in a rocky cove is a male preserve and women are not welcome. Periodically though the men are outraged by a female invasion. Its name comes from the nineteenth-century gun battery above the cove where the Fortieth Regiment of Foot were stationed.

**FOSTER, JOHN, BARON ORIEL,**
(1740-1828). The last Speaker of the
House of Commons, 1785-1800, he opposed both CATHOLIC EMANCIPATION
and the ACT OF UNION. After the closing
of the Dublin parliament he refused to
surrender the Mace of Office and it remained in his family until the early twentieth century when the BANK OF IRELAND
bought it back from his descendants.

**FOUNTAINS.** The fountains which are
such a pleasant feature of European
cities have never been prominent in Dublin's streetscapes, and they constitute a
surprising omission for a Georgian city.
The Rutland Memorials in MERRION
SQUARE and Collins Barracks are the
only exceptions. Drinking fountains and
horse-trough fountains are in fact more
common, and numerous nineteenth-century versions of these are to be found
around the city. Late twentieth-century
fountains provide the most significant
group in Dublin, with the ANNA LIVIA
FOUNTAIN in O'Connell Street certainly
the most distinctive. The 'Heralds of the
Four Provinces' at College Green, the
'Children of Lir' in Parnell Square, and
'The Charioteer of Life' in Lower
Abbey Street are all works of consider-
able interest. Some of the modern foun-
tains are 'water features' rather than
conventional fountains but they are ga-
thered together here for convenience:
'Anna Livia', O'Connell Street.
Blackrock Park, Blackrock.
Cavendish Row, Parnell Square.
'Charioteer of Life', Lower Abbey
Street.
'Children of Lir', Parnell Square.
Croppies' Memorial Park, Wolfe Tone
Quay.
'Davis Monument', College Green.
Dublin Castle.
Earlsfort Piazza.

'Five Lamps', South Circular Road.
'Grattan Fountain', St. Stephen's Green
North.
Irish Life Mall, Talbot Street.
'Irish National War Memorial', Island-
bridge.
Millennium Gardens, Dame Street.
Newcomen's Bank, Lord Edward
Street.
People's Park, Dun Laoghaire.
'Rutland Fountain', Merrion Square.
'Three Fates', St. Stephen's Green.

**FOUR COURTS, THE,** Inns Quay,
D7, tel 725555. Designed by JAMES GAN-
DON to replace the decrepit Court buildings at CHRIST CHURCH, the Four Courts
dominate the western approaches to the
city as the most impressive and majestically situated building on the Liffey.
Begun in 1786 and completed by 1802,
the building is composed of a great central block and side wings linked by open
arcaded screen walls. The western wing
incorporates a building by THOMAS
COOLEY into the overall design. This
ponderous 134m (440ft) façade is
broken by a Corinthian portico and topped by a tall drum with shallow saucer
dome. During the Civil War the building
was severely damaged but has been substantially reconstructed as originally designed. In the burning of the Four
Courts, the Public Records Office was
also destroyed and with it a vast quantity
of irreplaceable Irish historical records.
The Four Courts is the seat of the Supreme and High Courts as well as subsidiary courts and may be visited when in
session, Mon-Fri 11-1.00, 2.00-4.00.

**FRANCINI, FILIPPO AND PAOLO,**
Italian stuccodores. They came to Ireland around 1739 from England, and
decorated many important mansions in
Dublin city and county, as well as in

other parts of the country. In the 1740s they went back to England, returning to Dublin twenty years later. Their work became influential in the development of Georgian plasterwork in Ireland, beginning with a style of Baroque high relief and later working in a Rococo manner. The Francini's particular significance is that they introduced the human figure into Irish plasterwork using Classical subjects based on Continental models such as Jean Antoine Watteau. Notable houses decorated by the Francini are, 85 ST. STEPHEN'S GREEN (NEWMAN HOUSE), 1739-40; TYRONE HOUSE, 1740; Carton and Russborough, Co. Wicklow, 1740; 9 St. Stephen's Green, 1760; CASTLETOWN, Co. Kildare.

**FREDERICK THE GREAT**, (1712-86). Hohenzollern King of Prussia, a number of Dublin streets are named in his honour, North and South Frederick Streets and also Prussia Street. The King's house in Potsdam, based on a design by Palladio, is thought to be the origin of the design for the PROVOST'S HOUSE, Trinity College.

**FREEMEN OF THE CITY OF DUBLIN.** Since 1876 the Corporation has had the right to grant the Freedom of the City to persons it wishes to honour, although the concept of Free Citizens in Dublin dates from the twelfth century. Amongst the fifty-nine Freemen elected since 1876 are only three women, Lady Sandhurst, 1889, Maureen Potter, 1984 and Princess Michiko of Japan, 1985. Clerics, politicians and administrators form the preponderance of the names, with a scattering of people from the arts. The most interesting of these recipients are: Ullysses S. Grant, 1879, SIR HUGH LANE, 1908; John Mc Cormack, 1923; Sir John Lavery, 1935, GEORGE BER-

*The Four Courts from Merchant's Quay.*

NARD SHAW, 1946; John F. Kennedy, 1963; MÍCHEÁL MAC LIAMMÓIR and HILTON EDWARDS, 1973; Nelson Mandela, 1988.

**FRESCATI LODGE**, Blackrock, Co. Dublin. Childhood home of LORD EDWARD FITZGERALD, the Roches Stores 'Frescati' shopping centre stands on the site of this house, demolished in 1983. Frescati, which had beautiful painted ceilings and decorative plasterwork, is mentioned with affection in Fitzgerald's letters to his mother, the Duchess of Leinster, written when he lived there during the years 1787-94.

**FRINK, DAME ELIZABETH**, (1930-). In a glade on the north side of MERRION SQUARE park stands a sculpture by Frink, called 'Tribute Head', 1975-6, donated by Artists for Amnesty in 1982. The inscription on the plinth reads:
Unveiled – on South Africa Freedom Day, June 26th 1983, in the 20th Year

of Imprisonment of Nelson Mandela. Leader of the African National Congress of South Africa.

This is the only memorial to a living person in Dublin, an honour in the past bestowed only on monarchs. Mandela visited Dublin in June 1990 to accept the honour of FREEMAN OF THE CITY, which had been conferred on him in 1988 by Dublin Corporation while he was still a prisoner in South Africa. See MONUMENTS AND SCULPTURES.

**FURNITURE.** Eighteenth-century Irish furniture is one of the areas in which the superlative standards of the craftsmanship of the time are particularly evident. Although many institutions such as the NATIONAL GALLERY and NATIONAL MUSEUM possess collections of Irish furniture, generally only occasional pieces are on display. Houses like CASTLETOWN HOUSE, MALAHIDE CASTLE and NEWBRIDGE HOUSE contain many fascinating pieces of furniture, some made specifically for those houses, and they provide the opportunity to see a wide range of pieces in appropriate settings. In Dublin, furnished interiors are to be found in more official rather than domestic contexts. MARSH'S LIBRARY, the HOUSE OF LORDS, the PROVOST'S HOUSE, Trinity College, and NEWMAN HOUSE are the most significant.

**G**AELIC ATHLETIC ASSO-CIATION (GAA). Founded by Michael Cusack in 1885 for the promotion of native Irish athletic sports, Gaelic football, hurling and handball, in order to diminish the influence of what were then perceived as 'foreign games', that is rugby, soccer, cricket or anything not known to have been played by the Fianna in the Late Bronze Age! 'Foreign games' were placed under a ban which prohibited anyone who wished to play GAA sports from also playing the proscribed ones. Cusack was taken by JAMES JOYCE as the model for the irascible 'Citizen' in *Ulysses*, a man more in tune with the Ireland of 1014 or 1798 than that of the late Victorian era. The influence of the GAA was widespread throughout the country and today the GAA still successfully promotes Gaelic games, but without the chauvinism of a century ago. The All Ireland Gaelic Football and Hurling Finals held in Croke Park in September are among the principal sports fixtures of the year. Games under the auspices of the GAA are also played in the United States and Australia. See SPORT.

**GAELIC LEAGUE, THE.** Founded in 1893 by DOUGLAS HYDE, who was later to become the first President of an independent Ireland, the Gaelic League generated enthusiasm for the Irish language and encouraged its members to study and to speak it. The League was an important influence on the movement of cultural nationalism which swept the country at the end of the nineteenth century and, coupled with the philosophy of an Irish Ireland, laid the groundwork for subsequent political developments. Although the aims of the organisation were cultural rather than political, in the climate of the times the two were virtually inseparable. The League was instrumental in introducing the Irish language into the educational curriculum at both school and university level in an effort to make it the primary language of the country.

**GALILEI, ALESSANDRO,** (1691-1737). Florentine architect, whose principal work in Rome is the Church of St. John in Lateran. He designed the central block of CASTLETOWN HOUSE, Celbridge, Co. Kildare, the largest Palladian house in Ireland. The building was completed by SIR EDWARD LOVETT PEARCE. A portrait of Galilei by Giuseppe Berti now hangs in Castletown. It is thought that the Temple in the grounds of All Hallows College, Drumcondra is also by Galilei.

**GALLERIES.** See ART GALLERIES.

**GANDON, JAMES,** (1743-1823). Architect, born in London where he was apprenticed to SIR WILLIAM CHAMBERS, the leading Palladian architect of the day. Chambers had designed a number of important buildings for Dublin clients – LORD CHARLEMONT and TRINITY COLLEGE – and this may have served as Gandon's introduction to work in Dublin. Gandon became the foremost architect working in Dublin during the late eighteenth century and was responsible for some of the city's greatest public buildings. His work is characterised by finely proportioned massing of the elements of the building, crisp and simple detailing and the use of sculptural decorations in stone to enhance the structure. He was brought to Dublin by the Rt. Hon. John Beresford and Lord Carlow to design the CUSTOM HOUSE, begun in 1781 amid much opposition from sectors of the city's merchants. The merchants foresaw an inevitable move of the centre of trade away from the existing Custom House on Essex Quay. This building was followed by the FOUR COURTS, 1786, alterations to the Houses of Parliament, 1782, and the KING'S INNS, 1786. Gandon retired from public practice in 1808. All Gandon's major buildings are based on variations to the same arrangement of blocks, spaces and screens. The Custom House and Four Courts have the same massing of the blocks but with closed screens in the former and open in the latter. The King's Inns takes the principle of one wing of its predecessor, the Four Courts, and again uses a screen to unite the separate blocks. Virtually all Gandon's buildings are embellished with sculptural decorations by EDWARD SMYTH which greatly enhance their roof lines. The Custom House and Four Courts are among the most important Georgian public buildings to be seen anywhere in the British Isles, and are synonymous with eighteenth-century Dublin. Gandon, despite being the foremost architect of his age in Dublin, did not become a wealthy man. He is buried in DRUMCONDRA churchyard in the grave of his friend, the antiquarian Francis Grose.

## GARDA HEADQUARTERS,
Phoenix Park, D8, tel 771156. Designed by Jacob Owen in 1839, the building, now the centre of Garda activity and crime prevention, was built as a police training depot. It also houses the GARDA MUSEUM.

## GARDEN OF REMEMBRANCE.
See CHILDREN OF LIR and WAR MEMORIALS.

## GARDENS.
Dublin and its environs contain some spectacular gardens which cover a wide range of approaches to the idea of landscape and the very purpose of maintaining a garden. The NATIONAL BOTANIC GARDENS at Glasnevin deal with the scholarly and botanical aspects of plants. FERN HILL at Sandyford is an internationally renowned alpine garden created in 1860. While ST. ANNE'S, CLONTARF with its recently introduced Rose Garden is an example of nineteenth-century landscaping. The demesnes of MALAHIDE and Newbridge exploit the eighteenth-century concept of landscaping on the grand scale, while Mount Usher, Ashford, Co. Wicklow, in its arboretum, explores the decorative aspects of landscape. The Japanese Gardens at Tully Co. Kildare are concerned with the symbolic aspects of nature as a reflection of life and death. See PARKS.

## GARDINER, LUKE, (d1755).
Landowner and developer, he was instrumental in directing the growth of the aristocratic residential quarters in the north-east of the city during its Georgian heyday. Gardiner Street bears his name and he was responsible for developing HENRIETTA STREET, some of Parnell Square and Sackville (now O'Connell) Street, the central walkway of which was called GARDINER'S MALL.

## GARDINER'S MALL.
In its fully developed eighteenth-century form, O'CONNELL STREET was as broad as it is today but ran only from where the PARNELL MONUMENT now stands as far as Henry Street and did not connect through to the Liffey. The central walking area, 15.24m (50ft) wide in the 45.72m (150ft) wide street, known as Gardiner's Mall, was cordoned off from the surrounding thoroughfare and decorated with obelisks carrying street lights. An equestrian statue of General

Blakeney by JOHN VAN NOST stood at the north end, the first public monument on a street which was to become crowded with sculptures by the end of the twentieth century.

**GASOMETER**, Sir John Rogerson's Quay, D2. Looking from Holles Street Hospital south along MERRION SQUARE, there is a half mile of Georgian architecture stretching towards the Dublin Mountains, certainly one of the finest views in the city. Looking the other way, from Leeson Street towards the Hospital you see the Gasometer. It was built in 1934, and at a height of 76.2m (250 ft) was, prior to the building of LIBERTY HALL in 1964, the tallest and most dominant structure in the city. With the discovery of natural gas off the Kinsale coast in the 1970s, the Gasometer became redundant. Two skeletal cast iron frames of the ornate gasometers of the 1870s still stand on South Lotts Road and invite imaginative re-use.

**GATES OF THE MEDIEVAL CITY OF DUBLIN.** The Medieval walls of Dublin as they stood in the sixteenth century were bounded by the Liffey on the north, and roughly followed a line up PARLIAMENT STREET to the Castle. Then south along the line of the Castle walls at Little Ship Street where the most extensive remnants may be seen, to the top of Patrick's Street and then ran west and north along Francis Street to meet the river wall at Bridge Street. The walls were regularly punctuated by towers, with gates at prominent points of access. Small postern gates existed occasionally along the wall independently of the towers. ST. AUDOEN'S GATE, the only one still standing, was not in the perimeter wall but on an intermediate wall which bisected the city from west to east, fol-

lowing the line of the tenth- to thirteenth-century Viking and Anglo-Norman city wall. The City Gates and their relationship to current streets are as follows:

Dame Gate on DAME STREET.
Pole Gate on Werburgh Street.
St. Nicholas's Gate on Patrick Street.
Newgate on Thomas Street.
Gormond's Gate on Cook Street.
Bridge Gate on Bridge Street.

They were all swept away during the eighteenth century.

**GENERAL POST OFFICE** (GPO), O'Connell Street, D1, tel 728888. Designed by FRANCIS JOHNSTON and built between 1814 and 1818, it is the only really important building on O'Connell Street and forms a centrepiece for the 45.72m (150ft) wide street with an Ionic portico projecting out over the pavement into the street. The portico is built of Portland stone while the building is of granite, creating a subtle contrast of colour and texture in the façade. On the pediment are statues by Thomas Kirk of Fidelity, Hibernia and Mercury. The GPO was used as the headquarters of the 1916 RISING and it was from the steps of the portico that the PROCLAMATION OF THE REPUBLIC was read by PATRICK PEARSE. Considered today as the birthplace of the Republic, commemorative and political rallies are held outside it, and the reviewing platform for parades is usually located here. The Post Office, and much of O'Connell street, was destroyed and the portico still bears bullet marks from the conflict. The GPO is the headquarters of An Post, the Irish postal service. In the main public office of the building is a sculpture of CÚCHULAINN, erected as a memorial to 1916. The GPO is open seven days a week, Mon-Sat 8.00-8.00, and Sun 10.00-6.30.

**GEORGE II**, (1727-1760). JOHN VAN NOST'S bronze equestrian statue of the King stood in St. Stephen's Green from the eighteenth century until it was blown up by Republicans in 1937. The massive limestone plinth bore the following inscription, suggesting a parallel between Imperial Rome and Georgian Dublin: S.P.Q.D. (*Senatus Populusque Dubliensis*).

**GEORGIAN DUBLIN.** Eighteenth-century Dublin was an altogether remarkable place and at its zenith was the second city of the British Isles, one of the most important cultural centres in Europe. During the long, relatively peaceful and productive period which marks the reigns of the four Georges, 1714-1830, the entire phenomenon of Georgian Dublin was created on what had previously been open land on the eastern limits of the city. These developments were made possible by a group of forceful, wealthy and ambitious individuals whose combined efforts totally changed the face of Dublin. The planning of new streets and squares was carried out with a spirit and vision which moved the centre of the city away from the confining and chaotic environs of Dublin Castle and allowed it to grow on a grand scale. The results which can be seen today are wide streets, splendid residential squares, and an urban quality missing from any other city in Ireland. Expansion developed in two directions, civic architecture to the west of the city and residential to the east and north. Music, theatre, painting and, above all, architecture flourished in Georgian Dublin, making the new city a place of luxury and intellect. The houses, or palaces as they sometimes were, of the nobility and gentry were opulently furnished and decorated with the work of Dublin

*The Peppercanister Church from Merrion Square.*

craftsmen, and the plasterwork, stone and marble carving, glass and furniture of the period are probably the finest that the country has ever produced. The combination of wealthy clients of refined and educated taste with a thriving manufacturing area provided ideal conditions for maintaining high standards in the decorative arts. However, the converse was also to be found – the bucks and the duels, extraordinary feats of hospitality and excessive drinking, fantastic expenditure on fashions and general frivolity. The fact that this city of culture and taste also harboured teeming slums and had, as its economic base, tenant farmers of rural Ireland whose lives were lived in marked contrast to that of the aristocracy, guaranteed the end of this Golden Age. The rebellion of 1798, followed by the ACT OF UNION in 1801, brought the great days of Georgian Dublin to a close, although it continued to flourish in a more modest manner into the first quarter of the nineteenth century. The best of the Georgian city survives in areas like FITZWILLIAM, MERRION, MOUNTJOY and PARNELL SQUARES where the fabric of the eighteenth century is almost intact, and in the individual town mansions of the nobility – CHARLEMONT, LEINSTER, NEWMAN and POWERSCOURT HOUSES, all of them containing lavishly decorated interiors – and in characteristic Georgian elements which may be found in the quays and the Temple Bar area. Other public buildings of the period, like the ROTUNDA HOSPITAL, the CUSTOM HOUSE and FOUR COURTS, the Parliament House and TRINITY COLLEGE, speak of the assurance and sense of purpose that guided the promoters and builders of eighteenth-century Dublin, enabling them to leave such an impressive legacy of public and private architecture.

**GEORGIAN HERITAGE TRAIL.** Signposted walks in the city centre, beginning from the west front of TRINITY COLLEGE, which guide the viewer to the main areas of interest and landmark buildings in the eighteenth-century quarters of Dublin. However, this walk deals only with buildings south of the river. An illustrated booklet to accompany the walks is available from the Tourist Office, 14 Upper O'Connell Street, D1, tel 747733.

**GEORGIAN PERIOD.** The reigns of the four Georges, 1714-1830:
George I, 1714-27.
George II, 1727-60.
George III, 1760-1820.
George IV, 1820-30.

**GEORGIAN VILLAS.** An attractive and characteristic development in the Georgian idiom which became common in the suburbs during the mid-nineteenth century, in both terrace and free-standing examples. Elements of the style of the eighteenth century, the entrance flight of granite steps with ironwork, a symmetrical brick or stuccoed façade, panelled doorway with fanlight and low roof lines were combined to make a type of two-storey house, modest in scale yet having considerable presence. With the entrance situated on the first floor, the Villa reverses the conventional arrangement of small houses, and the reception rooms are above while the bedrooms remain below. Many variations on this theme can be found throughout the nineteenth-century suburbs and around the shores of Dublin Bay.

**GERALDINES.** The Geraldines or Fitzgeralds, ANGLO-NORMAN Barons who came to Ireland with the Norman invasion of the late twelfth century and established themselves as one of the most powerful families throughout six hundred years of Irish history. Made Earls of Kildare in the fifteenth century, they held the office of Lord Deputy, representative of the British monarch in Ireland. The family were elevated to the Dukedom of Leinster during the eighteenth century.

**GLASNEVIN CEMETERY**, Finglas Road, D11. The Irish National Cemetery, where famous names of Irish political history are buried. Since the foundation of the cemetery by DANIEL O'CONNELL in 1832, it has grown from three-and-a-half to fifty hectares, and while principally regarded as a Catholic burial ground it is open to all denominations. The older parts of Glasnevin are surrounded by high walls marked by watch towers, a necessity due to the prevalence of body snatching in the early nineteenth century. The cemetery is dominated by the O'CONNELL MONUMENT, a 51.2m (168ft) replica round tower designed by the antiquarian, GEORGE PETRIE, and in fact taller than any of the actual ROUND TOWERS. Grouped around the tower are Republican and Nationalist memorials, the famous as well as the notorious. Memorials to the perpetrators of the PHOENIX PARK MURDERS, and many other outrageous deeds, are gathered here, as are the remains of ROGER CASEMENT, Michael Collins, EAMON DE VALERA, COUNTESS MARKIEVICZ, and many others. Victorian taste in funerary monuments sets the tone of Glasnevin – forests of Celtic crosses, with Hibernia weeping for her slain sons at frequent intervals. A remarkably powerful example is the 1916 memorial by the sculptor Dora Sigerson Shorter, which blends Christian and Nationalist symbolism. This takes the form of an austere white marble pietà in which a Victorian Hibernia supports the slain Christ-like body of her dead son, who has the face of PATRICK PEARSE. Nationalist imagery in Glasnevin receives no stronger representation than this extraordinary work. Poets, actors, writers, academics are all here, scattered over the many acres of the cemetery. GERARD MANLEY HOPKINS and JAMES CLARENCE MANGAN, both poets who died in their forties, are buried here as are BRENDAN BEHAN and Margaret Burke-Sheridan. Some other distinguished monuments are the restrained Regency tomb of John Philpott Curran, the rough granite boulder from Avondale for CHARLES STEWART PARNELL which has replaced the topiary harps and round towers that previously marked the spot, and THOMAS FARRELL's statue of the actor Barry Sullivan in the role of Hamlet, complete with doublet and skull. Maps, giving the location of all the burials and monuments of interest in the cemetery, are available. The National Graves Association organises tours of Glasnevin at 11.30 every Sunday morning throughout the summer. These tours deal only with the Republican and political monuments. In a contrasting funerary style, MOUNT JEROME exploits the Classical tradition in most of its fine monuments.

**GLASS**. Eighteenth-century maps such as Rocque's map of the city 1757, show numerous circular buildings, glass houses, scattered around the backs of the main streets, and in these were produced the high quality crystal and more utilitarian domestic glass of the period. Ringsend is the only area of Dublin which still continues to manufacture glass but what is produced there today is sheet glass. Glassmakers achieved high standards in cutting and engraving, and much Dublin glass was exported to North America, Britain and Europe during the Georgian period. Collections of Dublin glass can be seen in the NATIONAL MUSEUM, the CIVIC MUSEUM, and the chandelier of the HOUSE OF LORDS is a superb example, still in its original setting.

**GLENDALOUGH,** Co. Wicklow. (51.5km [32 miles] from Dublin). Glendalough or *Gleann dá Locha*, (the Valley of the Two Lakes) is a secluded, wooded valley where the Early Christian Saint Kevin established his monastery in the seventh century AD. There are seven ecclesiastical buildings in the narrow valley scattered around the Lower Lake, (known as The Seven Churches of Glendalough) as well as the ROUND TOWER and numerous crosses. The church buildings which date from between the ninth and twelfth centuries are quite varied, and all roofless with the exception of what is known as St. Kevin's Kitchen, a miniature church of the ninth century with steep stone roof and bell cote in the form of a round tower. The main round tower which is excellently preserved, including its reconstructed cap, rises above the huddle of monastic buildings among the trees with a majestic presence. Access, St. Kevin's Bus Service from St. Stephen's Green.

**GOETHE INSTITUTE,** 37 Merrion Square East, D2, tel 611155. German Cultural Institute, involved in the promotion of the German language and culture. Events and courses organised include art, music, literature and film.

**GOGARTY, OLIVER ST. JOHN,** (1878-1957). Poet, wit, surgeon, Senator and athlete, born at 5 Parnell Square (plaque). The figure of 'stately, plump

*Early Christian remains, Glendalough.*

Buck Mulligan' in *Ulysses* is a portrait of Gogarty during the period when he and Joyce were close friends. Throughout his professional career in Dublin, Gogarty, as a man of wide culture and achievements, was involved in most of the intellectual and political movements of the time. He has left his mark in fields as disparate as medicine, literature and athletics. In 1923, when a

Senator of the Irish Free State, he was kidnapped by the IRA and only escaped death by swimming to safety in the wintry waters of the Liffey at Islandbridge. In gratitude to the spirits of the river for having preserved his life he presented the Liffey with a pair of swans on 24 March 1924, in the presence of the President, DOUGLAS HYDE, and W. B. YEATS.

> Keep you these calm and lovely
> things,
> And float them on your clearest
> water;
> For one would not disgrace a King's
> Transformed beloved and buoyant
> daughter.

('To the Liffey with Swans', 1924, Oliver St John Gogarty.)

## GOLDSMITH, OLIVER, (1728-1774).

Playwright, poet and novelist, he was a sizar or poor scholar at TRINITY COLLEGE, where his career was undistinguished, yet his statue is one of only two alumni of the university to grace the lawns of the West Front. With Edmund Burke, his contemporary at Trinity and the subject of the other statue, he was a member of the intellectual circle which gathered around Dr. Johnson in London. Goldsmith's considerable success in different branches of literature, *The Vicar of Wakefield*, 1766, *The Deserted Village*, 1770, and *She Stoops to Conquer*, 1773, brought him fame but little fortune.

> The morn was cold, he views with
> keen desire
> The rusty grate unconscious of a fire:
> With beer and milk arrears the frieze
> was scor'd,
> And five crack'd tea cups dress'd the
> chimney board

('A description of an author's bedchamber', Oliver Goldsmith.)

## GOTHIC ARCHITECTURE.

Of the many civil and ecclesiastical Gothic buildings known to have stood in Dublin, not many are still in existence. The two cathedrals, CHRIST CHURCH and ST. PATRICK'S, and ST. AUDOEN'S parish church are notably intact examples; everything else is mere fragments. The Chapter House of ST. MARY'S ABBEY is the only other fragment within the city, while outside it are HOWTH ABBEY, HOWTH CASTLE, and MALAHIDE CASTLE, all of which have Gothic elements, but are buildings of many periods.

## GOTHIC REVIVAL.

A romantic admiration for the ecclesiastical architecture of the Middle Ages led in the late eighteenth century to a revival of build-

*Swans on the Liffey at Islandbridge.*

ing in the Gothic style. Dublin, as a city clearly identified with the Classicism of the Georgian era never became Gothicised, nonetheless it did produce some outstanding examples of Gothic Revival and many business premises designed in a medievalist manner were introduced into the Georgian streets. The CHAPEL ROYAL at Dublin Castle, the Augustinian church ST. AUGUSTINE AND JOHN and the medievalist buildings of architects DEANE and WOODWARD are all fine examples of Gothic Revival and there are many lesser churches throughout the city also in this idiom.

**GOVERNMENT BUILDINGS**, Merrion Street, D2. Designed by T. M. Deane, and Sir Aston Webb, 1904-1922, as the Royal College of Science, the building now houses the Department of the Taoiseach and other civil service departments. Conceived on the grand scale, somewhat in the manner of one of JAMES GANDON'S buildings, this essay in Edwardian Baroque fails to make the impression it warrants due to its narrow siting with no room to view it from any distance. The roofline of Government Buildings is decorated with massive allegorical figures, by Oliver Sheppard and Albert Power, representing the arts and sciences. Government Buildings was among the last buildings in the Classic idiom to be erected in Dublin, bringing to a close over three hundred years of continuity in the decorative language of architecture in Dublin.

**GRAFTON STREET**, D2. The most popular shopping street south of the Liffey and the heart of Dublin's fashionable business quarter. The principal stores of Grafton Street – BROWN THOMAS, BEWLEY'S, Switzers and Weirs – are names synonymous with quality and tradition

in the city, in the same way that the many nearby pubs – DAVY BYRNE'S, the BAILEY and MCDAIDS – are synonymous with Dublin drinking habits. From Grafton Street, side streets and alleyways radiate, and much of this area is now a splendidly paved pedestrian precinct, attracting boulevardiers, BUSKERS, street artists and throngs of pedestrians to see and be seen. Grafton Street's origin was as a wandering country road linking the Medieval commons of St. Stephen with HOGGEN GREEN, and its curved un-Georgian contour reflects this beginning. It was named for the Duke of Grafton, illegitimate son of Charles II. With the exception of the PROVOST'S HOUSE at the northern end, the architecture of the street is largely nineteenth-century, with many examples of floridly designed business premises contributing to the street's rather exotic appearance.

**GRAND CANAL**. The two canals, Grand and Royal, which were built during the eighteenth century to connect Dublin to the Shannon and Irish midlands, are major examples of the engineering skills of the period. The Grand Canal enters the LIFFEY at Ringsend and from the vast Canal Basin the waterway cuts through the city in a gentle arc to Dolphin's Barn from where it proceeds inland. The canals mark the extent of the Georgian city on the south of the Liffey. The towpath on either side of the canal has a rustic character and many sections of it are among the loveliest quarters of the city, with terraces of small brick houses, wildfowl and swans on the water and humpbacked eighteenth-century bridges. Two sections of the original canal system, the harbour at Portobello and the spur section at Rialto, have regrettably been filled in and were built upon during the 1960s. Today, with a greater appreciation of the value of open water as potential areas of recreation and nature, such changes would be less likely.

**GRATTAN, HENRY,** (1746-1820). Parliamentarian and orator, born in Raheny, Dublin. Grattan was the dominant figure in Irish politics during the last years of the Dublin parliament known as 'Grattan's Parliament'. He campaigned for Irish legislative independence from Britain and the removal of restrictions on Irish trade. He favoured Catholic Emancipation and voted against the ACT OF UNION (1800) but the events of the 1798 rebellion precluded the possibility of the independence he fought for. Ironically, he is buried in Westminster Abbey. Grattan's statue, by JOHN FOLEY, stands opposite the old Parliament House and he is shown in oratorical pose, hand held high, gesturing to the harassed Dublin pedestrians who have been the inheritors of his dream.

**GRAVING DOCK,** Dublin Port, D1. The earlier of a pair of dry docks for ship repairs in the port, built during the mid-nineteenth century and constructed with stepped sides and steep ramps for the lowering of materials. One of the finest and visually most interesting examples of marine architecture in Dublin.

**GREAT PALM HOUSE,** National Botanic Gardens, Glasnevin. Built in 1884, it houses the Garden's collection of tropical plants.

**GREAT SOUTH WALL,** Poolbeg, D4. The South Bull or river wall was the first part of a vast engineering enterprise which between 1717 and 1768 attempted to tackle the serious problem of access to Dublin Port. Prior to this time,

*Crowds on Grafton Street.*

because of a shifting harbour bar and continuous silting up of the LIFFEY channel, the quays and docks of the city were often inaccessible to shipping except at high tide. The Great South Wall was 5.6km (3.5 miles) long, running from Sir John Rogerson's Quay on the south bank of the Liffey, out into the bay, and ending at the POOLBEG LIGHTHOUSE. This wall prevented the clockwise motion of the tides in the Bay from carrying sand into the channel and largely solved the navigational problems. However it was not until the construction of the corresponding wall on the north side of the river, the NORTH BULL WALL, in the nineteenth century that Dublin Port became freely accessible. The combined effect of the two walls was to speed the flow of the ebb tide in the river, thus causing it to scour the bed of the channel. The portion of the Great South Wall which projects from the Poolbeg Electricity Generating Station is the only area of the wall which has not been overtaken by building developments and dockland expansion. On it one can walk out virtually into the centre of Dublin Bay, to the Lighthouse, and it is a perfect spot from which to watch the sun set across the city, for saltwater bathing, or to observe at close quarters the movement of shipping into and out of the Port. Bus 1 from Townsend Street to ESB Power Station, Poolbeg.

**GREENS.** Of the four historic Medieval Greens which were originally common grazing land, HOGGEN, OXMANTOWN, St. Stephen's and Fair Green, three survive to some degree as open spaces, but only ST. STEPHEN'S GREEN remains as public parkland. Hoggen Green has become College Green, a busy street intersection, and a portion of Oxmantown Green survives at the back of the Incorporated Law Society Buildings at the Blue Coat School, Blackhall Place. The fourth, Fair Green, which was a market area outside the western wall of the city, has completely disappeared, but its function is maintained by the IVEAGH MARKET which stands on part of the lands which it covered. The VIKING origins of Dublin are recorded in the naming of both Hoggen and Oxmantown Greens. The name Green Street derives from ST. MARY'S ABBEY Green.

**GREGORY, LADY AUGUSTA**, (1852-1932). Folklorist, playwright and translator, she was, with EDWARD MARTYN and W. B. YEATS, a founder of the ABBEY THEATRE. The art dealer SIR HUGH LANE was her nephew and she supported his plans for a gallery of modern art in Dublin. Lady Gregory wrote over twenty plays of Irish folklife, based on her knowledge of the people of the west of Ireland. A portrait of Lady Gregory by AE hangs in the Abbey.

*Huband Bridge, Grand Canal.*

**GREYSTONES**, Co. Wicklow. Village on the coast south of Dublin, 29km (18 miles) from the city. It is popular during the summer months for bathing and walks in the surrounding countryside. The beach which extends for miles south of the village is ideal for walking. DART to Bray. Bus 84A from city centre.

**GUILD HALLS.** The various Dublin crafts, weavers, bakers, tailors and silversmiths, all had their own professional Guilds and usually concentrated their work in a particular area of the city. Guild halls were common during the eighteenth and nineteenth centuries and many of these stood until the 1950s. The TAILORS' HALL, 1701, in Back Lane, now the offices of AN TAISCE, The National Trust, is the only one to survive. The WEAVERS' HALL, 1745, in THE COOMBE was well known for a statue of George II which stood in a niche on the façade, and the enormous LINEN HALL complex, which has also totally vanished, was the largest Guild establishment in the city. Another Guild Hall, the Bricklayers' Hall in Cuffe Street, survived until around 1984.

**GUINNESS, ARTHUR EDWARD.** See LORD ARDILAUN.

**GUINNESS, BENJAMIN LEE, SIR,** (1798-1868). Son of Arthur Guinness, the founder of the brewery, he bought IVEAGH HOUSE in 1856 as a town house, restored ST. PATRICK'S CATHEDRAL, 1860-63, at the cost of £110,000, and sponsored the Dublin Exhibition Palace project in 1856. His statue by JOHN FOLEY is in the precincts of St. Patrick's Cathedral.

**GUINNESS BREWERY,** St. James's Gate, Thomas Street, D8, tel 536700 ex 5230. Founded by Arthur Guinness in 1759, and then one of some fifty small breweries in Dublin, it eventually survived or bought out all the others to become by the 1930s the largest brewery in the world. It is now the only large industry in Dublin's inner city area and its brew is synonymous with the city. The brewery began on the south side of St. James's Street, expanding during the nineteenth century to the Liffey and now covering an area of 24 hectares (60 acres). The Guinness ships, the *Lady Patricia* and *Miranda Guinness*, painted in the company's colours of dark blue and cream, are usually to be seen berthed at City Quay. They replaced the open topped Guinness barges which were a familiar sight on the Liffey. The GUINNESS HOP STORE AND VISITORS' CENTRE in Crane Lane off Thomas Street is open to the public. Mon-Fri 10.00-4.00.

**GUINNESS, EDWARD CECIL,** First Earl of Iveagh, (1847-1927). Philanthropist, he founded the IVEAGH TRUST in 1890 for the provision of artisans dwellings. The Trust cleared a large area of slums from the LIBERTIES, and built the IVEAGH BUILDINGS, Baths and Hostel, and laid out ST. PATRICK'S Park.

**GUINNESS HOP STORE.** See MUSEUMS.

**GUNPOWDER PLOTTERS.** All the equestrian statues of British monarchs and military leaders in Dublin, including those who were Irish, have suffered the fate of being blown up by those to whom their memorials were potent symbols of oppression. Other standing figures suffered the same fate, and the massive statue of Queen Victoria, which sat before Leinster House, was recently sold to the City of Victoria in New South Wales where it has a better chance of survival.

GEORGE II: St. Stephen's Green, 1937.

'King': shop sign in Civic Museum depicting the figure of a king, blown up during Emmet rebellion, 1803.

Lord Gough: Phoenix Park, attempts, 1944, 1956, 1957.

Prince Albert: Unsuccessful attempt in 1927; the statue was then moved for protection to the Leinster Lawn enclosure.

Seventh Earl Of Carlisle: People's Gardens, Phoenix Park, 1958.

Thirteenth Earl Of Eglington: St. Stephen's Green, 1958.

NELSON PILLAR: O'Connell Street, 1966.

William III: College Green, 1836, 1929.

HAMILTON, HUGH DOUGLAS, (1739-1808). Artist, born in Dublin, he studied under Robert West, and subsequently in London, 1764, and Rome, 1778. On his return to Dublin in 1791 he became a fashionable portrait painter, and artist of lyrical Neo-Classical subjects. The NATIONAL GALLERY has portraits by him of John Philpott Curran, LORD EDWARD FITZGERALD, and Richard Lovell Edgeworth, as well as the remarkable 'Cupid and Psyche in the Nuptial Bower', a delicate and romantic treatment of a Classical theme, and a double portrait of the Earl Bishop of Derry and his granddaughter. The Earl, an inveterate builder, collector and traveller was one of the Georgian era's great Irish eccentrics and is shown in Hamilton's painting admiring antiquities in the Villa Borghese gardens. This painting is one of the finest eighteenth-century portraits in the Gallery as it expresses as much about the preoccupations of the period as it does about its subjects.

## HAMILTON, SIR WILLIAM ROWAN, (1805-1865). Mathematician and astronomer, born 36 Lower Dominick Street. Hamilton was appointed Professor of Astronomy of TRINITY COLLEGE at the age of twenty, while still a student there, and in rapid succession he became superintendent of DUNSINK OBSERVATORY and in 1828 Astronomer Royal. In 1843 he discovered the formula of Quaternion Multiplication when out walking with his wife and inscribed it with a penknife into the parapet of Broom Bridge on the Royal Canal, an unusually inspired example of graffiti. A plaque on the bridge commemorates the occasion.

HANDEL, GEORGE FREDERICK, (1685-1759). Composer and musician, born in Germany, he settled in England in 1712. Handel lived in Abbey Street for nine months during 1741-42, giving public concerts for the charitable institutions of the city, a common practice during the eighteenth century when hospitals, orphanages and other charities depended on public subscriptions for their maintenance. Handel arrived on Wednesday, 18 November 1741, at the invitation of the Lord Lieutenant and the following month he played an Organ Concerto in the Round Church in Suffolk Street to raise funds for Mercer's Hospital. This was followed by a series of subscription concerts in Neal's Music Hall in FISHAMBLE STREET, and his visit culminated with the first performance of the Oratorio, *Messiah,* in the same venue on Tuesday, 13 April 1742. So vast a crowd was expected at the performance that the public were requested in the local newspapers 'ladies not to come with hoops – and gentlemen to come without their swords'. The occasion was a triumph, with the composer performing on the organ, the choirs of Christ Church and St. Patrick's Cathedrals, and soloists brought from London taking part. Four hundred pounds was raised and one hundred and forty-two unfortunate debtors were released from the Debtors Prison. The Music Hall, or rather its shell, survives in Fishamble Street as Kennan's Ironworks and there is a commemorative plaque on the adjoining building. Handel left Dublin in August, 1742, intending to return but further successes in London claimed his attention. His visit to Dublin proved to be one of the great moments in the city's cultural history and it is reassuring to know that those who attended the first performance of *Messiah* appreciated that they were in the company of genius.

**HANLON, REV. JACK**, (1913-1968). Artist, born in Templeogue, Dublin. He studied in Dublin, Belgium and Paris, and then became a priest and served for the rest of his life in the Dublin diocese. Hanlon was a founder member of the IRISH EXHIBITION OF LIVING ART. He painted in a light-hearted, School of Paris manner, using watercolours decoratively in thin effervescent light washes, and dealing mainly with religious and landscape themes. He also painted in oils and decorated a number of churches, representing Ireland abroad in international exhibitions. There are many of his light and airy pictures in the NATIONAL and HUGH LANE GALLERY collections.

*The Ha'penny Bridge.*

**HA'PENNY BRIDGE**, connecting Ormond Quay with Wellington Quay, D1 and D2. Also known as Wellington,

Metal and Liffey Bridge, it was designed in 1816 by John Windsor, an iron foreman from the Coalbrookdale Company in Shropshire and is an early and important example of cast-iron bridge building. The single-span elliptical arched bridge has endeared itself to Dubliners both for its convenience and for its graceful outline, spanning the Liffey in a filigree of delicate lines. The Ha'penny Bridge acts as an alternative axis to O'CONNELL BRIDGE, connecting DAME STREET through Merchant's Arch to North Abbey Street. Its curious name derives from the fact that it was a toll bridge from its opening in 1816 until 1918, and could be crossed for the uninflationary sum of one halfpenny for all of that period. In 1913, during the controversy surrounding the proposal to build an art gallery in Dublin to house HUGH LANE'S gift of paintings to the city, EDWIN LUTYENS produced a design which would have replaced the Ha'penny Bridge with a pair of Classical pavilions projecting into the Liffey, with a colonnaded bridge connecting them. As a piece of architecture, like anything from the hand of Lutyens, this scheme was of considerable interest, but as an art gallery it was inappropriate and found few supporters.

**HARCOURT STREET**, D2. Gently curving Georgian street which connects the south-west corner of St. Stephen's Green with ADELAIDE ROAD. Its character as an eighteenth-century residential street has been partially maintained, although many of the buildings are merely Georgianesque façades fronting modern offices rather than real Georgian houses. The Harcourt Street Station, 1859, is the most significant individual building at the eastern end of Harcourt Street. Many famous Dubliners lived in the street: George Fitzmaurice, playwright, at No.

3, his plaque carries the line 'for him the flowers smile'; Sir JONAH BARRINGTON at No. 14; Sir EDWARD CARSON was born at No. 4; Lord Clonmel lived at No. 17 and a plaque there commemorates the fact that the Municipal Gallery of Modern Art was housed here from 1908-1932; No. 87 is The National Children's Hospital. The Gardens of Clonmel House, No. 17, extended across to where Earlsfort Terrace is today, a remnant surviving as the IVEAGH GARDENS.

**HARCOURT STREET STATION**, Harcourt Street, D2. Terminus of the Harcourt Street Line which was closed in 1958 as part of the 'rationalisation' of the railway system, in the misguided belief that this form of travel would be superseded by road transport. The station was designed by George Wilkinson in 1859 for the Dublin and Wicklow Railway and belongs to a group of imposing railway buildings in Dublin, all constructed during the early years of steam travel and designed in remarkably disparate styles. Harcourt Street is in the Roman Baroque manner with a Tuscan colonnade and large arched entrance way surmounted by a monumental inscription in Roman numerals giving the date, MDCCCLIX. The exterior of the platform sheds seen from Hatch Street are also of interest. The building is now used as offices.

**HARCOURT TERRACE**, off Adelaide Road, D2. Mid-nineteenth-century terrace of Regency stucco-fronted houses which look like refugees from the Regents Park area of London. Although the detailing on the buildings is rather heavy, they merit notice as the only such centralised composition of Regency buildings in the city. HILTON EDWARDS and MÍCHEÁL MAC LIAMMÓIR

lived at No. 4 (plaque), and SARAH PURSER at No. 11 (plaque). The single-storey extension to this house which ends the street was her studio. Harcourt Terrace is now officially called Mac Liammóir Terrace but this change of name has yet to aquire popular usage.

**HAROLD'S CROSS**, D6. The village of Harold's Cross, eighteenth- and nineteenth-century houses surrounding a triangular green, retains all the character of the place as it must have been a century or more ago, but heavy traffic on the Harold's Cross Road, on one side of the green, ruins what would otherwise be a village within the city. MOUNT JEROME Cemetery, on the southern side of the village is full of interesting nineteenth-century memorials to famous Dubliners. Bus 16, 16A from O'Connell Street; 49, 49A from Crampton Quay.

**HARP, BRIAN BORU**, Trinity College Library. Date uncertain, but probably fourteenth-century, the earliest surviving Irish harp. Constructed of oak and willow with brass and rock crystal fittings, it is decorated with interlace and animals in roundels, carved in low relief. No relationship can be established between the harp and BRIAN BORU. The Irish government official emblem which appears on the national coinage and government publications is based on the Brian Boru Harp, as is the harp which is the emblem of the GUINNESS BREWERY. The harp makes another appearance in the Maclise painting of the 'Marriage of Strongbow and Aoife' in the NATIONAL GALLERY.

**HARTY, SIR HERBERT HAMILTON**, (1879-1941). Composer, musician and conductor, born at Hillsborough, Co. Down, he worked as an organist from the age of twelve and was appointed to Christ Church, Bray, Co. Wicklow, when he was sixteen. Harty, who had been trained by his father, a church organist, came under the influence of Michael Esposito in Dublin. He had a successful career internationally as conductor of the Halle and London Symphony Orchestras. His 'Irish Symphony', an accomplished orchestral treatment of melodies from Irish traditional airs, is frequently performed. Harty was knighted in 1925.

**HAWKINS STREET**, D2. Connects Burgh Quay with Townsend Street. At the north end of the street is a Gothic Revival monument, topped by a Celtic cross on a rather spiky coronet. A lengthy inscription on the east side of the monument gives the reason for its erection:

This memorial was erected in memory of Patrick Sheahan a constable in the Dublin Metropolitan Police Force who lost his life on the sixth day of May 1905 in a noble and self-sacrificing effort to rescue John Fleming who had in the discharge of his duties descended the Main Sewer close by this spot and was overcome by sewer gas. It was also intended to commemorate the bravery of a number of other citizens who also descended the sewer to assist in rescuing the beforementioned, thereby risking their lives to save those of their fellow men.

Further along the street is the mock-Tudor Gas Company premises. A plaque set into the wall displays a figure of Hibernia with harp and the inscription, 'Dublin Gaslight Company 1825'. Below Hawkins House, an uninteresting office building, is the Screen Cinema and standing in its forecourt a witty sheet-copper sculpture 'Mister Screen'

by Vincent Browne. With a gesture of his outstretched arm this tribute to generations of cinema commissionaires, outfitted like a South American general, gestures every night to the queueing cinemagoers.

**HEALY, MICHAEL**, (1873-1941). Artist, born at 40 Bishop Street, he studied in Dublin and Florence. Healy's work had a public and a private aspect, the former in the stained glass for which he is best known, and the latter for the execution of small very free and beautifully observed watercolours of Dublin's street characters. Healy joined SARAH PURSER'S '*AN TÚR GLOINE*' stained-glass studios at its foundation in 1903 and worked there for the rest of his life. Although his windows are widely dispersed, some significant ones are in churches around Dublin and display his lively draughtsmanship and command of colour.

Rathmines (Cof I), 1909.
Donnybrook (RC), 1914.
Mount Jerome Cemetery, 1915.
James's Street (Cof I), 1916.
Dundrum (RC), 1919,
Donore Avenue (Cof I), 1923.
Incorporated Law Society, 1930.
Augustinian Church, 1934.
Blackrock College, 1938.

**HEALY, ROBERT**, (1743-1771). Artist, studied in Dublin, he specialised in monochrome studies of horses and people, and his series of drawings in grisaille of the CASTLETOWN Conolly household are among the most charming and relaxed images of Irish eighteenth-century life, showing members of the Castletown household in scenes of ice skating, getting ready for the hunt, and generally enjoying country life. The NATIONAL GALLERY has three self portraits by Healy, intense and uncomfortable works in which the artist appears to scrutinise the viewer.

**HEARN, LAFCADIO**, (1850-1904). Writer of Irish extraction, he was born on the Greek island of Levkas and he grew up in Dublin. Hearn went to live in Japan in 1890 and became a pioneering Japanese folklorist, publishing a rapid succession of books on all aspects of Japanese culture. He is regarded in Japan as a writer of immense importance in the study of oriental culture, religion and philosophy. There is a plaque on 21 Leinster Square, Rathmines.

*HELGA*. Gunboat built in Dublin, 1908, as a Fishery Protection Vessel, it was used on the Liffey by the British Forces during the 1916 RISING to shell the GPO, the trades union headquarters, the Four Courts, Liberty Hall and Boland's Mills in Ringsend, all garrisoned by the rebels. In 1947, after continuing service as a fishery vessel for the Free State service, it sank on its way to being broken up.

**HELL FIRE CLUB**, Montpelier Hill, Co. Dublin. Built by Speaker Conolly of CASTLETOWN HOUSE in 1720 as a hunting lodge, this gaunt and curious building stands on the peak of a previously barren but now wooded mountain, with spectacular views over Dublin and the east coast. The connection between this building and the Hell Fire Club seems to be tenuously based on popular rumour rather than any proven association, although the location certainly does recommend itself to nefarious doings. The members of this Club were dissolute young bucks of the aristocracy and gentry of the countryside, who used to carouse in the Eagle Tavern on Cork Hill, and were reputed to resort to Mont-

pelier Hill in order to perform Black Masses and to engage in occult rituals. Whether they went there for drinking or more sinister pastimes, Montpelier Hill is not the sort of place where one would be likely to bump into passersby, so isolated is the building. In 1849 a massive bonfire was lit on the vaulted roof of the Hell Fire Club to welcome Queen Victoria to Dublin. Four miles from Rathfarnham, Bus 16, 16A from O'Connell Street, and 47 from Hawkins Street to Rathfarnham.

*Hell Fire Club.*

**HENRIETTA STREET**, D7. The earliest of the great Georgian streets to be developed on the north side of the Liffey, it was laid out by LUKE GARDINER in the 1730s and became known as Primate's Hill because of the number of bishops who had their town houses there. The scale of the thirteen houses remaining is larger than that of any subsequent development and although now showing the signs of a century of neglect and having declined into tenements, there is still a remarkable grandeur about the street which survives in a state of heroic decrepitude. Two houses at the top, Nos. 9 and 10 designed by Sir EDWARD LOVETT PEARCE, and now functioning as convents, are well preserved. No. 9 is of particular interest, with one of the most individual doorways in Dublin as well as some fine interiors. Nos. 5 and 7 are by Nathaniel Clements. The

*Henrietta Street and the King's Inns.*

KING'S INNS, 1785, JAMES GANDON'S last public building, effectively completes the street, its library by FREDERICK DARLEY, 1827, occupying the position of the last two houses on the southern side of the street. The courtyard of the Inns leads through to a small park on the top of the hill. The Pipers' Club occupies a building on the southern side of the street at No. 15, also the headquarters of the Folk Music Society of Ireland.

**HENRY II**, (1154-1189). In the wake of the Anglo-Norman invasion of 1169, which had been conducted by the Norman barons, Henry II arrived to ensure that his vassals did not set up a separate kingdom in Ireland. His arrival in October of 1171 with a large army curbed any ideas of independence the barons may have had. Henry remained in Ireland for six months, spending Christmas in a temporary palace outside the city of Dublin where he entertained the Irish chieftains. Before returning to England he granted the city by Charter to the citizens of Bristol, thereby tying it firmly to rule from England.

Henry II, King of England, Duke of Normandy and Aquitaine, and Earl of Anjou, notifies that he has granted and confirmed to his men of Bristowe his city of Duvelina.

This Charter, as well as many later ones, is in the CITY ARCHIVES at CITY HALL.

**HENRY VIII**, (1491-1547). The dissolution of the monasteries, which occurred during the reign of Henry VIII, had the effect of freeing large tracts of land in the immediate vicinity of Dublin, which were then given by grant to those who had served the Crown. From these origins developed all the great aristocratic estates, which later became the focus for the growth of the city from the end of the seventeenth century. Ten Charters of Henry VIII are in the CITY ARCHIVES.

**HENRY STREET,** D1. On the west side of O'Connell Street, which it connects with Capel Street, and now pedestrianised is Dublin's main shopping street on the north side of the river with the greatest concentration of department stores, retail clothes outlets and shoe shops. The ILAC Centre and the MOORE STREET open-air fruit and vegetable market are on the north side of Henry Street, and street vendors with mobile shops mounted on old-fashioned perambulators weave their way in among the crowds crying their wares. These street vendors synchronise their cries to follow one another in a manner which has to be considered an art form, like singing rounds, and they represent a tradition of street life that must be as old as the city itself.

> Tomatoes, mush-er-rooms, the last of the collies,
> Iceberg leuttice, thirty a head,
> Keukin apples, five for fifty,
> Fresh fleurs.
> Tobler, Tobler, get the big Tobler-owen,
> Nointy-noine P,
> Any choc-alet ba-ers, five for a pou-end,
> To-bler-owen, get the big Tobler.

At Christmas, Henry Street is like Bedlam, with choirs singing carols outside the department stores, adding more strains to the cacophony, and raising the volume to one of seasonal hysteria.

**'HERALDS OF THE FOUR PROVINCES',** College Green, D2. Fountain by the sculptor EDWARD DELANEY (1966), which is part of the THOMAS DAVIS memorial. The Heralds are surrounded by six granite slabs suggestive

*Henry Street traders.*

of a Neolithic stone circle and bearing bronze plaques which illustrate themes from DAVIS'S most significant poems, 'The Penal Days', 'Wolfe Tone's Grave', 'The Burial', 'We must not fail' and 'The Famine'.

**HEUSTON, SEÁN,** (1891-1916). Revolutionary, he commanded the garrison of the Mendicity Institute during the 1916 RISING and prevented the arrival by rail of British army reinforcements in Dublin. Heuston Station, formerly Kingsbridge, is named in his honour. A vigorous statue of Heuston, shown as the archetypal proletarian revolutionary with enormous veined hands, by Laurence Campbell, stands in the People's Gardens, PHOENIX PARK.

**HEUSTON STATION,** Kingsbridge, D8. The terminus for all trains to the west and south, Heuston retains the atmosphere of the age of steam while functioning as a thoroughly modern railway station. The station building, 1844, is by Santon Wood and looks like a Florentine Palazzo with a façade overladen with ornament, columns, pedimented windows, swags and festoons, and flanked by two miniature pavilions topped with domed cupolas. The cast-iron railway shed is by Sir John Mac Neill. There is a direct bus connection from Heuston to the airport. Bus 23, 24, 26 from Essex Quay and 51 from Connolly Station.

**HEWETSON, CHRISTOPHER**, (1739-1798). Sculptor, born in Kilkenny, he studied under JOHN VAN NOST in Dublin before going to Rome in 1765 for further study. He remained there for the rest of his life. Hewetson is the greatest Irish sculptor of the eighteenth century, specialising in portraiture of a Classical mode. He worked in bronze, marble and terracotta and executed accomplished portraits of the aristocrats and intellectuals who visited Rome, amongst them Leibnitz, Anjelica Kauffmann and Pope Clement XIV. Little of Hewetson's work is in Dublin as his commissions were dispatched all over Europe. His memorial to Provost Baldwin in the TRINITY COLLEGE Examination Hall, with the figures in Carrara marble, was executed in Rome in 1771 and shipped to Dublin. Also in the PROVOST'S HOUSE, Trinity, is a bust of Richard Rigby, Lord Lieutenant, and a terracotta bust of Sir William Wynn stands in the NATIONAL GALLERY.

**HIGGINS, FRANCIS**, (1746-1802). Known as the 'Sham Squire', he conducted a lucrative and dubious career in Dublin as con-man, newspaper proprietor, gaming house owner and informer. DUBLIN CASTLE records suggest that he was the person who revealed (for £1,000) the hiding place of LORD EDWARD FITZGERALD in 1798. His gaming house on Crane Lane, off Dame Street, was intriguingly known as 'Pandemonium'. Higgins is buried in the graveyard at Kilbarrack.

**HIGH CROSS, THE**. Up to the end of the eighteenth century, in what is now Christchurch Place in front of St. Michael's Arch, stood the High or Market Cross. Sometime after this period it was removed and its remains have not survived. More a pillar than a cross, it took the form of a set of octagonal steps on which was mounted a square pillar with tiered panels of carving, and topped by a small cross on an orb. This monument, probably dating from Medieval times, was used as the place from which to read public proclamations, and perform a public penance.

**HIGH STREET**, D8. Between Cornmarket and Christchurch Place, High Street today has a rather disorganised look, as many of its original buildings have been demolished over the last twenty years and are only now beginning to be replaced. This was the main thoroughfare of Viking and Medieval Dublin, the principal street of the city within the walls up to the seventeenth century, and more recently an important shopping street. Excavations carried out here by the NATIONAL MUSEUM in the 1970s revealed the intense life of the area from the tenth century and many important finds from the excavations can be seen at the Museum. Grouped around High Street are a number of Medieval ecclesiastical foundations and remains of the Medieval and later city. CHRIST CHURCH CATHEDRAL, ST. AUDOEN'S, and the tower of ST. MICHAEL'S are substantially intact while the church of ST. NICHOLAS WITHOUT is a ruin. St Audoen's Gate and three sections of the Medieval CITY WALL lie to the north and south of High Street, and from later periods are the TAILORS' HALL, 1706, and ST. AUDOEN'S, RC, 1841. Bus 21A, 78, 78A from Fleet Street.

**HOEY'S COURT**, off Werburgh Street, D8. The birthplace of the greatest of all Dubliners, JONATHAN SWIFT, was at No. 7, now occupied by an Employment Exchange. No monument or plaque marks this street, nor is there any figure of Swift in Dublin other than contemporary busts in buildings associated with him – the DEANERY, TRINITY LIBRARY and in his Cathedral. In nearby Little Ship Street on the left-hand pier of the entrance to DUBLIN CASTLE is a commemorative inscription which reads:

IN No 7 Hoey's Court [now demolished] about 100 feet NW of this spot it is reputed that Jonathan Swift Dean of St. Patrick's Cathedral was born on the 30th day of Novr 1667 He died on the 19th day of Octr 1745 MCMXIII.

**HOGAN, JOHN**, (1800-1858). Sculptor, he was apprenticed to SIR THOMAS DEANE, architect in Cork. In 1824 he was sent by a subscription of admirers to study in Rome where he remained for over twenty years, receiving many important commissions from Ireland. After the departure of Bertel Thorwaldsen from Rome, Hogan was regarded as the finest Neo-Classical sculptor working there. In 1849 the revolution in Rome caused him to return permanently to Dublin, but his career suffered a reverse and he had some difficulty in getting commissions, the Protestants regarding him as a Catholic artist, while to the Catholics he was tainted by the stigma of Continental Liberalism and revolution.

Hogan did receive other important commissions but was embittered at being rejected for the Thomas Moore statue (College Street) in favour of a work by a much inferior sculptor. There is a significant number of Hogan's principal works in Dublin which display his superb command of naturalism and power as a portrait artist:

'THE DEAD CHRIST', 1829: Carmelite Church, Clarendon Street, D2.

'FARRELL MEMORIAL', 1842: St. Andrew's Church, Westland Row, D2.

'HEAD OF ERIN', 1842: National Museum, Kildare Street, D2.

THOMAS DRUMMOND, 1843: City Hall, D2.

'HIBERNIA' with the bust of Cloncurry, 1845: National Gallery, Merrion Sq. D2.

'ITALIAN SHEPHERD BOY', 1846: Iveagh House, St. Stephen's Green, D2.

DANIEL O'CONNELL, 1846: City Hall, D2.

PURCELL MEMORIAL, 1848: Pro Cathedral, Marlborough Street, D2.

THOMAS DAVIS, 1853: City Hall, D2.

THOMAS MOORE, 1853: National Gallery, Merrion Sq. D2.

WILLIAM CARLETON, 1855: National Gallery, Merrion Sq. D2.

'CIVIL AND RELIGIOUS LIBERTY, 1858: Wellington Testimonial, Phoenix Park.

**HOGARTH, WILLIAM**, (1697-1764). Artist, eighteenth-century master of satire and social realism in portraiture and narrative painting. He is well represented in the NATIONAL GALLERY with six paintings, two of which were bequeathed by SIR HUGH LANE. Of these 'The Mackinnon Children', a study of an elegantly dressed young boy and girl on a terrace with their pet dog, is among Hogarth's finest studies of children and one of the masterpieces of English painting in the Gallery.

**HOLYHEAD MAILBOAT.** Speedy communication of the mail between Dublin and London was a government priority from the sixteenth century, and the Packet Boat from Dublin to Holyhead in Wales or other British ports remained a constant cause of concern due to the inadequate harbour facilities at the Dublin end of the journey and the general unreliability of the ships plying this route. Small sailing ships of sixty tons were used up to the end of the eighteenth century as they were less restricted by the tides. By this time the service had become a daily one, operating under charter to individual ship owners who also carried passengers. The Packet Station was transferred from Ringsend to HOWTH in 1818 when the new harbour was opened there, but this was superseded by DUN LAOGHAIRE in 1832. Although the mail now travels by air, the Sealink Ferry which docks at Dun Laoghaire is still known as 'the Mailboat'. Two passenger, car and freight services now operate from Dublin to England, B&I from Dublin Port and Sealink from Dun Laoghaire. See FERRIES.

**HOME RULE.** From the mid-nineteenth century the widespread aspiration for a separate legislature for Ireland became a preoccupation which found a formal leader in the Home Government Association founded by ISAAC BUTT. This movement developed into the IRISH PARLIAMENTARY PARTY under the leadership of CHARLES STEWART PARNELL. By the end of the century this party had succeeded in convincing at least a portion of the British establishment of the necessity of Home Rule. Successive Home Rule Bills were introduced in Westminster in 1886 and 1893 under Gladstone and in 1912 under Asquith and a third of them passed into law in 1914, but due to the outbreak of the First World War their implementation was suspended. In fact the relevance of this Bill was overtaken by events when in the aftermath of the 1916 RISING the first DÁIL was established in 1919 by MPs unwilling to sit at Westminster. With the emergence of the Irish Free State in 1921 the objectives of the Home Rule movement were in a large measure achieved.

**HONE, EVIE,** (1894-1955). Artist, born at Roebuck Grove, Rathfarnham, she studied in London and Paris and developed a style strongly influenced by Cubism. Hone was a founder member of the Irish Exhibition of Living Art. In 1932 she began to work in STAINED GLASS and it is in this area that some of her finest work was done. The intense colours and imagery of Medieval art and the work of Georges Rouault inspired her later work which moved away from Cubism towards a more figurative manner. Hone's most important commission was for the 'Crucifixion and Last Supper' window at Eton College Chapel, Berkshire. Her work is well represented around Dublin:

INCORPORATED LAW SOCIETY, 1936: Blackhall Place, D7.

UNIVERSITY HALL CHAPEL, 1947: Hatch Street, D2.

NATIONAL GALLERY, 1947-51: Merrion Square, D2.

HUGH LANE MUNICIPAL GALLERY, 1948-54: Parnell Square, D1.

ST. ANNE'S HOSPITAL, 1948: Northbrook Road.

SUBURBAN CHURCHES WITH WINDOWS BY HONE:

ALL HALLOWS: Drumcondra
BLACKROCK COLLEGE
BLACKROCK (RC)

CLONSILLA (Cof I)
DRUMCONDRA
DUNDRUM (Cof I)
FOSTER AVENUE (Cof I)
HOLY GHOST COLLEGE: Kimmage
MILLTOWN PARK
SANDYMOUNT: (Methodist)

## HONE, NATHANIEL (THE ELDER), (1718-1784).

Artist, born Dublin, studied in London 1742, and Rome 1750. He became a successful portrait painter and founder member of the Royal Academy in London. In 1775 his satirical painting 'The Conjuror' was removed from exhibition at the Academy because of its savage portrayal of Sir Joshua Reynolds as the Conjuror and Anjelica Kauffmann as his apprentice, creating their works from prints of the Italian masters. The painting is now in the NATIONAL GALLERY of Ireland, which also has three provocative self portraits by Hone. No one could accuse Hone of plagiarism.

## HONE, NATHANIEL (THE YOUNGER), (1831-1917).

Artist, born Fitzwilliam Place, D2, he was a descendant of his eighteenth-century namesake. He qualified as an engineer in TRINITY COLLEGE and worked briefly on the railways in Ireland but then went to Paris and studied painting, settling in Barbizone where he lived amongst a community of artists. Hone returned to Dublin in 1875 and lived in Malahide. In 1901 an exhibition of paintings by Hone and JOHN BUTLER YEATS which had been organised by SARAH PURSER focused the interest of HUGH LANE on contemporary Irish art with results which were to be of momentous importance for the development of the visual arts in Dublin. Principally a landscape and seascape artist, Hone painted in the muted colour range favoured by Jean Baptiste Corot and Jean-François Millet with whom he had worked at Barbizone. His work is concerned with light and atmosphere and can be considered a precursor of Impressionism. The Hone bequest, presented by his widow to the NATIONAL GALLERY, contains a vast number of his works, some three thousand drawings and watercolours, and two hundred and fifty oil paintings.

## HOPKINS, GERARD MANLEY, (1844-1889).

Poet and academic, he was Professor of Classics in University College Dublin from 1884 for five years until his death from typhoid. He is buried in GLASNEVIN CEMETERY. Hopkins, a Jesuit, was the most significant religious poet of the nineteenth century and his innovative use of language is a precursor of later experimental writers. There is an echo of his interest in the internal music of words in the work of James Joyce whose period in University missed Hopkins's by a year. Hopkins was ill at ease in Dublin and felt isolated for, as an English patriot, he opposed Home Rule and had little sympathy with Irish public or clerical opinion:

> I am in Ireland now; now I am at a
>     third
> Remove. Not but in all removes I can
> Kind love both give and get. Only
>     what word
> Wisest my heart breeds dark
>     heaven's baffling ban
> Bars or hell's spell thwarts. This to
>     hoard unheard,
> Heard unheeded, leaves me a lonely
>     began.

('To seem a stranger lies my lot, my life', Gerard Manley Hopkins.)

## HORSE SHOW, THE.

Held as a six-day event in August at the ROYAL DUB-

LIN SOCIETY show grounds in BALLS-BRIDGE, it is the main show jumping occasion of the year, with international teams competing for the AGA KHAN TROPHY and the Nation's Cup. Crowds of over 100,000 watch the competitions for all classes of bloodstock, although the style of the fashions on display seems to attract as much attention as the quality of the horses. See ANNUAL EVENTS IN DUBLIN.

## HORSE-DRAWN TRANSPORT.

Horses have not quite left the streets of Dublin, and the traders who deal in scrap seem to favour a horse and cart to ferry old baths and redundant aluminium sinks around the city. During the DUBLIN MILLENNIUM of 1988 horse-drawn carriages began to appear on the streets and there is now what amounts to a cab rank of Broughams, Landaus and Victorias, some of them eighteenth- and nineteenth-century and others reproductions, at the GRAFTON STREET corner of Stephen's Green. On a Sunday, with little motor traffic around the Green or Merrion Square, the clip-clop of horses' hooves on the streets transports one back to a century ago when the great squares of Dublin were still residential oases of privileged living. Today the carriages give hour and half-hour tours of historic parts of the city, as pleasant a way as any to see Dublin, and for the enthusiast of the Georgian era, absolutely appropriate.

**HOSTELS** (See MAP). For cheap, convivial and convenient accommodation, hostels provide the city with a network of accommodation geared towards the young. With the advent of the Independent Hostel Owners Association, staying in a hostel has begun to lose some of the atmosphere of a genial but rules-bound boarding school, and to provide open access and better facilities, with less emphasis on the virtues of spartan living. Simplicity, friendliness and economy are the keynotes of this form of accommodation.

DUBLIN INTERNATIONAL YOUTH HOSTEL (An Óige), Mountjoy Street, D1, tel 301766. Very well equipped hostel accommodation in atmospheric old buildings within walking distance of city-centre train and bus termini. Facilities include information centre, restaurant, recreation rooms, all-day opening and secure car and bicycle parking. An Óige also have a hostel at 78 Morehampton Road, D4, tel 680325, and at Scoil Lorcáin, Eaton Square, Monkstown, but this is open only during holiday months.

ISAAC'S, The Dublin Tourist Hostel, 2-5 Frenchman's Lane, D1, tel 363877/ 749321. The most conveniently located hostel, virtually around the corner from the city-centre bus station. Restaurant as well as self-catering kitchen and music sessions are among the facilities.

KINLAY HOUSE (USIT), 2-12 Lord Edward Street, D2, tel 6796644. In the heart of the historic centre of old Dublin, next door to CHRIST CHURCH CATHEDRAL, across the road from DUBLIN CASTLE and housed in an attractive converted Victorian school building. Facilities include launderette, study rooms, self-catering kitchen, bicycle park and left luggage.

KINLAY VILLAGE (USIT), Belfield, tel 6796644. Self-catering apartments, with individual rooms, available between June and September, 5km (3.1 miles) from city centre.

THE YOUNG TRAVELLER (IHO), St. Mary's Place, D7, tel 305000/ 305319. IYO hostels are generally smaller than those of other organisations, independently owned and family run. There is no membership requirement.

YWCA, Radcliff Hall, St. John's Road, Sandymount, D4, tel 694251. Accommodation for women only in an attractive location on the edge of Dublin Bay.

## HOTELS AND GUESTHOUSES

(See MAP). Hotel accommodation ranges from the most luxurious and consequently expensive, to the more modest establishments which also provide an excellent quality of service, to the bed and breakfast type of guesthouse which is homely, unpretentiously comfortable and generally excellent value. Charges vary in accordance with the facilities and scale of the establishment, but a rough division of cheap, C, medium priced, M, and expensive, E, indicates a price range of roughly £30, £50, and £100 per night respectively. Virtually all hotels accept major credit cards.

ASHLING HOTEL, Parkgate Street, D8, tel 772324. Conveniently located across the bridge from Heuston Station and within a few minutes walk of the Phoenix Park. Fifty-six beds, C.

BARRYS' HOTEL, Great Denmark Street, D1, tel 746943. Commercial hotel, long established and traditional, close to O'Connell Street and Municipal Gallery of Modern Art. Fifteen beds, M.

BERKELEY COURT HOTEL, Lansdowne Road, D4, tel 601711. Luxury hotel in embassy quarter of city, adjacent to Lansdowne Road IRISH RUGBY FOOTBALL UNION (IRFU) grounds, two restaurants, bars, shopping arcade. Two hundred beds, E.

BLOOMS HOTEL, Anglesea Street, D2, tel 715622. City-centre location, Joycean bar. Eighty-six beds, M.

BURLINGTON HOTEL, THE, Upper Leeson Street, D4, tel 605222. Luxury hotel with extensive recreational facilities, lavish restaurants and bars. Four-hundred-and-twenty beds, M.

BUSWELLS HOTEL, Molesworth Street, D2, tel 764013. Outside the gates of Leinster House and popular with politicians and business people, a long-established hotel. One-hundred-and-fifty beds, M.

CLARENCE HOTEL, Wellington Quay, D2, tel 776178. Traditional hotel in the heart of the city overlooking the Liffey, hosts ballroom dancing, the Elvis Fan Club and other nostalgic activities. Sixty-six beds, C.

CONRAD HILTON HOTEL, Earlsfort Terrace, D2, tel 765555. Part of the Hilton chain, luxury and lavish interiors with two restaurants, the Alexandra and the Plurabelle. Opposite the National Concert Hall, and just off the corner of St. Stephen's Green. One-hundred-and-ninety beds, E.

DALKEY ISLAND HOTEL, THE, Dalkey, Co. Dublin, tel 850377. Located on the edge of DUBLIN BAY, in the centre of the watersports and angling area, modernised small hotel with fine restaurant and bars overlooking the coast. Twenty beds, C.

DUBLIN INTERNATIONAL HOTEL, Dublin Airport, tel 379211. Modern well equipped hotel on Airport Road. One-hundred-and-ninety-five beds, C.

FITZPATRICK'S CASTLE HOTEL, Co. Dublin, tel 851533. Set into the delightfully wooded slopes of Killiney Hill Park, a luxurious environment with restaurant, bars and nighclub. Ninety-four beds, M.

GRESHAM HOTEL, Upper O'Connell Street, D1, tel 746881. Nineteenth-century historic hotel, extensively modernised with all the facilities of a grade A hotel. Situated in the centre of the shopping district. One-hundred-and-eighty-two beds, M.

JURY'S HOTEL, Pembroke Road, Ballsbridge, D4, tel 605000. Adjacent to US Embassy, all night restaurant and noted cabaret, indoor swimming pools. Three-hundred-and-ninety beds, E.

KILLINEY COURT HOTEL, Killiney Bay, Co. Dublin, tel 851622. Small Victorian hotel beautifully sited a few minutes from the seacoast. Eighty-six beds, M.

MONTROSE HOTEL, Stillorgan Road, D4, tel 693311. Modern hotel close to TV and Radio studios, and opposite the Belfield campus of UCD. Bar and restaurant and shopping facilities. One-hundred-and-ninety-five beds, M.

NEW ORMOND HOTEL, THE, Upper Ormond Quay, D7, tel 721811. Old established city-centre hotel on the quays overlooking the Liffey. Sixty-three beds, Sixty-three beds, C.

ORWELL LODGE HOTEL, Orwell Road, Rathgar, D6, tel 977256. Suburban small hotel and restaurant. C.

POWERS HOTEL, Kildare Street, D2, tel 605244. Overlooking College Park in city centre, disco. M.

ROYAL DUBLIN HOTEL, Upper O'Connell Street, D1, tel 733666. Hotel and ballroom in modern building in heart of shopping district. One hundred beds, M.

ROYAL MARINE HOTEL, Dun Laoghaire, Co. Dublin, tel 801911. Victorian hotel, extensively modernised, a few minutes' walk from the Sealink Ferryport, with a combination of period and contemporary decor. One-hundred-and-four beds, M.

SACHS HOTEL, Morehampton Road, D4, tel 680995. Elegant suburban hotel and fashionable bar and restaurant in Regency terrace buildings. Twenty beds, M.

SHELBOURNE HOTEL, THE, St. Stephen's Green, D2, tel 766471. The most prestigious hotel in Dublin, splendidly located overlooking St. Stephen's Green. An hotel with many historic associations and a popular meeting place. E.

SKYLON HOTEL, Drumcondra Road, D9, tel 379121. Modern hotel on Airport Road with banqueting and shopping facilities. M.

TARA TOWERS HOTEL, Merrion Road, D4, tel 694666. High rise hotel overlooking Dublin Bay with the most splendid views of any Dublin hotel; bar, restaurant and conference room. One-hundred beds, M.

WESTBURY HOTEL, Balfe Street, (off Grafton Street), D2, tel 791122. Modern luxury hotel tucked into the busiest part of the city with bar, restaurants and conference rooms. Two hundred beds, E.

WYNN'S HOTEL, Lower Abbey Street, D1, tel 745131. Old-fashioned hotel in central position, on same street as Abbey Theatre. C.

**HOWTH**. Fifteen kilometres (9.5 miles) north-east of Dublin, the rocky mass of the Howth peninsula forms the northern limit of DUBLIN BAY and, being virtually an island connected to the mainland by the isthmus of Sutton, it maintains an individual identity as well as a singular history, separate from the adjacent city and countryside. The name derives from *Hoved,* Norse for a headland, and it was one of the areas outside the city of Dublin settled during the Viking era. At the Battle of Evora in 1177 the Vikings were conquered by the next wave of invaders, the Anglo Normans, who established the lordship of Howth and the eight-hundred-year connection between Howth and the St. Lawrence family of HOWTH CASTLE, the most important building on the peninsula. The other buildings of historic interest on Howth are the Early Christian church of ST. FINTAN at SHIELMARTIN and HOWTH ABBEY and College in the village. The village itself has a fine harbour constructed 1807-14 as the Mail Packet Station but it was superseded by DUN LAOGHAIRE in 1836. Today it is the home port for a fleet of trawlers and also the base of the Howth Yacht Club with a yacht marina. Above the steeply winding streets of the village the landscape opens out to Howth Summit and the Ben of Howth, areas of windswept natural beauty, carpeted in gorse and bracken with spectacular views of Dublin Bay and the undulating mountains of Wicklow on the far side. Around the perimeter of the peninsula, starting from BALSCADDEN BAY there is a Cliff Walk by which the whole seaward side of Howth can be traversed before emerging at the MARTELLO TOWER of RED ROCK in Sutton. This is without a doubt the most invigorating and 'away from it all' place to go in Dublin, with gulls whirling about your head and the deep pellucid greens of the Irish Sea at your feet. DART to Howth. Bus 31 from Lower Abbey Street.

## HOWTH CASTLE.
In unbroken succession through the male line, the St. Lawrence family had been Lords of Howth from 1177 to 1909 when the descent passed to the sister of the last Lord Howth. The family, now Gaisford St. Lawrence, still live in the castle and their eight-hundred-year association with the

*Howth Summit.*

peninsula is the most enduring in Ireland. The original castle, built by the Anglo-Norman St. Lawrence family, was probably a motte and bailey on Castle Hill above the village where the MARTELLO TOWER now stands. Older parts of the castle date from the fifteenth century and it was considerably altered in the eighteenth century by FRANCIS BINDON, who organised the buildings into a symmetrical composition around the present entrance courtyard. SIR EDWIN LUTYENS added extensively to the castle in 1911, emulating the Medieval style of the earlier towers to provide a convincingly rambling range of buildings on the southern side, one of these a tower to house the important library. The demesne of Howth Castle was laid out in the eighteenth century and there are fine areas of mature planting and a magnificent rhododendron grove, with some 400 varieties of plant. Two public golf courses have been laid out in the demesne and a transport museum is housed in the stables.

On the terrace of the castle are the fifteenth-century bells from Howth Abbey and in the rhododendron grove is the megalithic portal dolmen 'AIDEEN'S GRAVE' one of the largest prehistoric tombs in the country. DART to Howth. Bus 31 from Lower Abbey Street.

**HUBAND BRIDGE**, Grand Canal, D2. Hump-backed canal bridge, built in 1791, linking Upper Mount Street to Percy Place, it is the most attractive of the bridges spanning the canals, and central to a canal-bank quarter of late Georgian houses and tree lined towpaths.

**HUGHES, JOHN**, (1865-1941). Sculptor, born in Dublin, studied in Dublin and on the Continent. His principal work in Dublin, a colossal and unattractive seated bronze figure of Victoria, sat in the Kildare Street forecourt of Leinster House from 1909 until it was removed in 1948 to storage at the Royal Hospital and more recently sold to Victoria, New South Wales. The figures at the base of this monument, battle-weary soldiers supported by Erin, Peace and Fame, were much more successful than the central subject of the Queen, executed in obese realism. Hughes lived from 1890 to 1901 at 28 Lennox Street, D8, (plaque).

**HUGUENOT CEMETERY**, Merrion Row, D2. Nestling between the office on a busy corner of ST. STEPHEN'S GREEN is a break in the line of buildings, with a railing and a granite entranceway which bears the inscription 'Huguenot Cemetery 1693'. In this little graveyard, recently restored by the French Government – doubtless in an act of reparation for the ill treatment of these seventeenth-century French Protestants – lie the family tombs of the refugees who rose to prominence in eighteenth-century Dublin. Their names, such as D'Olier and La Touche, are commemorated around the city in street names and other associations.

**HUGUENOTS**. In 1685 the EDICT OF NANTES of 1598, which had guaranteed freedom of worship in France, was revoked and almost half a million Calvinists became refugees, leaving France to avoid persecution. Many settled in England and a community gradually developed in Dublin. The Lady Chapel of ST. PATRICK'S CATHEDRAL was put at their disposal and for this reason the Huguenots settled in the area surrounding the Cathedral, beginning the association between the LIBERTIES and the Huguenots. They brought with them many trades among the most prominent of which was weaving, and they set up workshops producing poplin, silk and woollens. Weaving thrived until punitive legislation favouring English manufacture caused it to decline, transforming the Liberties from an area of prosperity to one of slums and poverty. Associated with the Huguenots are the gabled houses known as 'DUTCH BILLIES', but only one of these still stands in the Liberties – No. 35 on Kevin Street. Many Huguenot remains from what was once French Peter's graveyard have been re-interred in Mount Jerome. There is also a HUGUENOT CEMETERY at Merrion Row.

**HUME STREET, BATTLE OF**. In December 1969, architectural students from UCD and Bolton Street College of Technology occupied a group of Georgian buildings in Hume Street on the corner of St. Stephen's Green in an effort to prevent their imminent demolition for re-development purposes. The occupation lasted for six months while AN TAISCE, THE IRISH GEORGIAN SOCIETY, the Dublin Civic Group and other concerned bodies attempted to have the buildings preserved. The battle was at length won by the developers who agreed to preserve the character of one of the highest amenity value areas in the city by restoring brick rather than using steel and glass façades. In the twenty years since 1969, the idea that the Georgian character of Dublin is of vital importance to the city has received more widespread acceptance, and new schemes tend to be more in harmony with the old. However, areas of eighteenth-century interest which might be preserved continue to decline through neglect and insensitive development.

## HUNGERFORD POLLEN, JOHN, (1820-1902).

Architect and artist, he came to Dublin in 1855 and lived at 62 Rathmines Road for three years while he worked on the design and decoration of the UNIVERSITY CHURCH in St. Stephen's Green for JOHN HENRY NEWMAN, rector of the recently established Catholic University. Newman's expressed aim was to 'build a large barn and decorate it in the style of a basilica'; what he got was the most individual church building in Dublin, and Pollen's masterpiece. In contrast to the prevailing mode of church building in Dublin at the time – Neo Classical and Gothic Revival – Pollen's University Church is a miniature Byzantine-Romanesque building with no significant exterior but a richly decorated interior. The idea was to dispense with the elaborate architectural devices of contemporary churches and create an effect by the use of surface decoration, painting and varied materials. Pollen painted much of the interior himself and encouraged his masons to work on the decorated Byzantine capitals as though they were Medieval masons, making each one different and an expression of the individual craftsman. During the period that he was working on the University Church, Pollen held the Chair of Fine Art in the Catholic University.

## HYDE, DOUGLAS, (1860-1949).

Folklorist and translator, linguist and academic, he was influential in the founding of the GAELIC LEAGUE in 1893 and became its first President, an office he held until 1915. The object of the League was to encourage the use of Irish in everyday life. Hyde's involvement in language and folklore had a significant influence on the early work of W.B. YEATS and LADY GREGORY, directing them towards the Irish tradition as a source of literary inspiration. Hyde became the first Professor of Modern Irish at UCD in 1909 and first President of Ireland in 1937. After his retirement in 1945, he was given an official residence in the Phoenix Park. This house, previously known as 'The Little Lodge', he renamed 'Ratra' after his birthplace in Co. Roscommon. (During the 1870s the infant Winston Churchill lived in The Little Lodge for a number of years and records it as his earliest childhood memories.)

ICE SKATING. There are only two small rinks in Dublin, both located in the inner city:

DUBLIN ICE RINK: Dolphin's Barn, D8, tel 534154. Open seven days, 2.30-5.30, 8.30-11.00.

SILVER SKATE ICE RINK: North Circular Road, D7, tel 301263. Open seven days, 4.00-6.00, 8.00-10.30.

**ILLUMINATED MANUSCRIPTS.** The Golden Age of Early Christian art in Ireland is represented in Dublin by many objects in the museums and libraries but by nothing so well as THE BOOK OF KELLS, the finest manuscript to survive anywhere from the Early Middle Ages. There are in fact seven manuscript Gospel books from the sixth to ninth centuries in the TRINITY COLLEGE LIBRARY, respectively THE BOOKS OF ARMAGH, DIMMA, DURRO, THE GARLANDS OF HOWTH, BOOKS OF KELLS, MOLING and USERIANUS PRIMUS. These manuscripts – the products of the scriptoria of Irish monasteries in Ireland and Scotland – display various stages in the development of the style of illumination which came to be associated with the Irish monastic tradition. The Book of Kells differs from the others in its sheer sumptuousness of decoration, with virtually every one of over six hundred pages embellished. The ROYAL IRISH ACADEMY has a large and important manuscript collection housed at Academy House in Dawson Street, the most famous of which are the Cathach Psalter and the Stowe Missal, dating from the Early Christian Period. At the CHESTER BEATTY LIBRARY in Shrewsbury Road, the concentration is on Oriental manuscripts with some notable Christian texts, the Walsingham Bible and St. Augustine's De Civitate Dei, both from the

twelfth century, and the fifteenth-century Books of Hours, magnificently illuminated, the Coetivy Hours and the Rosarium of Philip II. Korans do not tend to be illuminated in the sense in which Western manuscripts are, but rather in terms of elaborate calligraphy, and the Library contains particularly rare examples of Korans in the early vertical Cufic script, as well as masterpieces by famous scribes. Persian manuscripts with their pictorial illumination of the Sha Nama from the fourteenth century are particularly rich, and of course the Chester Beatty also houses Indian, Chinese and Japanese manuscripts.

**IMPRESSIONISTS.** Although both the NATIONAL GALLERY and HUGH LANE GALLERY between them have a fine collection of small works from painters of the Impressionist school, only one of these is of outstanding importance, Claude Monet's 'Waterloo Bridge' in the Hugh Lane Gallery and a masterwork of the period. The Monet, painted in 1900, belongs to one of his major Series Paintings, and its shimmering and evanescent colours epitomise the attempt to capture the fugitive moment with which Impressionism was concerned. It is probably the single most important painting of the modern era in Dublin, certainly more important in a seminal sense than even the National Gallery's great early Picasso. It was from a painting by Monet that the Impressionist movement acquired its name. Small works by other Impressionist painters, Edgar Degas, Paul Cezanne, Berthe Morisot, Camille Pissarro and Alfred Sisley are in both Galleries, principally the National, and often, not surprisingly the gift of people such as EVIE HONE or EDWARD MARTYN. Associations of a contentious nature between the Impressionists and Dublin arise from the controversy over the still unresolved (since 1917) ownership of the 'LANE PICTURES', claimed by both the London National Gallery and the Hugh Lane Gallery in Dublin. The Lane Pictures include some world famous Impressionist paintings but they are not on permanent display in Dublin. See also POST IMPRESSIONISTS.

**INDUSTRIAL REVOLUTION.** There is little evidence of the type of industrial development of the eighteenth and nineteenth centuries so characteristic of many British cities. The GUINNESS BREWERY at St. James's Gate and some interesting warehouse buildings associated with the canals are the most significant examples. As the administrative and cultural centre of the country, the city did not develop a large-scale industrial base until well into the twentieth century.

**INGRAM, REX,** (1893-1950). Film director, born (as Reginald Ingram Hitchcock) at 58 Grosvenor Square, Rathmines. Ingram worked in the United States from 1911, and became an important early Hollywood director of silent movies whose work spanned the emergence of the talkies. Both Rudolph Valentino and Ramon Novarro were introduced to the screen in films directed by Ingram. A multi-faceted individual, he also sculpted and wrote a number of novels. Among his principal films are, *The Four Horsemen of the Apocalypse, The Prisoner of Zenda* and *Scaramouche.*

**INKBOTTLE SCHOOL.** Whimsically designed eighteenth-century circular school building at Glasnevin which was demolished in 1901. JONATHAN SWIFT is credited with the inspiration for its shape, which closely resembled an old-fashioned ink bottle. The body of the two-storey building was of stone, with a conical slated roof and a circular plain brick chimneystack. Its popular name was most apt.

**INLAND WATERWAYS ASSOCIATION OF IRELAND,** Stone Cottage, Claremont Road, Killiney, Co. Dublin, tel 852258. The Association, which has published two excellent guides to the GRAND and ROYAL CANALS, is concerned with the development, use and maintenance of the country's navigable waterways.

**INTERIORS.** Very few of the Georgian houses noted for their spectacular interior decoration are open to the public. Some, BELVEDERE HOUSE, IVEAGH HOUSE, LEINSTER HOUSE, the PROVOST'S HOUSE (Trinity College) may be visited by appointment, while others, CHARLEMONT HOUSE, POWERSCOURT HOUSE and the CITY HALL are used for public functions. Clanwilliam House, which is part of NEWMAN HOUSE on St. Stephen's Green and was recently restored by UCD, has the finest interiors accessible to the public, and here may be seen major examples of the decorative arts of the eighteenth century. Individual houses throughout the city, in HENRIETTA STREET, NORTH GREAT GEORGE'S STREET, PARNELL and MERRION SQUARES have fine plasterwork but are not usually accessible. Important interiors of other periods from the Medieval to the twentieth century include such buildings as ST. PATRICK'S CATHEDRAL, the ROYAL HOSPITAL, KILMAINHAM JAIL, the Chapel Royal, the Church of Saints Augustine and John and the Atrium in Trinity College. Of all periods, the twentieth century seems to have the least esteem for great or significant internal spaces and many buildings which are externally impressive offer little internally.

**INVINCIBLES.** Shortlived revolutionary secret society whose activities prompted the British government to introduce the 1882 Coercion Act. The society was founded in 1881 when the Invincibles planned a campaign of political assassinations which culminated in the PHOENIX PARK MURDERS for which five of the perpetrators were hanged.

**IRELAND'S EYE.** Island off the coast of the HOWTH peninsula, opposite the entrance to Howth Harbour. Ireland's Eye is now a nature reserve under the care of AN TAISCE. The gannetry at the eastern end where the birds breed can be overlooked at close quarters and the island is a popular resort for bird watchers. The Early Christian church of CILL MAC NESSAN was considerably reconstructed in the nineteenth century but is thought to have had a miniature round tower as belfry over the apse, like St. Kevin's Kitchen in GLENDALOUGH. On the western end is the only other building on the island, a MARTELLO TOWER, part of the series which were built along the east coast in 1804 to guard against a threatened Napoleonic invasion. In 1852, Ireland's Eye was the scene of a tragedy which caused much interest at the time. An artist, William Kirwan, went with his wife Maria to the island for the day where she met her death in suspicious circumstances – Kirwan maintained by drowning. The jury at his subsequent trial decided on a verdict of murder. Kirwan was sentenced to life imprisonment and served twenty-seven years' hard labour on Spike Island in Cork

Harbour. It was stated at his trial that during the twelve years he was married to Maria Kirwan, he had maintained a relationship with a Miss Kenny who had borne him eight children! DENIS JOHNSTON wrote a play on the subject. Ireland's Eye can be reached in calm weather by boat from the East Pier of Howth Harbour. DART to Howth.

**IRISH ACADEMY OF LETTERS.** Thirty-five member Literary Academy, founded in 1932 by G.B.SHAW and W.B.YEATS in response to the new CENSORSHIP Laws introduced by the Irish Free State in 1929. Of the twenty-five writers initially invited to become members, some declined the honour, among them JAMES JOYCE and SEÁN O'CASEY. The aim of the Academy is to promote literature in both English and Irish and it makes awards for work of exceptional merit.

**IRISH ARCHITECTURAL ARCHIVE,** 63 Merrion Square, D2, tel 763430. The archive was established in 1976 with the object of recording the historic architecture of Ireland, on a thirty-two-county basis. Since then its brief has expanded to include all periods of architecture up to the present. The archive houses a library and a constantly growing collection of some 40,000 drawings of Irish buildings from the eighteenth century onwards, as well as photographic and documentary records and models. The archive, which exists on private sponsorship, is the principal national resource for information on the architectural heritage of the country and provides an expert consultative service to public bodies and the architectural profession. It also publishes monographs on endangered or neglected aspects of architecture and architects. The material of the archive is available for consultation in the reading room. Tue-Fri 10.00-1.00, 2.00-5.00.

**IRISH ARTS REVIEW**. An annual journal of contemporary and historic arts founded in 1984 by the architectural historian Brian de Breffny. The profusely illustrated *Review* is the only Irish publication to deal with all aspects of the visual arts in Ireland and publishes scholarly assessments of the work of individuals, of periods and institutions. The *Review* is published in November.

**IRISH ASTRONOMICAL SOCIETY**, PO Box 2547, D15, tel 344869. Founded in 1937, the Society organises an annual programme of lectures and meetings for both the amateur and the advanced student of astronomy. In coordination with the DUNSINK OBSERVATORY, regular weekly telescope nights are held and the 12-inch aperture refractor telescope, the largest in Ireland, is available to members for studying the night sky and the wonders of the universe.

**IRISH CITIZEN ARMY**. Founded in 1913 by JAMES CONNOLLY and JIM LARKIN, with SEAN O'CASEY as secretary, during the Lock Out Strike. The Irish Citizen Army's purpose was to protect the strikers from intimidation by thugs hired by employers and from attack by the police. The headquarters of the Citizen Army were at LIBERTY HALL and the orientation of the organisation was Socialist rather than revolutionary. During 1916 the Citizen Army joined with the IRISH VOLUNTEERS in the Easter RISING. After the Treaty with Britain the Citizen Army rejected the agreement. During the Civil War in 1922 they occupied the FOUR COURTS.

**IRISH EXHIBITION OF LIVING ART** (IELA). Founded in 1943 as a reaction to the conservatism of the RHA, it became the vanguard of contemporary art in Dublin for forty years. The founding members included Norah Mc Guinness, JACK HANLON, EVIE HONE, MAINIE JELLETT, Louis Le Broquy, and Laurence Campbell. Continental artists such as Giorgio de Chirico, Max Ernst, David Hockney, Juan Miro and Pablo Picasso exhibited with the Living Art during their annual exhibitions. The IELA ceased to hold annual exhibitions in the 1980s when the objectives for which it had been established had been achieved.

**IRISH FILM CENTRE**, 6 Eustace Street, D2, tel 6795744. The Irish Film Institute which is based at the centre is the principal body concerned with film in the Irish Republic. An archive of Irish film is being built up and the centre is in the process of developing a two-screen art house cinema complex in the old Quaker Meeting Hall and adjacent buildings.

**IRISH FOLKLORE COMMISSION, THE**. The Folklore Commission was established in 1927 to record the traditional way of life of the Irish people. It maintains an archive of manuscripts, sound recordings, photographs and a library dealing with social life, belief, customs, crafts and culture as existing or remembered in rural Ireland. The Commission publishes an annual journal on folklore research.

**IRISH FREE STATE**. Officially called SAORSTÁT ÉIREANN, the Irish State existed within the British Commonwealth from 1922 to 1937, when its name was changed to ÉIRE. The Republic of Ireland officially came into existence in 1949.

## IRISH GEORGIAN SOCIETY

(IGS), Leixlip Castle, Leixlip, Co. Dublin, tel 6244211. The Society was founded in 1958 by Desmond Guinness, a member of the famous brewing family, and is a revival of an organisation formed in 1909 which issued a valuable set of publications on Irish Georgian architecture. The object of the current Society is the study, conservation and preservation of Georgian architecture throughout Ireland. In fact the Society's influence goes beyond the limits of the arts of the eighteenth-century and has spread an interest among the public in the conservation of heritage generally and a wider appreciation of Ireland's rich stock of historic architecture. The Georgian Society owns a number of mansions which it is in the course of restoring, the most important of which is CASTLETOWN HOUSE. This house was rescued from imminent demolition by the Society and is being restored and refurnished. The IGS publishes a bulletin dealing with architecture, art, cartography, furniture, glass, landscape and all aspects of the arts of the Georgian Era.

## IRISH GIANT, THE. Patrick Cotter

O'Brien, (1760-1806), from Co. Kilkenny was exhibited in Ireland and England because of his phenomenal height. He had reached 254cm (8ft 4in) by the age of seventeen. His shoes are on display in the CIVIC MUSEUM, looking more like giant versions of the Viking leatherwork at the NATIONAL MUSEUM than any contemporary footwear.

## IRISH MANUSCRIPT COMMISSION, 73 Merrion Square, D2, tel

761610. The Commission, which was established in 1928, publishes an annual report – *Analecta Hibernia* – dealing with research into the field of Irish manuscript resources, principally those of literary, historic and linguistic interest.

## IRISH NATIONAL WAR MEMORIAL, Colbert Road, Islandbridge, D8.

On a sloping site falling down to the Liffey and opposite the Phoenix Park, this War Memorial created by EDWIN LUTYENS is the most beautifully designed park in the city. Built between 1933 and 1939, as a memorial to the fifty thousand Irishmen who died in the First World War while serving in the British Army, the architecture and landscaping of the memorial provide a tranquil and austere setting on a site which had been, nearly a thousand years before, a burial ground for warriors during the Viking Age. Four small Classical pavilions joined by pergolas form a courtyard around the Stone of Remembrance, on either side of which are two brimming and almost silent fountains. One of the pavilions contains the volumes recording the names of the dead, and another, a cross which was fashioned from spars at Ginchy on the battle field at the Somme. The cenotaph which rises above the memorial is backed by plantations of evergreen oaks, the dark leaves of which form a beautiful contrast to the lightness of the stonework. Having suffered years of neglect during which the only frequent visitors were itinerants' piebald ponies, the Memorial Park has recently been restored and the gardens replanted. Part of the original design was for a footbridge to provide a connection over the river to the Phoenix Park and this idea is again being considered. Although Islandbridge is not architecture in the conventional sense of a building, it ranks with the CUSTOM HOUSE and the CASINO at Marino as one of the true architectural masterpieces in Dublin. Bus 23, 25, 26 from Essex Quay, 51 from Aston Quay.

**IRISH PARLIAMENTARY PARTY.** This Party developed from the HOME RULE League, founded by ISAAC BUTT in 1873 with a view to promoting the establishment of Irish parliamentary independence through constitutional means. CHARLES STEWART PARNELL became leader of the group of Westminster MPs in 1879 and by adroit manipulation of the balance of power in English politics gradually began to gain concessions for the Party's aims. Following the scandal of Parnell's divorce case in 1890 the party split with the minority following Parnell. By the time of his death in 1891 the impetus of the Party had been dissipated and other groups took up the cause of Home Rule.

**IRISH PEATLAND CONSERVATION COUNCIL** (IPCC), 3 Lower Mount Street, D2, tel 616645. Conservation body involved with the study and preservation of selected Irish boglands which form a unique and threatened aspect of the landscape. These bogs, which are amongst the last surviving extensive peatlands in Europe, form a natural habitat for a wide range of plants and animals. The IPCC purchases bogs threatened by development and is involved in the monitoring and protection of bogs throughout the country, from the immediate hinterland of Dublin to the west coast. A range of publications relating to Irish peatlands is available from the IPCC.

**IRISH VOLUNTEERS.** Both the eighteenth and twentieth centuries produced Volunteer organisations in Dublin, the earlier, led by members of the nobility, had the ostensible object of resisting the threat of a French invasion, but also wished to indicate to the British government the self determination of the Dublin parliament. The twentieth-century Volunteers, seeking independence from England, were formed in 1913 in response to the existence of a similar body in Ulster opposed to HOME RULE, the Ulster Volunteers. In 1920 the Dublin Volunteers became the Irish Republican Army – the military wing of the recently proclaimed Irish Republic – although at the time the Republic had no legal standing.

**IRISH WILDBIRD CONSERVANCY**, 8 Longford Place, Monkstown, Co. Dublin, tel 804322. The organisation is concerned with the recording and study of wildbirds and their habitats throughout Ireland.

**IRISH WILDLIFE FEDERATION** (IWF), The Conservation Centre, 132A East Wall Road, D3, tel 366821. The whole spectrum of wildlife falls within the brief of the Federation. Of special concern is the education of both the public and administrators in conservation about the many species of the countryside. Wildlife surveys are conducted by the IWF and their programmes with children and schools are designed to develop active environmental awareness.

**ISLAM.** With no significant immigrant community from Muslim countries in the past, any relationship between Dublin and Islam would seem tenuous in the extreme. However, the presence of the CHESTER BEATTY LIBRARY with its unrivalled collection of early Korans makes Dublin important for the student of Islamic literature. For economic and educational reasons a Muslim community has developed in Dublin since the 1970s and a MOSQUE has opened in a converted church on the South Circular Road, forming a cultural focus for the growing Muslim community.

**IVEAGH HOUSE**, 80 St. Stephen's Green South, D2, tel 780822. Now the Department of Foreign Affairs, the original house was built for Robert Clayton, Bishop of Cork, and was designed by RICHARD CASTLE in 1736. The eighteenth-century town house has been much adapted and enlarged by subsequent owners and externally nothing of Castle's building, which occupies the four lefthand bays of the façade, can be seen. Inside, the old music room and the saloon, both on the first floor, are the most important parts of the Georgian building still intact. The ceiling of the music room is decorated with motifs of musical instruments and dates from the 1770s, and on the walls is a set of three romantic views of Roman Antiquities, from roughly the same date, by the Irish painter George Barret. The saloon, the principal reception room of the eighteenth-century house, has a deeply coffered coved ceiling dating from 1736 which expresses the same robust Classicism as the HOUSE OF LORDS interior. SIR BENJAMIN LEE GUINNESS bought the house in 1866 and began to transform it, largely to his own designs. The original building and Guinness's additions were unified by a façade also designed by Guinness. In contrast to these is the ballroom, the largest and most richly decorated room in the house. It was added by Sir Benjamin in 1896 and designed by William Young. Domed and with the look of Roman baths, the walls of the ballroom are inlaid with marbles and

*Newcomen's Bank, by Thomas Ivory.*

onyx and hung with curtains of damask and velvet. In 1939, Rupert Guinness, the Second Earl of Iveagh, presented Iveagh House to the Irish nation when it became the Department of External Affairs, and subsequently Foreign Affairs. Two ministers of the Department, EAMON DE VALERA in 1959, and Patrick Hillery in 1969, became Presidents of Ireland.

**IVEAGH MARKET**, Francis Street, D8. Built in 1907 on the site of the Medieval Fair Green which existed outside the western walls of the city, to provide housing for street traders. The handsome limestone and brick building is, on the Francis Street side, an old clothes market with a sprinkling of bric-a-brac stalls, while at the rear is the fish market. A grinning sculptured head over an archway on the southern façade is said to represent Lord Iveagh, the benefactor.

**IVEAGH TRUST,** Patrick Street, D8. Public housing complex erected by the Guinness Family Trust between 1894 and 1915, in an ambitious scheme of slum clearance. The development, entirely in red brick with terracotta tile embellishments, consists of numerous apartment blocks, a hostel, baths in an Art Nouveau style and the BAYNO, the Iveagh Play Centre in Dutch Baroque manner. St. Patrick's Park was also laid out at the same time by the Trust.

**IVORY, THOMAS,** (1720-1786). Architect, born in Cork, master of the Dublin Society's Drawing School from 1759 until his death. Two of his buildings in Dublin still survive and are among the most distinguished of the Georgian period for their delicacy of proportion and detailing, although both have been altered from the original designs. The BLUE COAT SCHOOL in Blackhall Place, now the Incorporated Law Society, is an impressive Palladian composition which in the proportions of the blocks and their connecting arcades has a graceful lightness. Its spire was never completed, but replaced in the nineteenth century by a small cupola. NEWCOMEN'S BANK in Castle Street, now the Corporation Rates Department, was built as a banking house in the eighteenth century and its rooms are designed to impress, with the principal suite on the first floor based on an oval form. Externally the limestone detailing is in an Adamesque manner, the low relief of the window bays suggesting a more malleable material than stone. In the nineteenth century, the area of the building was doubled, with an identical block being added to the north of the original, and a canopied porch uniting them on Cork Street.

JAMES II, (1633-1701). The first British monarch since Henry VIII to be a Catholic, his reign was exceptionally brief, lasting from 1685 to 1688 when he was deposed in the 'Glorious Revolution', and fled to France. He arrived in Kinsale in 1689 at the head of a French army and on coming to Dublin he called a parliament and attempted to restore Catholic power and interests. He installed a Catholic provost in TRINITY COLLEGE, using much of the College as a barracks for his troops. James remained in Dublin until he and his army were defeated by Prince William of Orange at the Battle of the Boyne on 1 July 1690. The theatre of European conflict had transferred itself to Ireland and two multinational armies faced each other at the Boyne. The speed of James's departure from Ireland, three days after the battle, enabled his opponents to regard him with ridicule. During his year in Ireland, James replaced Ormond, the Lord Deputy, with Richard Talbot, Earl of Tyrconnell. Permanently desperate for money James set up a Royal Mint in Capel Street and coined millions of pounds of largely worthless money.

**JAMES JOYCE CULTURAL CENTRE**, 35 North Great George's Street, D2, tel 731984. During the fifth International James Joyce Symposium, held in Dublin in 1977, the idea of a Cultural Centre was first considered but it did not become a reality until 1986 when this 1784 Georgian mansion was leased from Dublin Corporation for the purpose of having a study centre, archive, and museum devoted to Joyce in the city centre. Still in the throes of a lengthy restoration project, this fine building will provide a focus for Joycean studies and information. Tours of the little-known Joyce associations with the north side of the city are given from the Centre by Joyce's nephew, Ken Monaghan.

**JAMES JOYCE'S DUBLIN HOMES.** The eight Joyce children were ferried around the city by their alcoholic and improvident father, moving from house to house in a rapidly decreasing economic spiral. This unsettling itinerant existence probably made the sensitive Joyce more aware of the different aspects of Dublin than he would otherwise have been. The list of houses begins with a comfortable suburban middle class residence in a triangular 'square' and ends with a circular gun battery on the inhospitable sea coast, with all shapes and sizes of houses in between.

41 Brighton Square, Rathgar (plaque).
23 Castlewood Avenue, Rathmines.
1 Martello Terrace, Bray.
23 Carysfort Avenue, Blackrock (plaque).
14 Fitzgibbon Street.
29 Hardwicke Street.
2 Millbourne Avenue, Drumcondra.
17 North Richmond Street.
29 Windsor Avenue, Fairview.
7 Convent Avenue, Fairview.
15 Richmond Avenue, Fairview.
8 Inverness Terrace, Fairview.
32 Glengarriff Parade, North Circular Road.
7 St. Peter's Terrace, Phibsboro.
60 Shelbourne Road, Ballsbridge.
35 Strand Road, Sandymount.
44 Fontenoy Street
103 Strand Road, Sandymount.
The Martello Tower, Sandycove (now the James Joyce Museum).

**JAPANESE ARTS.** Both the NATIONAL MUSEUM and CHESTER BEATTY LIBRARY have extensive collections of the arts of Japan. The Museum collection of decorative and domestic objects, to which a room is devoted, consists mainly of the rather florid works of the Meiji Period, (1868-1912). There are also fine Netsuke and Inro from the Edo period, (1600-1868), and an extremely rare bronze bell, Dotaku, of the Yayoi period, (200BC-AD250), of which very few examples exist, and which is interesting to compare with the Early Christian bronze bells in the same Museum for the subtle low-relief decoration. The Chester Beatty Japanese collection is primarily a manuscript one, the main body of which consists of picture scrolls and albums from the seventeenth and eighteenth centuries, many of them of considerable rarity. All the principal polychrome wood block artists of the Edo and Meiji periods are represented by superb examples of their work.

**JELLETT, MAINIE,** (1897-1944). Artist, born 36 Fitzwilliam Square, she studied in Dublin, London and Paris under Sikert, André L'Hote and Albert Gleizes. Like her friend EVIE HONE she was influenced by the concept of Cubism, and continued to paint in an adaptation of these principles. She was a founder member of the IRISH EXHIBITION OF LIVING ART. Jellett's work has a strong decorative and religious approach, as demonstrated by the many examples of her work in public collections, such as the 'Virgin of Éire' and 'I Have Trodden the Winepress Alone' in the NATIONAL GALLERY.

**JERVAS, CHARLES,** (1675-1739). Artist, born in Co. Offaly, studied under Sir Godfrey Kneller in London and succeeded him as painter to King George I in 1723. He visited Ireland frequently and executed many portrait commissions. Jervas's portrait of JONATHAN SWIFT in the NATIONAL GALLERY is one of the most attractive images of the writer, showing him in a benign mood unlike the more common severe portraits by FRANCIS BINDON and others.

**JOHNSON, HESTER** (Stella) (1681-1728). This formidable and charming 'bluestocking' was the child of a servant or member of the household of Sir William Temple at Moore Park in Staffordshire where JONATHAN SWIFT was employed as secretary from 1689. Swift became attached to her and acted as her tutor while he lived at Moore Park. With a lady companion, Rebecca Dingley, Stella moved to Dublin in 1701 to be near Swift, and it was to her that the *Journal to Stella,* 1710-13, was composed after Swift had returned to England. In this intimate series of letters he gives a detailed picture of his daily life, interspersed with a babytalk-like private language. As much attention has been given to the question of whether or not Swift and Stella were married as has been to the curious affairs of great figures from the past. The matter has never been resolved, but with general opinion on the side of assuming that they were. Stella is buried beside Swift in ST. PATRICK'S Cathedral.

**JOHNSTON, DENNIS,** 1901-1984. Playwright, war correspondent and novelist, his most well known play, *The Old Lady Says 'No'*, 1929, is an Expressionist drama based on the life of ROBERT EMMET. It was rejected by the ABBEY THEATRE and produced by with considerable success by the GATE and many other theatres. The title is supposed to have come from a variation on the conventional rejection slip, in this case, W.B. YEATS's reference to LADY GREGORY's opinion of the play. Amongst his other plays is *Strange Occurrence on Ireland's Eye*, 1956, based on the notorious Kirwan murder case. See IRELAND'S EYE.

**JOHNSTON, FRANCIS**, 1760-1829. Architect, born in Armagh, he came to Dublin in 1793. Johnston shares with JAMES GANDON the unfortunate posthumous experience of having his major buildings occupying centre stage in the battles which waged in Dublin during the early twentieth century and suffering accordingly. Johnston was an exceptionally gifted and versatile architect, capable of designing equally well in different styles, and all his major works have remarkable public presence. ST. GEORGE'S, Hardwicke Place, 1802, the finest Georgian church in the city was followed in 1807 by the CHAPEL ROYAL in DUBLIN CASTLE, executed in an extravagant Gothic Revival manner, and in 1812 he began the GENERAL POST OFFICE on O'CONNELL STREET in a severe Greek Revival style, showing in all cases an accomplished mastery of form and proportion. Johnston lived at 64 Eccles Street, a house notable for its relief plaques set into the front wall and also for a circular room at the rear. He erected a belfry with a peal of bells in his rear garden, something which was not appreciated by his neighbours. A painting by Henry Kirchoffer in the NATIONAL GALLERY shows the view from Johnston's house in 1832, giving the impression that he had created a whole monastic settlement at the bottom of his garden. Johnston worked on the old Parliament House after the Act of Union (1800), transforming it into the Bank of Ireland by a deft balancing of the work of his predecessors. His Academy House in Abbey Street, which he had designed for the RHA was destroyed in the fighting of 1916, but unlike the GPO which was also gutted, it was not rebuilt. Other smaller works by Johnston are the gateway of the King's Inns at Henrietta Street, appropriately classical to blend with Gandon's buildings, and the Scots Baronial entranceway to the RHK from Kilmainham, originally spanning the quay at Rory O'More Bridge from which it was moved.

**JOYCE, JAMES**, 1882-1941. Writer, born at 41 Brighton Square, Rathgar, his life and work – which are in themselves inseparable – became totally involved in creating one of the masterworks of twentieth-century imaginative literature out of memories of the Dublin of his youth. The declining fortunes of the Joyce family, which caused them to move house frequently, seems to have activated a nomadic instinct which possessed him for the rest of his life. From Brighton Square the family moved first upwards, to better addresses, then rapidly downwards in a succession of houses around

*James Joyce on Sandymount Strand.*

the North Circular Road area of the north city, forever fleeing from landlords and debts. Joyce left Dublin, aged twenty-two, in 1902, and remained abroad for the rest of his life, living in Trieste, Zurich, Paris and finally Zurich again, where he died. One of his rare return visits to Dublin was in 1909, when he came as the manager of the Volta Cinema in Mary Street, the first cinema to open in Ireland. Cinemas had been thriving in Trieste and Joyce convinced a group of Triestean businessmen to establish one in Dublin. The venure failed, and Joyce abandoned any further attempts to engage in business. After the publication of *Dubliners* in 1914, and *A Portrait of the Artist as a Young Man* in 1916, Joyce began to receive critical acclaim, but his life was increasingly fraught with difficulties – physical illness, poverty and the disorientation of his children. In 1922, ULYSSES was published and was instantly accepted by the intellectual world as a work of genius, but its fate at the hands of customs and the law courts was worthy of the behaviour of the Inquisition, the book being banned, burned, and, the final irony, pirated. *Ulysses* is a celebration of eighteen hours in the life of Dublin, seen through the eyes of LEOPOLD BLOOM, a Jewish advertising canvasser for *The Freeman's Journal*. This proletarian Everyman is the lens through which Joyce scrutinises the minutiae of everyday life, showing extraordinary powers of total recall and great imaginative resources in conjuring up the matrix of ordinary life in the Dublin of 1904. Nothing from Joyce's family life, recollections and personal history was wasted, no experience was too trivial to be re-fashioned into the details of his characters' lives. Joyce's experiments with technique, which encompassed stream-of-con-

ciousness, surrealism and parody in *Ulysses,* were developed to their ultimate extremity in *Finnegans Wake*, 1939, to the extent of virtually re-creating the English language as a personalised Esperanto. Joyce is buried in Fluntern Friedhof, Zurich, with a life-size sculpture of him by Milton Hebald on the grave, glancing quizzically at passersby. Increasingly honoured in his native city, Joyce's memory is preserved in the spirit by the celebration of BLOOMSDAY, 16 June, and physically by the JAMES JOYCE MUSEUM at Sandycove, and the JAMES JOYCE CULTURAL CENTRE in North Great George's Street, and most curiously of all by the way in which his creations have taken on a life of their own. Bloom, a figment of Joyce's witty and sardonic imagination, is commemorated by a plaque on the house in Clanbrassil Street where Joyce decided that he should be born, as well as by many other allusions in the naming of everything from a hotel (Blooms, of course) to a flower shop, (Molly Bloom, the wife in this instance). Joyce would be amused – perhaps. Unlike other great Dublin writers, Joyce has never graduated to the schoolbook curriculum, there being a strong body of opinion that the image he presents of Dublin life is still, at the end of the century, too close to reality. See JOYCE'S DUBLIN HOUSES and BLOOM.

**JURY'S HOTEL.** Prior to moving to BALLSBRIDGE, Jury's Hotel was originally located on Dame Street and was noted for it's 'Antique Bar'. In a nice piece of symmetry, the relics of James Joyce which have found their way from Zurich to Dublin have been balanced by the migration of the interior of the 'Antique Bar' to Zurich where it was installed there in the James Joyce Pub.

**K**AUFFMAN, ANJELICA, (1740-1807). Artist, born in Switzerland, she achieved a success remarkable for a woman painter of that period. Kauffman excelled as a painter of allegorical subjects and society portraits. In England under the patronage of Sir Joshua Reynolds she became one of the leading artists of her day. Anjelica Kauffman is credited with painting more works in Ireland during her brief six months visit in 1771 than could have been accomplished by the entire Royal Academy. Any vestige of a decayed painted ceiling in a Dublin tenement was commonly attributed to her. She stayed as a guest of Mrs Clayton, wife of Bishop Clayton, builder of what has now become IVEAGH HOUSE in St. Stephen's Green, and with the Ely family at RATHFARNHAM CASTLE. A group portrait of the Elys, which includes a self portrait of the artist, is in the NATIONAL GALLERY. Her inclusion in the painting indicates that the social position she held was above that of a tradesman expected to dine in the servant's hall, a social level common among contemporary artists. Most of the house decorations attributed to Kauffman are in fact by others though based on engravings of her work. Although the painted ceilings at Rathfarnham have been ascribed to her, even this attribution is now doubted.

**KAVANAGH, JOSEPH MALACHY,** (1856-1918). Artist, born Dublin, he studied at the RHA Schools and on the Continent. He belongs to a group of Irish artists, including Walter Osborne and Dermod O'Brien, who were heavily influenced by contemporary Dutch painting, producing small pictures showing corners of old towns, church interiors, and rustic characters. Kavanagh's most interesting work is a series of studies for the painting 'Cockle Pickers', painted around DUBLIN BAY, and showing wide expanses of sky with the distant and lonely figures of the cockle women. An unlikely victim of the 1916 RISING, Kavanagh only barely escaped with his life when he rescued the RHA regalia from the burning Academy House in Abbey Street. He never recovered from the shock of this experience, and died two years later. There are characteristic examples of his work in the NATIONAL GALLERY, of which 'The Old Convent Gate, Dinan' shows a peddler pausing in deep shadows before an arched entranceway through which the sun is streaming.

**KAVANAGH, PATRICK,** (1905-1967). Poet, born on a small farm in Iniskeen, Co. Monaghan. Having published two books, *Ploughman and Other Poems* and *The Green Fool*, 1936, he moved to Dublin in the unpropitious year of 1939 and lived there in comparative poverty for the rest of his life. The major Irish poet of the mid-century, Kavanagh also published prose and articles, all of which are imbued with his acute sense of the spiritual dimension of ordinary life. He drew his subject matter from the dark landscape of his origins and from the canalbank area of Dublin where he lived, and where he is now commemorated by a bench on the canal at Baggot Street bridge. *The Great Hunger*, a long poem concerned with the degrading poverty of rural life, was published in 1942, and forms a powerful antidote to the romantic presentation of rural Ireland characteristic of those Irish writers (the majority), whose background was urban. Kavanagh was involved in two disastrous court cases, both of which he lost. The first of these was in 1939 when he was sued by

OLIVER ST. JOHN GOGARTY whom he had mentioned in *The Green Fool*, and the second in 1954 when he sued *The Leader*, a Dublin newspaper, for what he regarded as an uncomplimentary profile. In a short-lived attempt to find a platform for his views, Kavanagh and his brother launched their own newspaper in 1952, *Kavanagh's Weekly*, which was almost entirely written by the poet and was published from his flat at 62 Pembroke Road. Author and publisher then distributed the journal by bicycle. *Kavanagh's Weekly* lasted for thirteen issues before funds ran out and the paper folded.

> On Pembroke Road look out for my
> ghost,
> Dishevelled with shoes untied,
> Playing through railings with little
> children
> Whose children have long since died.

('If you ever go to Dublin Town', Patrick Kavanagh.)

**KEATING, SEAN,** (1889-1987). Artist, born in Limerick, he studied under SIR WILLIAM ORPEN at the Metropolitan School of Art. An ardent Nationalist, Keating treated west of Ireland and Republican subject matter in a somewhat Soviet Social Realist manner. Throughout his life he painted fine self portraits of his rugged features and appears as a character in many of his own group paintings. The Hugh Lane Gallery holds a very characteristic work, 'Men of The West', 1915, which shows a group of revolutionaries, clad in the homespun garments of the Aran Islands, posing on a hillside with their guns at the ready. 'An Allegory' in the NATIONAL GALLERY of Ireland gives a more complex or perhaps more jaundiced treatment of revolutionary themes. In this strange painting a tableau is enacted be-

*Jim Larkin, by Oisin Kelly.*

fore the gutted remains of a Great House, in which a dead comrade is being buried by soldiers beneath a tree, while politician, cleric, woman, child and old man stand in mutual isolation.

**KELLY, OISIN,** (1915-1981). Sculptor, he studied languages at TRINITY COLLEGE, and sculpture briefly in Frankfurt, and in London with HENRY MOORE. Working in wood, stone and bronze, Kelly's fine feeling for birds, animals, and the human figure has created an interesting body of small-scale works which often deal with group subjects, such as people marching or cows in a herd with a drover. His large-scale public works include some of the most ambitious modern monuments in Dublin, which through their sense of movement enliven the spaces they occupy. 'THE CHILDREN OF LIR' in the Garden of Remembrance, Parnell Square, 1971, shows the children at the point of metamorphosis into swans, a tremendous achievement in weightlessness. Likewise, the 'Charioteer of Life' at the Irish Life Plaza, Lower Abbey Street, conveys a sense of speed and effortless movement. On O'Connell Street, 'JIM LARKIN', is the most recent addition to the notables who jostle for prominence along the central mall, except of course the recumbent Anna Livia. Larkin the labour leader is shown, arms raised, rallying the downtrodden, in memory of the many rallies he addressed in O'Connell Street during the unrest of the early years of the century. Other works by Kelly are two saints in St. Francis Xavier, Gardiner Street. Another excellent sculpture by Oisin Kelly, a humorous pair of figures called 'Two Working Men', commissioned by the Irish Transport and General Worker's Union (ITGWU) and intended to stand on the pavement outside Liberty Hall on Eden Quay gazing up at what Labour had achieved, was refused planning permission by the government's Paving Department who considered that it would 'cause an obstruction'. Dublin's loss was Cork's gain and these figures now stand gazing up at County Hall in Cork.

**KENILWORTH SQUARE**, Rathgar, D6. Late nineteenth-century houses of red brick, arranged singly and in pairs. These substantial houses maintain the trademarks of the Georgian period – flights of granite steps and impressive ironwork, and stucco quoins on the brick façades. The large central park is now used by a school as a sportsground.

**KERNOFF, HARRY**, (1900-1974). Artist, born London, his family moved to Dublin in 1914 and he studied at the Metropolitan School. A prolific artist, and although he did paint landscapes, primarily an urban artist who strongly identified with the themes of city life. His oils are painted in a bold and colourful manner with much emphasis on patterns of shapes in trees and buildings. Kernoff produced a large collection of wood and lino cuts and published two collections of prints in 1942 and 1951. These prints are among his best-known work, covering a wide range of subjects from west of Ireland beauties to Expressionist treatments of Dublin street life, pubs and characters. These prints are still frequently found in secondhand bookshops and are characterised by Kernoff's strange habit of signing them in green ink, doubtless a statement of his Nationalist sentiments.

**KILDARE STREET, D2**. A street of contrasting styles, with everything from the great treasures of the past stored in the NATIONAL LIBRARY and MUSEUM through a magisterial Georgian mansion to the gamut of nineteenth- and twentieth-century architectural taste. The first great house laid out in this quarter of Dublin during the eighteenth century was Kildare House, built by the Duke of Leinster and now known as LEINSTER HOUSE, seat of the DÁIL. The forecourt of Leinster House is occupied to the north and south, by the National Library and Museum respectively. On the east side of the street, the industry and commerce building of the 1940s has an interesting bas relief frieze by Gabriel Hayes, and at the north end of the street is the KILDARE STREET CLUB.

**KILDARE STREET CLUB**, Kildare Street, D2. Now the premises of Alliance Française and the State Heraldic Museum. The Club is an imposing brick building, designed by BENJAMIN WOOD-WARD of the Deane and Woodward collaboration, with elaborate limestone carving by the Harrisons, O'Shea brothers and others. Built between 1858 and 1861, this was one of the the most important nineteenth-century buildings in Dublin to come from the scholarly interest in Medieval architecture inspired by the work of Augustus Pugin and John Ruskin. The chief internal feature of the Club was the magnificent central staircase, unfortunately removed when the building was divided in 1967. The Coffee Room of the Club is now the exhibition area of the HERALDIC MUSEUM, and its cornice carved in a rich foliage pattern is especially interesting. On the outside of the building are carved column bases with sporting and animal motifs, the most amusing and well observed of which are those on the Kildare Street frontage, satirising the club members, who are shown as a pair of monkeys at a billiard table and other comic animals. The Kildare Street Club was a pillar of Establishment life during the latter end of the nineteenth century and its members, country gentlemen, were noted for their philistine conservatism.

This club is a sort of oyster-bed into which all the eldest sons of the landed gentry fall as a matter of course. There they remain spending their days, drinking sherry and cursing Gladstone in a sort of dialect, a dead language which the larva-like stupidity of the club has preserved. The green banners of the League are passing, the cries of a new Ireland awaken the dormant air, the oysters rush to the window – they stand there open-mouthed, real pantomime oysters ...

(*Parnell and His Island*, George Moore.)

**KILLINEY BAY.** Between BRAY and DALKEY the coast curves in a long gentle sweep, terminated at either end by Bray Head and Killiney Hill. This stretch of coastline was constantly compared during the nineteenth century to the Bay of Naples, a resemblance which may have been more apposite when the landscape was one of widely dispersed villas set in trees, with the hills rising into the distant Dublin and Wicklow Mountains. Whatever about Naples, Killiney Bay is a beautiful stretch of coastline and the journey round it by DART is an exhilarating beginning or end to the day for those who commute into the city. Bordered by quiet pebbly beaches, golf courses, and more recently burgeoning suburbs, the shores of the Bay are best seen from the height of Killiney Hill. DART to Killiney.

**KILMAINHAM.** Centred around the ROYAL HOSPITAL, the Kilmainham area encompasses a number of important buildings of civil, military and charitable purpose, dating from the seventeenth to twentieth centuries and largely concerned with the serious themes of life, death, crime and retribution. The Royal Hospital is of course the architectural showpiece of the quarter, but DR. STEEVENS' HOSPITAL, from 1721, is a diminutive variation on the same theme of an arcaded cloistral courtyard and steeply roofed ranges of building dominated by a clock tower. Next to Dr. Steevens' is Jonathan Swift's Hospital, called St. Patrick's, set up with a bequest from the Dean and containing a museum of Swiftian memorabilia. The KILMAINHAM PRISON MUSEUM, where many Irish revolutionaries were guests of the nation, houses relics of those incarcerated in these grim surroundings. Between the prison and the rear entrance to the Royal Hospital is Kilmainham Court House, an

official link in the processing of those
bound for Botany Bay. In the eighteenth-century ballad, 'The Night before
Larry was Stretched', a clergyman
comes into the cell as Larry and his
friends are playing cards to celebrate the
prisoner's last night. 'Larry tipped him
a Kilmainham look/And he pitched his
big wig to the devil.' Between Kilmainham and the Liffey is the Irish National
War Memorial at Islandbridge. Bus 79
from Aston Quay.

**KILMAINHAM CROSS,** Bully's
Acre. Base of an Early Christian high
cross of which the upper portions have
disappeared.

**KILMAINHAM MINUET, THE.** A
characteristic Dublin slang ballad of the
eighteenth century, concerned with a
felon's last hours. The minuet in question is that danced on air by the hanged
man. The surgeons of anatomy, or 'surgents of ottamy' are invoked in the belief
that a cut to the jugular could revive the
hanged man.

> When I dance twixt de ert and de
>   skies,
> De clargy may bleet for de struggler,
> Bud when on de ground your friend
>   lies.
> Oh, tip him a snig in de jugglar;
> Ye know dat is all my last hope,

As de surgents of ottamy tell us,
Dat when I'm cut down from de rope,
You'd bring back de puff to my bel-
  lows,
And set me once more on my pins.

**KING'S INNS, THE,** Henrietta Street,
D1. The last major building by JAMES
GANDON, 1785, it can be approached
obliquely from HENRIETTA STREET,
where one enters a tall narrow three-
sided courtyard, or from Constitution
Hill on the other side of the building,
where it stands back from a park and
expresses a very different character.
There is an element of the unexpected –
rare in Dublin – in the Henrietta Street
approach, as little of the Inns can be seen
from the hill leading up to it. The composition of twin pedimented wings, rising from the cobbled yard, with a
graceful columned cupola facing an arched screen combines these elements
with great power. The Constitution Hill
façade has two CARYATID entrances,
male and female, another feature of this
interesting building unusual in Dublin
architecture. The library of the Inns,
housed in a separate building in Henrietta Street, is by FREDERICK DARLEY. In the
park of the Inns are splendid examples
of Empire-style furnishings in the cast
iron benches.

**LA TÈNE.** European Celtic culture lasting from approximately 500 BC to, in Ireland, the Early Christian period. The style is characterised by fine metalwork with curviliniar and stylised bird and animal motifs as surface decorations. Some outstanding examples of La Tène objects are in the NATIONAL MUSEUM collection. The bronze trumpet from Loughnashade is of quite Homeric magnificence, and from it and the Petrie Crown, horse trappings and other functional objects, a substantial idea of the severe beauty and absolutely modern sense of design can be seen. Elements of the La Tène style of decoration lasted into the era of the Ardagh Chalice and Tara Brooch where, infused with the Viking elements of their Ringerike style, they have been absorbed into the elaborate decorative schemes of Irish Medieval art.

**LAMBAY ISLAND.** Private estate on an island off the north county Dublin coast at Portraine, 6km (4 miles) from Rush and 24km (15 miles) from Dublin. The gardens were laid out for Cecil Baring, Lord Revelstoke, 1907, by EDWIN LUTYENS, with planting by Gertrude Jekyll, the foremost garden designers of their day. The house, which incorporates some existing ruins, is laid out in a Greek cross plan surrounded by enclosed gardens with a rampart wall to give protection from the fierce winds which sweep over the island. Lord and Lady Revelstoke are buried on Lambay within the formal gardens in a tomb also designed by Lutyens. Private but may be visited by appointment.

**LANE PICTURES, THE.** Thirty-nine paintings, the ownership of which is a matter of dispute between the National Gallery in London, and the HUGH LANE MUNICIPAL GALLERY of Modern Art in Dublin. In 1907 HUGH LANE presented a 'conditional gift' of paintings to Dublin Corporation provided that a promised permanent building to house them was erected within a few years. Growing impatient with the dilatory behaviour of the Corporation and the Dublin public's lukewarm reception of the paintings, Lane withdrew them from the temporary gallery in Clonmel House, Harcourt Street in 1913 and lent them to the National Gallery in London for an exhibition, after which they were consigned to storage in the London gallery's basement. Lane bequeathed these paintings to London in his will, but prior to leaving for the United States in 1915, he added a codicil to the will, re-allocating them to Dublin. This codicil was not witnessed. Lane died in the sinking of the *Lusitania* and the paintings were claimed by London. A rapprochement was achieved in 1959 when it was agreed to share the paintings between Dublin and London on a five-year rotating basis. This arrangement is still in force. Amongst the Lane Pictures are works by Jean-Baptiste Corot, Gustave Courbet, Honoré Daumier, Edgar Degas, Jean-Auguste-Dominique Ingres, Edouard Manet, Claude Monet, Camille Pissarro, Pierre-Auguste Renoir, Henri Rousseau and Edouard Vuillard and include such major works as Renoir's 'Les Parapluies' and Puvis de Chavannes' 'Beheading of St. John Baptist'.

**LANE, SIR HUGH,** (1875-1915). Art dealer and philanthropist, born in Cork. The son of LADY GREGORY's sister, he went to London and established himself as a dealer whose judgement became widely respected, and in retrospect the quality of his purchases and bequests testify to the breadth of his interests and the soundness of his judgement. In 1901 he saw an exhibition of paintings by JOHN BUTLER YEATS and NATHANIEL HONE in Dublin which activated his involvement in contemporary Irish art. He commissioned Yeats to paint a series of portraits of prominent Irish figures but became dissatisfied with his slow progress and gave the remainder of the commission to WILLIAM ORPEN. The idea which Lane promoted of establishing a gallery of modern art in Dublin was surrounded by controversy and was not to be permanently achieved until 1932 when CHARLEMONT HOUSE was opened as the HUGH LANE MUNICIPAL GALLERY OF MODERN ART, called after the donor, a gesture he had specifically forbidden. Lane was accorded the Freedom of the City of Dublin in 1908, knighted for his services to Irish art in 1909 and became Director of the NATIONAL GALLERY of Ireland in 1914. His death on the *Lusitania* in 1915 deprived the Irish art world of its most outward looking and generous spirit.

**LANSDOWNE ROAD STADIUM**, Lansdowne Road, D4. Headquarters of the Irish Rugby Football Union (IRFU), and the venue for national and international rugby tournaments. The stadium, a functional concrete structure, stands in the midst of a red-brick Victorian suburb of Ballsbridge. See SPORT.

**LANYON, SIR CHARLES**, (1813-1889). Architect, born in England. He formed a prolific partnership in 1854 with W.H. Lynn, which lasted for over twenty years. Works by him in Dublin include the campanile in Trinity College, 1852-56, the Unitarian Church on St. Stephen's Green, 1860, and Prince of Wales Terrace in Bray, 1861. Lanyon

was also involved in the early stages of the NATIONAL GALLERY design.

**LARKIN, JAMES**, (1876-1947). Labour leader, born of Irish parents in Liverpool, he began work at the age of nine. The living and working conditions of Dublin's poor at the beginning of the twentieth century were appalling. Unskilled labour composed a third of the population, and Larkin, who came to Dublin in 1908, organised these workers, carters, labourers and dockers into the Irish Transport and General Workers Union (ITGWU) in 1909, a movement which was opposed by the employers. The Lockout Strike of 1913, which brought Dublin to a standstill, was caused by the employers' demand that workers sign a statement guaranteeing they would not join Larkin's union. The strike, which lasted from August 1913 to February 1914, caused devastating hardship and many families were actually starving. The police took the side of the employers and attacked the striking workers. This action and Larkin's arrest prompted JAMES CONNOLLY to found the IRISH CITIZEN ARMY to protect the workers from assault. Plans to take the children of destitute families to England where they would be cared for by sympathetic British workers' families were thwarted by the Catholic archbishop and the organisers were arrested on charges of kidnapping. The strike eventually collapsed when support from England and the United States diminished, but the absolute power of the employers had been broken and working conditions gradually began to improve. Larkin also founded the Workers Union of Ireland (WUI) in 1924. OISIN KELLY'S heroic statue of Larkin stands in O'Connell Street, arms raised in dramatic expression of his oratorical powers as leader of

Dublin's powerless poor.
  What Larkin bawled to hungry
     crowds
  Is murmured now in dining-hall and
     study
('Inscription for a Headstone', Austin
Clarke.)

**LATHAM, JAMES**, (1696-1747). Artist, who after considerable Continental travels, established himself as a portrait painter in Dublin, receiving many important society commissions. The NATIONAL GALLERY has a characteristic collection of his work, strong on sour and arrogant looking bewigged aristos, doubtless his bread-and-butter work. More interesting is the double portrait of Bishop Clayton and his wife. The Bishop with his beautifully painted clothes, Latham's forte, is represented as a worldly divine, which as the builder of what became IVEAGH HOUSE, he certainly was. Latham's portrait of ESTHER JOHNSON is more enigmatic and tells little of the vivacious and intellectual Stella who captivated JONATHAN SWIFT.

**LE FANU, JOSEPH SHERIDAN**, (1814-1873). Prolific writer, born 45 Lower Dominick Street, D1. Le Fanu produced sixteen novels and much journalism. One of the founding fathers of the Gothic novel, his writing is concerned with the strange and the macabre. Significant among his large volume of work are, *Turlogh O'Brien*, 1847; *The House by the Churchyard*, 1863; *Uncle Silas*, 1864; and *In a Glass Darkly*, 1872.

**LECKY, WILLIAM HARTPOLE**, (1838-1903). Historian, born Newtown Park, Blackrock, Co. Dublin, he lived in London from 1871. Lecky published *A History of England in the Eighteenth Century* much of which was devoted to Ireland and was an important attempt to reassess Irish history as it was then seen. Lecky became MP for TRINITY COLLEGE in 1895.

**LEECH, WILLIAM JOHN**, (1881-1968). Artist, born at 45 Parnell Square, D1. Leech belongs with JACK B. YEATS and RODERICK O'CONNOR as one of the most significant Irish artists of the first half of the twentieth century. Influenced by French painting, he worked in a Post Impressionist manner, producing coolly observed and beautifully composed and painted studies of figures and landscape. Leech lived in Brittany from 1903-1916 and his work from that period uses the characteristic subject matter of the area, made familiar by the work of many better known Continental artists. Both the NATIONAL GALLERY and the HUGH LANE GALLERY have outstanding examples of Leech's work which has in recent years become immensely popular with the public and sought after by collectors. Amongst the National Gallery's paintings of particular note are, 'A Convent Garden, Brittany'; 'The Goose Girl, Quimperle'; and 'The Sunshade'.

**LEESON STREET, UPPER AND LOWER**, D4 and D1. Leeson Street, formerly known as Suesey Street, is bisected by the Grand Canal and clearly defined into two areas and periods, the eighteenth century graduating into the nineteenth from west to east. Lower Leeson Street runs from the south east corner of St. Stephen's Green as an undistinguished Georgian street, now known as 'the Strip' and the centre of Dublin's fluctuating population of basement night clubs which only come to life after the rest of the city has put up its collective shutters. Beyond the canal, the street becomes nineteenth-century suburban, with Christ Church, Leeson Park, as its most distinguishing feature.

**LEINSTER HOUSE**, Kildare Street, D2. At the age of twenty-two, James Fitzgerald succeeded to the earldom of Kildare in 1744 and the following year he began to build what was to be the largest Georgian town house in Dublin. Designed by RICHARD CASTLE and known as Kildare House, the eleven-bay, 43m (140ft) façade with a central pediment and Corinthian columns became a characteristic form echoed by other later Georgian buildings in the city, and is even seen as the genesis of the White House in Washington, designed by Dubliner James Hoban. Inside, the house is of many phases and there are rooms designed by Richard Castle, WILLIAM CHAMBERS and JAMES WYATT. The house is now so crowded in by the NATIONAL LIBRARY and MUSEUM that it is difficult to appreciate that it was built in open countryside in a then un-fashionable area on the outskirts of the city. JAMES MALTON in the late eighteenth century described it as 'enjoying in the tumult of a noisy metropolis all the retirement of the country'. In 1766 the Earl of Kildare became First Duke of Leinster and the name of the house was changed to Leinster House, a name it has retained through subsequent history, although the street continued to be called Kildare Street. The Third Duke sold the house to the Royal Dublin Society (RDS) in 1815 who developed it as the core of a national cultural complex with the National Museum and Library flanking its Kildare Street façade and the NATIONAL GALLERY and Natural History Museum flanking the Leinster Lawn front. This brilliantly conceived concentration of scholarship was undermined by the ac-

*Leinster House, from the National Library.*

quisition of Leinster House in 1924 by the Irish Free State Government as a parliament house now called the DÁIL. For the functions of the parliament, see DÁIL.

**LEVER, CHARLES**, (1806-1872). Novelist, born 35 Amiens Street. Lever studied medicine at TRINITY COLLEGE and practised as a doctor for a number of years until he became sufficiently successful as a writer to be able to abandon the profession in 1842. His comic novels depict life in Ireland in a humorous manner for which he has been accused of creating the Stage Irishman. The *Confessions of Harry Lorrequer* was published in 1839 and *Charles O'Malley, the Irish Dragoon*, which gives a picture of his student life in Trinity, in 1841.

Were the lamps of the squares extinguished, and the college left in total darkness, we were summoned before the dean; was the Vice-Provost serenaded with a chorus of trombones and French horns, to our taste in music was the attention ascribed; did a sudden alarm of fire disturb the congregation at morning chapel, Messrs. Webber and O'Malley were brought before the board; – Reading men avoided the building where we resided as they would have done the plague. – Within, the noise and confusion resembled rather the mess room of a regiment towards eleven at night, than the chambers of a college student;

(*Charles O'Malley*, Charles Lever.)

**LIBERTIES, THE.** Historically the Liberties represent areas lying to the south and west of the walled city which were outside the civil jurisdiction of the mayor and council of Medieval Dublin. In present-day terms the area implied by the name is roughly that between Fishamble Street on the east and Bridgefoot Street on the west, stretching south from the Liffey as far as a line running from Long Lane, Malpas Street, Mill Street, and turning at Ardee Street back towards the river. The Liberties were those of the Archbishop, Christ Church, Donore, Earl of Meath, and St. Patrick, but they were also known by other names. Within the walls was the Lord Mayor's Liberty.

The Liberties, as the first areas to develop outside the city walls are important for many reasons, among them the fact that post-Medieval Dublin began here, and only later grew to the north and east. The timber frame cagework houses of the Liberties, the Huguenot Dutch Billies, and nearly all the early eighteenth-century architecture are now long gone, and the area is one of nineteenth-century ARTISANS' DWELLINGS, philanthropic flat developments like those of the IVEAGH TRUST, and a certain number of fine stonebuilt eighteenth- and nineteenth-century warehouses. In the midst of all this are the Medieval CATHEDRALS, ST. AUDOEN'S and remnants of the WALLS OF THE CITY. The restored Queen Anne period TAILORS' HALL is a unique survival in an area of Dublin which has only now begun to be rescued from centuries of economic decline and municipal neglect. The street pattern of the Liberties suggests more of the past than much of what is to be seen today, but despite decline and decay there is still a vitality about the Liberties which gives some sense of the vigorous street life for which it was known. Today, as portfolio-laden art students en route to the National College of Art and Design (NCAD) weave their way through the Thomas Street fruit and vegetable market, one can see that this part of the inner city is beginning to return to its former role as a hive of creativity and craftsmanship in Dublin.

**LIBERTY HALL,** Beresford Place, D1. Designed by Desmond Rea O'Kelly in 1964, the first and only high rise building in Dublin. Liberty Hall, which houses the offices of the Irish Transport and General Workers Union (ITGWU), takes its name from the Union building which was destroyed during the 1916

RISING. Unlike many of the contemporary office developments of the 1960s and 1970s, Liberty Hall has a clearly defined personality, its simple glass sheeted exterior relieved by a rather frivolous corrugated topknot. The irony of this palace becoming the office of the inheritor of Larkin's followers has been acidly commented upon by poet Austin Clarke.

On top, a green pagoda
Has glorified cement,
Umbrella'd the sun. Go, da,
And shiver in your tenement.
('New Liberty Hall', Austin Clarke.)

**LIBRARIES** (See MAP). Dublin city and county public libraries are administered from Cumberland House, Fenian Street, tel 619000, and the system covers individual libraries, and those in schools, institutions, prisons and the mobile service. The principal, and best equipped, branch is in the ILAC Centre, Henry Street, Dublin 1.

AUSTIN CLARKE LIBRARY, Poetry Ireland, 44 Upper Mount Street, D2, tel 684875. The personal library of the poet Austin Clarke forms the core of this collection of books on poetry and general literature. Mon-Fri 2.00-5.00.

BERKELEY LIBRARY, Trinity College. Designed in 1967 by Paul Koralek as the result of an international competition, the new library building fits neatly between the east end of the old library and the Museum building. Faced in granite and concrete, the scale and proportions harmonise successfully with the disparate styles of its neighbours, and internally it has many pleasing features. Access by reader's ticket.

CENTRAL CATHOLIC LIBRARY, 74 Merrion Square, D2, tel 761264. Irish and international Catholic literature in books, magazines and journals, reference and lending library. Mon-Sat 12.00-7.30.

THE CHESTER BEATTY LIBRARY AND GALLERY OF ORIENTAL ART, 20 Shrewsbury Road, Ballsbridge, D4, tel 692386. This library, accumulated by SIR ALFRED CHESTER BEATTY, is one of the finest manuscript collections in the world, and at any one time only a fraction of the extensive collection can be shown. The Chester Beatty is particularly strong in early manuscripts of the Koran, European illuminated manuscripts and books of hours and early printed books. The library building, which was constructed by Sir Alfred Chester Beatty, has been added to with a modern exhibition space designed by MICHAEL SCOTT. As well as manuscript material, the library has an extensive collection of related objects from Eastern cultures. Tue-Fri 10.00-5.00, Sat 2.00-5.00.

DUBLIN PUBLIC LIBRARIES, Central Library, ILAC Centre, Henry Street, D1, tel 734333. The best equipped modern public library in the city, housed on the first floor of the ILAC Centre shopping complex. Computer, video and language laboratory are among the facilities which also include a children's library, Irish and foreign newspapers, journals and magazines, and a music and record library. Mon-Thur 10.00am-8.00pm, Fri-Sat 10.00am-5.00pm.

GILBERT LIBRARY, Pearse Street, D2, tel 777662. Housed in the top floor of the Dublin Corporation branch library, it is based on the personal collection of the historian SIR JOHN GILBERT who over a period of thirty years edited for publication the Royal Irish Academy's collection of Irish manuscripts. The Gilbert Library has the most comprehensive specialist collection of books

*Marsh's Library.*

available relating to Dublin and its history.

GOETHE INSTITUTE, 37 Merrion Square, D2, tel 611155. German cultural centre with library relating to German art, literature and music. Mon-Tue-Thur 4.00-8.00, Wed-Fri 10.00-6.00; Sat 10.00-1.00.

KING'S INNS LIBRARY, Henrietta Street, D1, tel 747134. Law library of the Inns, accessible only to members.

MARSH'S LIBRARY, St. Patrick's Close, off Patrick's Street, D8, tel 753917. SIR WILLIAM ROBINSON who designed the Royal Hospital is also responsible for this delightful building, erected in 1705 to contain the library of Archbishop Narcissus Marsh. When it opened in 1707 it was the first public library in Ireland. It contains around 25,000 books of history, classics, religion and philosophy dating from the sixteenth to eighteenth centuries. Although the building has been smartened up on the outside during

the nineteenth century refurbishment of ST. PATRICK'S CATHEDRAL complex, internally it was not altered and has the atmosphere of a collegiate library. Furnished with dark oak bookcases, and divided into bays by Gothic screens bearing the Archbishop's arms, the users of the library could be locked into the cubicles in order to safeguard the immensely valuable collection of books and manuscripts. Mon-Wed-Thur-Fri 10.00-12.45, 2.00-5.00, Sat 10.30-12.30.

THE NATIONAL LIBRARY OF IRELAND, Kildare Street, D2, tel 765521. The Library and NATIONAL MUSEUM form a pair of buildings flanking the main façade of LEINSTER HOUSE, and were conceived as forming a cultural complex when the Royal Dublin Society (RDS) occupied the house, now the seat of the DÁIL. For security reasons the access to both Library and Museum is now by way of heavily railed off passageways like a henrun! Both buildings were designed by T. N. DEANE and Sons, 1895-90, in a Victorian interpretation of the Palladian style, and they harmonise well with RICHARD CASTLE'S Leinster House of 1745. The National Library is the principal repository of books, newspapers, maps and manuscript material relating to Ireland. More recent newspapers are available on microfiche. The remarkable photographic archives of the Library, including the Lawrence Collection, record all parts of Ireland from virtually the invention of this medium in the mid-nineteenth century. Access to the collection only by reader's card. Mon-Fri 10.00-9.00pm, Sat 10.00-1.00.

ROYAL DUBLIN SOCIETY LIBRARY, RDS, Ballsbridge, D4, tel 680645. The Society, which was established in the eighteenth century to promote the improvement of agriculture in Ireland, has always fostered an interest in all branches of natural philosophy and study of the environment. The members' library is principally of scientific and agricultural interest. Mon-Fri, by arrangement.

ROYAL IRISH ACADEMY LIBRARY, Dawson Street, D2, tel 764222. The Academy, established during the eighteenth century with LORD CHARLEMONT as its first president, is a scholarly body devoted to the study and publication of Irish manuscript sources. Their collection of early Irish manuscripts is the most important in the country. The results of research into topics of antiquarian interest are published in the proceedings of the Royal Irish Academy. Mon-Fri 9.30-5.30.

TRINITY COLLEGE LIBRARY, TCD, D2. The Long Room of Trinity Library can justly claim to be the greatest architectural interior in Ireland, in many ways far more immediately impressive than the treasures which it contains. Famous as the repository of the BOOK OF KELLS, the space itself is a breathtaking achievement which evolved not from the work of a single designer, but as a result of alterations and refinements carried out over a period of 150 years. The Library was designed by Thomas Burgh in 1712-23 as a three-storey building with an open ground-floor arcade above which was the library. Internally, the 64m (210ft) long 'Long Room' had floor to ceiling bookcases on the first floor with an open walkway above, covered by a flat compartmented ceiling. This was transformed between 1856 and 1861 by DEANE and WOODWARD who carried the bookcases up to the second floor and united the two ranges with a timber-sheeted barrel vault. For the purist of Georgian or Victorian architecture

*The Long Room, Trinity College Library.*

the changes may lead to a confusion of styles, but despite that the result is undeniably an imaginative triumph. A collection of marble busts of Classical and eighteenth-century worthies decorate the library, mounted on plinths between each bay and representing, along with the Greek and Latin authors, famous Trinity names like BERKELEY and SWIFT. These busts were originally placed along the balcony of the upper part of the library but are much more accessible where they now stand. The Book of Kells which is the finest illuminated manuscript of the early Middle Ages to survive is displayed in two sections so that four pages can be seen at any one time. Other manuscripts on view are the Books of Durrow and Dimma and also the Medieval BRIAN BORU HARP. Mon-Fri 9.30-4.45, Sat 9.30-12.45.

**LIFFEY, THE.** The river of Dublin, historically the section which runs through the city was known as *Ruirteach* (tempestuous), and the term 'Liffey' referred to the plain, beginning at Islandbridge, through which the river flows. The Classical personification of the river as Anna Livia or Anna Liffey was common usage into the beginning of the twentieth century, and appears thus on eighteenth- and nineteenth-century maps. Joyce developed this anthropomorphic treatment of the river to create ANNA LIVIA PLURABELLE which association seems to have permanently attached itself to the river. The Liffey rises near Liffey Head Bridge on the road from the Sally Gap to Glencree in Co. Wicklow, some 113km (70 miles) from where it flows into the Bay. A spring on the slopes between the Djouce and Kippure Mountains, surrounded by bogland, is its source. The Liffey is interrupted by three reservoirs which greatly diminish its flow, as do the weirs at Lucan and Islandbridge. As the principal freshwater supply to Dublin Bay, the condition of the water is crucial to fish life and recreational activities on the Bay. At the beginning of the twentieth century all the city reach of the Liffey was heavily polluted with direct input of sewage from housing causing an appalling stench between O'Connell Bridge and Ringsend. This situation was much improved by the building of the Ringsend treatment plant and despite occasional lapses, usually caused by industry, the water quality of the Liffey has continued to improve. Among the tributaries of the Liffey, the Camac, DODDER, PODDLE and Tolka have seriously contributed to pollution problems as their general volume of water is unable to cope with the growing suburban demand in their valleys, however this also is being improved with the development of linear parks along the river

*The Source of the Liffey.*

banks and stricter controlling of industrial and domestic emissions. Angling and skiff racing are popular on the Islandbridge stretch of the Liffey, as is angling all the way up the river to the mountains.

**LINEN HALL, THE**. Vast eighteenth-century complex of buildings in the North King Street area of the city, now demolished. Built for the linen traders in 1728, the initial building resembled the ROYAL HOSPITAL on a smaller scale with a courtyard surrounded by two-storey ranges of storerooms and offices, with pedimented and arcaded entranceways. The Linen Hall was a clearing house for fabric mainly manufactured in Ulster, and at its total extent by the early nineteenth century, covered an area of three acres, with six interconnecting courtyards. The decline in the linen trade caused the buildings to become redundant and they were used for a variety of purposes including the Dublin Civic Exhibition of 1914. Seriously damaged during the fighting in the 1916 RISING, the complex was finally demolished to be replaced by corporation housing. Surrounding streets, Coleraine, Lisburn and Lurgan, still bear names relating to the northern dominance of the linen industry.

**LITERARY PUBS.** The Dublin literary drinking places which flourished from the 1940s-1960s, associated with the names of BRENDAN BEHAN, PATRICK KAVANAGH and Flann O'Brien (BRIAN O'NOLAN), and which gained a dubious reputation as pubs in which literary lions 'performed', have now been taken over by a more affluent and less flamboyant generation. Of contemporary Dublin writers there are plenty, but they do not now seek this sort of limelight. The hostelries which were famous for intellectual company – THE BAILEY and DAVY BYRNE'S in Duke Street, MCDAIDS in Harry Street and Mulligans in Townsend Street, all within the Grafton Street orbit – are still worth visiting, but that person in the black sombrero with an abstracted expression is more likely to be a clerk in a record shop than a writer of poetry or of the Great Irish Novel.

**LITTLE JERUSALEM.** Area of the city centred on the South Circular Road and Clanbrassil Street, where Jewish immigrants, refugees of the anti semitic pogroms in Eastern Europe, settled during the late nineteenth century. Today, although the Jewish community has migrated to the suburbs, a Jewish presence is maintained in the area by the IRISH -JEWISH MUSEUM at the old Walworth Road synagogue, and by plaques, one on a house in Clanbrassil Street commemorating the fictitious birthplace of LEOPOLD BLOOM, and another in Bloomfield Avenue, the actual birthplace of Chief Rabbi Hertzog and also in such street names as Rehoboth Avenue.

**LONGFORD, LORD,** (1902-1961). Edward Pakenham, Sixth Earl of Longford, theatrical producer and writer, became involved in the GATE THEATRE in 1931 during a financial crisis, beginning his lifelong association with theatre in Ireland. In 1936 he set up his own company, Longford Productions, sharing the Gate with EDWARDS/MAC LIAMMÓIR, each spending six months in Dublin and the rest of the year touring. Longford produced many translations of his own, from French and Greek Classics, plays by his wife, Christine Longford, and a cross section of modern Irish and European drama. Much of the strength of the amateur dramatic movement in rural Ireland owes its inspiration to the quarter century of touring by the Longford Company which brought professional theatre to village halls all over the country. Lord Longford's translations include some from the Irish, Brian Merriman's *Midnight Court*, and Early Christian poetry. His most successful play, *Yahoo*, was based on the life of JONATHAN SWIFT. He was a member of the Senate, 1946-48. After his death in 1961, Longford Productions ceased to function; their last play was performed the previous year.

**LOOP LINE BRIDGE.** The link between Amiens Street Station and Westland Row, it was built in 1891 and cuts an unfortunate swathe through the heart of the city, obscuring the important western view of the Custom House. The opportunity to place the link under, rather than over the Liffey, as had been successfully done in London, was lost when the city stations were built in an elevated position. If this elevated rail link were considered as a feature rather than an embarrassment, then the offence would be less great. Without advertising hoardings and cleverly painted it could become a visual unit, instead of a neglected eyesore.

**LORD CHANCELLOR'S COACH,** Newbridge Traditional Farm, Newbridge House, Donabate, Co. Dublin, tel 436064. This eighteenth-century coach which is on loan from the NATIONAL MUSEUM is a stunning relic of the opulent lifestyle of a Georgian grandee. Built in London in 1791 for Lord Fitzgibbon, it required a team of six matched horses to pull it.

**LORD EDWARD STREET** and **CORK HILL,** D2. The western continuation of DAME STREET and COLLEGE GREEN, on the north side is Kinlay House Youth Hostel formerly the 'Dublin Working Boys Home and Harding Technical School', by ALBERT E. MURRAY, 1890, and to the west the twelfth-century CHRIST CHURCH CATHEDRAL with restoration by G.E.Street of 1871. On the south side, the Carnegie Trust by MACDONNELL & DIXON, 1927, NEWCOMMEN'S BANK, a 1781 building by THOMAS IVORY of which the Lord Edward Street replica extension is of 1886. Facing down Parliament Street is the CITY HALL by Thomas Cooley, 1768.

**LORD MAYOR, THE.** The Charter of Henry III in 1229 allowed for the appointment of 'a loyal and discreet Mayor', and this office lasted until 1641 when it was reconstituted as Lord Mayor. Two hundred years later, in 1841, the mayoralty was again reorganised, DANIEL O'CONNELL being the first to hold the new office. The Lord Mayor is elected annually from amongst the members of the City Council and he or she chairs the meetings of the Council held at CITY HALL. The office tends by agreement to rotate between the political parties represented on the Council and it has become current practice for office holders not to be re-elected. The last Lord Mayor to hold office for more than two years was Alfie Byrne from 1930 to 1939.

**LOTTS, THE.** Areas to the east of the city centre, north and south of the river, reclaimed from the tidal reaches of the Liffey during the eighteenth century and divided amongst the City Councillors by 'lott'. All the land between Amiens Street, North Strand Road and East Wall Road is artificial landfill created during this period, and was known as the North Lotts. The corresponding area south of the river between Sir John Rogerson's Quay and Pearse Street was the South Lotts. These reclamation schemes were longterm but successful developments which greatly expanded the eastern quarters of the city, simultaneously providing river walls to 'train' the Liffey. The land was reclaimed by enclosing the area with a boundary wall within which building rubble and urban refuse were dumped until a land surface had been created. Brooking's map of 1728, referring to the North Lotts, states 'This part is walled in but as yet over flowd by ye tide.'

**LOVER, SAMUEL,** (1797-1868). Novelist, artist and entertainer, he was born at 60 Grafton Street. From 1835 he lived in London where he successfully pursued a joint career as novelist and artist, illustrating some of his own writing, composing songs and opera libretti. Although better known as a miniaturist, he painted full-scale portraits, one of which, in the NATIONAL GALLERY, must be among the stranger images of Victorian life. Titled 'Mrs Lover and her Daughter Meta', it shows a woman in an enormous garden-party hat, observing a doll-like child she is holding on a pedestal. Although presumably intended to

*Lusk Round Tower.*

represent motherhood – as the floral elements in the painting, hollyhocks and a lily, are symbolic of fecundity and purity – the impression this painting gives is of the child as museum specimen. Lover's novels, *Rory O More*, 1836 and *Handy Andy*, 1842, like those of his contemporary, CHARLES LEVER, give a romantic picture of rural Irish life in the mid-century and were immensely popular in their day.

**LUPPI, ERMENEGILDO**, (1877-1937). Sculptor. A monumental figure group 'La Deposizione' (1930), stands in the grounds of the Department of Education on Marlborough Street, between Tyrone House and its replica building. This finely carved and somewhat surreal white marble sculpture was presented to the Irish people by the government of Italy in gratitude for relief supplies sent to Italy after the Second World War. It was transported to Ireland at the expense of the Italian community in Dublin in 1948. Other than wayside shrines of plaster madonnas put up by local groups and found on many city housing estates and in places like the traffic island at the taxi rank on O'Connell Street, this is one of the few major pieces of religious sculpture on display in Dublin.

**LUSK ROUND TOWER**, Co. Dublin, 24km (15 miles) from city centre. The Medieval bell tower attached to the nineteenth-century Church of Ireland parish church has an Early Christian round tower adapted into its composition. The fifteenth-century tower has a turret at three corners, the fourth corner being occupied by the early round tower, possibly of the sixth century. This is complete to the cornice but lacks the conical cap. The church contains some fine Medieval tombs. See ROUND TOWERS. Bus 33 from Eden Quay.

**LUTYENS, SIR EDWIN**, (1869-1944). English architect and the last major architect to work in the Classical idiom. Three important and very different examples of Lutyen's work in Dublin are on LAMBAY ISLAND, at HOWTH CASTLE and the NATIONAL WAR MEMORIAL at Islandbridge. Another scheme for a building to house HUGH LANE'S collection of paintings was not built. See HA'PENNY BRIDGE.

MC ARDELL, JAMES, (1728-1765). Engraver, born in Cow Lane, he trained in Dublin but made his career in London as the leading mezzotint engraver of the day. He engraved the work of the major contemporary portrait painters such as Joshua Reynolds and Thomas Gainsborough and his work achieved a remarkable level of subtlety. The group of Dublin engravers who dominated mezzotint engraving in London were known as 'the Dublin Scrapers'.

MC CORMACK, COUNT JOHN, (1884-1945). Operatic singer, he won a gold medal in the 1902 FEIS CEOIL, sharing the stage with the unsuccessful contestant JAMES JOYCE. Mc Cormack made his debut in Covent Garden in 1907 and followed this with an outstandingly successful career in opera and as a concert performer. He retired to 'Glena' a large nineteenth-century house overlooking Dublin Bay at Rock Road, Booterstown. The house is marked with a plaque.

MC GRATH, RAYMOND, (1903-1977). Architect and artist, born in Australia in 1948, he became chief architect of the Board of Works in Dublin. An excellent artist and designer, he was working in a period of economic stagnation and many of his schemes remained unrealised. He designed the RHA Gallagher Gallery, the Leinster Lawn Obelisk and the Garda Memorial in the Phoenix Park. For state institutions he designed carpets in modern interpretations of eighteenth-century styles – examples survive at the State Apartments, ÁRAS AN UACHTARÁIN, TRINITY COLLEGE, IVEAGH HOUSE, and LEINSTER HOUSE. He was also responsible for much rebuilding work at DUBLIN CASTLE. Mc Grath was President of the RHA at the time of his death.

MC GUINNESS, NORAH, (1903-1980). Artist, born in Derry, she studied in Dublin and Paris and like NATHANIEL HONE and MAINIE JELLETT before her, developed a personal version of the School of Paris Cubism which she used to great effect in highly decorative and colourful landscapes, figure painting and animal studies. In the early forties, Senator E.A. Mc Guire of the BROWN THOMAS department store invited her to do window designs for the store. So successful were her designs and so strong her sense of Parisian style that she singlehandedly altered the perception of what was possible in this field, from mere window display to an art form. She also worked as an illustrator and stage designer. In her paintings of the birdlife of the sloblands of Dublin Bay, Mc Guinness created some of the finest twentieth-century images of the natural world which makes up Dublin's coastal regions.

MC GUIRE, EDWARD, (1932-1986). Portrait painter and still life artist, he has painted a remarkable series of literary and artistic portraits of the leading contemporary figures in the arts in Ireland. These paintings which grace many book covers and public collections, depict their subjects as ikons of art rather than as psychological studies. Among his subjects have been Patrick Collins, Eilís Dillon, Paul Durcan, Monk Gibbon, Seán Ó Faoláin, Michael Hartnett, Seamus Heaney and Francis Stuart.

MC QUAID, DR JOHN CHARLES, (1895-1973). From 1940, when he became Archbishop of Dublin, McQuaid remained in office for thirty-two years during a period of considerable social change in Ireland. McQuaid was committed to Catholic social welfare and education and instituted an extensive programme of school and church building in the Dublin diocese. He opposed the 1950 Mother and Child social welfare scheme as he considered that it did not pay sufficient heed to Catholic ethics. He had no interest in Ecumenism or changes in church ritual instituted in Rome and had little contact with other Christian denominations during his long period in office.

## MAC BRIDE, MAUD GONNE,

(1866-1953). Revolutionary, muse and social reformer. She was one of a small group of emancipated Irish women who were prominent in the cultural and Nationalist movements of the late nineteenth century. Her beauty, striking personality, and deeply held convictions inspired many to follow her leadership, including Yeats who wrote the play *Cathleen Ni Houlihan* for her, and in which she played the title role. Maude Gonne married Seán Mac Bride, one of the leaders shot after the 1916 RISING. Seán Mac Bride (below) was their son. She campaigned vigorously during her life for the underdog – political prisoners, children and the poor.

## MAC BRIDE, SEÁN, (1904-1988).

Politician and lawyer, son of Maude Gonne Mac Bride, a controversial figure in Irish and international affairs, he was Chief of Staff of the IRA 1936, Minister of External Affairs 1948, founding member of Amnesty International 1961, UN Commissioner for Namibia 1973, and recipient of both the Nobel Peace Prize 1974 and the Lenin Peace Prize 1977. He lived in 'Roebuck', a beautiful eighteenth-century house with a colonial style cast iron verandah.

## MAC LIAMMÓIR, MÍCHEÁL,

(1899-1978). Actor, artist and writer, he was born in Willesden, London, as Alfred Willmore and became a successful child actor on the London stage, playing opposite the equally young Noel Coward. Although not of Irish extraction, he adopted Ireland as his country and became deeply involved in the Irish language and in the founding of the TAIBHDHEARC theatre in Galway in 1928. With HILTON EDWARDS, Mac Liammóir founded the GATE THEATRE in 1928, and for just short of fifty years, acted in and designed a wide range of productions of classic and contemporary plays. A flamboyant personality, he excelled in character roles, ultimately finding the perfect vehicle for his talents as wit, monologist and aesthete in *The Importance of Being Oscar*, and *I Must be Talking to My Friends*, with which he toured the world. Mac Liammóir's artistic work in stage design and illustration, while derivative of Continental artists of the 1890s, was perfect for the presentation of modern theatre, and in this field as in everything else he worked with a great sense of style. The present-day Gate Theatre carries on the Edwards-Mac Liammóir tradition of brilliantly designed and produced contemporary drama.

> The real business of the Gate was with methods of acting, production, design and lighting; and it is in this direction that its influence, at its best and worst, has made itself most strongly felt.

(*Theatre in Ireland*, Micheál Mac Liammóir.)

## MACLISE, DANIEL, (1806-1870).

Artist, born in Cork, he studied there and

in London. Maclise became one of the leading painters of the early Victorian era, excelling in romantic genre and historical subjects. He decorated the Palace of Westminster with a series of murals which occupied him for much of the latter part of his life. The NATIONAL GALLERY houses his mammoth painting, 'The Marriage of the Princess Aoife of Leinster with Richard le Clare, Earl of Pembroke, (Strongbow)', 1854, which forms a catalogue of all the emotive symbols of Irish history as seen from the viewpoint of the mid-nineteenth century. Everything is here, dying Gaels, an aged harper, Hibernia wailing, monastic ruins and in the midst of all this the demure princess being married to the dark and masterful stranger. In the background are scenes of pillage and rapine, and the harp on which the blind harper rests his arm is none other than the BRIAN BORU HARP, symbol of a lost culture. Amongst other Maclise paintings in the Gallery collection is his 'Charles I and his Children before Oliver Cromwell',1836, a subject which received widespread popularity during the Victorian period through reproduction in steel engraving. It remains a classic of the nineteenth-century sentimentalised view of history.

**MADDEN-ARNHOLZ COLLECTION**, Royal Hospital Kilmainham, D8, tel 778526. Remarkable collection of prints presented in 1987 by Claire Madden in memory of her daughter Etain and son-in-law Dr Friedrich Arnholz, who formed the collection. The 1,200 works, which cover the history of European printmaking, represent the masters of the subject with work by Albrecht Dürer, Honoré Daumier, William Hogarth, Edouard Manet, Samuel Palmer, Auguste Renoir and many others. Periodically a selection from this marvellous collection, the only one of its kind in Dublin, is on display at the Royal Hospital. These are small works, virtually miniatures, but the sheer quality of the individual pieces makes the collection one of the most artistically satisfying groups of pictures in any Dublin gallery.

**MAGAZINE FORT**, Thomas Hill, Phoenix Park, D8. Powder and munitions magazine built by the Duke of Wharton in 1732. The fortifications are set into the top of the hill, surrounded by a moat, and largely concealed from view. The interior of what must be one of Dublin's least known buildings has a complex of very interesting diminutive Georgian houses, quarters for the garrison, and rows of vaulted magazines. Military establishments like this – even such archaic ones – for security reasons do not appear on ordnance maps, so a tantalising blank indicates where the fort stands. It was raided by the Republican forces for supplies during 1916 and also in 1939 by the IRA for a similar purpose. The Department of Defence handed the fort over to the Board of Works in 1989, and it is in the process of being restored and will eventually be opened to the public. Bus 23, 25, 26 from Essex Quay. A quatrain attributed to JONATHAN SWIFT casts doubt on the need for military expenditure in the early eighteenth century, half a century after the Boyne.

Behold! a proof of Irish sense!

Here Irish wit is seen!

When nothing's left that's worth
defence,

We build a magazine.

('Epigram', Jonathan Swift.)

**MAHAFFY, SIR JOHN PENTLAND**, (1839-1919). Classical scholar and conversationalist, he wrote in 1887

*Principles of the Art of Conversation*, and influenced the conversational style of OSCAR WILDE and OLIVER ST. JOHN GOGARTY. Mahaffy was a Fellow of TRINITY COLLEGE from 1868 to his death. A noted linguist he translated Egyptian hieroglyphic texts for the pioneer of modern archaeology, Flinders Petrie, as well as being Provost of Trinity, President of the first Georgian Society and of the Royal Irish Academy.

*Malahide Castle.*

**MALAHIDE CASTLE**, Malahide, D5, tel 452337. The Norman Talbot de Malahide family lived here from 1185 to 1976 when, after the death of the last male heir, the Castle and park were bought by Dublin County Council and subsequently opened to the public. The great hall of the Castle houses paintings of the Talbots, now part of the National Portrait Collection. The core of the building is fourteenth-century with Georgian and Victorian additions and there are some very fine oak panelled interiors and an important collection of eighteenth-century furniture. The FRY MODEL RAILWAY MUSEUM of O'Gague trains, tel 452758, is in the Castle outbuildings. Eight miles from Dublin. Mon-Fri 10.00-5.00, Sat, Sun, BH 2.00-5.00, April-October, Sat 11.00-6-00. By train from Connolly Station to Malahide, then a half-mile walk through the grounds. Bus 32A from Lower Abbey Street, 42 from Talbot Street.

**MALTON, JAMES**, (1760-1803). Artist, born in England, son of the architectural draughtsman, Thomas Malton, he was the finest topographical artist to work in Dublin during the eighteenth century. Malton came to Dublin in 1785 and worked for three years in the drawing office of JAMES GANDON during the period when the CUSTOM HOUSE was being built. In 1792 *A Picturesque and Descriptive View of the City of Dublin* was published, containing a set of twenty-five views of the principal public and private buildings in etching and aquatint. These prints, drawn and etched by Malton, represent Dublin in its Georgian heyday, and remain the single most important contemporary representation of what had been achieved during the eighteenth century in architecture and town planning. Shortly after their publication, Malton returned to London where he remained until his death. Original watercolours for the aquatints as well as other views of Dublin are in the National Gallery Collection. A framed set of the prints is on permanent display in the CIVIC MUSEUM and also at the Malton Gallery, 23 St. Stephen's Green. Modern reproductions may be bought at the NATIONAL GALLERY and elsewhere.

**MANDELA, NELSON.** See DAME ELI-ZABETH FRINK.

**MANGAN, JAMES CLARENCE,** (1803-1849). Poet, born in poverty in Fishamble Street and during his brief lifetime never escaped from a situation of acute misery. Despite his background Mangan received a good Classical education in a local school in the Liberties and obtained work as a scrivener in the Ordnance Survey Office and in TRINITY COLLEGE LIBRARY. Without any Irish, Mangan created spirited translations or rather versions of Irish poetry, based on prose transcriptions of Eugene O'Curry, the antiquarian, and other scholars. These translations became the accepted renderings of the originals and were much anthologised until relatively recently, but in fact are as much Mangan's own compositions as translations. Translations from German, Ottoman, Arabic and Coptic make up the body of his work, which like his life is exceptionally melancholy. John Mitchell describes his first sight of the poet, of bizarre and emaciated appearance, in Trinity Library and wondered whether his fame was 'as a magician, a poet, or as a murderer'. Mangan, wasted by opium and alcohol, died in a cholera epidemic. Regarded in his day as The National Poet, he is buried in Glasnevin.

O, the rain, the weary, dreary rain,
How it plashes on the window-sill!
Night, I guess, too, must be on the
  wane,
Strass and Gass around are grown so
  still.
Here I sit, with coffee in my cup —
Ah! 'twas rarely I beheld it flow
In the tavern where I loved to sup
Twenty golden years ago!

('Twenty Golden Years Ago', James Clarence Mangan.)

**MANSION HOUSE, THE,** Dawson Street, D2, tel 761845. The official residence of the Lord Mayor. Despite the Victorian stucco and cast-iron embellishments on the exterior, this is the oldest house in continuous occupation in the city, having been built by a merchant, Joshua Dawson, in 1710, and purchased by the Corporation as a house for the Lord Mayor in 1715. Actually a Queen Anne townhouse, the front façade of red brick was altered in 1851 by Hugh Byrne, and the cast-iron porch added in 1886. Internally much of the original style survives, with heavy dark oak panelling and regal portraits in ornate frames. The Round Room, designed by FRANCIS JOHNSTON, was added in 1821 as a setting for receptions during the visit of George IV. In continual use for fairs and functions, the Round Room comprises, with the supper room, some of the most attractive interior spaces of the late Georgian period in the city. The forecourt of the Mansion House was re-paved during the millennium year with appropriate cobbles and granite paving slabs, restoring just the right balance of detail and texture to give the feel of a Georgian street. Viewing by appointment only.

**MARINO CRESCENT,** Clontarf. Built in 1792 this fine late Georgian crescent originally looked directly onto the Bay, but its view now is obscured by new buildings on the reclaimed land of Clontarf's shore. The only major Georgian crescent in Dublin, the presence of these houses emphasises the gradual westward spread of the city.

**MARKETS.** Street markets anywhere in the world have a shared sense of liveliness and impending chaos. It is just this chaotic confusion, babble of voices and flash of colour which makes them attractive, nowhere more so than in Dublin where the decorous and restrained architecture of the city gives little hint of disorder. Camden Street, Meath Street and Thomas Street, south of the river, Moore Street and Parnell Street on the north side are the principal open air fruit and vegetable markets, and the cheapest places to buy from. They also provide an unrivalled opportunity to listen to the local patois. Smithfield, in the area of the city, Oxmantown (or Eastmantown), to which the Vikings were dislodged after the Normans conquered Dublin in the twelfth century, still hosts an occasional horse fair. On the first Sunday of the month, early in the morning, piebald ponies and potential flat racers are traded here, an unlikely survival in such urban surroundings. Indoor markets tend to deal in secondhand goods, antiques and junk. The Iveagh Market, the oldest, is beginning to graduate from rags and bones to bric-a-brac. Nearby, Christ-Church Market sells principally antiques and secondhand goods, as does Portobello Market in Rathmines and the Blackrock Market. The Corporation Fruit and Vegetable Market for wholesale traders in Chancery Street is, like the Iveagh Market, housed in an imposing Victorian building.

## MARKIEVICZ, COUNTESS CONSTANCE, (1868-1927). Revolutionary,

born into landowning family, the Gore-Booths in Co. Sligo. She went to Paris to study art and in 1900 married a fellow artist, Count Casimir Markievicz of Polish Ukrainian background. A wealthy, beautiful and passionate figure, she became centrally involved in the emerging Nationalist movement in Dublin and in 1909 founded Na Fianna Éireann, a kind of boy scout organisation which trained

*Moore Street.*

boys in drill and the use of arms. Later during the 1913 Lockout, she worked to provide food relief for the strikers' families. In 1916 the Countess was second-in-command of the College of Surgeon's garrison, for which she was condemned to death, but the sentence was commuted to life imprisonment. Released during the amnesty of 1917, she was in the following year elected to Westminster as MP for the borough of St. Patrick's. Although the first woman elected to the London parliament, she did not take her seat. Her opposition to Partition brought her further terms in jail and she continued to be a determined opponent of the status quo for the rest of her life. Public esteem for Constance Markievicz's social involvements was not shared by W. B. YEATS, who presents an exceptionally arid picture of her in his memorable poem on the RISING.

That woman's days were spent
In ignorant good-will,

Her nights in argument
Until her voice grew shrill.
What voice more sweet than hers
When, young and beautiful,
She rode to harriers?
('Easter 1916', W.B. Yeats.)

## MARLAY CRAFT COURTYARD,
Marlay Park, Rathfarnham, D14. Craft complex, established by the Industrial Development Authority (IDA), in the old courtyard of Marlay House. In separate studios are interesting mixtures of craftsman's workshops varying from clock restoration to the carving of inscriptions, pottery, engraving and glassware. EVIE HONE had her studio in this courtyard (plaque). Bus 47B from Hawkins Street.

## MARTELLO TOWERS. Between
Balbriggan and Bray, north and south of DUBLIN BAY, there are now twenty martello towers dotted along the coastline in positions of maximum visibility although there were originally twenty-five. This defensive chain of gun batteries, of which examples are also found around other potentially vulnerable landing points such as the Shannon Estuary and the south coast, was built in 1804 in preparation for an expected French invasion. In fact, they never saw any action and by the time, a century later, when JAMES JOYCE stayed briefly and memorably in the Sandycove martello, they were redundant. Although individual towers differ in detail and in quality of construction, the general form is of a squat round tower of fine granite masonry, with slightly inclined walls. The entrance is always some 2m (7½ft) off the ground, over which is positioned a corbelled machicolation. On the roof terrace a swivel-mounted traversing cannon was positioned, and below this the tower contained two rooms, quarters on the entrance floor and a powder magazine beneath it. Their name is supposed to have come from a similarly constructed tower on Cap Mortella in Corsica which was unsuccessfully besieged by the British navy in 1793. Martellos at DALKEY ISLAND and IRELAND'S EYE can be easily inspected, but the most accessible one is the JOYCE MUSEUM in Sandycove, although alterations have been made here to create an entrance on the ground floor.

## MARTYN, EDWARD, (1859-1924).
Playwright, he was instrumental, with W. B. YEATS and GEORGE MOORE in establishing the Irish Literary Theatre, precursor of the ABBEY THEATRE, in 1899. He also founded the Palestrina Choir at the Pro Cathedral for the performance of liturgical music, and it still sings at an 11.00am Latin Mass on Sundays. But the single most important effort made by this multi-directional individual was to invite Christopher Whall, the pioneer of stained glass revival in England, to design windows for a church on Martyn's family estate in Co. Galway. This move inaugurated Martyn's seminal influence on a school of brilliant Irish stained-glass artists which led to the establishment in Dublin in 1903 of AN TÚR GLOINE, a professional glass studio, directed by A. E. CHILD. Every Irish stained-glass artist of significance was either taught by Child at the Metropolitan Schools, or worked under him at An Túr Gloine.

## MASONIC HALL, Grand Lodge, 17
Molesworth Street, D2, tel 761337. Behind the dignified nineteenth-century façade, bearing Masonic emblems on the tympanum, is a number of impressive interiors concerned with Masonic rit-

uals, in particular the Grand Lodge Hall, which compares favourably with the reception rooms of DUBLIN CASTLE or the Great Hall of the ROYAL HOSPITAL

**MATURIN, CHARLES**, (1782-1824). Gothic novelist and prolific writer, he published *Melmoth the Wanderer*, his finest work, in 1820. OSCAR WILDE, a descendant of Maturin, travelled under the name of Sebastian Melmoth after his release from Reading Jail.

**MERCHANT'S HALL**, Merchant's Quay, D2. Designed by FREDERICK DARLEY in 1821, and despite its small size, the most distinguished building on this rather bland section of the south quays. Merchant's Arch, the passageway under the building, that connects the Crown Alley area to the HA'PENNY BRIDGE, is a permanent location and echo chamber for buskers.

**MERRION SQUARE**, D2. Laid out by JOHN ENSOR for the Fitzwilliam Estate in the 1760s, the square forms the core of the best preserved section of Georgian Dublin. The finest houses and also the first to be developed are on the north and east sides. The south side is much more regular in its roofline and detailing, while the west is dominated by the garden façade of LEINSTER HOUSE, the NATIONAL GALLERY and the NATURAL HISTORY MUSEUM. From Merrion Square the finest eighteenth-century street vistas are to be seen, along the south of the square and Upper Mount Street to the PEPPERCANISTER CHURCH, and along the east side of the square for half a mile of Georgian streets looking south towards the Dublin Mountains. While there are intrusions of modern infill in the area – the ESB buildings in Fitzwilliam Street for instance – in most cases roof and

building lines have been maintained so that one gets a sense of completeness not possible in other parts of the city. Built as townhouses for the nobility and gentry, the houses had become the homes of doctors and lawyers by the nineteenth century and today are almost exclusively offices. The square suffered a narrow escape when the parkland was purchased by the Catholic hierarchy with the intention of building a Catholic cathedral on the site. Fortunately this plan was not proceeded with and although it was officially renamed Bishop Ryan Park in 1974, the land was leased to the Corporation Parks Department who opened it for public use. The principal monument in the square is the Rutland Fountain on the west side, commemorating a Viceroy, and designed by HENRY AARON BAKER in 1791. Within the park a number of small sculptures are set apart in the glades and these have to be sought out. Sundays are the best days to view this part of Dublin, and the Georgian streets generally, as the hazards and obstruction of traffic are absent.

**MIGHT HAVE BEENS**. The buildings which were proposed for Dublin but never built form an interesting area for speculation. In some cases the loss is to be regretted, in others it may be greeted with a deep sigh of relief. The great eighteenth-century architect, Sir John Soane, was asked by the Bank of Ireland to provide designs for a building to occupy the island site bounded by D'Olier, College and Westmoreland Streets. The drawings show a very handsome Classical building, but fate intervened and the sudden availability of the old Parliament House, redundant after the ACT OF UNION in 1801, solved the bank's problem. This may be regarded as a loss for Dublin.

Another exciting, if inappropriate, proposal was for SIR EDWIN LUTYEN'S Modern Art Gallery spanning the Liffey at the Ha'penny bridge. This scheme had few supporters and was quickly abandoned. In 1914 the Abercrombie plan was entered in an architectural competition for two new major public buildings, a Catholic cathedral and national theatre. But due to the intervention of the 1916 RISING nothing was decided until 1922 when this scheme was awarded first prize. This was as close as the plans came to realisation. The planned cathedral, a Florentine Basilica with Celtic round tower as campanile, faced down Capel Street towards the Liffey. Behind it a piazza occupied the space where Henrietta Street now stands. For the national theatre, the whole east side of Parnell Square was to be demolished and a building like the Paris Opera erected to face into O'Connell Street. There are of course many more such might-have-been schemes, and a recurring theme among them is the practical desire to use up what their promoters evidently perceived as wasted land, Merrion Square, Mountjoy Square, St. Stephen's Green and Parnell Square.

**MITCHELL, FLORA,** (1890-1973). Artist, born in the United States, she lived in Dublin from the time of her marriage. Her book *Vanishing Dublin*, 1967, captures the atmosphere of the city prior to the sudden surge of development which occurred in the sixties and seventies, and is an attractive record of old brick façades, alleyways, courts and archways which have indeed vanished. There is a large collection of her drawings and watercolours in the NATIONAL GALLERY, including original material for her book.

**MODEST PROPOSAL, A.** JONATHAN SWIFT'S most savage satirical pamphlet, published in 1729, in which he calmly suggested that the children of the poor might be profitably fattened for consumption at the tables of the rich. The conspicuous waste of human lives, engendered by the desperate conditions in which the poor lived, must have been daily evident to Swift, who lived in a Dublin teeming with beggars and the destitute in stark contrast to the opulent lives of the rich.

**MOLESWORTH STREET,** D2. A street of some early eighteenth-century houses with heavy stone doorcases and gables facing the street, which runs west to east on an axis with the main front of LEINSTER HOUSE. The nineteenth-century MASONIC LODGE has some very interesting interiors, particularly its Grand Hall.

**MOLLY MALONE,** Grafton Street, D2. Opposite the PROVOST'S HOUSE on a street corner stands the rather brazen figure of this famous Dublin street trader with her barrow of 'Cockles and Mussels, Alive, Alive Oh!' The larger than life bronze sculpture by Jeanne Rynhart was erected in 1988 for the DUBLIN MILLENNIUM and at once aroused controversy between those who loved its humour and those who would have preferred something less overtly vulgar. Dressed in early eighteenth-century clothes and with considerable attention to historic details the image of Molly Malone has established itself as a popular meeting place and monument against which to be photographed. The sculpture is popularly known as 'The tart with the cart'.

**MONKSTOWN.** During the eighteenth century an aristocratic suburb of gentlemen's residences and marine villas, today it is an attractive mix of Georgian, Victorian and modern developments and a sought-after residential area. The most significant building in Monkstown is the extraordinary MONKSTOWN CHURCH by JOHN SEMPLE which dominates the approach from the city. This remarkable building, in some hybrid style of its designer's fancy, part Scots Baronial, part Moorish, is one of the few exotics of Dublin's considerable collection of churches, its sheer eccentricity a continual surprise. DART to Monkstown, Bus 7A, 8 from Eden Quay.

**MONTENEGRO.** On the southern side of the ambulatory of Christ Church Cathedral, on the sill of a blind window is a casket with the following inscription, 'This urn contains the ashes of Major Marko Zekov Popovich, Hereditary Royal Standard Bearer of Montenegro who died in London on Oct 26 1934.'

**MONTO**, D1. The notorious brothel quarter of Dublin, the name is Dublin slang for Montgomery Street. From Amiens Street, the block extending between Mecklenburgh Street and Montgomery Street was the centre of Monto and in the period between 1800 and the 1920s was considered to be one of the worst red light districts in any European city, with at least a thousand prostitutes working there openly and without police interference. The large numbers of soldiers garrisoned in the city formed a substantial part of Monto's clientele. In the Circe episode of *Ulysses*, which takes place in the brothel quarter, Joyce describes in graphic detail the sordidness of the area. Monto was closed down in the 1920s and even the street names were changed, Mecklenburgh became Railway Street, and Montgomery, Foley Street.

See the Dublin Fusiliers, the bloody
   ould bamboozeleers
De Wet'll kill the chiselers, Wan,
   two, three:
Marchin' from the Linenhall, there's
   wan for every cannonball,
And Vicky's going to send 'em all
   over the sea; but first,
Send 'em up to Monto, Monto,
   Monto,
Send 'em up to Monto, langeroo to
   you.

('Monto', Boer War period Dublin ballad.)

**MONTPELIER PARADE**, Monkstown Road, Co Dublin. Built between 1795 and 1805, this major terrace of eighteenth-century houses was the first to be developed outside the city in what were then the wilds of Monkstown. The terrace originally commanded an uninterrupted view of DUBLIN BAY.

**MONUMENTS AND SCULPTURES.** One can learn a great deal about any city or culture by an examination of the monuments which it has created, and Dublin's collection of monuments forms an instructive introduction to the local and national preoccupations of the last few centuries. The colonial and post colonial experience that Ireland shares with many other countries has been the cause of an unfortunate atavism which desires the destruction of those monuments commemorating the departed conquerors. In this way Dublin has lost many interesting figures from the past. All its equestrian monuments have trotted off into oblivion, spurred on by a few kegs of gunpowder, and many others have gone in the same way. It is a pity that the affection with which the conquerors of the more distant past, such as the Vikings, are now regarded cannot be ex-

*Famine Monument, by Edward Delaney.*

tended to those of more recent vintage. Among the works by twentieth-century artists, ALEXANDER CALDER, ELIZABETH FRINK, HENRY MOORE, Arnaldo Pomodoro and Richard Serra are found with a strong representation of Irish sculptors, JOHN HENRY FOLEY, Sir Thomas Farrell, John Hogan, EDWARD DELANEY, John Behan, Eamon O'Doherty and many more. ST. STEPHEN'S GREEN, O'CONNELL STREET, TRINITY COLLEGE, ST. PATRICK'S CATHEDRAL and MERRION SQUARE between them account for most of the monuments and sculptures in the city with the greatest concentration at the Green.

'ADULT AND CHILD SEAT', 1988, Jim Flavin: St. Catherine's Park.

AE (George William Russell), 1925, Jerome Connor: 8 Merrion Square.

ALBERT, PRINCE, 1871, John Henry Foley: Leinster Lawn, Merrion Square.

'ANNA LIVIA', 1988, Eamon O'Doherty & Seán Mulcahy: O'Connell Street.

'ARCHER II', 1985, Niall O'Neill: Sandycove.

ARDILAUN, LORD, 1892, Sir Thomas Farrell: St. Stephen's Green.

'THE AWAKENING', 1990, Linda Brunker: Earlsfort Piazza.

'BAITE', 1988, Betty Maguire: Essex Quay.

BALDWIN, PROVOST, 1784, Christopher Hewetson: Trinity College.

'THE BLACK ROCK', 1986, Rowan Gillespie: Blackrock Village.

BOER WAR, 1907: St. Stephen's Green.

BOYD, CAPTAIN J. MCNEILL, 1861: East Pier, Dun Laoghaire.

BOYLE, RICHARD (Earl of Cork), 1632, Edmond Tingham: St. Patrick's Cathedral.

BUCKINGHAM, MARQUIS OF, 1813, Edward Smyth: St. Patrick's Cathedral.

BURKE, EDMUND, 1868, John Henry Foley: College Green.

'CACTUS', 1967, Alexander Calder: Trinity College.

'CARNAC', Bob Mulcahy: Leeson Street Upper.

'CELEBRATION', 1986, Dick Joynt: Glasthule.

'CHARIOT OF LIFE', 1982, Oisin Kelly: Talbot Street.

CHARLES II 17th C, William de Keyser: Crypt, Christ Church Cathedral.

'CHILDREN OF LIR', 1971, Oisin Kelly: Parnell Square.

'CHRIST THE KING' & WORLD WAR I, 1926, Andrew O'Connor: Dun Laoghaire.

COLLINS, GRIFFITH, O'HIGGINS, 1950, Raymond McGrath: Leinster Lawn, Merrion Square.

CONYNGHAM, ARCHBISHOP, 1901, Sir Hamo Thorneycroft: Kildare Street.

'THE CRAFTS', 1863: Millennium Garden, Dame Street.

'CÚCHULAINN', 1911, Oliver Sheppard: GPO, O'Connell Street.

CULLEN, CARDINAL, 1881, Sir Thomas Farrell: Pro Cathedral, Marlborough Street.

CUSTOM HOUSE GARRISON, 1955, Yann Renard Goulet: North Façade, Custom House.

'CUT OUT PEOPLE', 1986, Dan Mc Carthy: Blackrock Park.

DARGAN, WILLIAM, 1864, Sir Thomas Farrell: Forecourt, National Gallery.

'DARK NIGHT', 1981, Michael Warren: Dublin Port.

'DARK ROSALEEN', 1916, William Pearce: St. Stephen's Green.

DAVIS, THOMAS, 1966, Edward Delaney: College Green.

DAVIS, THOMAS, 1853, John Hogan: City Hall.

'LA DEPOSIZONE', 1937, Ermenegildo Luppi: Marlborough Street.

DONERAILE, ELIZABETH, c1761, Simon Vierpyl: St. Patrick's Cathedral.

DRUMMOND, THOMAS, 1843, John Hogan: City Hall.

'ÉIRE' (Kerry Poets Memorial), 1926, Jerome Connor: Merrion Square.

EMMET, ROBERT, 1917, Jerome Connor: St. Stephen's Green.

'FAMINE', 1967, Edward Delaney: St. Stephen's Green.

FARRELL, JEANETTE MARY, 1841, John Hogan: St. Andrew's, Westland Row.     FIANNA ÉIREANN, 1966 A.J. Breen: St. Stephen's Green.

FIELD, JOHN, 1988, Colum Brennan and Leo Higgins: Golden Lane.

'FOR PEACE COMES DROPPING SLOW', 1989, Colm Brennan: Earlsfort Piazza.

'THE FOUR MASTERS', 1876: Eccles Street.

'FREEDOM', 1985, Alexandra Wejchert: AIB Bankcentre, Ballsbridge.

'AN GALLÁN GRÉINE DO JAMES JOYCE' 1983, Cliodna Cussen: Sandymount Beach Road.

GARDA SIOCHÁNA, 1972, Raymond McGrath: Garda Headquarters, Phoenix Park.

GEORGE IV, 1821: Marine Road, Dun Laoghaire.

'GEORGE IV'S FOOTPRINTS', 1821, Robert Campbell: West Pier, Howth.

'GOATS', 1986, Cathy Goodhue: Dillon Park, Dalkey.

GOLDSMITH, OLIVER, 1861, John Henry Foley: College Green.

GRATTAN, HENRY, 1879, John Henry Foley: College Green.

GRATTAN, HENRY, 1982, Peter Grant: Merrion Square.

GRATTAN, HENRY, 1829, Sir Francis Chantrey: City Hall.

'GREENWELLS GLORY', 1983, Sean Adamson: East Link Bridge.

GREY, SIR JOHN, 1879, Sir Thomas Farrell: O'Connell Street.

GUINNESS, SIR BENJAMIN LEE, 1875, John Henry Foley: St Patrick's Cathedral.

'HEAD', 1985, Tom Glendon: Swan's Hollow, Glenageary.

'HERALDS OF THE FOUR PROVINCES', 1966, Edward Delaney: College Green.

HEUSTON, SEÁN, 1943, Lawrence Campbell: People's Gardens, Phoenix Park.

JAMES II, William de Keyser: Crypt, Christ Church Cathedral.

JOYCE, JAMES, 1990, Marjorie Fitzgibbon: North Earl Street.

JOYCE, JAMES, 1982, Marjorie Fitzgibbon: St. Stephen's Green.

KETTLE, T.M., 1937, Albert Power: St. Stephen's Green.

KILDARE, EARL OF, c1743, Sir Henry Cheere: Christ Church Cathedral.

'THE KISS', 1989, Rowan Gillespie: Earlsfort Piazza.

'KNIFE EDGE' (In memory of W.B.Yeats), 1967, Henry Moore: St. Stephen's Green.

LARKIN, JAMES, 1981, Oisin Kelly: O'Connell Street.

LECKY, WILLIAM H, 1906, W. Goscombe John: Trinity College.

'LIBERTY BELL', 1988, Vivienne Roche: St. Patrick's Park.

LUCAS, DR. CHARLES, 1772, Edward Smyth: City Hall.

'MAN ON TRESTLE', 1987, Carolyn Mulholland: Wilton Place.

MANGAN, JAMES CLARENCE, 1909, Oliver Sheppard: St. Stephen's Green.

'THE MARINER', 1973, John Behan: North Wall Quay.

MARKIEVICZ, CONSTANCE, 1956, Seamus Murphy: St. Stephen's Green.

MATHEW, FATHER THEOBALD, 1891, Miss Redmond: O'Connell Street.

'MEETING PLACE', 1988, Jakki McKenna: Lower Liffey Street.

MERCHANT SHIPPING, 1990, Anon: City Quay.

MISTER SCREEN, 1988, Vincent Browne: Townsend Street.

'MOLLY MALONE', 1988, Jeanne Rynhart: Grafton Street.

'MONUMENT TO THE AXE', 1983, Niall O'Neill: East Link Bridge.

MOORE, THOMAS, 1854, Christopher Moore: College Street.

'MOUNT STREET MEMORIES', 1988, Derek A. Fitzsimons: Upper Mount Street.

MURRAY, ARCHBISHOP, Sir Thomas Farrell: Pro Cathedral, Marlborough Street.

O'CAROLAN, TURLOUGH, 1824, John Hogan: St. Patrick's Cathedral.

O'CONNELL, DANIEL, 1932, Andrew O'Connor: National Bank, Dame Street.

*Tribute Head, in honour of Nelson Mandela, by Elizabeth Frink*

O'CONNELL, DANIEL 1854, John Henry Foley: O'Connell Street.

O'CONNELL, DANIEL, 1846, John Hogan: City Hall.

O'DONOVAN ROSSA, JEREMIAH, 1954, Seamus Murphy: St. Stephen's Green.

PARKE, T.H., 1896, Percy Wood: Leinster Lawn, Merrion Square.

PARNELL, CHARLES STEWART, 1911, Augustus Saint-Gaudens & Henry Bacon: O'Connell Street.

'PEOPLE'S ISLAND', 1988, Rachel Joynt: traffic island at the junction of Westmoreland Street and D'Olier Street.

'PHOENIX COLUMN', 1745: Main Avenue, Phoenix Park.

'RECLINING CONNECTED FORMS', 1969, Henry Moore: Trinity College.

'RED SAILS AT SUNSET', 1986, Bernard Mortell: Seapoint.

'REFLECTIONS', 1975, Michael Bulfin: Bank of Ireland, Baggot Street.

'RELEASE' 1983, Jim Buckley: East Link Bridge.

ROYAL ZOOLOGICAL SOCIETY OF IRE-LAND, 1980, Colm Brennan: Dublin Zoo, Phoenix Park.

SALMON, PROVOST GEORGE, 1911, John Hughes: Trinity College.

'SEÁN'S SPIRAL', 1984, Richard Serra: Crane Street, off Thomas Street.

SHAW, G.B, 1927, Paul Troubetzkoy: Forecourt, National Gallery.

SMITH O'BRIEN, WILLIAM, 1870, Sir Thomas Farrell: O'Connell Street.

'AN SPÉIR BHEAN', 1990, Robin Buick: Windsor Place.

'SPHERE WITH SPHERE', 1982, Arnaldo Pomodoro: Trinity College.

'STELE FOR CECIL KING', 1986, Colm Brennan: Temple Hill, Blackrock.

STEWART, SIR RICHARD, 1875, Sir Thomas Farrell: Leinster Lawn.

'STEYNE', 1984, Cliodna Cussen: College Street.

STRONGBOW, 13th C: St. Patrick's Cathedral.

SWIFT, JONATHAN, 1766, Patrick Cunningham: St. Patrick's Cathedral.

TALBOT, MATT, 1988, James Power: Talbot Memorial Bridge.

'THREE FATES', 1956, Josef Wackerle: St. Stephen's Green.

'THUS DAEDALUS FLEW', 1986, Niall O'Neill: Killiney Hill.

TONE, THEOBALD WOLFE, 1967, Edward Delaney: St. Stephen's Green.

'TOWER', 1976, Edward Delaney: Lower Mount Street.

'TRACE', 1988, Grace Weir: traffic island, St. Stephen's Green.

'TREE CHAIR', 1988, Carolyn Mulholland: South Great George's Street.

'TRIBUTE HEAD', 1975, Elizabeth Frink: Merrion Square.

'UNTITLED', 1974, Gerda Fromel: Setanta Centre, Nassau Street.

'UNTITLED', 1978, John Burke: Bank of Ireland Headquarters, Baggot Street.

'THE VICTIMS', 1920, Andrew O'Connor: Merrion Square.

WELLINGTON, DUKE OF, 1817, Robert Smirke: Phoenix Park.

'WIND SCULPTURE', 1988, Eamon O'Doherty: Clontarf Promenade.

YEATS, W.B. 1925, Albert Power: Sandymount Green.

## MOORE, GEORGE, (1852-1933).

Novelist and playwright, born to a Co. Mayo landowning family, he lived in London and Paris and established a reputation with his realistic novels of contemporary life, *A Drama in Muslin*, 1887, and *Esther Waters*, 1894. He became involved in the Irish Literary Revival and moved to Dublin in 1900 where he lived for ten years, but eventually became disillusioned with the prospects for any further achievement and returned to London. His autobiographical *Hail and Farewell*, 1911-14, gives an amusing and jaundiced picture of Dublin during his years there. Moore lived at 4 Ely Place (plaque), and the RHA Gallagher Gallery is partially built on his gardens.

## MOORE, HENRY, (1898-1986). The

most celebrated British sculptor of the twentieth century, there are two characteristic works of his in Dublin, the W.B.YEATS memorial, 'Knife Edge', 1967, in St. Stephen's Green, and a reclining figure, 'Reclining Connected Forms', 1969, on the lawns in front of the Rubrics in Trinity College. Despite the existence of these two important works in Dublin, very few of the recent monuments around the city can be said to show any evidence of Moore's influence, with the possible exception of the sculpture by Jim Flavin in St. Catherine's Park.

## MOORE STREET. See HENRY STREET.

## MOORE, THOMAS, (1779-1852).

Poet and songwriter, born at 17 Aungier Street (plaque). His songs, set to Irish airs, have proved to be of enduring popularity, both as ballads and on the concert hall stage, and have been arranged by many composers from Mendelssohn to Hindemith. He published these songs as *Irish Melodies* from 1808 onwards, and they brought him considerable wealth and social acclaim. As a biographer he wrote lives of LORD EDWARD FITZGERALD and Byron, the latter of whom left Moore his memoirs, which Moore subsequently destroyed.

## MORGAN, SYDNEY OWENSEN, LADY, (1775-1859). Novelist, she

popularised a romantic image of Irish life in her work, presenting the dispossessed Gaelic nobleman as a tragic rather than villainous individual. The fine O'Carolan relief by JOHN HOGAN in ST. PATRICK'S CATHEDRAL, erected as a memorial to the musician, was carved as a result of a bequest in Lady Morgan's will, left specifically for this purpose.

## MORRISON, SIR RICHARD,

(1767-1849), and his son WILLIAM VITRUVIUS MORRISON, (1794-1838). Architects, they had an extensive practice designing notable country houses such as Fota, Co. Cork. In Dublin their principle buildings are the Georgian Sir Patrick Dun's Hospital, 1803, located in Grand Canal Street, designed by Sir Richard, and CLONTARF CASTLE, designed as a country house in the Gothic Revival manner by William Vitruvius, 1836.

## MOUNT JEROME CEMETERY,

Harold's Cross, D8. In this cemetery, first opened in 1836, are gathered the most interesting funerary monuments in Dublin. Established as a non-denominational cemetery a few years after GLASNEVIN, it became principally a Protestant burial place. The style of monument here is predominantly Neo-Classical in contrast with the Celtic imagery of Glasnevin and there are many finely designed family vaults and individual memorials. Amongst the famous Dubliners buried in Mount Jerome are AE, Thomas Davis, Edmund Dowden, Thomas Gresham of hotel fame, WILLIAM LECKY, SHERIDAN LE FANU, Thomas Kirk, Walter Osborne, George Petrie, JOHN MILLINGTON SYNGE and SIR WILLIAM WILDE. A group of Huguenot re-interments from 'French Peter's' in Peter Street are commemorated on a slab bearing an exhaustive list of Huguenot names, although the plot, like much of the cemetery is quite neglected. There are also some fine Neo-Egyptian vaults designed by John Mulvany, designer of the BROADSTONE Railway Station and other fine nineteenth-century buildings. Bus 16, 16A from O'Connell Street, 54, 54A from Burgh Quay.

## MOUNT PLEASANT SQUARE,

Ranelagh, D6. Fine two- and three-storey brick houses around three sides of a square with gently bowed sides. This delightful example of late Georgian architecture, built around 1830, has all the essentials of the mansions of Merrion Square, but scaled down to dolls' house proportions. The central park has mostly been cannibalised for tennis facilities. From Ranelagh Road, looking along the west side of the square, the magnificent dome of Rathmines Church provides one of the finest examples of streetscape in Dublin.

**MOUNTJOY JAIL**, North Circular Road, D7. Mountjoy is the setting for BRENDAN BEHAN's play, *The Quare Fellow*, and the dramatic silhouette and oppressive presence of Mountjoy dominate a stretch of the Grand Canal. Built in 1847 as an example of enlightened penal architecture, five wings of cells branch from a central block and what appear as tall chimney stacks are in fact air vents designed to improve the usually fetid atmosphere. The jails, which Mountjoy was built to replace, such as the Marshalsea, Newgate Gaol and Smithfield Penitentiary where the living conditions were utterly appalling, have all been demolished. Only KILMAINHAM PRISON, now a museum of political history, remains as an example of earlier prison conditions. Bus 10, 22, 22A from O'Connell Street.

**MOUNTJOY SQUARE**, D1. Laid out by LUKE GARDINER, Lord Mountjoy, between 1780 and 1798 but not completed until the 1820s, it is the only one of Dublin's Georgian squares to have sides of equal length. Unlike Merrion Square where the visible fabric, if not the interiors, has been preserved, Mountjoy Square has been seriously diminished by demolition on the south and west sides of the square, without adequate replacement of the buildings removed. The square as originally conceived had a church, ST. GEORGE'S, later built in Hardwicke Place, in the centre of the park. The streets were monumental composi-

tions, each side developed into a unified façade with end pavilions and a domed and pedimented central block. None of this materialised, the square as eventually built being much more modest. More so than the bustling area south of the river, an aura of calm pervaded these Georgian streets as when all the houses were lived in. Not being manicured like Merrion Square adds to the sense of reality.

> Tall brick houses, browbeating each other in gloomy respectability across the white streets; broad pavements, promenaded mainly by the nomadic cat; stifling squares, wherein the infant of unfashionable parentage is taken for the daily baking that is its substitute for the breezes and press of perambulators on the Bray Esplanade or the Kingstown Pier. Few towns are duller out of season than Dublin, but the dullness of its north side neither waxes nor wanes; it is immutable, fixed as the stars.

(*The Real Charlotte*, Somerville and Ross, 1894.)

**MOVING CRIB**, St. Martin's Apostolate, 42 Parnell Square, D1, tel 730147. This display is rather more than its name implies and consists of a series of separate tableaux including over eighty figures presenting biblical and new testament scenes. The animated figures carved in Germany in the 1950s by J. Hoffman are in a combination of Walt Disney and traditional German puppetry styles. Included in the display is 'Fred', a stuffed pet dog who saved many people from drowning in the Liffey! The best free show for small children in Dublin. Dec-Jan, Mon-Sat 1.00-6.00, Sun 11.30-6.00, other times by appointment.

**MULVANY, JOHN SKIPTON**, (1813-1870). Architect, he designed a number of important late Georgian buildings around the city. BROADSTONE and DUN LAOGHAIRE Railway Stations, and the Royal Irish Yacht Club are the most well known of his buildings but he also designed many private houses in the suburbs. Mulvany designed his own house, No. 5 Brighton Vale, Monkstown, many Egyptianesque funerary monuments in MOUNT JEROME and also the mausoleum-like ANEMOMETER on the East Pier in DUN LAOGHAIRE, the smallest major building in Dublin.

## MUSEUMS AND COLLECTIONS

(See MAPS). Museums are both publicly and privately run, in state institutions and private houses, and vary in scale and intimacy, as well as in the standards of display and scholarship of the exhibits. Frustratingly, financial considerations have forced many of the national institutions to maintain only skeleton staff levels, with a consequent closing down of whole sections of the museums. It is advisable to check beforehand, if one wishes to view a particular section of any state collection other than the most important ones. Admission to all museums is free, unless otherwise stated.

ARMY MUSEUM, Department of Defence, Infirmary Road, D8, tel 771881. Collection related to the history of the national army since its inception at the foundation of the state, to service during the Emergency and overseas with the UN forces. Open by arrangement. Bus 10 O'Connell Street, 26 Middle Abbey Street.

BEWLEY'S MUSEUM CAFÉ. See BEWLEY'S.

BRAY MUSEUM, Town Hall, Bray, Co. Wicklow, tel 862539. Museum of local history housed in the Tudor Revival town hall, concentrating on the life of the people with examples of domestic and

*In the National Museum.*

agricultural artifacts. Wed-Sat-Sun, 2.30-5.00. DART to Bray.

BROADCASTING MUSEUM, Lower Rathmines Road, D6, tel 932789. Old broadcasting equipment and memorabilia of the early days of RTE when its call sign was 2 RN. Tue-Sat by arrangement.

CHESTER BEATTY LIBRARY AND GALLERY OF ORIENTAL ART. See LIBRARIES.

CIVIC MUSEUM, 58 South William Street, D2, tel 794260. Devoted to the history of Dublin and housed in the old City Assembly House, built for the Society of Artists in 1765, a rather dowdy eighteenth-century building which was opened as a museum in 1953. Permanent collection of artifacts relating to all aspects of the city's development. Changing exhibitions are held which deal with specialist areas of Dublin history. The permanent collection traces the city's growth and change in maps, prints and relics of social and political events. The battered head by Thomas Kirk from the ill-fated NELSON PILLAR is here, as is a shop sign damaged when a secret arms depot blew up during the EMMET rebellion of 1803, and the gargantuan shoes of the IRISH GIANT. JAMES MALTON'S celebrated views of Georgian Dublin can be compared with prints by other artists and the individual exhibits complement the artistic impressions with functional items from the Georgian and many other periods. Tue-Sat 10.00-6.00, Sun 11.00-2.00. Free.

CLASSICAL MUSEUM, UCD, Belfield, D4, tel 693244, ext 8218. Classical antiquities from the Graeco-Roman world.

DUBLIN CORPORATION ARCHIVES, City Hall, Dame Street, D2, tel 6796111, ext 2818. Housed in the City Hall, the archive contains historic records of the municipal government of Dublin from the first Charter issued in 1192 by John, King of England and Lord of Ireland, up to the present day. Manuscript records, maps, charters, correspondence and deeds are stored in the archives and are available for research purpose. Much of this material has been published but a substantial body remains only in manuscript form and these documents constitute the most comprehensive collection of documents relating to the history of Dublin available. Mon-Fri 10.00-1.00, 2.15-5.00. An advance appointment is desirable.

DUBLIN WRITERS' MUSEUM, 18-19 Parnell Square North, D1. Opened in 1991 to celebrate Dublin's year as European City of Culture, the Writers' Museum is housed in two adjoining eighteenth-century houses which have been restored but retain many original features. The museum incorporates a library, exhibition of memorabilia of Dublin writers, rare books, children's section, sound library, café and shop. A living writer's workshop is an integral part of the centre and poetry readings and other literary events take place. Mon-Fri 10.00-5.00, Sat 12.00-5.00.

EGESTORFF COLLECTION, 25 Wellington Place, D2, tel 689325. Private collection of early scientific instruments. View by appointment only.

ESB GEORGIAN RESIDENCE MUSEUM, 29 Lower Fitzwilliam Street, D2, tel 765831. The National Museum collection of eighteenth-century furniture is the basis for this display which demonstrates the workings of a Georgian house. Housed in a Georgian house which has been restored by the ESB, the museum also contains a restaurant and audio visual display. Mon-Fri 9.00-5.00.

FRY MODEL RAILWAY, Malahide Castle, Malahide, Co. Dublin, tel 452337. Working O'Gague scale models of railway layout, with many old Dublin trams and trains represented as well as curiosities from other parts of the country. Stations, sidings, bridges and the Liffey are all part of the extensive layout, with the DART and other trains shunting and running around miles of track. Mon-Fri, 10.00-5.00, Apr-Oct, Sat 11.00-6.00, Sun 2.00-6.00, Nov-Mar, Sat Sun 2.00-6.00. Admission charge. Train from Connolly Station. Bus 32A from Lower Abbey Street, 42 from Talbot Street.

GARDA MUSEUM, Garda Headquarters, Phoenix Park, D8, tel 771156. The history of the national police force since 1922, with many interesting exhibits showing the changing image of the policeman by way of uniforms, photographs and documents. View by arrangement only. Bus 10 O'Connell Street, 26 Middle Abbey Street.

GEOLOGICAL MUSEUM, TCD, D2, tel 772941. Collection of mineralogical and palaeontological specimens showing the development of the earth's geological formation.

GEOLOGICAL SURVEY OF IRELAND, Beggar's Bush Barracks, Haddington Road, D4, tel 609511. Collection of specimens relating to the geology of Ireland. Mon-Fri 2.30-4.30.

GEOLOGY MUSEUM, Museum Building, TCD, D2, tel 772941 ex 1477. Collection of fossils and minerals, primarily of Irish origin, also some interesting specimens from other countries, in particular Dinosaur fragments from Mongolia. Wed 2.00-4.00. School parties by appointment.

GUINNESS MUSEUM, The Hop Store, Crane Street, off Thomas Street, D8, tel 536700. The history of the great brewing firm is shown here in buildings formerly used in the production of Guinness. Fine equipment from the nineteenth century is surrounded by posters and objects relating to the development of brewing in Dublin. Mon-Fri 10.00-4.00. Bus 21A, 78, 78A, 78B from Fleet Street.

IRISH MUSEUM OF MODERN ART (IMMA), Royal Hospital Kilmainham, D8, tel 718666. The museum, housed in the seventeenth-century Royal Hospital, opened in 1991 as a centre for visual arts of the twentieth century. Work by the key figures in the Irish modern art movement is shown in the context of exhibitions of international contemporary art and a number of important individual collections, such as the Sidney Nolan Bequest and the O'Malley-Roelofs collection, are displayed in the museum. The emphasis is on the art of the latter part of the century, the earlier part being dealt with by the HUGH LANE GALLERY and also to a lesser degree by the NATIONAL GALLERY. Tue-Sat 2.00-5.00, Sun 12.00-5.00. Admission charge. Bus 23, 25, 26 from Essex Quay.

THE IRISH NATIONAL MARITIME MUSEUM, Haig Terrace, Dun Laoghaire, Co. Dublin, tel 800969. Appropriately housed in the old Mariner's Church and concerned with Ireland's involvement with the sea. The exhibits which fill the nave and galleries of the church display with paintings, photographs, models, and actual marine objects, the dangers and heroism of those who sail around Ireland's coast and on the high seas. In the apse the magical optic of the Baily Lighthouse continues to rotate, flashing its prismatic light across the French longboat from the ill fated 1796 Bantry expedition of which WOLFE TONE was a member, and reflecting on all manner of interesting exhibits, each representing a chapter in the still continuing struggle with the seas. Models of lifeboats, a diving suit, the uniform of Robert Charles Halpin, chief officer of the Great Eastern – which made the first transatlantic crossing under steam – and many documents elaborate the fascinating story. May-Sept, Tue-Sun 2.30-5.30, Apr, Oct, Nov, Sat, Sun 2.30-5.00. Closed Dec - Mar. Admission charge. DART to Sandycove.

IRISH PRINT MUSEUM, 35 Lower Gardiner Street, D1, tel 743662. Run by the Irish Print Union, the museum covers the history of printing and has examples of printing presses, documents and photographs relating to the development of printing technique. Mon-Fri, by arrangement.

IRISH RAILWAY RECORDS SOCIETY, Heuston Station, D8. For the railway enthusiast Heuston Station remains a favourite because of its relatively well preserved buildings and trainsheds. The society's collection of photographs and 'age of steam' relics evoke the great days of railway travel in Ireland. Tue 8.00pm by arrangement. David Murray, hon sec, 24 Avondale Lawn, Blackrock, Co. Dublin. Bus 23, 24, 26 from Essex Quay.

IRISH WHISKEY CORNER, Bow Street, D7, tel 725566. The last remnants of what was one of Dublin's most important industries – distilling – were preserved at Irish Distillers after the actual manufacturing processes of whiskey were moved out of the city. All the curious distilling equipment, looking like an alchemist's lair, is on display here – pot stills, cooperage, and the many brands of bottles in which the brew was marketed. Mon-Fri 3.30 tour.

IRISH-JEWISH MUSEUM, 3-4 Walworth Road, off Victoria Street, Portobello, D8, In the centre of what used to be the Jewish quarter of nineteenth-century Dublin, the now redundant Walworth Road synagogue has been restored and below it the building has been transformed into a museum which records the life of the Jewish community in Dublin. As well as a fascinating collection of objects relating to Jewish life and rituals, the larger European context is also dealt with. May-Sept, Sun-Tue-Thur 11-00-3.30, Oct-Apr, Sun 10.30-2.30. Closed on Jewish holidays. Bus 16, 16A, 19, 19A from O'Connell Street.

JAMES JOYCE MUSEUM, Sandycove Martello Tower, Sandycove, Co. Dublin, tel 809265. The opening scenes of *ULYSSES* take place in the interior and on the roof terrace of the Sandycove martello tower which now houses the James Joyce Museum, and the collection is a fascinating assemblage of objects associated with Joyce. The museum is in the nature of a shrine to the writer, his family and circle, and the personal quality of some of the exhibits – Joyce's cane, guitar and a waistcoat embroidered by his grandmother – create a palpable sense of his presence. A library of books by and about Joyce, manuscripts, letters and photographs fill in much more of the picture of the writer in exile conjuring up his native city in mythological form while living in a European ambiance which could hardly have been less like Dublin. Joyce lived in the tower for only six days in 1904, as the guest of OLIVER ST. JOHN GOGARTY who was then renting it. Many years later the circular shape of the building provided Joyce with the symbolism he required for a pivotal structure in *Ulysses*, and those few days were immortalised. The martello tower was built in 1804 as part of a coastal defence network being constructed by the War Office to withstand an expected French invasion. Built of local granite with two vaulted rooms, the lower of which was the powder magazine, the armament was a traversing cannon mounted on the roof. The martellos never saw any action and were redundant exactly a century later when Gogarty took over the Sandycove one. In the 1950s the architect MICHAEL SCOTT bought the tower and it was opened in 1962 by Sylvia Beach, the publisher of *Ulysses*, as a Joyce museum. Since then an extension has been added to provide additional exhibition space and a bookshop. Apr-Oct, Mon-Sat 10.00-1.00, 2.00-5.00, Sun 2.30-6.00. Admission charge. DART to Sandycove, bus 8 from Eden Quay.

KILMAINHAM JAIL MUSEUM, Inchicore, D8, tel 535984. Museum of Irish political history displayed within a prison building which was built shortly after the 1798 rebellion and where many of the rebels of subsequent times were incarcerated. The guest list of Kilmainham is a virtual who's who of Irish nineteenth- and early twentieth-century revolutionary history, and everybody from CHARLES STEWART PARNELL to PATRICK PEARSE and the other 1916 leaders spent time there. The architecture of the prison with its companionways, caged staircases and glazed barrel vault is impressive in an intimidating manner, as are the individual cells. Over the entrance to the prison is a bas relief suggestive of the building's purpose, should one be in any doubts about the matter. This shows five squirming and enraged serpents, heavily chained. It is not clear whether this was intended to assure the public that the villains were appropriately incarcerated, or to impress their impending fate upon the inmates. From either point of view the message is chilling. June-Sept, 7 days, 11.00-6.00. Tours by arrangement, Oct-May, Wed & Sun 2.00-6.00. Admission charge. Bus 79 from Aston Quay.

MUSEUM OF CHILDHOOD, 20 Palmerstown Park, Rathmines, D6, tel 973223. Private collection of dolls and childhood toys from the eighteenth century onwards, with all the strange fascination of the artifacts of a Pharaoh's tomb – tiny tea sets and miniature prams, rocking horses which have rocked in the nurseries of great houses – relics of another lost world like many of the houses themselves. The earliest doll is an Irish one of 1730, limbless but still smiling. This museum is an utterly charming place best appreciated in the company of small children. Sun 2.30-5.30 throughout the year, July-Aug, Sun & Wed 2.30-5.30. Admission charge. Bus 13, 14, 14A from O'Connell Street.

*James Joyce Museum, Sandycove.*

MUSEUM OF LABOUR HISTORY, Beggar's Bush Barracks, Haddington Road, D4. The museum, opened in 1990, contains a small display of documents relating to labour history in Dublin during the nineteenth and twentieth centuries. Mon-Fri 10.00-5.00, closed 1.00-2.00.

THE NATIONAL MUSEUM, Kildare Street, D2, tel 765521. One of the world's great national museums, its collection of gold artifacts from Ireland's past forms a unique and stunning display of the craftsmanship and the ostentatious wealth of early civilizations in Ireland. The Bronze Age exhibits, particularly the gold dress ornaments, utilise simplicity of design with mastery of materials to produce artifacts worthy of the protagonists of the Celtic legends. From the Early Christian period the objects are no less wonderful, although here ecclesiastical rituals have produced the dominant items – the Ardagh and Derrynaflan Chalices, and crosses, croziers and shrines. These are richly ornamented in a manner that exhibits a profound sense of order and the high point reached by the decorative arts as practised in the monastic settlements of the period. A change of emphasis occurs during the Viking Age, and the exhibits from excavations in Dublin are predominantly domestic, giving the viewer a remarkable feeling for the nature of daily life in tenth-century Dublin. Here are leather children's shoes, cut down from adult ones, bone combs, fishing hooks, needles and pins, the fabrics and pottery which represent the very texture of Viking households. Other collections within the museum are of Irish furniture, ceramics, militaria, Irish political history, musical instruments, costume, coins and stamps which due to staff shortages are not permanently open. The museum building, designed by T. N. DEANE, 1885, was built in a soft sandstone which has weathered badly and much of the exterior of the building is crumbling away. Tue-Sat 10.00-5.00, Sun 2.00-5.00. Small charge for some exhibitions.

THE NATIONAL MUSEUM ANNEX, Merrion Row, D2, tel 765521. Houses occasional exhibitions from the main collection in Kildare Street, same opening hours.

NATIONAL WAX MUSEUM, Granby Row, off Parnell Square, D1, tel 726340. Not a national institution, the museum illustrates the famous and infamous from history with life-size individual wax figures and tableaux covering everything from the Chamber of Horrors to the Hall of Presidents. The children's world of fairy tales and fantasy, popes and megastars, Irish and international figures from politics and the arts, all jostle for your attention with their unnerving glassy stares. Mon-Sat 10.00-5.30, Sun 1.00-6.00. Admission charge.

*St. Patrick's Bell, National Museum.*

PEARSE MUSEUM, St. Enda's Park, Grange Road, Rathfarnham, D14, tel 934208. In this Georgian house PATRICK PEARSE, one of the leaders of the 1916 RISING, lived and ran an experimental school. Now a museum to the Pearse legend, with his study preserved as it was during his lifetime, the display covers Pearse's work as educationalist, revolutionary and mystical writer. Open 10.00-12.30, seven days all year, winter afternoons 2.00-3.30, spring afternoons 2.00-4.30, summer afternoons 2.00-6.00. Bus 16 O'Connell Street and 47B Hawkins Street.

THE NATURAL HISTORY MUSEUM, Merrion Square, D2, tel 765521. This museum is unique among Dublin collections in that the manner of display is as interesting as the exhibits themselves. Designed by Frederick Villiers Clarendon, 1856, the museum's handsome virtually windowless granite façade faces on to Leinster Lawn, and is mirrored by the NATIONAL GALLERY on the opposite side. Internally it is more an eighteenth-century antiquarian's cabinet of curiosities than a conventional modern museum. Photographs of the exhibits in the 1890s show the arrangement little different from today, with tier upon tier of birds, fish and animals in stuffed and skeletal form mounting to the ceiling in extraordinary profusion, all lit from above in a great stream of light. The elk skeletons are among the most fascinating exhibits, standing majestically inside the main doors, their enormous antler span stretching one's credibility – as do many of the other strange exhibits in the museum, seeming more figments of human imagination than products of nature. Tue-Sat 10.00-5.00, Sun 2.00-5.00. Bus 7, 7A, 8 Eden Quay.

PLUNKET MUSEUM OF IRISH EDUCATION, Church of Ireland College of Education, 96 Upper Rathmines Road, D6, tel 970033. With a collection of documents, photographs and artifacts, the museum traces the development of education from 1811 under the auspices of the Kildare Place Society. Wed 2.00-5.00.

ST. PATRICK'S HOSPITAL, Bow Lane West, James's Street, D8, tel 775423. This hospital was built with a bequest from JONATHAN SWIFT'S will, as he himself wrote,

He gave the little Wealth he had
To build a House for Fools and Mad.

It is now an important psychiatric hospital which has pioneered the humane treatment of the mentally disturbed. Poet Austin Clarke, a onetime patient there, has described it as

The Mansion of Forgetfulness
Swift gave us for a jest.

The museum collection of Swift's personal possessions and items is small but of immense interest to all who admire

him. Viewing by arrangement. Swift's death mask is on display in ST. PATRICK'S CATHEDRAL, with other memorabilia of the writer's time as Dean of the Cathedral. Bus 21A, 78, 78A from Fleet Street.

STATE HERALDIC MUSEUM, 2 Kildare Street, D2, tel 614877. Housed in a portion of the old Kildare Street Club, the main exhibition area was the coffee room of the Club. The museum was opened in 1909 at DUBLIN CASTLE and located in the Genealogical Office until it was moved to Kildare Street in 1987. The exhibits trace the use of heraldic devices in all sorts of forms from suits of armour to domestic china. Many of the aristocratic families of Ireland during the eighteenth century had specially made dinner services embellished with their armorials, and examples are shown. During the last two centuries heraldic devices could be used to decorate practically any useful object as is shown by the wide range on display in the museum, from coins to snuff boxes. The Genealogical Office operates a consultancy service at the museum for those wishing to trace their family origins. Mon-Fri 10.00-12.30, 2.00-4.30.

TRANSPORT MUSEUM, Howth Castle, Howth, D13, tel 475623. Housed in the farm buildings of Howth Castle, with hardly room to move between the vehicles, are bygones of Irish transport history. The Howth tram is here as are a few others at present being restored, and early double-decker buses, lorries, trucks, bread vans, army vehicles, and a Victorian fire engine. Sat-Sun 2.00-6.00. Admission charge. DART to Howth.

TRINITY MUSEUM, Engineering Building, Trinity College, D2, tel 772941. The museum housed in DEANE and WOOD-WARD'S major Dublin building has a small but interesting geological collection, some fine nineteenth-century engineering models, including a contemporary one of the DIVING BELL, and two elk skeletons which preside like a pair of guardians over the faded Byzantine splendours of the interior.

WEINGREEN MUSEUM OF BIBLICAL ANTIQUITIES, Arts Block, TCD, tel 772941 ex 2229. Pottery and artifacts from the ancient Near East, as well as Greek and Roman antiquities. Mon-Fri by appointment. School groups by arrangement.

WILLIE MONKS MUSEUM, Lusk, Co. Dublin, tel 437276. Collection of artifacts from the folk life of the area, domestic and agricultural implements and cottage furnishings. Easter-Oct, Sun 2.30-6.00 and by arrangement. Bus 33, Eden Quay.

## MUSIC AND MUSIC VENUES (See MAPS).

Music is the most popular form of entertainment in Dublin and the sheer number of venues, as well as the variety of styles of music available, puts the listener in the pleasurable situation of being spoiled for choice. On any night of the week throughout the year, somewhere in the city the grand piano or the electric guitar is being tuned up for formal concert or informal gig, in environments as appropriately varied. The majority of music venues hosting popular music are of the informal variety, pubs and clubs, some dedicated to supporting music, others merely providing light entertainment for their patrons. Classical music, opera, chamber and choral music are more confined in the number of outlets, but a steadily increasing audience indicates that more venues may become available. A considerable amount of overlap occurs between venues, and the following list only suggests general trends in particular locations. The current events columns of the daily papers and *In Dublin* are the only adequate guide to what is happening where at any particular time. Some pubs have a cover charge for their music sessions.

CLASSICAL MUSIC

HUGH LANE MUNICIPAL GALLERY, Parnell Square, D1, tel 741903. During the winter the gallery hosts an excellent series of free chamber music concerts, generally held at 12.00pm on Sundays.

*O'Carolan relief, St. Patrick's Cathedral.*

THE NATIONAL CONCERT HALL (NCH), Earlsfort Terrace, D2, tel 711888, credit card bookings 711533. The principal classical music venue in Dublin and the only one with a year-round programme of international celebrity and orchestral concerts. The RTE Concert Orchestra and the National Symphony Orchestra are based at the National Concert Hall. The concert hall also hosts jazz, opera, and traditional concerts.

THE ROYAL HOSPITAL KILMAINHAM (RHK), D8, tel 778526. Although not principally a music venue, as the National Centre for Culture and the Arts, almost anything cultural comes within the ambit of the RHK and it hosts an interesting occasional music programme in the great hall.

ST. STEPHEN'S CHURCH, Mount Street Crescent, D2. Occasional concerts.

TRINITY COLLEGE, D2. The college chapel is an occasional venue for chamber music.

## COUNTRY MUSIC

BAD BOB'S BACKSTAGE BAR, Essex Street East, D2, tel 775482.
TILTED WIG, Chancery Street, D7, tel 735627.

## CHORAL MUSIC.

There are a number of choral societies – Our Lady's Choral Society, The Palestrina Choir, The Guinness Choir among others – which perform in the churches and cathedrals, as well as giving concert performances at the National Concert Hall, and their activities are listed in the regular newspaper advertisements.

## EARLY MUSIC.

The Early Music Festival, held annually in the spring, is really the only time to hear a concentrated programme. However, early music (classical music before 1700) performances occur in the National Concert Hall from time to time. The Early Music Organisation of Ireland can be contacted at tel 696484.

## FOLK/BALLADS

ABBEY TAVERN, Howth, tel 390307.
BARK KITCHEN, 1 Sarsfield Quay, D7, tel 776980.
EMBANKMENT, Tallaght, D24, tel 516116.
LOWER DECK, Portobello, D8, tel 751423.
WEXFORD INN, Wexford Street, D2, tel 751588.

## JAZZ/BLUES

BARGE INN, Charlemont Street, D2, tel 780005.
BRAZEN HEAD, Lower Bridge Street, D8, tel 779549
BRUXELLES, Harry Street, D2, tel 778731.
GRATTAN, Capel Street, D1, tel 733049.
HARCOURT HOTEL, Harcourt Street, D2, tel 7520134.
INTERNATIONAL BAR, Wicklow Street, D2, tel 779250.
SACH'S HOTEL, Morehampton Road, D4, tel 680955.

## OPERA

THE DUBLIN GRAND OPERA SOCIETY (DGOS), holds two seasons annually, spring and winter, at the Gaiety Theatre, South King Street. The programme consists of the standard repertoire of Continental opera, with an occasional modern or obscure work. Irish and international singers take the solo roles and the chorus is provided by the DGOS.

## ROCK

BAGGOT INN, Lower Baggot Street, D2, tel 761430.
McGONAGLE'S, 21a South Anne Street, D2, tel 774402.
NATIONAL STADIUM, South Circular Road, D8, tel 533371.
NEW INN, D8.
POINT DEPOT, East Link Bridge, D1, tel

366777.

SFX CENTRE, 23 Upper Sherrard Street, D1, tel 740550.

THE WATERFRONT, 14 Sir John Rogerson's Quay, D2, tel 513366.

THE WILDEBEEST, tel 712276.


TRADITIONAL MUSIC

AN BÉAL BOCHT, 58 Charlemont Street, D2, tel 755614.

THE BRAZEN HEAD, Lower Bridge Street, D8, tel 779549.

COMHALTAS CEOLTÓIRÍ ÉIREANN, 32 Belgrave Square, Monkstown, tel 800295.

HUGHES', Chancery Street, D7, tel 746945.

KITTY O'SHEA'S, Upper Canal Street, D4, tel 609965.

MOTHER REDCAP'S TAVERN, Back Lane, High Street, D8, tel 538306.

O'DONOGHUE'S, Merrion Row, D2, tel 762807.

THE PIPER'S CLUB, Henrietta Street, D7, tel 744447.

THE PURTY KITCHEN, Dun Laoghaire, tel 801257.

SLATTERY'S, 129 Capel Street, D1, tel 740416.

**N**ARROW **ESCAPES.** Any city's development can be directed along different paths by a particular turn of events, a single generative occasion which can subsequently be seen as a beginning. Such events may take all manner of forms and may be the result of decisions taken within or outside Ireland, or the result of an error in the chain of command. Such a narrow escape was the fatal bombing of the North Strand area of Dublin in January and May 1941 by German aircraft although Ireland was a neutral country throughout the war. In the May bombing thirty-four people were killed and over three hundred houses either destroyed or damaged. Whether the bombing was accidental or planned has not been established, but the former is more likely. In a less determinedly noncombatant period such an event could only have been a prelude to Ireland's involvement in the war. Another escape was the failure of a municipal proposal around 1900 to build local authority housing on St. Stephen's Green, a development which would in all probability have been the beginning of the elimination of all the green spaces within the city. There are many more examples of near misses, both good and bad, political, cultural and architectural from which the city's fate seems to bounce like a ping pong ball, veering between opportunity and disaster. See MIGHT HAVE BEENS.

**NATIONAL COLLEGE OF ART AND DESIGN** (NCAD), 100 Thomas Street, D8, tel 711377. The redundant Jameson's Distillery buildings, a complex of fine nineteenth-century brick-built warehouses, granaries and oats houses were converted in 1984 by the architects Burke Kennedy Doyle into spacious studio and lecture room accommodation for the National College of Art. The college had previously existed in very cramped quarters at the back of the National Library in Kildare Street. The heart of the Thomas Street complex is an open piazza known as 'Red Square', a brick-paved courtyard surrounding the old copper distilling vats whose eccentric shapes are reminiscent of the domes of the Kremlin and which were exposed by the demolition of the distillery buildings. To the west of Red Square is the Granary, a five-storey block of fine art, fashion and design studios. The NCAD is the present form of the drawing academy established in 1746 by the DUBLIN SOCIETY, which has continued to exist under a variety of different titles and in different locations ever since. It is now a degree and diploma awarding institution in the fine arts, design and related disciplines. Bus 21A, 78, 78A, 78B from Fleet Street.

**NATIONAL CONCERT HALL**, Earlsfort Terrace, D2, tel 711533. The absence of a major concert hall had inhibited musical activity in Dublin for many years and much discussion had produced no results by as late as the 1960s. Following the assassination in 1964 of J.F. Kennedy, President of the United States, who was of Irish extraction, the Government decided to build a Kennedy Memorial Concert Hall. The building was designed by RAYMOND MC GRATH for the Beggar's Bush Barracks site on Haddington Road, but in 1974 after many different proposals had been put forward for an alternative location, including the Phoenix Park, the plan was suspended. Mc Grath's design was finally abandoned in favour of converting the old UCD Examination Hall at Earlsfort Terrace. The University Buildings, designed by R.M. Butler in 1912, incorporated an earlier structure by Alfred Gresham Jones left over from the 1865 Dublin Exhibition, and it is this which became what is now the National Concert Hall. The new hall, which has filled the gap in the musical life of the city splendidly, provides a centre for classical music in Dublin and was designed by the Office of Public Works architects, de Chenu, O'Doherty and Smith and opened in 1981. The accoustics consultant was V.L Jordan, who worked on the Metropolitan Opera House, New York, and Sydney Opera House. See MUSIC. Bus 14, 14A, 14B from D'Olier Street.

**NATIONAL HERITAGE COUNCIL**, Department of the Taoiseach, Government Buildings, Upper Merrion Street, D2, tel 763546. Established in 1988 to co-ordinate all heritage activities on a national scale, its brief covers everything from architecture to waterways. Much of Ireland's archaeological and natural heritage is at risk and the Council helps existing voluntary groups and also advises government bodies on the development of a co-ordinated national protection and conservation policy.

**NATURE TRAILS**. The major nature trail in the Dublin hinterland is the WICKLOW WAY, an 128km (80 miles) walking route which begins in Marlay Park in Rathfarnham and traverses the foothills and highlands of the Dublin and Wicklow mountains as far as Carlow. Much of this route demands experience. On a less ambitious scale, nature trails exist in many of the parkland areas around Dublin such as KILLINEY HILL PARK, the PHOENIX PARK and ST. ANNE'S PARK, Clontarf, and guide maps of these are

*Nelson Pillar, blown up in 1966.*

displayed nearby or the routes are directly signposted.

**NELSON PILLAR**. Erected to commemorate Admiral Lord Horatio Nelson who was killed at the Battle of Trafalgar in 1805, 'The Pillar' as it was popularly known in Dublin was the chief landmark of O'Connell Street, and a general meeting place as well as the tram terminus.

The Lord Lieutenant, the Duke of Richmond, laid the foundation stone on 15 February 1908 and it predated Nelson's Column in London by over thirty years, but at 40.2m (134ft) high the Dublin pillar was considerably shorter than the 60.6m (202ft) London column. Standing on a massive rectangular base, the fluted Doric pillar had an internal spiral staircase which led to a viewing balcony below the statue. Designed by William Wilkins, Nelson Pillar was erected under the supervision of FRANCIS JOHNSTON. The Portland stone figure of the Admiral was by Thomas Kirk who also carved the sculptures on Johnston's Post Office nearby. On the fiftieth anniversary of the 1916 RISING, in March 1966, the column was blown up at night by the IRA. The battered head of Nelson is on display in the CIVIC MUSEUM.

## NEWBRIDGE DEMESNE TRADITIONAL FARM, Donabate, Co Dublin, tel 436064.

The eighteenth-century farm buildings of NEWBRIDGE HOUSE have been transformed into a living museum of farming where the history of Irish agriculture is demonstrated by a fascinating collection of farm equipment and animals. Among endangered or rare species of Irish farm animals being bred at Newbridge are Connemara ponies, Jacob sheep and Kerry cows. Different areas of the farmyard are laid out as they would have been during the eighteenth century when everything needed on the estate had to be made locally, and include a forge, joinery workshop and tack room. The LORD CHANCELLOR'S COACH is on display in the coachhouse. The combination of the traditional farm with the mansion gives a clear insight into the workings of great estates as well as smaller farms during the past. Mon-Fri 10.00-1.00, 2.00-6.00. Sun & BH 2.00-

5.00. Train from Connolly Station to Donabate. Bus 33B, Eden Quay.

## NEWBRIDGE HOUSE, Newbridge Demesne, Donabate, Co. Dublin, tel 436064.

This eighteenth-century house was designed by RICHARD CASTLE in 1737 for Archbishop Cobbe whose descendants lived there until the estate was bought by Dublin County Council in 1985. The principal room in Newbridge House is the red drawing room which contains a particularly fine collection of seventeenth- and eighteenth-century paintings, and is decorated with a splendid Rococo ceiling. Other rooms are the museum of curiosities, dining room and library. In the courtyard of the house is NEWBRIDGE DEMESNE TRADITIONAL FARM. In the village of Donabate, the Church of Ireland Church has a private gallery decorated with Rococo plasterwork for the use of the Cobbe family. Mon-Fri 10.00-1.00, 2.00-6.00. Sun & BH 2.00-5.00. Admission charge. Bus 33B from Eden Quay, or by train from Connolly Station, both to Donabate village and ten-minute walk through the demesne.

## NEWCOMEN'S BANK, Castle Street, D2.

Now used as the Rates Office by Dublin Corporation, the house was built by Thomas Ivory in 1791 for Sir William Newcomen, the banker, and the principal internal feature of the house is a majestic oval banking hall on the first floor, reached by an oval main staircase. Of the architects working in Dublin during the eighteenth century, Ivory is noted for his fine draughtsmanship and the delicacy of detailing on his buildings. Newcomen's Bank shows this latter quality to perfection in the shallow recesses and decoration of the Portland stone façade which shows the influence of Robert Adam. In 1856 the size of the building was doubled by extending the original block in replica to the north, and joining the parts with a projecting Victorian porch on Castle Street. Bus 50, 50A, 36A from Aston Quay.

*The burial mound, Newgrange.*

**NEWGRANGE,** Co. Meath. The most impressive prehistoric monument in Ireland and part of a group of Neolithic

(*circa* 3000 BC) passage graves located in the Boyne Valley. The three principal mounds are Dowth, Knowth and Newgrange, all within sight of each other and surrounded by smaller mounds and other features. Newgrange, which has been extensively excavated and reconstructed, consists of an acre of piled river boulders, topped with grass, in the interior of which was constructed a tomb approached by a 18m (60ft) passageway lined and roofed with monoliths. On the perimeter of the mound is a kerb of massive stones lying on their sides, decorated with elaborate and quite beautiful abstract designs, the significance of which has not been established. During the winter solstice on 21 December and the days surrounding it, the sun's rays penetrate into the burial chamber of the tomb through a slit in the roof of the passageway, indicating the sophisticated ability of the builders of Newgrange in the alignment of this great tomb. This extraordinary phenomenon was observed by Professor M. J. O'Kelly, the excavator of Newgrange on 21 December, 1967, perhaps for the first time in 5,000 years:

> A narrow beam of light entered the passage through the roof box, gradually the whole chamber became illuminated and this lasted for about 17 minutes. I was absolutely astonished, I hadn't expected anything so dramatic. I could feel the spirits of the dead all around me. I really expected a voice to speak.

**NEWMAN HOUSE,** 85 & 86 St. Stephen's Green, D2, tel 757255. Newman House is composed of two significant eighteenth-century mansions, No. 85, Clanwilliam House and its neighbour No. 86, which were connected when they were used in the late nineteenth century for Newman's Catholic

University. Clanwilliam is the earlier, being built in 1738 by RICHARD CASTLE, and it contains the most ravishing FRANCINI plasterwork in Dublin. It was the first townhouse to be designed by Castle and one of the earliest to be faced with cut stone. On the ground floor, to the right of the main hall is the Apollo room which is absolutely unique among masterpieces of the Italian stuccodores in Dublin houses, and compares with the stairhall of ELY HOUSE for the power of its Classical imagery. Over the mantelpiece and dominating the room is the majestic figure of Apollo, Greek God of physical beauty, and in separate panels around the room are figures of the nine muses, all executed in high relief. The saloon on the first floor occupies the entire front of the building and it too was decorated by the Francinis with an extravagant ceiling unequalled in any other Dublin house. No. 86 is a later eighteenth-century townhouse built in 1765 for the MP, RICHARD CHAPELL WHALEY, father of the notorious BUCK WHALEY. The house is extensively decorated with plasterwork by ROBERT WEST who may also have designed it. The stairhall, with its sustained musical instrument motifs, is particularly impressive. Newman House has recently been restored by University College Dublin (UCD) and individual rooms have been decorated in the style of the various periods of the building's occupation. The bishop's room was used for meetings of the Irish bishops up to the late nineteenth century, the president's room was used for official receptions of the president of UCD. Tue-Fri 10.00-4.00, Sat 2.00-4.30, Sun 11.00-2.00. Admission charge..

**NEWMAN, JOHN HENRY,** (1801-1890). English theologian and educationalist who converted from the Church

*Newman House, St. Stephen's Green.*

of England to the Catholic Church in which he ultimately became a cardinal. Appointed Rector of the Catholic University in Dublin in 1851, although the University was not actually established until 1854. Newman delivered a series of 'Discourses' at the ROTUNDA during 1852 and there formed the basis of his most influential writing, *The Idea of a University Defined and Illustrated,* 1873, in which he proposed that the function of a university was to train the mind rather than to impart knowledge. His position in Dublin was an unsatisfactory one as he was head of an institution with little funding and one that, because it was not recognised by the government, was unable to confer degrees. The Catholic University had been established by the Catholic bishops in opposition to the 'Godless' National University of Ireland, which was non-denominational. Newman resigned in 1858 and returned to England.

**NOBEL PRIZE.** Dublin is the only European city to be the birthplace of three writers who were recipients of the Nobel Prize for Literature during the twentieth century. W.B.YEATS in 1923, GEORGE BERNARD SHAW in 1926 and SAMUEL BECKETT in 1969. The work of these and many other Dublin writers are commemorated in the DUBLIN WRITERS' MUSEUM. Other Nobel Prize winners who lived in Dublin are SEÁN MAC BRIDE, winner of the Nobel Peace Prize in 1974 and ERWIN SCHRÖDINGER, physics, 1933.

**NOLDE, EMIL,** (1867-1956). German Expressionist painter, his vividly coloured 'Women in the Garden' in the NATIONAL GALLERY of Ireland is one of the examples of 'Degenerate Art' confiscated by the Nazis from public collections in Germany during 1937-38. It was purchased by the National Gallery in 1984.

**NORTH GREAT GEORGE'S STREET**, D1. Major eighteenth-century street with fine houses dating from the 1780s. Like Henrietta Street, it is steeply inclined, with BELVEDERE HOUSE completing the vista at the top of the hill. The lower part of the street declined into tenements during this century, and some of these were demolished. However those remaining are being restored and this street represents an anomaly among Georgian areas of Dublin – a street which is returning to residential use. Many of the houses have fine plasterwork. The JAMES JOYCE CULTURAL CENTRE is at No. 35 and there are plaques on other houses to John Dillon, Sir Samuel Ferguson and Sir John Mahaffy.

Ah me, the aspidistra grows dusty behind the window pane,
And the delicate tracery of the fanlight is obscured from light;
Yet these shall, perchance be dusted, and shine brightly again;
But they, the gallant, the witty and the brave,
Whaley and Egan, and all who fought the oncoming of death and night,
These death has taken. They lie forever, each in a forgotten grave.
('In North Great George's Street', Seamus O'Sullivan.)

**NORTH STRAND.** A continuation of Amiens Street, and as its name implies it at one stage formed the north western shore of DUBLIN BAY. The land reclamation begun in the eighteenth century has gradually moved the foreshore further east. Bus 12A, 20B from Eden Quay, 30 from Lower Abbey Street.

**NORTH WALL.** Traditionally the embarkation point for sailing between Ireland and England, but the Ferry Port from which the B&I Line runs a daily service to England has been moved out into the deeper waters of the port on recently created landfill. Bus 53A from Liberty Hall.

**NUBIAN MAIDENS.** The front balustrade of the Shelbourne Hotel on St. Stephen's Green is ornamented by four life-size lampholding nubile Nubian maidens, the outer pair being negroid attendants to the inner pair of princesses. This foursome is among the most attractive sculptural decorations on any Dublin building. The hotel, designed by John Mc Curdy in 1867 is a typically opulent Victorian palace hotel, built to entertain the fashionable and be the centre of the social season.

Obelisks. A popular form of monument during the Georgian era, based on Egyptian remains transported to Europe during the Renaissance. There are some outstanding examples of this type of structure, part folly and part memorial around Dublin. The WELLINGTON TESTIMONIAL, (Sir Robert Smirke, 1817) in the Phoenix Park is the largest obelisk in Europe, and at 68.3m (205ft), its massive bulk can be seen towering over the trees of the park from many parts of the city. The most interesting of the obelisks are eighteenth-century, and the two most notable are the Conolly Folly at CASTLETOWN (RICHARD CASTLE, 1739) and that at Obelisk Park, Stillorgan (SIR EDWARD LOVETT PEARCE, 1732). The obelisk on Killiney Hill (1742), is distinguished more for its location than for design, but it shares a common cause with the Conolly monument – both were erected to provide relief work for the poor. The Boyd Obelisk in Dun Laoghaire (1861), is another fine example of the end of the period during which this form of monument was common. Further obelisks are located at Anglesea Road and at Main Street, Bray, a pair in the forecourt of Charlemont House (Sir William Chambers, 1762), Thomas Street (Francis Sandys), Dundrum Village. On Leinster Lawn in front of the DÁIL is a modern variation on the theme, commemorating Michael Collins, Arthur Griffith and Kevin O'Higgins (RAYMOND MC GRATH, 1950). Perhaps not an obelisk at all but a related monument is the Steyne in College Street (Cliodna Cussen, 1984), a recreation of the Viking Long Stone which stood here from the ninth century until it disappeared during the eighteenth. MOUNT JEROME CEMETERY provides a veritable library

*Obelisk on Killiney Hill.*

of obelisks, used in this instance as Victorian funerary monuments.

## O'CAROLAN, TURLOUGH, (1670-1738).

Blind harper and composer, the most significant Irish musician of his period who, having been trained in the traditional manner of a seven-year apprenticeship, spent his life travelling between the houses of aristocratic patrons to whom he dedicated most of his compositions. O'Carolan's music shows an awareness of contemporary European composers and many of his compositions are still performed, having passed into both the traditional and Classical repertoire. He is reputed to have been friendly with JONATHAN SWIFT, his direct contemporary. The O'Carolan memorial in ST. PATRICK'S CATHEDRAL, a white marble bas relief by JOHN HOGAN, 1824, depicts the harpist as a handsome young man, elegantly dressed, and is one of the most attractive memorials, not just in St. Patrick's, but anywhere in Dublin.

## O'CASEY, SEÁN, (1880-1964).
Playwright, his trilogy of Dublin plays performed at the ABBEY THEATRE between 1923 and 1926, *The Shadow of a Gunman*, *Juno and the Paycock* and *The Plough and the Stars* are written from the point of view of a committed Socialist, and deal with the life of the TENEMENT dwellers of the city during the years of revolution. In this sequence of tragi-comedies, O'Casey captured something of the essence of the humour and pragmatic philosophy of the inner-city Dubliners, as well as dealing with social and political issues. O'Casey became disillusioned with the triumph of Irish Nationalist over Socialist ideas in the years after the foundation of the Irish Free State and after the Abbey rejected his experimental play about the First World War, *The Silver Tassie*, he moved to England, where he lived for the rest of his life. A considerable amount of the subject matter of O'Casey's later work is based on his early life in Dublin, particularly his *Autobiographies*, a lengthy series which depict the background from which his work emerged.

## O'CONNELL BRIDGE. Originally
Carlisle Bridge and called after the Lord Lieutenant, it was designed by JAMES GANDON in 1790. Widened and altered in 1876 by Bindon Blood Stoney in order to line up with the extension of Sackville Street to the Liffey.

## O'CONNELL, DANIEL, (1775-1847).
Political leader, he was a member of a wealthy landowning family in Co. Kerry and one of the first Catholics to be called to the Bar in 1798, a year after the removal of professional restrictions. He practised successfully as a lawyer and gradually assumed leadership of the campaign for Catholic Emancipation. As a pacifist he opposed the pursuit of concessions through violent means and harnessed an enormous popular movement to campaign for repeal of the Penal Laws. O'Connell's election as MP in 1828 spelled the end of the old order and the Emancipation Act was passed the following year, signifying the most fundamental change in British legislation in Ireland since the seventeenth century. For his part in this achievement, O'Connell became known as 'The Liberator'. The second major project which he embraced was repeal of the ACT OF UNION, for which he organised monster meetings of up to three quarters of a million people around the country, culminating in a proposed meeting at Clontarf in 1843. The British government, fearing this growing militancy, proscribed the meeting and jailed O'Connell. Younger leaders, dissatisfied with O'Connell's tactics, had emerged in the YOUNG IRELAND MOVEMENT and the combination of this dissention, the advent of the Famine and O'Connell's age brought an end to the tremendous achievements of O'Connell's career. Lord Mayor of Dublin in 1841, his statue stands in the Rotunda of the CITY HALL, as well as on O'Connell Street which is named in his honour. He lived at 58 Merrion Square (plaque).

## O'CONNELL MONUMENT,
O'Connell Street Lower, D1. By JOHN HENRY FOLEY, 1854. Since the demise of NELSON PILLAR, the figure of DANIEL O'CONNELL, half as high as the pillar, is the dominant monument on the street. A heroic bronze of 'The Liberator' stands

above allegorical and naturalistic references to aspects of his life. The four-winged female Victories which occupy the corners represent attributes of O'Connell's character, courage, eloquence, fidelity and patriotism. These Victories were in the line of fire during the 1916 fighting on O'Connell Street and bullet holes can clearly be seen in the bronze breasts of those facing the GPO. Around the drum, the most successful part of the monument, are gathered civil and religious figures, the professions and the peasantry, with Erin in the centre holding the scroll of Catholic Emancipation. Foley died before completing the monument which was not unveiled until 1882. The O'Connell Monument forms an interesting contrast to that of CHARLES PARNELL at the other end of the street, erected some fifty years later. In the O'Connell Monument, the subject is dominated by symbolism, whereas it is the figure of Parnell which is the focus of that monument.

**O'CONNELL STREET,** D1. The finest street in Dublin and its focal point, the massive portico of the General Post Office is the location of state and civic functions and political rallies. The northern end of O'Connell Street was laid out in the 1750s by LUKE GARDINER on open lands previously belonging to ST. MARY'S ABBEY. The character of this street was more that of an elongated square, with sides resembling the present-day appearance of Merrion Square. Then known as Sackville Street and 45m (150ft) wide, it ran from where the Parnell Monument now stands to Henry Street, divided down the middle by GARDINER'S MALL, a precursor of the parks of later Georgian squares. The east side became the more fashionable, and many members of parliament lived here,

*O'Connell Monument.*

building substantial mansions, none of which now remains. In fact only one house from the original Sackville Street survives, No. 46 on the west side. The WIDE STREETS COMMISSIONERS extended Sackville Street to the Liffey in 1790, maintaining the width of the original street, and continuing the idea of a central mall. This mall was reinstated in 1988. Carlisle Bridge was constructed to link with the developments on the south bank of the river. By the end of the nineteenth century the street was entirely commercial with hotels and substantial business premises gradually replacing the houses. In 1916 a large section of the street was destroyed during the fighting, but this was rebuilt during the 1920s, with uniform building heights and maintaining related materials and design with a result which has considerable dignity, even if at present it is rather tawdry at street level. O'Connell Street today is a street of monuments, although the principal of these,

NELSON PILLAR, was destroyed in 1966. From O'Connell Bridge, looking north, the monuments are to DANIEL O'CONNELL, William Smith O'Brien, John Gray, FATHER MATHEW, JAMES LARKIN, ANNA LIVIA, and CHARLES STEWART PARNELL. See MONUMENTS.

**O'CONNOR, ANDREW,** (1874-1941). Irish-American sculptor, he lived in Dublin in the latter part of his life. O'Connor was influenced by Auguste Rodin, and his 1914-1918 War Memorial, now called 'Christ The King' at Haig Terrace, Dun Laoghaire, is possibly the single finest piece of outdoor sculpture in Dublin, imaginatively conceived and vigorously modelled. The obscurity of its siting prevents it from being better known. Other works by O'Connor in Dublin are the figure of DANIEL O'CONNELL in the National Bank on Dame Street and another war memorial 'Les Debarqueme', MERRION SQUARE, both of which are infused with a heroic sense of the human figure. THE HUGH LANE GALLERY has a fine equestrian figure of General Lafayette 1922; the original is in Baltimore, USA.

**O'CONOR, RODERIC,** (1860-1940). Artist, born in Co. Roscommon, spent most of his life in France where he came under the influence of the POST IMPRESSIONIST movement. Both the NATIONAL GALLERY and HUGH LANE GALLERY have outstanding examples of O'Conor's work and he ranks as one of the leading Irish artists of the early twentieth century. As a member of an Irish landowning family he possessed independent means and never sought publicity so his work is little known, but the best of it can be compared with that of Paul Signac and Paul Gauguin who were his friends.

**OLD DUBLIN SOCIETY.** Devoted to all aspects of the history of the city, with its headquarters at the City Assembly House, 58 South William Street, D2, where it holds monthly meetings. The Society publishes a quarterly journal, the *Dublin Historical Record*.

**O'NOLAN, BRIAN,** (1911-1966). Writer, who published under the aliases Flann O'Brien and Myles Na gCopaleen, the latter a character from DION BOUCICAULT. O'Nolan was one of the cleverest and least conventional Dublin writers of his time and his work is a blending of surrealism, satire and bizarre imaginative flights of fancy. He wrote a column 'Cruiskeen Lawn' for twenty years in *The Irish Times* in which he savagely satirised contemporary society. For much of his life O'Nolan was a civil servant but there is little indication of this in his extraordinary novels, *At Swim-Two-Birds*, *An Béal Bocht*, *The Dalkey Archive* and *The Third Policeman*. As in the writings of JAMES JOYCE, O'Nolan's work captured essences of the city in a manner which has given his characters a life beyond the printed page.

**ORDNANCE SURVEY,** Phoenix Park, D8. The Ordnance Survey has been the national authority for the mapping of the country since the mid-nineteenth century, and its headquarters since 1825 have been an eighteenth-century house in the park.

**ORMOND, JAMES BUTLER, DUKE OF,** (1610-1688). Viceroy, born in London to the powerful Butler family of Kilkenny Castle, he succeeded to the earldom in 1632. Ormond upheld the position of the Crown during the 1641 rebellion, being made Lord Lieutenant by Charles I in 1643. During the Cromwellian period he lived in France with the future Charles II and with the Restoration Ormond again returned to Dublin as Lord Lieutenant in 1662. He became the most influential cultural figure in Dublin during the seventeenth century, and two of the city's most important features, the PHOENIX PARK and the ROYAL HOSPITAL KILMAINHAM were instigated by him. During his years in France, Ormond had absorbed the cultural influences of the French court and his second period of office in Dublin brought Continental culture in its wake. As the monarch's representative in Dublin, Ormond believed that it was important to maintain a regal court, and music, one of the principal entertainments of the day, flourished during his viceroyalty.

**ORMOND QUAY**, D1. Between O'Donovan Rossa Bridge and the Ha'penny Bridge on the north side of the Liffey, and the first section of the river bank to be developed in the form of the stone quays which now flank the river.

**ORPEN, SIR WILLIAM**, (1878-1931). Artist, born in Dublin, he studied in Dublin and London where he eventually settled and where he achieved success as war artist and society painter. Orpen taught for over ten years at the Metropolitan School of Art in Kildare Street, and an entire generation of Irish artists, among them SEÁN KEATING, PATRICK TUOHY and Margaret Clarke were influenced by him. Orpen is one of the few major figures of the Dublin art world who did not identify with the cultural Nationalism of the time, and very little of his major work reflects upon Irish affairs. During summer holidays at Howth before the outbreak of the First World War, he painted a series of Impressionist figure and landscape studies overlooking DUBLIN BAY, capturing the billowing clouds and shimmering sea in pictures full of the light and space of the location. One painting from this series, 'Looking at the Sea' is among the examples of his work in the NATIONAL GALLERY collection.

**OSBORNE, WALTER**, (1859-1903). Artist, although known in his lifetime as a portrait painter, he is now highly regarded for small Impressionist and informal street scenes, many of them from the Liberties area of Dublin, as well as for his studies of children. Osborne died in the pneumonia epidemic of 1903, aged forty-four. There are fine examples of his work in both the NATIONAL GALLERY and the HUGH LANE GALLERY.

**O'SHEA BROTHERS**. Stonecarvers from Co. Cork employed by BENJAMIN WOODWARD on his University Museum, Oxford, 1854, they had already worked for him in Dublin on the Trinity Museum Building of 1852 and also possibly on the Kildare Street Club, 1858. The eccentric vigour, humour and freedom of the O'Shea brothers' work greatly enhances these buildings, taking the idea of mere decoration into the realm of applied sculpture like the work of the stonecarvers of the Medieval cathedrals.

**OUR LADY OF DUBLIN**, Carmelite Friary, Whitefriars Street, D2. Due to the destruction of the religious foundations in Dublin during the Reformation, little of the art of the period remains intact. An exception is the fine oak carved fifteenth-century Madonna and Child which is displayed on a side altar at the rear of the Carmelite church. This figure, which is believed to have originally come from ST. MARY'S ABBEY, has had a chequered history, its survival apparently being due to the fact that its hollowed-out back was used as an animal trough. It returned to church use after it was found in a junk shop in the nineteenth century.

**OUZEL GALLEY SOCIETY.** One of the most distinctive memorial plaques to be found on the wall of any Dublin building is over the side door to the COMMERCIAL BUILDINGS on Dame Street. This plaque, dated 1799, shows a ship in full sail and commemorates a Dublin merchant ship, the *Ouzel Galley* which left the quays in 1695 and, having been captured by pirates, failed to return. The owners claimed the insurance, and were duly paid. Some years later the ship re-appeared with its captain and crew having escaped from captivity. A controversy arose as to the current ownership of the *Ouzel Galley*, did it belong to the merchants or to the insurance company? The Ouzel Galley Society was set up in 1700 to arbitrate over such disputes. The plaque, now on Dame Street, was originally over a doorway in the internal courtyard of the old Commercial Buildings, replaced in 1976 by a replica building.

**OXMANTOWN.** A corruption of Ostmantown (Eastmantown), the Viking settlement north of the Liffey between Smithfield and the Blue Coat School. The Vikings who moved here after the Norman conquest of Dublin, are well commemorated around Oxmantown Road by the names of streets of nineteenth-century artisans' dwellings, with Olaf Road, Sitric Place, Sigurd Road and Ivar Street. Blackhall Place and the playing fields behind the Bluecoat School are remnants of Oxmantown Green.

**P**AGANINI, NICCOLÓ, (1728-1840). One of the leading virtuoso pianists of the nineteenth century, and an exceptionally flamboyant performer, he played at the Dublin Music Festival on 30 August 1831.

**PALACE OF SAINT SEPULCHRE**, Kevin Street, D8. Formerly the palace of the Protestant archbishop of Dublin, and now occupied by Kevin Street Garda Station, the two-storey battlemented building, arranged around an open courtyard, is largely seventeenth-century and of little architectural distinction. Separating it from Kevin Street is an eighteenth-century wall with a magnificent pair of gate piers, now alas gateless. Not open to the public except for Garda business.

**PALE, THE**. Area of land centred on Dublin but with fluctuating boundaries, which had come under English influence when Henry II declared the 'Lordship of Ireland' in 1171. This territory, fortified with Anglo-Norman settlements along its borders, was first referred to as The Pale Settlement in 1446. Within The Pale, English laws, language and customs prevailed, although not consistently, and prior to the Elizabethan conquests it was the only part of Ireland which had been effectively colonised.

**PAPAL CROSS**. Erected in the Fifteen Acres of the Phoenix Park as the centrepiece for the Papal Mass during the visit of Pope John Paul II to Dublin in 1979. The cross was retained after the ceremony and has caused some controversy.

**PARKE, SURGEON MAJOR T.H.**, (1857-1893). Explorer, he was involved in the unsuccessful attempt to rescue General Gordon at Khartoum and later accompanied H. M. Stanley on his expedition to the Congo Basin in 1887. Among Parke's other heroic journeys was a trans-African expedition in 1889. The statue of Parke by Percy Wood which stands in front of the NATURAL HISTORY MUSEUM shows the explorer dressed for equatorial adventures, with one foot resting on a bleached animal skull, and it is one of the most expressive Victorian monuments in the city.

## PARKS AND GARDENS

BLESSINGTON STREET / BROADSTONE PARK, North Circular Road, D7. A spur of the Royal Canal was filled in to provide a linear park which is connected through a small gateway to the still water-filled City Basin on Blessington Street.

CABBAGE GARDEN, Kevin Street, D8. The gardens of JONATHAN SWIFT'S Deanery were located near a Huguenot graveyard. This graveyard is now a small park tucked in between the Iveagh Trust flats and new houses on Kevin Street. It is called the Cabbage Garden in memory of Swift's gardens.

CLONTARF PROMENADE, Clontarf, D3. A green belt running from Fairview Park to Bull Island along the northern shore of Clontarf Pool, the westernmost extent of DUBLIN BAY.

FAIRVIEW PARK, North Strand, D3. Park developed on reclaimed land between the railway embankment and the original shoreline, the North Strand Road. The Children's Traffic School is in the portion of the park to the east of the embankment.

HERBERT PARK, Ballsbridge, D4. The site of the Dublin International Exhibition of 1907, and much of the park's layout and fixtures remain from that time, the ponds, bandstand and pergolas. A cruciform iron and glass pavilion occupied the centre of the park for the Exhibition, with the arms of the cross occupied by the four provinces. There are facilities for bowling, fishing and tennis, as well as an extensive herbaceous area.

IVEAGH GARDENS, Earlsfort Terrace, D2. The only secret garden in the city centre, concealed behind the buildings of HARCOURT STREET, ST. STEPHEN'S GREEN South and EARLSFORT TERRACE, the tops of the trees appear over a wall in Hatch Street. Access to the gardens is through a gate at the rear to the right of the UCD Earlsfort Terrace building. The parkland, two-thirds the size of Merrion Square, is now used by students of the National University which maintains some faculties at Earlsfort Terrace. The gardens were originally the private lands of Clonmel House, which still stands at No. 15 on the west side of Harcourt Street. In 1817 the lands became separated from the house and were re-named Coburg Gardens and run as public pleasure grounds, rather like the Rotunda Gardens in Parnell Square and Ranelagh Gardens in Ranelagh. In 1863 the Dublin Exhibition Palace was built here and the gardens were designed by Ninian Niven. Some of the features of Niven's design still remain. Later these grounds became the private gardens of Iveagh House, and when the house was presented to the state, the gardens were given to the University.

KILLINEY HILL PARK, Killiney, Co. Dublin. The estate and former deerpark of Killiney Castle, now the Killiney Castle Hotel, comprises the major part of what is today the public park. Called Victoria Park to commemorate the Queen's Jubilee, it opened to the public in 1887. Although covering only an area of 64 hectares (153.6 acres), there is remarkable variety of terrain in this park, and it shares with the Hill of Howth the claim to provide the finest views over DUBLIN BAY. Interesting features of the park are the eighteenth-century obelisk on the summit of the hill, and a smaller obelisk and mid-nineteenth-century WISHING STONE just below the summit. Dalkey Quarry, from which the granite for Dun Laoghaire harbour was quarried, is also part of the park, and is popular with rock climbers in training. Telegraph Hill, on the rim of the quarry, has an old signalling tower, and further down the slope on the seaward side, a Victorian Celtic cross marks the burial site of a local resident who didn't wish to be parted from the magnificent view of KILLINEY BAY and the coast of Wicklow. Standing there, one can appreciate his sentiments. DART to Killiney.

KING'S INNS, Constitution Hill, D7. Small park belonging to the King's Inns, approached either from Constitution Hill, or more attractively, up HENRIETTA STREET, and through the hushed courtyard of the Inns. The most interesting feature of the park is its remarkable Empire-style cast iron park benches, like props from a painting by Jacques Louis David. A tree has grown around one of these benches, enveloping the seat back in a caress of sinuous bark.

LONGMEADOW PARK, Islandbridge, D8. On the southern bank of the Liffey, and opposite the Phoenix Park. The National War Memorial is on the higher ground of the park, and the riverbank is a popular spot for anglers. Skiff racing also takes place on this reach of the river.

*Merrion Square.*

MERRION SQUARE, D2. The private gardens of Merrion Square were taken over by Dublin Corporation and opened to the public in 1974. The planting at that time resembled what the park must have looked like during the eighteenth century, a screen of trees inside the railings, and the rest of the landscape open like the parkland of a country house. Since 1974, this expanse has been filled in and copiously planted to divide up the space between the trees and today it is the most tranquil area of greenery in central Dublin, filling with sunbathers during lunchtime on a sunny day, but otherwise an oasis of quiet.

MILLENNIUM GARDENS, Dame Street, D2. Pocket handkerchief-sized garden next to the CITY HALL, with nineteenth-century figures of the crafts from the 1865 Dublin Exhibition Buildings at Earlsfort Terrace, and a small fountain.

NORTH BULL ISLAND, Dollymount, D3. Spectacular 3km (1.8 miles) long strand with sand dune nature reserve and wetland area which is the most important bird-watching site in Dublin. The Interpretive Centre on the island provides information on all aspects of the flora and fauna of the area. Bus 30 from Lower Abbey Street.

PALMERSTON PARK, Rathmines, D6. Tiny semi-circular park in the midst of fine red-brick Victorian residential quarter.

PEOPLE'S PARK, George's Street, Dun Laoghaire. Small Victorian park with two cherub encrusted fountains, a bandstand, children's play area and usually quite stunning flower arrangements. This little park, a few minutes' walk from the East Pier is the epitome of the civilised standards of nineteenth-century Kingstown, lacking only the regimental band and the high Victorian prams guarded by nannies. DART to Sandycove.

PHOENIX PARK, D7. A little over a mile from O'Connell Street, and with a circumference of 11.2km (7 miles), this pear-shaped expanse of landscape is the largest enclosed park in Europe. These lands, which belonged to the Knights Hospitallers of Kilmainham up to the dissolution of the monasteries, extended south of the Liffey to where the ROYAL HOSPITAL now stands. The Park was first enclosed in 1662 by order of the DUKE OF ORMOND and constituted as a public park by the Viceroy, LORD CHESTERFIELD, in 1747. Charles II attempted to present the land to one of his favourites, the Duchess of Cleveland in 1665, but fortunately this plan miscarried. Three quarters of the Park is now public, the remainder being occupied by a number of miniature island estates, all of which have government or executive functions. The principal of these is ÁRAS AN UACHTARÁIN, now the official residence of the President. This house was built for the Park Ranger in the eighteenth century and later became, as the Viceregal Lodge, the residence of the Viceroy. Also in the Park is the residence of the US Ambassador, Ashtown Castle, which was part of the now demolished Apostolic Nunciature, the Cheshire Home, the Civil Defence Headquarters, Garda Siochána Headquarters, the Magazine Fort, the ORDNANCE SURVEY, St. Mary's Hospital and the ZOO. Two of the finest public monuments in Dublin are set in the Phoenix Park, the PHOENIX COLUMN, 1747, and the WELLINGTON TESTIMONIAL, 1817. The name of the Park, which might reasonably be thought to derive from the Phoenix Column, in fact predates it and is a corruption of an Irish topographical name 'Fionn Uisce', the clear water, referring to a spring within the Park, and it was first applied to Phoenix House which stood on Thomas Hill and is now the location of the Magazine Fort. Within the park are extensive stretches of open parkland, contrasting with wooded areas, and a 300 head herd of fallow deer still roams as freely as in the eighteenth century. At the narrower, city end of the Park are athletic grounds catering for everything from hurling to polo, but no matter what activity is taking place in the Phoenix Park, it always seems large enough to accommodate much more, and still to appear uncrowded. Bus 10 from O'Connell Street and 25, 26 from Middle Abbey Street.

RANELAGH GARDENS, Ranelagh, D6. Hidden from the street and accessible through an arch in the old Harcourt Street Line embankment on Ranelagh Road is a small open space, now developed as a residential estate. This is the remains of one of the great eighteenth-century pleasure gardens, called after the Ranelagh Gardens in London. Bus 11, 11A, 13 from O'Connell Street, 48A from Hawkins Street.

ST. ANNE'S PARK, Clontarf, D3. Five hundred-acre park which was originally the estate of LORD ARDILAUN, the house was accidentally burned down in 1943 and the grounds were purchased by the Corporation. The rose gardens which have been developed in St. Anne's are spectacular when the flowers are in bloom, and have become one of the most popular features of any Dublin park. Many elements remain from the days when St. Anne's was a private estate and, after the Phoenix Park, this is the most extensive park within the greater Dublin area. Bus 29A, 30 Lower Abbey Street.

ST. AUDOEN'S PARK, Cornmarket, High Street, D8. Small park developed in what was the graveyard of the Medieval St. Audoen's Church, in the heart of the most historic area of the city. The park is bounded on the north by the Medieval city wall, and approached through the only surviving city gate, St. Audoen's Arch.

ST. CATHERINE'S PARK, Thomas Street, D8. To the rear of the eighteenth-century St. Catherine's Church, the old church-yard has been turned into a little park, shaded by mature trees, one of the few open spaces in this densely built up area surrounding the Guinness Brewery. Bus 21A, 78 Fleet Street.

ST. PATRICK'S PARK, Patrick Street, D8. This park, the only one of any significance in the LIBERTIES, was laid out by the IVEAGH TRUST during the 1890s as part of an admirable philanthropic scheme to improve the living standards of the local population. An extensive area of tenements between Bull Alley and St. Patrick's Close was cleared in order to make room for the park which now lies between the Cathedral and the extraordinary Victorian Baroque building known locally as the 'BAYNO', the Iveagh Play Centre, which is now the Liberties Vocational College. Along the eastern side of the park is a literary parade of plaques commemorating famous Dublin writers from JONATHAN SWIFT to SAMUEL BECKETT. A recent addition to the park is the 'Liberty Bell', a sculpture which derives its form from the Early Christian St. Patrick's Bell in the NATIONAL MUSEUM. An idea of what the area looked like before the park was developed can be had from WALTER OSBORNE'S painting 'St. Patrick's Close' which is in the NATIONAL GALLERY. To the left of the main entrance to the park from Patrick's Street a stone marks the presumed position of St. Patrick's Well, and an Early Christian cross stone found there is displayed in the Cathedral. Tradition states that the saint founded a church on this spot. Bus 50, 50A Aston Quay, 54, 54A Burgh Quay.

ST. STEPHEN'S GREEN, D2. The oldest of the Dublin squares, it was originally a Medieval commonage which was first enclosed in 1670 and is now the most popular and frequented city-centre park, providing an area for relaxation in the very centre of the business and shopping heart of the city. Screened by mature trees, the park has a great variety of different and attractive features, the principal of which is a large ornamental lake on which mallard and moorhens breed. Feeding the ducks on the Green is a favourite pastime with small children, and there is also a special children's section of the Green with swings and climbing frames for the more energetic. A garden for the blind is one of the more unusual features of the Green, with the planting identified in Braille inscriptions. The collection of sculptural monuments in St. Stephen's Green is the largest of any park or street in Dublin, apart from the NATIONAL GALLERY. The monuments are distributed around the park, both within and outside the railings, and can be found in detail under MONUMENTS and BENCHMARKS, but the most important of these are the Yeats memorial by HENRY MOORE, and busts or statues of ROBERT EMMET, JAMES JOYCE, JAMES CLARENCE MANGAN and THEOBALD WOLFE TONE. During the summer months concerts are given on the south side of the Green where there is a Victorian bandstand and wide expanses of grass for the audience to lounge upon. In essence, St. Stephen's Green is a Victorian park and its layout reflects the landscape ideas of the 1890s when Lord Ardilaun, whose statue is on the west side, restored the park and opened it for public use. Two attractive conical gazebos have recently been added to the central enclosure as shelters. During the hostilities of 1916, the battle raged across the Green, with rival outposts at the Shelbourne Hotel and the College of Surgeons. In an account written afterwards by the park superintendant, he reported that 'six of our

*St. Stephen's Green.*

waterfowl were killed or shot'. Since then the twenty-two acres of the Green have enjoyed a more tranquil existence, and despite the crowds which invade it daily, it continues to provide a fragment of fresh and untroubled countryside to delight all those who pass through it.

SANDYMOUNT BEACH ROAD, Ringsend, D4. Linear park running between Beach Road and the strand, and a popular point from which to gaze at the ever-changing conditions on DUBLIN BAY, or to walk on the fine hard sand which extends for miles along the coast.

SANDYMOUNT GREEN, Sandymount, D4. Triangular village green, surrounded by nineteenth-century houses and some attractive Victorian shopfronts. The Green has a fine bust of W.B.YEATS who was born in a house nearby, 5 Sandymount Avenue.

**PARNELL, CHARLES STEWART,** (1846-1891). Leader of the IRISH PARLIAMENTARY PARTY at Westminster and the most effective Irish political leader of the late nineteenth century. Parnell, a landowner from Co. Wicklow, became in 1879 the leader of the HOME RULE Party and his campaign in the House of Commons was paralleled by the Land

War in Ireland. This agitation, which sought to deprive landlords of their estates and redistribute their land amongst the tenant farmers, was accompanied by considerable violence. An attempt to smear Parnell's reputation in 1887 linked him to the murder of the Chief Secretary, Lord Frederick Cavendish, but this was subsequently shown to be based on forged letters. In 1890, Parnell became involved in another scandal, this time a divorce case which caused outrage amongst his parliamentary supporters both in Britain and Ireland, and led to a split in the Home Rule movement, with Parnell's supporters in the minority. The split, and the damage caused to Parnell's reputation, brought about the end of his absolute mastery of the Irish political situation. Home Rule, which had seemed to Parnell and his supporters to be within reach, was not achieved until thirty years after his death in 1891. He is buried in GLASNEVIN and, like a Bronze Age hero, his grave is marked by a granite boulder brought from his birthplace, Avondale in Co. Wicklow. In the years following his death, support for or antagonism towards Parnell's cause was a source of widespread contention, and it surfaces in the work of many later writers such as W.B. YEATS and JAMES JOYCE.

'Twas Irish humour, wet and dry flung
quicklime into Parnell's eye.
(*Gas from a Burner*, James Joyce.)

**PARNELL MONUMENT**, Upper
O'Connell Street, D1. A three-sided granite obelisk, surmounted by a flaming
torch, dominating the northern end of
O'Connell Street with a monumental
figure of CHARLES STEWART PARNELL by
Augustus Saint-Gaudens, 1907, standing in oratorical pose, arm outstretched
as though in the heat of a parliamentary
debate. The figure of Parnell is the finest
of any of the individual sculptures on
O'Connell Street and was erected in
1911 on the twentieth anniversary of his
death. Saint-Gaudens, the leading sculptor of the American Beaux Arts movement, had been born in Dublin, and this
factor was influential in his selection as
sculptor. The New York architect,
Henry Bacon, who is best known for the
Lincoln Memorial in Washington, designed the monument in collaboration
with the sculptor. The monument, with
the exception of the bronze components,
was executed in Ireland of Shantalla granite from Galway. Around its base is an
animal skull and swag motif frieze
which reflects that on the drum of the
ROTUNDA behind it.

**PARNELL SQUARE**, D1. Previously
known as Rutland Square and called
after the Lord Lieutenant, the Duke of
Rutland, it was laid out in the 1760s and
after ST. STEPHEN'S GREEN was the second Georgian square to be laid out. From
the very beginning the park of Parnell
Square was partially occupied by buildings along its southern side. This was Dr
Mosse's Lying-In Hospital, now known
as the ROTUNDA, and built by Mosse as
the first maternity hospital for the poor
in the British Isles. Following its com-

*Pavement Artists.*

pletion in 1752, the park was opened as
pleasure gardens to raise funds for the
hospital. The Rotunda itself followed in
1764 and the Assembly Rooms in 1784,
to provide a complex of elegant public
places of entertainment, all devoted to
the maintenance of the hospital. At the
same time housing was being developed
around the other sides of the square.
Lord Charlemont built a house in the
centre of the north side, CHARLEMONT
HOUSE, which gave the name Palace
Row to that group of houses, two of
which are now occupied by the DUBLIN
WRITERS' MUSEUM. The Garden of Remembrance, which now occupies the
area of the square opposite Charlemont
House, was opened in 1966 for the fiftieth anniversary of the 1916 RISING.
There are some fine Georgian doorways
on the east side of the square on Cavendish Row, and the end of the row houses
the GATE THEATRE as part of the Rotunda
complex.

**PAVEMENT ARTISTS.** Wherever there seems to be a throng of pedestrians and some area of vacant pavement, the street artist will establish his pitch, (it appears to be a male profession). The top of Grafton Street, further down beside the Molly Malone statue and the corner of College Green and Grafton Street are reliable locations. The central mall of O'Connell Street opposite the GPO is another suitable space. The pictures produced by these artists are generally enlargements of well-known works from European masters such as Caravaggio and the Impressionists and the practitioners tend to be either art students or the self-taught. Whatever their academic backgrounds the results are often well executed and lively interpretations of the originals. These artists have been mimicked by Traveller children also drawing on the streets, usually outside the Kilkenny Design shop on Nassau Street, sometimes on Baggot Street. The subject matter of their charming pictures are the universal children's themes of home, people and animals, except that they always draw caravans where a child from a settled community would draw a house. The creativity of their work tends to diminish the dismal spectacle of small children begging for a livelihood.

**PEARCE, SIR EDWARD LOVETT**, (1699-1733). Architect, the most brilliant and individual designer working in Ireland during the early eighteenth century. In his brief career (he died at thirty-four), he was responsible for some of the finest country houses, Cashel Palace and Bellamont Forest, and in Dublin, the Parliament House, begun in 1929 and completed after his death. Also from his hand is 9 HENRIETTA STREET, 1731, built for the Master of the Rolls, and the finest mansion on what was the earliest Geor-

gian street to be laid out in Dublin, and the Stillorgan Obelisk, 1732. Pearce, the first Irish-born architect to study in Italy, demonstrates by his robustly Classical work, his fine command of the language of Graeco-Roman architecture. His most important interior to survive intact in Dublin is the House of Lords in the old PARLIAMENT HOUSE, which has all the massive strength of an ante room of a Roman imperial baths.

**PEARSE, PATRICK**, (1879-1916). Revolutionary, writer and radical educationalist, born at 27 Great Brunswick Street (now Pearse Street). Having been educated as a barrister, he became involved in the Nationalist movement and the Irish language, founding St. Enda's, a bilingual experimental school in Ranelagh in 1908. This school he later moved to Rathfarnham to the building which is now the Pearse Museum. Gradually becoming more convinced of the need for symbolic action, in 1913 he joined the IRISH REPUBLICAN BROTHERHOOD (IRB) and the VOLUNTEERS, and in 1915 delivered an oration at the burial of JEREMIAH O'DONOVAN ROSSA, the Fenian. Commander-in-Chief during the 1916 RISING, his subsequent execution with the other leaders fulfilled his belief in the necessity of blood sacrifice. Regarded in the early years of the Irish Free State as a sacred revolutionary figure, sanctified in death, in recent years his role as educationalist and writer is attracting more attention.

**PEMBROKE ESTATE.** Prior to 1930 when it became part of the Greater Dublin Area, Pembroke was a separate township centred around the Pembroke Town Hall in Ballsbridge, which had been set up in 1853 on the estate of the Earl of Pembroke. Pembroke Town Hall belongs to a fine group of Victorian municipal buildings erected in varying styles by the separate townships. Interesting examples are to be found in Bray, Ballsbridge, Dun Laoghaire, and Rathmines.

**PHOENIX COLUMN**, Phoenix Park, D7. Erected in 1742 by the Viceroy, Lord Chesterfield, who is now remembered for his *Letters* to his son presented as a guide to good manners, and for the fact that Dr Johnson declined to dedicate his *Dictionary of the English Language* to him. The Column is the only free-standing eighteenth-century sculptural monument, other than decorations on buildings, to remain intact in central Dublin. On the top of a Corinthian column set on a stepped plinth, the Phoenix rises from stone flames which, because of the general greyness of the material, tend to merge with the bird's feathers. The Column is roughly equidistant from the Castleknock and Parkgate entrances to the Park, at a roundabout on the main roadway.

**PHOENIX PARK MURDERS**. In 1882, following the Land War and the imprisonment of CHARLES STEWART PARNELL and his followers in Kilmainham, Lord Frederick Cavendish was sent to Ireland as Viceroy in an attempt at conciliation. On his second day in Dublin, 6 May, while walking in the Phoenix Park with T.H. Burke, the Under Secretary, they were both attacked by assassins with surgical knives and murdered. The perpetrators were members of the INVINCIBLES, a splinter group of the Fenians and a secret society. The deed outraged public opinion and five of the Invincibles were hanged for the crime, having been informed upon by James Carey, one of their number. The Invincible organisation was not

heard of subsequently. The poet, SIR SAMUEL FERGUSON, wrote an account of the event, remarkable for its period, in which he imagines the thoughts of Carey concerning the murder.

> By this time all is over with them both.
>
> Ten minutes more, the Castle has the news,
>
> And haughty Downing Street in half an hour
>
> Is struck with palsy.

('At the Polo Ground', Sir Samuel Ferguson.)

**PIGEON HOUSE HOTEL**, South Bull Wall, D4. Fine granite eighteenth-century hotel building, standing on the edge of the Pigeon House harbour – once the port for the packet boats between Dublin and Chester in England. For many years used as ESB offices, it was transferred in 1986 to the Bolton Trust as an information technology resource centre. Its curious name comes from John Pidgeon who opened the first hostelry on this spot.

**PIKE THEATRE**, Herbert Lane, D2. Tiny experimental theatre in a converted mews garage, founded in 1953 by Alan Simpson and Carolyn Swift. In a not very vital theatrical period in Dublin, the Pike was for ten years the centre of innovative and exciting productions with, among other firsts, the premier of BRENDAN BEHAN's *Quare Fellow* in 1954 and the first Irish production of SAMUEL BECKETT's *Waiting for Godot* in 1955. Within the almost impossible constraints of a sixty-seat auditorium and minute stage, modern drama and late-night reviews continued to be produced in rapid succession until the theatre fell foul of public over-reaction to its production in 1953 of Tennessee Williams's *The Rose Tattoo*. This involved the director in a long drawn-out court case concerning the supposed indecency of the production. The off-stage drama eventually led to the closure of the Pike in 1964.

**PINKINDINDIES.** Eighteenth-century aristocratic thugs who created mayhem in the streets and taverns of Dublin. These bucks used to allow the points of their swords to protrude from the bottom of the scabbard. This enabled them to slash or 'pink' any passerby who attracted their unwelcome attention. As the majority of the Pinkindindies were well-off army officers or from noble families they normally escaped prosecution.

**PLAQUES.** Erected by Dublin Tourism and by other bodies and individuals since the late eighteenth century, these memorials to famous people and memorable events provide a tangible link between the present and those who have contributed in some manner to the life and legend of Dublin since the eighteenth century, recording the presence of many of the great names in the history of the city – JONATHAN SWIFT, HENRY GRATTAN, OSCAR WILDE and W.B. YEATS – the names one would expect to see remembered, but also surprises like LAFCADIO HEARN, ERWIN SCHRÖDINGER and LUDWIG WITTGENSTEIN. In most cases the plaques mark a building, or the site of one, in which an individual lived or worked, in others merely the approximate location of a presumed event, for example, the 1803 memorial to Swift in Little Ship Street where the wording states that 'it is reputed that' Swift was born nearby. With the frequent demolition and rebuilding of areas of the city over the centuries, this caution is often warranted. The following list identifies the subject and location of the memorials, but cannot claim to be totally comprehensive, as every year adds further plaques to the streets in honour of another important figure from the past whose life and works have attracted the attention of some admirers, and inevitably there are those which have escaped attention. Excluded from this list are, with a few exceptions, funerary monuments, foundation inscriptions, (three alone on the BALLAST OFFICE) and plaques on bridges which indicate a change of name. Occasionally the relevant inscription is carved into the stones of the structure (PARNELL, Dawson Street) and these, like some of the older plaques can be very hard to spot. Other buildings mentioned may in the course of time be demolished without the plaque being replaced nearby. As remarkable as this list is for the variety of its contents, remarkable also are the names of those who wait to be honoured, BISHOP BERKELEY, JAMES GANDON and PEG WOFFINGTON are three random examples.

AE (George William Russell), 5 Harcourt Terrace, D2.

AE, 84 Merrion Square, D2.

AE, 17 Rathgar Avenue, D6.

Balfe, Michael, Westbury Hotel, Harry Street, D2.

Barnardo, Dr Thomas, Millennium Garden, Dame Street, D2.

Barrington, Sir Jonah, 14 Harcourt Street, D2.

Barry, Kevin, 8 Fleet Street, D2.

Béaslaí Piaras, Parnell Square D1.

Beckett, Samuel, St. Patrick's Park, D8.

Behan, Brendan, 14 Russell Street, D3.

Behan, Brendan, St. Patrick's Park, D8.

Bloom, Leopold, 52 Clanbrassil Street, D8.

Bloom, Leopold, Sculpture trail, begins Easons, Middle Abbey Street, D1.

Bond, Oliver, Bond House, Lower Bridge Street, D8.

Bowen, Elizabeth, 15 Herbert Place, D2.

Burke-Sheridan, Margaret, 6 Lower Fitzwilliam Street, D2.

Butt, Isaac, Clonskeagh Road, Clonskeagh, D14.

Casement, Sir Roger, 29 Lawson Terrace, Sandycove Road, Co. Dublin.

Ceannt, Eamonn, 10 Ardee Street, D8.

Clancy, Peadar, Exchange Court, Dame Street, D2.

Clare, Earl of, Great Ship Street, D8.

Clarke, Austin, 83 Manor Street, Stonybatter, D7.

Clarke, Tom, 74 Parnell Street, D1.

Clonmel House, 17 Harcourt street, D2.

Clune, Conor, Exchange Court, Dame street, D2.

Colles, Abraham, Dr. Steevens's Hospital, D8.

Colum, Padraic, Eden Road, Glasthule, Dun Laoghaire.

Colum, Padraic, 11 Edenvale Road, Ranelagh, D6.

Coombe Lying-In Hospital, Coombe Portico, The Coombe, D8.

Cosgrave, T.W. 174 Mount Brown, D8.

Crosbie, Richard, Northbrook Road, Ranelagh, D6.

Cusack, Michael, 4 Gardiner Place, D1.

Dargan, William, 2 Fitzwilliam Square, D2.

Davis, Thomas, Independent Newspapers, Middle Abbey Street, D1.

Davis, Thomas, 67 Lower Baggot Street, D2.

Dillon, John, 2 North Great George's Street, D1.

Dillon, John Blake, Independent Newspapers, Middle Abbey Street, D2.

Donnelly, Dan, River House, Chancery Street, D1.

Duffy, Charles Gavan, Independent Newspapers, Middle Abbey Street, D1.

Dunlop, John Boyd, 67 Upper Stephen Street, D2.

Dunsany, Lady, 17 Harcourt Street, D2

Emmet Robert, Emmet Bridge, Clanbrassil Street, D8.

Emmet, Robert, 79 Grafton Street, D2.

Emmet, Robert, St. Catherine's Church, Thomas Street, D8.

Ferguson, Sir Samuel, 20 North Great George's Street, D1

Field, John, Golden Lane, D8.

Field, John, St. Werburgh's Church, Werburgh Street, D8.

Fitzgerald, Lord Edward, Frescati Shopping Centre, Blackrock, Co Dublin.

Fitzmaurice, Col. James, 33 Mountjoy Cottages, D1.

Fitzmaurice, George, 3 Harcourt Street, D2.

French Peter's, opposite Adelaide Hospital, Peter Street, D8.

Gibbon, William Monk, Tara Hall, Sandycove, Co. Dublin.

Godley, John Robert, Holles Street Hospital, Lower Mount Street, D2.

Gogarty, Oliver St. John, 5 Cavendish Row, D1.

Gogarty, Oliver St. John, The Shelbourne Hotel, St. Stephen's Green D2.

Grattan, Henry, Great Ship Street, D8.

Grattan, Henry, 56 St. Stephen's

Green, D2.

Griffith, Arthur, 122 St. Lawrence Road, Clontarf, D3.

Griffith, Sir Richard, 2 Fitzwilliam Place, D2.

Griffith, Sir Richard, 8 Hume Street, D2.

Hamilton, Sir William Rowan, Broom Bridge, Cabra.

Handel, George Frederick, Kennan's Ironworks, Fishamble Street, D2.

Hearn, Lafcadio, 21 Leinster Square, Rathmines, D6.

Hearn, Lafcadio, 73 Upper Leeson Street, D2.

Hertzog, Rabbi, 33 Bloomfield Avenue, D8.

Heuston, Seán, Platform 2, Heuston Station, D8.

Hopkins, Gerard Manley, Newman House, 86 St. Stephen's Green, D2.

Hughes, John, 28 Lennox Street, D8.

Hyde, Douglas, St. Patrick's Cathedral, D8.

IRA, 6 Gardiner's Row, D1.

Johnson, Hester, (Stella), St. Patrick's Cathedral.

Joyce, James, 41 Brighton Square, Rathgar, D6.

Joyce, James, 23 Carysford Avenue, Blackrock.

Joyce, James, Mullingar House, Chapelizod.

Joyce, James, Newman House, 86 St. Stephen's Green, D2.

Joyce, James, St. Patrick's Park, D8.

Joyce, James, 52 Upper Clanbrassil Street, D8.

Kavanagh, Patrick, 62 Pembroke Road, Ballsbridge, D4.

Kavanagh, Patrick, 19 Raglan Road, Ballsbridge, D4.

Kearney, Peadar, 68 Lower Dorset Street, D1.

Le Fanu, J. Sheridan, 70 Merrion

Square, D2.

Lord Mayor's Walk, Royal Hibernian Way, Dawson Street, D2.

MacBride, Major John, 8 Spenser Villas, Glenageary, Co. Dublin.

Mac Diarmada, Seán, Irish Times, 12 D'Olier Street, D2.

MacLiammóir, Mícheál, 4 Harcourt Terrace, D2.

McCormack, Count John, Glena, Rock Road, Booterstown, Co. Dublin.

Mc Kee, Dick, Exchange Court, Dame Street, D2.

Madden, Dr RR, 3 Booterstown Avenue, Blackrock, Co. Dublin.

Mahaffy, Sir John Pentland, 38 North Great George's Street, D1.

Mangan, James Clarence, St. Patrick's Park, D8.

Mangan, James Clarence, The Castle Inn, 5 Lord Edward Street, D8.

Monck, WHS, 16 Earlsfort Terrace, D1.

Moore, George, 4 Ely Place,D2.

Moore, Thomas, 79 Grafton Street, D2.

Morgan, Lady, Setanta House, Kildare Street, D2.

Murray, T.C., 11 Sandymount Avenue, Ballsbridge, D4.

*Nation, The*, Independent Newspapers, Middle Abbey Street, D1.

Newman, John Henry, Newman House, 86 St. Stephen's Green, D2.

O'Carolan, Turlough, St. Patrick's Cathedral, D8.

O'Casey, Seán, St. Patrick's Park, D8.

O'Casey, Seán, 85 Upper Dorset Street, D1.

O'Connell, Daniel, 58 Merrion Square, D2.

O'Connor, Andrew, 77 Merrion Square, D2.

O'Nolan, Brian (Flann O'Brien), Avoca Road, Blackrock, Co. Dublin.

O'Rahilly, The, O'Rahilly Parade, Moore Street, D1.

Ó Riada, Seán, 1 Galloping Green, Stillorgan, Co. Dublin.

Osborne, Walter, 5 Castlewood Avenue, Rathmines, D6.

O'Sullivan, Fr FJ, 32 Fitzwilliam Place, D2.

Ouzel Galley, Commercial Buildings, Dame Street, D2.

Parnell, Charles Stewart, Ulster Bank, 1 Dawson Street, D2.

Parnell, Sir John, Merrion Square, Dublin 2.

Pearse, Patrick and William, 27 Pearse Street, D2.

Petrie, George, 21 Great Charles Street, D1.

Praeger, Robert Lloyd, 19 Fitzwilliam Square, D2.

Proclamation of 1916, GPO, O'Connell Street, D1.

Purser, Sarah, 11 Harcourt Terrace, D2.

St. Michael le Pole, Great Ship Street, D8.

Schrödinger, Erwin, 65 Merrion Square, D2.

Shaw, George Bernard, St. Patrick's Park, D8.

Shaw, George Bernard, 33 Synge Street, D8.

Shaw, George Bernard, Torca Cottage, Dalkey Hill.

Sheridan, Richard Brinsley, 79 Grafton Street, D2.

Stanford, Sir Charles Villiers, 2 Herbert Street, D2.

Stoker, Bram, 30 Kildare Street, D2.

Synge, John Millington, 2 Newtown Villas, Rathfarnham, D 14.

Synge, John Millington, St. Patrick's Park, D8.

Swift, Jonathan, Little Ship Street, D2.

Swift, Jonathan, St. Patrick's Cathedral, D8.

Swift, Jonathan, St. Patrick's Park, D8.

Tandy, Napper, St. Audoen's Park, High Street, D8.

Tracey, Sean, 94 Talbot Street, D1.

Ulysses, (Aeolus - Lestrygonians episodes), 14 plaques set into the pavement, see BLOOM.

Ulysses, (Sirens episode), Ormond Hotel, Ormond Quay, D1.

Waxie's Dargle, Pembroke Street, Irishtown.

Wellington, Duke of, 79 Grafton Street, D2.

Whyte's Academy, 79 Grafton Street, D2.

Wilde, Oscar, St. Patrick's Park, D8.

Wilde, Oscar, 21 Westland Row, D2.

Wilde, Sir William, 1 Merrion Square, D2.

Wittgenstein, Ludwig, Ashling Hotel, Parkgate Street, D

Wolfe Tone, Theobald, PMPA Building, Wolfe Tone Street, D1.

Yeats, Jack B., 18 Fitzwilliam Square, D2.

Yeats, William Butler, 82 Merrion Square, D2.

Yeats, William Butler, St. Patrick's Park, D8

.

**PLASTERWORK.** Of all the decorative applied arts of the Georgian period, the most outstanding results were achieved by the stuccodores, and rich examples of their work covering different styles and developments can be seen in many of Dublin's buildings, although few are accessible to the public. So widespread was the use of decorated plaster ceilings that even the most unprepossessing eighteenth-century building can contain remarkable decoration. Landmarks in the stuccodores' art are the chapel ceiling in the ROYAL HOSPI-

TAL KILMAINHAM, which although now replaced by a replica, is an astonishing Carolean feast of floral decoration. The chapel of the ROTUNDA HOSPITAL is a Baroque extravaganza with the human figure as the chief motif and the CHAPEL ROYAL at Dublin Castle, a church interior from the very end of the Georgian period, is no less impressive for its vaulting and figure work. These plasterworkers, originally Continental, later developed as an indigenous group of master craftsmen. The work of the FRANCINI brothers, ROBERT WEST and MICHAEL STAPLETON is found principally in private houses of the period, and the Apollo Room in Clanwilliam House, 85 St. Stephen's Green, by the Francini, which has nearly life-size figures of the God and the nine Muses, is probably the most extraordinary of many remarkable rooms. POWERSCOURT HOUSE in South William Street, now a shopping centre, is the only Georgian mansion which can be seen in its entirety with fine examples of plasterwork in the Adams tradition.

**PODDLE.** Tributary of the Liffey, it rises in Tallaght, flowing through Templeogue, Kimmage and the Liberties before entering the river at Merchant's Quay. The Poddle expanded into a pool where the gardens of DUBLIN CASTLE are now, and this formed part of the defensive moat of the castle during the Medieval period. In the Viking era, the pool contributed to the strategic importance of the hill of Dublin, providing a safe mooring for shipping.

**POETS AND POETRY.** The concerns of Irish poetry up to relatively recent times have tended to be treated against a rural background, and despite the fact that the majority of writers today live in an urban environment, nature and life on the land continue to provide a significant inspiration for Irish poets. All the major figures of Irish poetry – JONATHAN SWIFT, W.B. YEATS, PATRICK KAVANAGH, LOUIS MAC NEICE, AUSTIN CLARKE – have either lived permanently in Dublin or been associated with it during some period of their lives, and taken the city as subject matter for their writing, yet few of them used the urban ambiance as their poetic landscape. In fact the Dublin ballad writers of the seventeenth to twentieth centuries have a stronger involvement with the place than any of the poets, with the possible exception of Austin Clarke. Brief yet memorable references to and descriptions of Dublin occur in the works of all the major poets, and give the reader compelling images of the changing personality of Dublin. Poetry Ireland, 44 Upper Mount Street, organises poetry readings throughout the year, and readings occur occasionally at other venues – pubs and bookshops – while in Grafton Street, pavement poets have joined the buskers and recite their own and others' work to appreciative crowds of passersby.

Grey brick upon brick,
Declamatory bronze
On sombre pedestals –
O'Connell, Grattan, Moore –
And the brewery tugs and the swans
On the balustraded stream.

('The Closing Album, Dublin', Louis Mac Neice.)

A swan goes by head low with many
    apologies,
Fantastic light looks through the eyes
    of bridges …

('Lines written on a Seat on the Grand Canal, Dublin, "Erected to the Memory of Mrs Dermot O'Brien"', Patrick Kavanagh.)

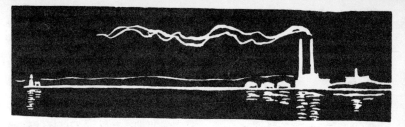

*Poolbeg Lighthouse and the South Bull Wall.*

**POOLBEG LIGHTHOUSE**, D4. The lighthouse, the construction of which began in 1761, is the culmination of an extensive harbour works programme which involved building 4.8km (3 miles) of granite causeway along the south of the Liffey channel in order to 'train' the river and to improve its navigability – a perpetual problem. The lighthouse replaces a lightship which was once moored at this spot marking the 'Little Pool', from which Poolbeg takes its name. The 'Great Pool' was at Clontarf. Prior to building the wall, a timber breakwater had been placed on the sandbanks in an effort to limit the amount of silt being carried by the clockwise motions of the currents in the bay, as this became deposited in the channel and on the harbour bar. Later when this breakwater, known as 'the piles', was made permanent the wall was constructed outwards from the city, and backwards from the lighthouse, meeting at the bend now known as the PIGEON HOUSE. The harbour is now part of the Corporation Sewage Works, but the eighteenth-century Pigeon House Hotel, built on the edge of the harbour, still stands. Bus 1 from Townsend Street.

**POPULATION OF DUBLIN.** To make a comparison between current population figures and those from the earliest periods of the city's history is not very useful, because the scale of modern cities bears little or no resemblance to those of the ancient world. No contemporary records exist for the old city and present-day estimates merely amount to an educated guess by archaeologists and historians based on the known size of the city, the possible number of habitations which it enclosed, and average family sizes. Figures for the later periods are derived from contemporary sources, and therefore can be considered as more accurate. The cartographer John Roque calculated the number of houses in Dublin in 1755 as being 12,060, and based on an average of eight occupants per house came up with a population figure for that year of 96,480. However, present-day estimates consider this figure to be far too small. In current population terms, the Viking city would be classed as a not very extensive town. By the eighteenth century Dublin had become one of the fastest-growing and largest cities in Europe, and this phenomenon continued in the following century at a slightly less accelerated pace. It was not until the mid-twentieth century that another great surge in growth occurred, which continues into the present.

Viking period, tenth century, 5,000
Norman period, twelfth century, 8,000

Late Medieval, fifteenth century,
50,000

Georgian, late eighteenth century,
150,000

Victorian, early nineteenth century
224,000

Victorian, mid nineteenth century,
370,000

Early twentieth century, 472,935

Late twentieth century (1990) greater
Dublin, 1,020,000

**PORTMARNOCK.** On a spit of sand-dunes running parallel to the coast north of Dublin Bay is the 4.8km (3 mile) long Silver Strand, one of the finest beaches in the Dublin area. Nearby is Portmarnock Golf Course. Bus 32, 32A from Abbey Street Lower.

**PORTOBELLO.** At Portobello Bridge on the Grand Canal was a typical complex of the industrial revolution – a canal harbour and hotel to facilitate the transport of freight and passengers. The harbour was filled in the 1960s, but the hotel, refurbished and converted into an office building, is still an important feature of the canal bank landscape. Behind the hotel and running along the banks of the canal is the nineteenth-century Portobello quarter, two-storey brick artisans' dwellings.

**POST IMPRESSIONISTS.** The first exhibition of the Post Impressionists in Dublin was held at the United Arts Club, Fitzwilliam Street, on 26 January 1911. This exhibition, which had been organised in London by Roger Fry, had caused a sensation there and is regarded as a significant milestone in the development of British twentieth-century painting. The reception of the exhibition in Dublin was more sedate, and the fact that paintings by Cezanne, Gauguin, Van Gogh, Matisse and Signac were hanging a few minutes' walk from St. Stephen's Green seems to have caused little excitement. The exhibition was organised in Dublin by Ellie Duncan, later to be the first curator of the Municipal Gallery of Modern Art. Artistically this exhibition must rank as one of the most important events in the city's cultural calendar, on a par with the well remembered visits to Dublin of Paganini or Handel.

**POST OFFICES.** The General Post Office (GPO), O'Connell Street has been, since its inception in 1812, the centre of postal services in the city and remains so today, with the longest opening hours and most extensive postal and philatelic services. Other city-centre post offices are at St. Andrew's Street, D2; Anne Street, D2; Ormond Quay, D1; Pearse Street, D2 and South King Street, (confined to the telephone service). Opening hours for the GPO, Mon-Sat, 8.00-8.00, Sun and BH, 10.00-6.30. All other post offices, Mon-Sat, 9.00-5.30, closed for lunch 12.30-2.00. All post offices are closed on Christmas Day and New Year's Day.

**POWERSCOURT DEMESNE,** Enniskerry, Co. Wicklow. The Powerscourt estate is one of the finest surviving examples of eighteenth- and nineteenth-century landscaping in Ireland. The central block of the Palladian house by RICHARD CASTLE was recently destroyed in a fire, but the grounds remain undiminished and their mature planting and elaborate formal terracing all appear to culminate in the stunning spectacle of the Sugarloaf Mountain, as though arranged by the garden designer for just that effect. Powerscourt is particularly rich in garden sculpture and ironwork. The 120m (400ft) waterfall in

*Powerscourt Demesne.*

the estate is the highest in Ireland. 22.5km (14 miles) from Dublin.

**POWERSCOURT HOUSE**, South William Street, D2. This is the only eighteenth-century mansion in Dublin in which the principal rooms are open to the public. Built in 1771 for Lord Powerscourt, it was designed by Robert Mack, with Rococo plasterwork in the stairhall by James Mc Cullagh, Adamesque plasterwork in the reception rooms by MICHAEL STAPLETON and an oak carving on the staircase by Ignatius Mc Donagh. In the narrow width of South William Street the heavily ornamented façade of the building comes as a surprise. Monumental gateways on either side of the façade led into the stable and kitchen blocks at the rear. After the ACT OF UNION, FRANCIS JOHNSTON added a courtyard to the back of the house for a Stamp Office. The entire complex of Powerscourt House and the Stamp Office courtyard was skilfully converted during the 1980s into a shopping centre, and represents one of the most successful reuses of a historic building in Dublin.

**PRINTING HOUSE**, TCD. By RICHARD CASTLE, 1734, small Doric temple built to house the college printing press. The Georgian Society Records, 1908-13, a landmark in the cause of Irish architectural heritage, were printed there.

**PROCLAMATION OF 1916**. Plaques inscribed with the complete wording of the PROCLAMATION, which was read by PATRICK PEARSE from the steps of the GPO on Easter Monday 24 April 1916, can be seen in Connolly, Heuston and Pearse Railway Stations and also under the portico of the GPO on O'Connell Street.

**PROVOST'S HOUSE**, Grafton Street Lower, D2. The only major Dublin townhouse to have been continually used for the purpose for which it was built. Constructed in 1759 as a residence for the Provost of Trinity, the house and furnishings have hardly changed since then. Similar to LEINSTER HOUSE as it was in the eighteenth century, the Provost's House stands back from the street concealed behind a high wall with a heavily rusticated entranceway. The façade of the building, which is flanked by a pair of single-storey pavilions, is also heavily rusticated and dominated by the central Venetian window on the first floor. Behind this window and running the full length of the first floor is the main apartment of the house, the Saloon, the magnificent plasterwork decoration of which is enhanced by a collection of splendid paintings by Gainsborough and others. The Provost's House is a private residence, but may occasionally be seen by appointment.

## PUBS

ALFIE BYRNE'S, 1 Chancery Place, off Inns' Quay, D1, tel 735627. Modernised late-eighteenth-century pub now called after Dublin's longest-serving Lord Mayor, who held office in the 1930s, it was previously known as the 'Legal Eagle' and the 'Tilted Wig'. Opposite the side of the Four Courts, it is busy with legal types and their clients during session times.

ANNA LIVIA, 58 Fleet Street, D2, tel 779393/711716. The ambiance of the old Theatre Royal in Hawkins Street is preserved here with its actual bar counter and fittings.

ASHTON'S, Clonskeagh Road, D6, tel 830045. Riverside pub on two levels where you can drink while watching the Dodder flow peacefully by.

BAGGOT INN, 143 Lower Baggot Street, D2, tel 761430. Important rock music venue in an otherwise undistinguished but very popular pub.

THE BAILEY, 2 Duke Street, D2, tel 770600. Bar with upstairs restaurant and dark glass arched façade embellished with eight horses' heads. It attracts the young business people from the surrounding area. In the 1940s to 1960s this was one of the haunts of the literary folk, and the front door of 7 Eccles Street, BLOOM'S house, is preserved in the hallway.

BARTLEY DUNNE'S, Lower Stephen Street, D2, tel 533137. Young black leather jacket crowd are to be found in throngs here, with bikers revving their engines on the pavement.

BOWE'S PUBLIC HOUSE, 31 Fleet Street, D1, tel 714038. Opposite the rear entrance to *The Irish Times*, a small and convivial drinking place with panelled and mirrored walls. Fleet Street, which connects D'Olier Street through Temple Bar and Essex Street with Parliament Street, has for what is an extremely unobtrusive street a great many pubs of distinction.

*The Brazen Head.*

THE BRAZEN HEAD, 20 Lower Bridge Street, D2, tel 6795156. The oldest pub in Dublin and still immensely popular for dining, music sessions (traditional), and plain old fashioned pint drinking. There has been a tavern on this spot since Medieval times, but the present building dates from the early eighteenth century. Approached from a small courtyard set back from the street, the bar and upper rooms in which revolution was plotted during the eighteenth and nineteenth centuries have lost none of their conspiratorial atmosphere.

BRUXELLES, 7 Harry Street, D2, tel 775362. Gothic Revival pub by J.J. O'Callaghan, 1890, and one of the best period interiors in the city. Fashionable youthful clientele.

BUTTERY BRASSERIE, 2 Royal Hibernian Way, off Dawson Street, D2, tel 6796259. Café-bar in sophisticated Continental style.

DAVY BYRNE'S, 21 Duke Street, D2, tel 775217. Pub with substantial literary associations. Here Mr BLOOM ate a gorgonzola sandwich and drank a glass of burgundy, a snack which is now traditionally served on 16 June, BLOOMSDAY. Fine Art Deco interior with murals of the Bohemian life from the 1930s by Cecil ffrench Salkeld, symbolist artist and father-in-law of BRENDAN BEHAN. Among other interesting artworks is a portrait of JOYCE by HARRY KERNOFF and a sketch of Davy Byrne's snug by WILLIAM ORPEN. Like the BAILEY on the opposite side of the street, relaxing business people account for most of the jam-packed crowd. Oysters are a speciality of the house.

DAWSON LOUNGE, 25 Dawson Street, D2, tel 775909. The only bar in this most civic of Dublin streets, and so well hidden as to be easily missed. Approached through an unobtrusive doorway, this is a basement bar, a rarity in the city. Well known for its range of individual cocktails.

DOHENY & NESBITT, 5 Lower Baggot Street, D2, tel 762945. A dark brown interior which looks like it has not changed since the Edwardian era. Snugs, glazed partitions and barstools provide the only decor in what must be among the most popular drinking places in the city. Famous for the patronage of economists, civil servants and moulders of opinion in politics. Upstairs is a rather more subdued and comfortable lounge.

DUKE LOUNGE, 9 Duke Street, D2, tel 774054. Popular and comfortable pub in which to negotiate business deals and relax afterwards.

FOGGY DEW, 1 Upper Fownes Street, D2, tel 779328. The Bohemian element of the Temple Bar area congregate here, with musicians and artists from the art and recording studios nearby.

GROGAN'S CASTLE LOUNGE, South William Street, D2, tel 779320. Dark and traditional interior with an equal mixture of Bohemian and local clients. Ideal for a more relaxed and private drink.

HARTIGANS, Lower Leeson Street, D2, tel 762280. Just round the corner from the NATIONAL CONCERT HALL and ST. STEPHEN'S GREEN, a traditional pub, popular with students and young people.

HUGHES, MICHAEL, Chancery Place, D1, tel 72654. Like Alfie Byrne's, barristers and those engaged in the law form much of the crowd here. Traditional and jazz sessions.

HUNTERS, South Frederick Street, D2, tel 775665. Sophisticated bar, part of the Pink Elephant night club.

THE INTERNATIONAL BAR, 23 Wicklow Street, D2, tel 779250. Well known for alternative theatre and comedy in the upstairs bar.

JUDGE ROY BEANS, 45 Nassau Street, D2, tel 679739. American-style wild-west decor and tex-mex restaurant in bar.

KEHOES, JOHN, 9 South Anne Street, D2. Arty crowd, where to go after an opening

*Handsome lamp outside Neary's Pub.*

in the nearby galleries.

KENNY'S PUBLIC HOUSE, 31 Westland Row, D2. The closest pub to the back entrance of TRINITY COLLEGE and consequently a haunt of academics and students.

THE LONG HALL, 51 South Great George's Street, D2, tel 751590. Fine Victorian interior of mirrors and polished wood, with snug at the rear; has the reputation of having the longest bar counter in the city.

McDAIDS, 3 Harry Street, D2, tel 6794395. High ceilinged pub, full of atmosphere and literary associations. A photograph exists of BRENDAN BEHAN seated at a table in McDaids, one pint glass empty, another at the ready, and a tiny typewriter wedged between them.

This antique typewriter is on display in the CIVIC MUSEUM with some of the manuscripts produced on it. The bar counter in McDaids was moved some years ago from one side of the pub to the other, a change guaranteed to disconcert the serious drinker.

McGRATHS PUB, 33 Upper O'Connell Street, D2, tel 787505. Convenient to the GATE THEATRE, a nineteenth-century pub given the opulent modern treatment, comfortable and spacious.

MOTHER REDCAPS TAVERN, Back Lane, off High Street, D8, tel 538306. Important country and traditional music venue in one of the most historic parts of the city.

MULLIGANS, J, 8 Poolbeg Street, D2, tel 775582. There has been a pub here since 1782, and the current Mulligans, which it has been known as since the mid-nineteenth century, has the reputation of serving the best pint in Dublin. Crowded and atmospheric, and favoured by the journalists of the nearby newspaper offices.

NEARY'S, 1 Chatham Street, D2, tel 777371. The severe brick and limestone front of Neary's is decorated with a pair of splendid lanterns on either side of the entrance, held aloft by cast-iron arms protruding from the wall, the signature of this famous pub. The stage door of the GAIETY THEATRE is nearby and whoever is appearing on stage may be seen relaxing here after the show.

THE NORSEMAN, Temple Bar, D2. Bustling with the life which inhabits the Temple Bar quarter, can Viking Dublin have been this crowded?

THE OAK, 81 Dame Street, D2, tel 772504. Quiet old-fashioned bar in the heart of the stockbroker belt.

O'DONOGHUES, 15 Merrion Row, D2, tel 614303. The most popular and populous traditional music venue in town with patrons spilling out on to the pavement. More a case of the atmosphere of traditional music than the real thing which can be heard in slightly less crowded circumstances elsewhere.

O'DWYERS BROS, 7 Lower Mount Street, D2, tel 762887. Tastefully modernised Victorian bar, with extensive pizza restaurant in the basement.

THE OLD STAND, 37 Exchequer Street, D1, tel 770821. Modernised but historic pub, now associated with people from the financial sector and rugby enthusiasts.

O'NEILL, MICHAEL, Suffolk Street, D2, tel 6793671. Large Victorian pub with five interconnecting bars inside, serving a very cosmopolitan clientele.

OVAL LOUNGE, 78 Middle Abbey Street, D1, tel 730905. One of those *tout le monde* pubs, always busy.

THE PALACE BAR, 1 Fleet Street, D2, tel 779290. Next to the Westmoreland Street Bewley's side entrance, a discreet exterior and traditional interior with snug at the rear which was a literary salon during the 1940s presided over by R.M. Smyllie, the editor of *The Irish Times*, with writers such as BRENDAN BEHAN and BRIAN O'NOLAN in attendance. A contemporary cartoon on display in the snug shows the entire personnel of literary and artistic Dublin congregating in the bar. Today it is as popular with bus drivers as Bohemians.

THE PEMBROKE, 31 Lower Pembroke Street, D2, tel 762980. Smart and sophisticated period interior with interesting fittings.

PETER'S PUB, 1 Johnson Place, off South King Street, D2, tel 778588. Small but attractive pub around the corner from the GAIETY THEATRE. The simplicity of the black and gold façade is unusual among the ornate fronts of Dublin pubs.

RYANS of Parkgate Street, D7. The finest traditional pub in Dublin for Victorian atmosphere and fittings, snugs, mirrors, engraved glass and dark wood. Outside the main gates of the PHOENIX PARK, the patrons are both local and passing trade.

SINNOTTS, South King Street, D2, tel 784698. Traditional pub which was demolished to make way for the St. Stephen's Green Centre, it has re-emerged as a basement bar with a remarkable display of literary portraits and theatrical memorabilia, and patrons of the GAIETY THEATRE across the street make a dash for refreshments to this convenient location during the interval.

SLATTERY'S, 129 Capel Street, D1, tel 727971. The most well known pub venue for traditional music in Dublin. Set dancing and ballads make up part of the diverse range of traditional entertainment which are an all-year-round feature.

STAG'S HEAD, 1 Dame Court, off Dame Street, D2, tel 6793701. Fine Victorian pub, by A.J. Mc Gloughlin, 1895, with brasswork, mirrors and stained glass.

TONERS VICTORIAN BAR, 139 Lower Baggot Street, D2, tel 763090. Dark interior with little snugs and glazed partitions, sensitively adapted to present-day needs. The plain Victorian façade is decorated with unusual fascia brackets of fruit. Without any of the opulence of the great nineteenth-century pub interiors, this remains one of the most attractive with an air of timeless simplicity.

**PURSER, SARAH,** (1848-1943). Artist, born in Dublin, studied there and in Paris. Throughout her very long life Sarah Purser was instrumental in promoting the arts in Dublin, as well as carrying on a career as a fine portrait painter. In 1903, and in collaboration with EDWARD MARTYN, she founded the co-operative stained glass studios, AN TÚR GLOINE, a venture which was to be of outstanding significance in the field of church art. In 1924, she founded the Friends of the National Collections to encourage people to present or bequeath significant works of art to the underfunded national institutions. She also prompted DOUGLAS HYDE, then President of Ireland to present CHARLEMONT HOUSE to the Corporation as an art gallery. It is now the home of the HUGH LANE GALLERY.

QUAKERS. The contribution of the Religious Society of Friends or Quaker community to social and economic life in Dublin is considerable and a number of prominent Quaker families have left a permanent mark on the history of the city. The Quakers were established in Dublin by the mid-seventeenth century, and the Eustace Street Meeting House was built in 1692 (it is now the theatre of the Irish Film Institute). During the nineteenth century they conducted relief work amongst the poor of the Liberties.

QUAYS. In the 1670s Ormond Quay was laid out in its present form, with a wide roadway between the houses and the river. This quay was later extended to include Bachelor's Walk and became the prototype of all the later developments of the riverside, leading to the construction of one of the city's most distinctive and attractive features, the Liffey Quays. Over two hundred years passed before the embanking of the city reach of the Liffey was completed by the construction of the north and south Bull Walls. North of the Liffey and from the west the quays are: Wolfe Tone, Sarsfield, Ellis, Arran, Inn's, Ormond, Bachelor's Walk, Eden, CUSTOM HOUSE and the North Wall. Within Dublin Port the quays are: Alexandra and Timber. South of the Liffey and from the west the quays are: Victoria, Usher's Island, Usher's, Merchant's, Wood, Essex, Wellington, Aston, Burgh, George's, City and Sir John Rogerson's . In Grand Canal Basin on the south bank of the Liffey the quays are: Britain, Hanover, Grand Canal and Charlotte.

QUEEN ANNE PERIOD, (1702-1714). The number of buildings which survive in Dublin from the period immediately prior to the great flowering of Georgian architecture is extremely small, but of considerable importance. The survival of these buildings is in all cases due to their being in state, municipal or charitable society ownership, and therefore subject to a continuity of function. Private houses in no longer fashionable areas frequently declined into tenements or warehouses. Two hospitals, an army barracks, two libraries, a Guildhall and an official residence comprise the group and with few exceptions they maintain their original appearance. Architectural style is no respecter of strict chronologies and there is an inevitable overlapping of period from the Restoration into the Queen Anne and subsequently into the early Georgian. Chronologically the buildings are the ROYAL HOSPITAL KILMAINHAM, 1668, the Rubrics TCD, 1701, MARSH'S LIBRARY, 1705, the TAILORS' HALL, 1706, Royal Barracks (now Collins), 1709, the MANSION HOUSE, 1710, the Library, TCD, 1712, and Dr. Steevens' Hospital, 1720, which although built within the Georgian period, stylistically belongs to the earlier era.

*QUERIST, THE.* Written by BISHOP BERKELEY between 1735 and 1737 with the practical objective of provoking thought amongst his complacent fellow countrymen. Berkeley felt the economic difficulties facing the country were due to the absence of a national bank and the scarcity of coinage, particularly of small denomination. The questions in *The Querist*, which deal with a wide range of economic as well as social issues are aimed at those in positions of power and certainly provoked widespread discussion, but Berkeley's objective was not achieved until after his death with the foundation of the Bank of Ireland in 1783.

Whether the industry of our people employed in foreign lands, while our own are left uncultivated, be not a great loss to the country?

Whether there be not every year more cash circulated at the card tables of Dublin than at all the fairs of Ireland?

**R**ADIO STATIONS. The national broadcasting authority, RTE has three stations, RTE 1 and 2, and Raidio na Gaeltachta broadcasting on respectively, 88.5 FM and 91.8 FM, and 92.5 FM. The RTE 1 station covers current affairs, the arts, discussion programmes and general social issues, RTE 2 is concerned with popular music. Raidio na Gaeltachta broadcasts Irish programmes during the day and classical music programmes in the evenings. Other commercial stations, all of which broadcast different categories of popular music are Capital Radio, 104.4 FM, Century Radio, 100 FM, Classic Hits on 98 FM, and Horizon Radio on 94.9 FM.

**RAILWAY RECORD SOCIETY OF IRELAND**, Box 9, Heuston Station, D8. Society devoted to the preservation of relics of the railways and the age of steam and has an extensive collection of Railwayana at its headquarters in the old Goods Offices at Heuston. Trips and lectures are organised throughout the year, travelling by steam and diesel locomotive to other parts of the country. The library is open on Tuesdays, 8.00pm-10.00pm except July and August.

**RAILWAYS.** The first railway in Ireland was the DUBLIN TO KINGSTOWN which opened in 1834, running from Westland Row to what is now DUN LAOGHAIRE, the route followed today by the most advanced railway in the country, the DART. The national rail network operates, for the east, west and south from HEUSTON STATION, and for the north from CONNOLLY STATION.

**RANELAGH**, D6. Former village outside the development of the eighteenth century canals, its name derives from the eighteenth-century RANELAGH GARDENS, a remnant of which survives between Ranelagh Road and Leeson Park. The area was extensively developed during the nineteenth century and has some fine late Georgian and Victorian architecture. Mount Pleasant, Belgrave and Dartmouth Squares are excellent examples of the changes which occurred during the period of suburban housing, from low Georgian to high Victorian. The Main Street still maintains a village atmosphere, although the character of individual buildings is not significant. Bus 11, 11A, 13 from O'Connell Street, 48A from Hawkins Street.

**RATHFARNHAM CASTLE**, Rathfarnham, D14. A castle was established here by Milo de Brett in the twelfth century as part of the defences of the Pale, but the present building was constructed in 1583 by Adam Loftus, Archbishop of Dublin. A rectangular fortified mansion, it has exceptionally fine eighteenth-century interiors by SIR WILLIAM CHAMBERS and James Stuart. The hallway is of particular interest and is decorated with a series of marble medallions of philosophers and other historic and intellectual figures. From 1915, after it became a Jesuit House of Studies, the Castle was the centre for seismological research in Ireland. Now owned by the state, there are plans to restore the Castle and open it to the public. Bus 16, 16A, 17 from O'Connell Street, 47 from Hawkins Street.

**RATHGAR**, D6. Nineteenth-century suburb with important large-scale houses in a variety of idioms. The residential character of the area has been maintained. Rathgar Road is a broad boulevard, which maintains its character despite modern infill, leading to Rathgar

*Record Tower, Dublin Castle.*

Village. KENILWORTH SQUARE has fine late Victorian houses designed individually or in pairs and BRIGHTON SQUARE, which is actually a triangle, represents the end of this concept of development, with the houses scaled down to two-storey typically twentieth-century proportions. JAMES JOYCE was born here in 1882. Bus 15A, 15B from College Street, 47 from Hawkins Street.

**RATHMINES**, D6. A separate township during the nineteenth century, the layout and architecture of Lower Rathmines Road represents a great boulevard, although this is rather hard to see now that the gardens of the houses have been encroached upon by shops. A number of significant individual buildings line this road, Patrick Byrne's fine Catholic Church, 1854, the Town Hall with its Italianate campanile, the Technical College, library and bank buildings. A recent addition is the Swan Centre, a well designed shopping mall which integrates successfully with the predominantly Victorian character of Rathmines. JOHN SEMPLE's Church of Ireland church, 1833, at Church Avenue is another building of interest. Bus 14, 14A D'Olier Street, 15A, 15B College Street.

**READ, THOMAS,** No. 4 Parliament Street, D2. The oldest shop premises in Dublin, established as a cutlers in 1670, the same trade has been carried on here ever since. The shop originally faced into Crane Lane but when Parliament Street was developed by the WIDE STREET COMMISSIONERS in 1762, the shopfront was moved to the now more fashionable side. Interior fittings include some fine eighteenth-century display cases and cabinets – unique examples in Dublin.

**RECORD TOWER,** Dublin Castle, D2. The most substantially intact of the external defensive towers of the Castle, dating from the Norman period. It was reconstructed early in the nineteenth century by FRANCIS JOHNSTON to harmonise with the CHAPEL ROYAL which he was building at the time, and the crenellation and windows date from this period. Known as the Wardrobe Tower in the eighteenth century, it was used to store the royal robes and regalia. Legend associates this tower with the escape from the Castle of Red Hugh O'Donnell during the sixteenth century. Bus 21A, 78, 78A from Fleet Street, 50, 50A from Aston Quay.

**REDMOND, JOHN,** (1856-1918). Politician, he became leader of the Irish

Parliamentary Party after CHARLES STEWART PARNELL. By 1912 he had succeeded in having a Home Rule Bill introduced at Westminster, which passed into law in 1914. However, the advent of war suspended the implementation of the Bill. Redmond supported Irish membership of the British Army during the war but this ran contrary to Nationalist opinion in the country. His attempt to keep Ireland peacefully within the British Empire was doomed to failure.

**REFORMATION.** The principal effect of the Reformation in Dublin was the dissolution of the monastic foundations which surrounded the city to the north, west and east. These monastic estates represented considerable wealth and the ecclesiastical power which went with it passed into civic and private hands. Subsequent development around Dublin took up much of this land – TRINITY COLLEGE on the lands of the Augustinian Priory of All Saints, 1592, the PHOENIX PARK, 1662, and the ROYAL HOSPITAL KILMAINHAM, 1680, both on land of the Knights Hospitallers of Kilmainham, and much of GEORGIAN DUBLIN north of the Liffey on the lands of ST. MARY'S ABBEY. See BACHALL ÍOSA.

**REFUGEES.** The only significant wave of refugees to come to Dublin was the Huguenots, whose arrival at the end of the seventeenth century introduced Continental ideas and standards of craftsmanship in many areas, most notably weaving, metalwork and woodcarving.

**REGINALD SQUARE**, Gray Street, D2. Artisans' cottages in the LIBERTIES dating from the 1870s, the humblest variant on a theme of Georgian magnificence. King Edward VIII visited Mrs Coady, the occupant of No. 18, during his visit to Dublin in 1885. The house was so clean that he asked to be shown a dirty one as well!

**RENNIE, JOHN,** (1761-1821). Pioneering English engineer who introduced many innovations into the design of canals, harbours and bridges, he was involved in the design of both HOWTH and DUN LAOGHAIRE harbours.

**RESTAURANTS.** Irish chefs have as fine natural ingredients at their disposal as are to be found anywhere in the world, and every year new restaurants devoted to imaginative or inspired use of this abundance of natural produce open in Dublin. As well as individual cafés and restaurants, all hotels, department stores and shopping centres have facilities ranging from scruffy in the down-at-heel locations to very lavish in the up-market ones. That sense of individuality which is the hallmark of a privately run speciality restaurant is difficult for even the most expensive hotel to equal and for quality or economy the private restaurants have a great deal to offer, capable of satisfying even the most discriminating palate or impecunious pocket, or a combination of both. The selection of restaurants given below, chosen from some hundreds of possibilities, covers a wide range of national cuisine and prices graduate from the cheap to the economic and from the moderate to the expensive.

CHEAP

BESHOFFS OCEAN FOODS, 14 Westmoreland Street, D2, tel 778026. Fish & Chips.
BURDOCKS, 2 Werburgh Street, D8, tel 540366. Fish & Chips.

McDONALDS, 9-10 Grafton Street, D2, tel 778393, and at six other locations. Hamburgers.

WELL FED CAFÉ, 6 Crow Street, D2, tel 771507. Vegetarian.

ECONOMY

BAD ASS CAFÉ, Crown Alley, D2, tel 712596. Pizza parlour.

BEWLEY'S, Grafton Street, D2, tel 776761, and other locations. Traditional.

BURGER KING, 39 Grafton Street, D2, tel 777170. Hamburgers.

CHICAGO PIZZA PIE FACTORY, St. Stephen's Green Shopping Centre, D2, tel 781233. Pizza parlour.

COFFEE INN, 6 South Anne Street, D2, tel 770107. Italian.

CORNUCOPIA WHOLEFOODS, 19 Wicklow Street, D2, tel 777583. Vegetarian.

KYLEMORE BAKERY, Upper O'Connell Street, D1. Traditional.

PRONTO RESTAURANT, Ranelagh, D6, tel 974174. Italian.

SALAD BOWL, THE, Powerscourt Town House, Clarendon Street, D2, tel 792405. Vegetarian.

MODERATE

BARRELL'S TRATTORIA, Monkstown, tel 801992. General.

BLAKES, The Grove, Stillorgan, tel 887678. General.

CAPTAIN AMERICA'S, 44 Grafton Street, D2, tel 715266. Pizza and hamburgers.

CASPER & GIUMBINIS, Wicklow Street, D2, tel 6794347. General.

CEDAR TREE, 11 St. Andrew's Street, D2, tel 772121. Lebanese.

CITY CENTRE, Moss Street, D2, tel 770643. General.

COOPER'S WINE BAR AND RESTAURANT, Monkstown, tel 842037. General.

*Table for one.*

ELEPHANT AND CASTLE, 18 Temple Bar, D2, tel 6791399. American.

FITZERS, National Gallery, Merrion Square, D2, tel 686481. General.

GALLAGHERS BOXTY HOUSE, 20 Temple Bar, D2, tel 772762. Irish.

IMPERIAL CHINESE RESTAURANT, 12a Wicklow Street, tel 772580. Chinese.

LITTLE LISBON, Fownes Street, D2, tel 711274. Portuguese.

NICO'S ITALIAN RESTAURANT, 53 Dame Street, D2, tel 773062. Italian.

THE OCTOPUS'S GARDEN, Main Street, Blackrock, tel 834663. Interesting gourmet.

PASTA FRESCA, Chatham Street, D2, tel 792402. Pastoria.

PERIWINKLE SEAFOOD BAR, Powerscourt Centre, South William Street, D2, tel 6794203. Fish.

PIER 3, Marine Parade, Dun Laoghaire, tel 842234. Informal gourmet.

SALTY DOG, THE, 3A Haddington Terrace, Dun Laoghaire, tel 808015. Indonesian.

TANTE ZOES, 1 Crow Street, D2, tel 679-4407. Creole.

EXPENSIVE

AYUMI-YA, Newtownpark Avenue, Blackrock, tel 831767. Japanese.

BAY TREE, THE, Carrickbrennan Road, Monkstown, tel 808642. General.

CAFÉ KLARA, 35 Dawson Street, D2, tel 778611.

DIGBY'S RESTAURANT AND WINE BAR, Windsor Terrace, Dun Laoghaire, tel 804600. General.

DILSHAD TANDOORI, George's Street, Dun Laoghaire, tel 844604. Indian.

GREY DOOR, THE, 23 Pembroke Street, D2, 763286. Russian.

GUINEA PIG, THE, Railway Road, Dalkey, tel 859055. Gourmet.

KING SITRIC FISH RESTAURANT, East Pier, Howth, tel 335235. Seafood and traditional.

LA VIE EN ROSE, 6 Upper Stephen Street, D2, tel 781771. French gourmet.

LE RELAIS DE MOUETTES, Marine Parade, Sandycove, tel 809873. French gourmet.

LOCKS RESTAURANT, Windsor Terrace, Portobello, D8, tel 538352. French provincial.

OISIN'S, 31 Upper Camden Street, D2, tel 753433. Irish.

OLD DUBLIN RESTAURANT, THE, 91 Francis Street, D8, tel 542028. Russian / Scandinavian.

PARK, THE, Main Street, Blackrock, tel 886177. Gourmet.

PATRICK GUILBAUD, 46 James Place, Lower Baggot Street, D2, tel 764192. French.

PAVANIS, George's Street, Dun Laoghaire, tel 809675. Greek.

PUERTO-BELLA, 1 Portobello Road, Portobello, D8, tel 720851. Gourmet sea food and game.

QUO VADIS, 15 Andrew Street, D2, tel 773363. Italian.

RAJDOOT TANDOORI, 26 Clarendon Street, D2, tel 6794274. Indian.

RESTAURANT NA MARA, Harbour Road, Dun Laoghaire, 806767. Fish gourmet.

SHAY BEANO, 37 Lower Stephen's Street, D2, tel 776384. French.

SOUTH BANK, Martello Terrace, Sandycove, tel 808788. Fresh from the locality.

TREE OF IDLENESS, THE, Sea Front, Bray, Co. Wicklow, tel 863498. Greek Cypriot.

TROCADERO RESTAURANT, 3 Andrew Street, D2, tel 775545. Italian.

TRUDIS, George's Street, Dun Laoghaire, tel 805318. Imaginative seasonal real food.

WHITES ON THE GREEN, 119 St. Stephen's Green, D2 tel 771181. French.

WINE EPERGNE, THE, Upper Rathmines Road, D6, tel 962348. Gourmet.

**RESTORATION.** The Restoration of Charles II in 1660 and the arrival of the Duke of Ormonde in Dublin as his Viceroy in 1662, brought, however belatedly, the Renaissance to Dublin as an established set of cultural ideas. Little is now to be seen from this period, although curiously what does remain is magnificent, having no relationship to anything previously existing in Dublin and overshadowing much of what was to follow. The ROYAL HOSPITAL KILMAINHAM, the only great Restoration building in Ireland, has, after extensive conservation, entered a new phase of life as the National Centre for Culture and the Arts while the PHOENIX PARK, instituted by the Duke of Ormonde in 1662, predates any of the other city parks by over two hundred years.

**RIDING THE FRANCHISES (OR FRINGES).** Ceremony in which the Mayor and Aldermen of the city, followed by members of the Guilds, traversed the area of the Mayor's jurisdiction, preceded by officers carrying the sword and mace. The ceremony was discontinued in 1841 when the office of Lord Mayor was instituted.

**RINGSEND.** In the seventeenth century a narrow spit of land, which projected from the south bank of the Liffey and had previously been uninhabited, was developed as a fishing village and disembarkation point for shipping, superseding DALKEY which had acted as the port of Dublin up to that point. Ringsend remained the effective port until harbour works constructed during the eighteenth century made the Liffey navigable. Ormond Quay, also laid out at this period, set the pattern for the rest of the quayside developments.

**RIVERINE AND OTHER HEADS.** EDWARD SMYTH, 1784, the sculptor and stonecarver who worked on most of JAMES GANDON'S buildings, carved for the CUSTOM HOUSE a series of fourteen keystones decorated with the heads of the deities of Irish rivers. Vigorously carved in high relief, these Riverine gods are Classical in inspiration, and each river is shown as a male or female head, crowned with the attributes of their locality. The only female deity is the Liffey. The identity of the individual rivers has been worked out by a process of elimination; some can be positively named but a few remain doubtful. Working anti-clockwise around the building, the heads represent, on the south river front, the Foyle, Erne and Liffey in the appropriately central position, then the Boyne and Barrow. On the east front the

Blackwater and the only maritime head, the Atlantic Ocean facing out to sea. On the north front, the Bann, Lagan, Lee in the centre, Shannon and Suir. Finally on the west front, the Nore and Slaney. The Nore and Barrow are the least definite identifications and may possibly be reversed. Wax models of twelve of the heads executed by John Smyth, son of the sculptor, may be examined at close quarters in the CIVIC MUSEUM. Two further Riverine heads from the old Carlisle Bridge (now O'Connell Bridge) are on a redbrick warehouse at 30-32 Sir John Rogerson's Quay. When the bridge was rebuilt they were replaced by replicas. These represent the Liffey and Atlantic Ocean. The tradition of decorating buildings with heads became very popular in Dublin during the nineteenth century, and many examples, although not Riverine ones, can be seen on the CHAPEL ROYAL in DUBLIN CASTLE, PEARSE STREET GARDA STATION, the IVEAGH MARKETS, GUINNESS BREWERY, 39 & 40 Dame Street, and the Irish Permanent Building Society, O'Connell Street. In CHRIST CHURCH and ST. PATRICK'S CATHEDRALS Medieval carved heads and Victorian versions of them give an alternative image to the prevailing Classical style of those around the city.

**ROBINSON, LENNOX,** (1886-1958). Playwright and manager of the ABBEY THEATRE with which he was associated for much of his life. His plays differ from those of SEAN O'CASEY and JOHN MILLINGTON SYNGE, the other playwrights prominent in the early days of the Abbey, in not being concerned with Dublin tenements or west of Ireland life, but with the Ireland of the small towns. Among his well known plays are, *The Whiteheaded Boy*, 1916, *The Far-Off Hills*, 1928 and *Drama at Inish*, 1933.

His rather disdainful portrait by James Slator hangs in the Abbey foyer.

**ROBINSON, SIR WILLIAM,** (1643-1712). Architect, appointed Surveyor General in 1670. Two of the finest buildings in Dublin, the ROYAL HOSPITAL KILMAINHAM and MARSH'S LIBRARY, 1702, are by Robinson. Combined with his work as a military engineer at Kinsale, Co. Cork, where he built Charles' and Rincurran Forts, his Dublin buildings show him to have been a designer of buildings which display great power and simplicity, using scale and Classical proportion rather than expensive materials to create an effect.

**ROCHE, SIR BOYLE,** (1743-1807). Member of parliament from 1776 to 1800, Boyle is credited with the perpetration of Classical examples of the 'Irish Bull' in the course of parliamentary debates. 'Why should we put ourselves out of our way to do anything for posterity; for what has posterity done for us?', and apropos the proposed Union between England and Ireland, 'I would have the two sisters embrace like one brother.' Boyle excelled in piling metaphor upon inappropriate metaphor, yet always succeeded in making his point. 'I smell a rat; I see him forming in the air and darkening the sky; but I'll nip him in the bud!'

**ROCQUE, JOHN,** (1705-1762). Huguenot cartographer, he was responsible for producing the finest eighteenth-century maps of Dublin and environs, which for their accuracy and wealth of detail form a fascinating archive of topographical information. Rocque had already produced maps of London, Paris and Rome when *An Exact Survey of the City and Suburbs of Dublin*, was published in 1756. It has the quality of a vast aerial photograph showing, unlike earlier maps of the city, all the incidental details of localities, much of which can still be traced in the fabric of present-day Dublin. The map on the £10 note is a detail from Rocque's map of 1756.

**ROSC.** Major exhibition of international contemporary art, held approximately every four years in Dublin at changing venues. ROSC was founded in 1967 by MICHAEL SCOTT, James Johnson Sweeney and Cecil King; the Old Irish word means 'the poetry of vision'. A selection committee of experts from around the world choose a group of artists whom they consider to represent the most important directions in contemporary art at that particular time. Related art history exhibitions are held in conjunction with the main ROSC show, and these have covered a wide field from Irish Celtic stone carving to the Russian Cubists.

**ROTUNDA ASSEMBLY ROOMS.** In 1766, JOHN ENSOR added a round building of plain brickwork to the east corner of the Lying-in Hospital, giving the hospital its name, The ROTUNDA, by which it has subsequently been known. Ensor's building was later improved externally by JAMES GANDON and sculptural decoration by EDWARD SMYTH was added. Inside, its fine spaces have been used as the Ambassador Cinema for many years but the cinema has now closed and the Rotunda is undergoing restoration. The building now occupied by the Gate Theatre and Pillar Room was added by RICHARD JOHNSTON and Frederick Trench, 1784-86, and the whole complex was used for entertainments designed to raise funds for Dr Bartholomew Mosse's Lying-in Hospital.

**ROTUNDA HOSPITAL.** Parnell Square, D1. Designed by RICHARD CASTLE in 1748 as Dr Bartholomew Mosse's Lying-in Hospital, the first maternity hospital in the British Isles, and remarkably, over two hundred years later, still performing its original function. A Palladian composition, which owes its inspiration to LEINSTER HOUSE designed by CASTLE a few years earlier, the ROTUNDA was extensively added to in the succeeding fifty years by a complex of public entertainment buildings. The GATE THEATRE now occupies part of the complex. The Rotunda was added by JOHN ENSOR in 1766, and extended by RICHARD JOHNSTON and Frederick Trench in 1784. Within the hospital is a chapel decorated in a Baroque manner, unique in Dublin church decoration of the period. The plasterwork by Barthelemy Cramillion is the most extravagant figurative work to be seen in any Georgian building in the city. Pleasure Gardens attached to the hospital, where fund-raising events were held, now house the Garden of Remembrance and other modern hospital buildings.

**ROUND TOWERS.** The only category of architecture unique to Ireland is the Early Christian round tower, and there are sixty-five of these singular monuments scattered across the countryside. Of these sixty-five towers some survive as mere foundations, while others are complete to their pointed caps and they form one of the most intriguing remnants of the country's architectural past. Three virtually complete towers stand within a few miles of the centre of Dublin, at CLONDALKIN, LUSK and SWORDS. Two others are known to have existed, one at Rathmichael, and another, St. Michael le Pole, overlooked Dublin Castle from the south but was demolished in 1778. Built between the ninth and thirteenth centuries, the towers are referred to in contemporary sources as *cloig theach* or the 'bell houses' of small monastic settlements, and this seems to have been their primary function, not as is generally believed a refuge from marauding Vikings, although doubtless they also performed this function. They were not conventional belfries, with a fixed peal of bells, but a tower from which a hand-held bell could be rung. St. Patrick's Bell in the NATIONAL MUSEUM dates from the same period. A unique feature of the round tower is that it is constructed with mortar in contrast to the Irish tradition of dry stone building, a factor which has contributed to its survival. The towers differ slightly in height and detail, but the general form is the same – a circular tapering tower, up to 30m (96ft) high, with the entrance door about 2m (6.5ft) above the external ground level, windows at the top facing the cardinal points, and capped by a conical roof. For structures of such height they have remarkably little foundations and extend not more than a metre below ground level. Of the Dublin examples, Clondalkin is unusual in having an external stairs, possibly contemporary, leading to the entrance door. Lusk has been cleverly adapted into a Medieval building which somewhat camouflages its identity, and Swords, although it is complete to the cone, is poorly constructed. A late addition to the body of Irish round towers is the O'Connell Memorial in GLASNEVIN CEMETERY, built in 1869 as a replica of the Early Christian towers, but at 52m (166ft), considerably taller than any of the originals. It is the most dominant feature on the north Dublin skyline. The round tower at the monastery of Glendalough gives a better idea of the original situation of these buildings than any of those in Dublin as it has not been encroached upon by later buildings.

## ROYAL COLLEGE OF PHYSICIANS OF IRELAND, 6 Kildare Street, D2, tel 616677.

Fine porticoed building of 1860 by W.G. Murray. The College contains a very important collection of portraits of eminent surgeons and physicians.

## ROYAL COLLEGE OF SURGEONS, St. Stephen's Green West, D2, tel 780200.

The College of Surgeons building is the most distinguished feature of the west side of the Green which is a great mixture of periods and has no clear identity. The building by Edward Parke has a central pediment which originally stood in front of the three bays on the right of the façade but was slid along to its present position when the building was enlarged in 1825. It contains some handsome interiors and possesses a fine collection of portraits. The college is the pre-eminent medical college in Ireland.

## ROYAL DUBLIN SOCIETY (RDS), Merrion Road, Ballsbridge, D4, tel 680645.

One of the great institutions of Dublin, the RDS was established as the Dublin Society in 1731 in the atmosphere of scientific enquiry which preoccupied the landowners and intellectuals of the period. Lord Chesterfield, the Viceroy, writing in 1747 said that its efforts had 'done more good to Ireland with regard to arts and industry than all the laws that could have been formed'. The RDS did not aquire royal status until 1820. From the beginning one of the Society's principal areas of interest has been agriculture and it strove to promote advances in the standards of farming by offering premiums for livestock breeding and crop improvements. The annual Spring Show and Horse Show are the two main traditional events in the RDS calendar, with the Young Scientist of the Year competitions an indication of the Society's involvement in a wide range of contemporary activities. Scholarly, cultural and artistic pursuits are also within the RDS ambit and it has been responsible for the establishment of a number of the most prominent academic institutions in the city, the NATIONAL LIBRARY and NATIONAL MUSEUM as well as the NATIONAL COLLEGE OF ART AND DESIGN (NCAD), which began as the Drawing Schools of the Dublin Society. Throughout the year the RDS grounds at Ballsbridge are the venue for an extraordinarily varied programme of concerts, conferences, exhibitions, lectures and trade fairs. Bus 5, 7, 7A from Eden Quay, 45 from Burgh Quay. See ANNUAL EVENTS.

## ROYAL HIBERNIAN ACADEMY OF ARTS (RHA), 15 Ely Place, D2, tel 612558.

Known to its members as 'The Academy', the RHA was founded in 1823, modelled on the Royal Academy in London, with a view to promoting the fine arts in Ireland. The landscape painter WILLIAM ASHFORD was its first president, Martin Creggan the portrait painter, secretary and FRANCIS JOHNSTON, architect, was treasurer. The annual exhibitions organised by the RHA began in 1826 and have run with few breaks up to the present time. The first premises were designed and paid for by Johnston and stood in Lower Abbey Street. This building, complete with the annual show of that year, was gutted during the fighting of 1916. The RHA was without a permanent home from then until the present GALLAGHER GALLERY, designed by RAYMOND McGRATH, was built in ELY PLACE. This project, the gift of Charles Gallagher, a property developer, remained unfinished for many years due to the death of the donor. Finally opened in 1989, it is the finest exhibition space in Dublin, with a magnificent series of well lit rooms on the upper floor and a sculpture gallery below. For generations the RHA represented the best artists practising in Ireland, but in the beginning of the twentieth century it reacted against experimentation and became a bastion of conservatism. This led directly to the establishment of the IRISH EXHIBITION OF LIVING ART in 1943 as a *Salon de Refuse*. In recent years the RHA has become less conservative and more representative of the many strands of opinion in the visual arts today. The opening of the annual Summer Show is one of the artistic social events of the year, with the academicians in their robes and a list of exhibitors running into hundreds, probably the largest group exhibition to be held annually in Dublin. See ART GALLERIES.

**ROYAL HOSPITAL KILMAIN-HAM** (RHK), Kilmainham, D8, tel 718666. This magnificent building, set in 48 acres of parkland and situated 1.6km (1 mile) from the city centre is the earliest Classical building of any importance in Ireland. It was built in 1680 at the direction of James Butler, the Great DUKE OF ORMOND, and owes its inspiration to Les Invalides in Paris. It was designed by the Surveyor General, Sir William Robinson, as a home for old soldiers and was used for this purpose until 1922. Externally it has a severe barrack-like appearance, but inside is an impressive courtyard, arcaded on three sides with the spire in the centre of the fourth and flanking it the Great Hall and

Chapel and Governor's residence. The Hall and Chapel interiors are among the finest in Dublin, the latter particularly notable for its extraordinary Carolean ceiling, ornamented in high relief with fruit and floral motifs. The Hall is hung with seventeenth- and eighteenth-century portraits of British monarchs and lords lieutenant. The particular charm of the Royal Hospital is in its restrained and dignified proportions, and it is an anomaly amongst Dublin's major architectural monuments in remaining as a single concept without additions or radical changes. The sheer size of the RHK recommends it for many uses and as the National Centre for Culture and the Arts it forms a venue for theatre, music, exhibitions, dance and children's activities and the permanent home for the IRISH MUSEUM OF MODERN ART and the Madden-Arnholz Print Collection. The RHK publishes a free monthly events guide which is available in city-centre galleries. Shop and restaurant. Tue-Sat 2.00-5.00, Sun 12.00-5.00. Admission charge, Tuesday free. Bus 23, 25, 26 Essex Quay.

**ROYAL INSTITUTE OF THE ARCHITECTS OF IRELAND** (RIAI), 8 Merrion Square, D2, tel 761703. The professional governing body which monitors architectural education and professional standards in Ireland. Among the Institute's publications is the very useful *RIAI Map Guide to the Architecture of Dublin* which gives basic information on all buildings of importance from every period up to the present.

**ROYAL IRISH ACADEMY** (RIA). Academy House, 19 Dawson Street, D2, tel 762570. After Trinity College, the Academy holds the most important collection of Irish manuscripts in Dublin. Founded in 1785 as an institution to promote the study of the sciences, literature and antiquities, its first president was the EARL OF CHARLEMONT. The 'Proceedings' of the Academy publishes papers on archaeology, history, science and literature. Academy House, which has fine interiors including a magnificent staircase hall, was designed by JOHN ENSOR in 1769 and has been occupied by the Academy since 1852.

**ROYAL IRISH ACADEMY OF MUSIC (RIAM)**, 36 Westland Row, D2, tel 764412. Founded in 1848, it is the premier musical institution in Ireland and is housed in a mansion built in 1771. The house is decorated in a restrained Adam manner as distinctively different from the heavy ornate plasterwork of other Dublin houses as is the façade on the first floor with a row of beautifully proportioned arched windows.

**ROYAL SOCIETY OF ANTI-QUARIES OF IRELAND**, 63 Merrion Square, D2, tel 761749. Founded in 1849, the Society promotes the study of historical and archaeological research.

**ROYAL TERRACE**, Dun Laoghaire. Like the nearby Crostwaithe Park and also dating from the mid-nineteenth century, Royal Terrace has only two formal sides, the remainder being infill of later periods – on the north side a Victorian orphanage, The Cottage Home for Little Children, and to the south, a clutter of 1940s suburbia.

**ROYAL ZOOLOGICAL SOCIETY OF IRELAND**, Phoenix Park, D8, tel 771425. The Zoological Society was founded in 1831 and is the governing body of the ZOO in the PHOENIX PARK.

**'RUIRTEACH'.** Pre-Viking name for the Liffey between Islandbridge and the river mouth. It means 'tempestuous'.

**S**T. PATRICK'S HOSPITAL, Bow Lane West, D8, tel 775423. George Semple designed this hospital for the mentally ill in 1749, and it was built with money bequeathed by DEAN SWIFT.

**ST. STEPHEN'S GREEN**, D2. The largest and also the oldest of the Dublin squares, with a central park of 8.8 hectares (22 acres), its architecture has suffered greater change than any other square in the city. Today there is more of the nineteenth and twentieth century to be seen and nothing at all of the seventeenth when it was originally laid out, but in fact representative buildings of many periods are jumbled together in a manner which provides an interesting mix in contrast to the uniformity of Merrion Square. The north side is dominated by the mid-nineteenth-century splendour of the SHELBOURNE HOTEL, and further to the west of it is the Friendly Brothers mansion at No. 22, and the Gentlemen's Clubs at Nos. 8, 9 and 17, in fine Georgian and Victorian premises, maintain the atmosphere of an exclusive enclave. These are representative of some of the most grandiose Georgian town houses ever built in Dublin. Much of the east side of the Green was rebuilt in the 1960s in a Georgianesque manner, but the central building, No. 51, now the Board of Works, is authentically Georgian. On the south side are three very important houses, IVEAGH HOUSE and Nos. 85 and 86 which are collectively known as NEWMAN HOUSE, next to which is the NEWMAN UNIVERSITY CHAPEL. Also on the south side are a number of surviving early eighteenth-century panelled houses. On the west of the Green only two Georgian buildings remain, the ROYAL COLLEGE OF SURGEONS and No. 119, after which the new St. Stephen's

Green Shopping Centre is the most interesting structure although its Victorian pastiche façade relates to none of its neighbours and suggests the ambiance of the Vieux Carré in New Orleans rather than late twentieth-century Dublin. See PARKS for the park of St. Stephen's Green.

**SACK 'EM UPS.** Eighteenth-century body snatchers who pillaged church graveyards to provide corpses for the college anatomy schools. This practice led to the defensive appearance of such nineteenth-century cemeteries as MOUNT JEROME and GLASNEVIN which is surrounded by a high wall punctuated by guard towers.

**SAINT-GAUDENS, AUGUSTUS**, (1848-1907). Dublin-born American sculptor (son of a French shoemaker and an Irish mother), who executed the vigorous statue on the PARNELL MONUMENT in O'Connell Street. Saint Gaudens was the foremost sculptor of the American Beaux Arts movement and became noted for his naturalistic public monuments. The figure of Parnell was one of his last commissions.

**SALLY GAP, THE.** Crossroads in the Dublin Mountains, the watershed between Kippure and Djouce Mountains. Rolling bogland covered with gorse and bracken extends to the horizon which appears to meet the clouds. Loughs Dan and Tay lie along the connecting roads, and the Liffey rises from a spring amongst the rocks.

**SANDYCOVE**, Co Dublin. A delightful suburb of Dublin, just beyond DUN LAOGHAIRE, with many fine early nineteenth-century houses hugging the coastline of Dublin Bay. The sandy cove is still an important feature of the area, safe and enclosed, and suitable for small children. Around the corner from the beach is that venerable bastion of male supremacy – the FORTYFOOT – where men bathe nude throughout the year and women are distinctly unwelcome. On Christmas Day, the stalwart bathers go for a ritual dip in the freezing waters. The Fortyfoot nestles under the walls of the Battery where the 40th Regiment of Foot were stationed, and from which it derives its popular name. Overlooking the Battery is the most distinguished of the MARTELLO TOWERS, now the JAMES JOYCE MUSEUM, next to which is a private house in the Corbusier idiom designed by MICHAEL SCOTT, architect of BUSÁRAS and the ABBEY THEATRE. In Sandycove Park, on a small unenclosed green area on the sea front at Marine Parade, a stone commemorates Joyce's centenary. Philatelists can enthuse over a post box on Sandycove Avenue West which has the SAORSTÁT ÉIREANN (1922-1949) logo, SE, a considerable rarity amongst boxes more commonly commemorating Victoria, Edward VII and George V. DART to Sandycove. Bus 8 Eden Quay.

**SANDYMOUNT, D4.** The village of Sandymount, a few minutes by DART from the city centre, preserves an old-world calm in contrast to the hectic traffic streaming along the roads on either side of it. The village green, a triangle of grass shaded by trees, and the very nineteenth-century look of the houses indicate a place which only came into existence after the brickfields which had been worked here in the eighteenth century had been exhausted. Sandymount Strand at low tide provides a vast expanse of sand which stretches almost to the horizon and has been a popular recreational area since the foundation of the city. Its position, minutes from COLLEGE GREEN, provides a remarkable resource of freedom and fresh air, a marine equivalent of the PHOENIX PARK. DART to Sandymount. Bus 3 O'Connell Street.

*Sandymount Strand.*

**SCHRÖDINGER, ERWIN,** (1887-1961). Austrian physicist who discovered wave mechanics, he worked from 1937 to 1954 at the Dublin Institute for Advanced Studies (DIAS), at 65 Merrion Square where he was professor of theoretical physics. In 1933 he was awarded the NOBEL PRIZE.

**SCOTT, MICHAEL,** (1905-1989). Architect, he was, from the 1930s, the leading designer of the modern movement in Dublin. He founded the firm of Scott, Tallon and Walker who are collectively responsible for many buildings of interest. Scott's first important commission was for the Irish Pavilion at the 1939 New York World Fair when he managed to produce a sophisticated modern building despite being in the shape of a shamrock! BUSÁRAS, 1946, Scott's most important early building in Ireland, is significant as the first public building in the international idiom to be built in central Dublin. Scott's other well-known works in Dublin are the ABBEY THEATRE, 1965, and his own house, 1937, which is next to the JAMES JOYCE MUSEUM at SANDYCOVE, the exhibition extension to which he also designed. See ARCHITECTURE OF THE TWENTIETH CENTURY.

**SCULPTORS SOCIETY OF IRELAND**, 23 Moss Street, D2, tel 718746. Founded in 1980 the Society has organised a number of symposia and workshops around Ireland and is involved in the promotion of sculpture for public and private locations. A recent publication, *Walker's Guide*, is a very useful handbook of contemporary sculpture in Dublin.

**SEANAD ÉIREANN** (Senate). See DÁIL.

**SEMPLE, JOHN**, (1801-1873). Architect. He was Dublin City Architect 1829-42, and also Architect to the Board of First Fruits, for whom he built a considerable number of churches which remain his principal achievement. The five Semple churches in Dublin built between the 1820s and 1830s – Anglesea Road, the Black Church, Blackrock, Kiltiernan, Tallaght and Whitechurch – show evidence of his curiously aggressive manner, all spikes and blank wall surfaces, and are instantly recognisable as his design. Semple came from a family with a tradition of building and architecture and he was great-grand nephew of the George

Semple who added the spiky spire to the Minot Tower at ST. PATRICK'S CATHEDRAL in 1749, which suggests a family regard for such things.

**SHAW, GEORGE BERNARD**, (1856-1950). Playwright, born at 33 Synge Street, D8. He left school at fifteen and worked as a clerk until his twenties when he moved to London with his family where he spent the remainder of his life. Shaw, who was two years younger than OSCAR WILDE, outlived all his Dublin literary contemporaries – OLIVER ST. JOHN GOGARTY, JAMES JOYCE, SEÁN O'CASEY, JAMES STEPHENS, J.M. SYNGE and W.B. YEATS. A perceptive music critic and social commentator on a multitude of issues, his principal achievement is as an intellectual dramatist rather than a poetic or comic playwright. His plays of ideas were to initiate a change in direction for English drama and a considerable number are still frequently performed, most notably *St. Joan*. Although he commented frequently in journalism on the Irish situation, only one of his plays, *John Bull's Other Island*, takes it as its principal theme. Shaw, who considered that his education had been formed by visits to the NATIONAL GALLERY in Merrion Square, left one-third of his royalties, known as the Shaw Fund, to the Gallery. His statue now stands on the lawn before the Gallery. Shaw won the NOBEL PRIZE for Literature in 1926.

**SHELLEY, PERCY BYSSHE**, (1792-1822). The English Romantic poet and champion of liberty espoused the cause of Irish freedom and published in 1812 *An Address to the Irish People* which favoured emancipation and repeal of the ACT OF UNION. He distributed his pamphlets in Dublin and was a speaker with DANIEL O'CONNELL at a public meeting in the Fishamble Street Theatre in February 1812.

**SHEPPARD, OLIVER,** (1865-1941). Sculptor, studied in Dublin and London. Himself influenced by the work of Rodin, he became an influential teacher in the Dublin Metropolitan Schools. Sheppard's fine head of the poet JAMES CLARENCE MANGAN, 1908, is in ST. STEPHEN'S GREEN, and his statue of THE FALL OF CÚCHULAINN, 1911, which stands in the public office of the GPO on O'Connell Street as a memorial to the dead of 1916, is one of the finest monuments in the city. He also executed the figures on the parapet of GOVERNMENT BUILDINGS. Sheppard was an unsuccessful entrant in the 1926 competition to design the national COINAGE which was won by Percy Metcalfe.

**SHERIDAN, RICHARD BRINSLEY,** (1751-1816). Playwright and politician, he was born at 12 Dorset Street, into a theatrical family, his father being an actor-manager and his mother a playwright and novelist. Sheridan's brief theatrical career was virtually over by the time he entered parliament at the age of twenty-nine, but his comic farces *The Rivals* and *The School for Scandal* ensured his reputation. His creation, Mrs Malaprop, whose conversation is littered with magnificently inappropriate words, represents a style of English still alive and flourishing in Dublin street markets, and a stock-in-trade of Dublin comedians.

She's as headstrong as an allegory on the banks of the Nile
(*The Rivals*, Richard Brinsley Sheridan.)

You're being a trifle previous with your device Mrs.
(*Moore Street*, street trader.)

**SHIP STREET**. To the west of DUBLIN CASTLE are Great and Little Ship Streets, canyon-like cobbled streets, paved with granite, running along the city walls and barrack buildings. The name comes not from some long-gone harbour, although the Castle moat would have once run along the city wall, but from the existence of a sheep market in the area.

**SHOPPING CENTRES**. The principal of the American shopping mall has been introduced successfully into the Irish shopping scene which was previously dominated by small shops. Although the new shopping centres do offer facilities for out-of-the-weather shopping and their carparks are convenient, their impact as environments is often fairly insubstantial, if not totally anonymous. The exceptions to this rule are characterised by an individual approach to the problem of space, style and variety of shops, and some of these solutions are indeed attractive to be in and to stroll around. Very few are distinguished externally.

BLACKROCK SHOPPING CENTRE, Main Street, Blackrock. Designed around an open atrium like a Roman villa with the noise of a cascading fountain the dominant sound, this is the most interesting of all the shopping centres and although far smaller than some of the others, its emphasis is on quality shops. These include a first class bookshop, photographic shop, well stocked supermarket and clothes shops. DART to Blackrock.

DUN LAOGHAIRE SHOPPING CENTRE, George's Street, Dun Laoghaire. Vast three-level centre with attached carpark and a grim and windowless exterior. Very little from a needle to an elephant is not included under this soaring roof-

and it is a pleasant place to walk around. Among the attractions are separate children's and adult bookshops, roof level pub with stunning views of DUBLIN BAY, and a number of different restaurants and cafés, at least one on each level. DART to Dun Laoghaire, Blackrock.

ILAC, Henry Street, D1. Dublin Corporation Library Service has its most well-equipped branch on the first floor of the centre and there is also a multi-storey carpark. The wide range of general shops covers all the principal chains.

POWERSCOURT TOWNHOUSE, South William Street, D2. Interesting adaptation of an eighteenth-century mansion and nineteenth-century courtyard to provide a multi-level centre, mainly occupied by restaurants. It also contains an art gallery and arcade of antique shops. The first such development in Ireland.

ST. STEPHEN'S GREEN SHOPPING CENTRE. Designed along the lines of a Victorian shopping arcade, the internal space is light and airy, with a glazed barrel-vaulted roof and balconies surrounding an open central space dominated by an enormous openwork clock. The impression on entering the centre is of a building refurbished from the past rather than something entirely new, although it was built in 1989. Here a primary concern has been the creation of a particular environment and there is a certain gaiety in the result. On the outside the Victorian theme has run riot and lacks the cohesion of the interior, clashing with this sedate nineteenth-century corner of the Green. The shops are principally fashion and clothing, with a large supermarket and variety goods shops.

STILLORGAN SHOPPING CENTRE. More like a modern village than a shopping centre, the wide variety of shops is arranged on streets in the open air, in contrast to the indoor environment of more recent developments.

THE SQUARE, Tallaght. This shopping centre, built 1990, twenty years after the housing developments, fills a considerable gulf in this area and provides a social service in the form of a centre to an otherwise focusless environment. Bus 65, 65A, 49 from Crampton Quay, 50 from Aston Quay.

SWAN CENTRE, Rathmines Road, D6. The brick façade of the shopping centre fits well into the Victorian ambiance of Rathmines. There is an interesting open-mechanism clock on the upper level of the centre.

## SICK AND INDIGENT ROOM-KEEPERS SOCIETY, Palace Street, D2.
The premises of this eighteenth-century non-denominational charitable institution are decorated on the façade with a monumental inscription giving its name and the date of its foundation, 1790. The charity was established to care for the destitute of the city and as the oldest charitable institution in Dublin it still carries out its work from this eighteenth-century building. The house now stands alone – the terrace of which it was part having been demolished.

## 'SILENCE, EXILE AND CUNNING'.
As early as 1916, when he published *A Portrait of the Artist as a Young Man*, JAMES JOYCE had established a dictum for his artistic and social development which he was to pursue rigorously throughout the rest of his life:

I will not serve that in which I no longer believe, whether it call itself my home,

my fatherland, or my church: and I will try to express myself in some mode of life or art as freely as I can and as wholly as I can, using for my defence the only arms which I allow myself to use – silence, exile and cunning.
(*A Portrait of the Artist as a Young Man,* James Joyce.)

**SILVER TASSIE, THE**. Play by Seán O'Casey which followed his Dublin trilogy in 1928. It was rejected by the ABBEY THEATRE, leading to an unfortunate breach between the playwright and the theatre. The experimental nature of the play, which deals with the First World War in a symbolic manner in total contrast to the realism of his earlier work, has made it difficult to perform successfully although it is periodically revived. O'Casey presented war as a dehumanising and destructive force, devoid of heroism, a view acceptable today but not when it was written.

**SIMNEL, LAMBERT**, (1475-1525). On 24 May 1487, the ten-year-old Simnel was crowned Edward VI, King of England, in CHRIST CHURCH CATHEDRAL. This coronation was in opposition to Henry VII who had become King in 1485 on the defeat of Richard III at the Battle of Bosworth. The new King claimed to be a nephew of the defeated Richard. According to legend, Simnel was crowned with a tiara borrowed from the statue of the Virgin from one of the Dublin churches, possibly that of ST. MARY'S ABBEY. A month later the boy pretender to the throne was captured by the actual occupant at the Battle of Stoke and was put to work as a scullion in the royal kitchens.

**SINN FÉIN**. Irish Nationalist organisation founded in 1905 which recommended the disassociation of Irish life and economics from British influence and interference. It was not until after the 1916 RISING that Sinn Féin came to prominence as a political force when its candidates won seventy-three out of the total of 105 Irish parliamentary seats at Westminster in 1918. The present-day DÁIL is a development of the assembly formed in Dublin in 1919 by the MPs who decided to boycott Westminster.

**SMIRKE, SIR ROBERT**, (1780-1867). Architect and the leading English Neo-Classicist of his day, his most famous building is the British Museum in London, the entrance portico of which was influenced by the design of the Old Parliament House, now the Bank of Ireland in Dublin. Smirke won the competition to design the Wellington Testimonial, 1817-61, in the PHOENIX PARK.

**SMITHFIELD**, D7. Cobbled market square to the north east of the city. A horse market is still held here on the first Sunday of the month. Nearby are the splendid but unused Jameson Distillery buildings. Bus 39, 39A Middle Abbey Street.

**SMYTH, EDWARD**, (1749-1812). Sculptor, associated with the buildings of JAMES GANDON, all the important ones of which are embellished with his work. Smyth was the most important sculptor working in Dublin during the eighteenth-century and much of his work survives, although a great deal of minor works probably remain unidentified or have been destroyed as he also worked as a stuccodore and carver of mantelpieces. He came to prominence when he won a competition for the Charles Lucas memorial in 1771. This Baroque statue now stands in the CITY HALL. Another Baroque figure is that of the Marquis of Buckingham, 1783, in ST. PATRICK'S CATHEDRAL. On the CUSTOM HOUSE, Smyth executed the RIVERINE HEADS, 1784, on the ground floor of the building, the armorials on the parapet of the end pavilions, two statues on the pediment which were destroyed in the fighting of 1922, and the colossal figure of Commerce on the dome. When Gandon was building a new portico for the PARLIAMENT HOUSE, Smyth provided the sculptures for the pediment, Justice, Wisdom and Liberty, 1787, but these have deteriorated due to pollution. A few years later when the Parliament House became the Bank of Ireland, Smyth executed three further statues, Fidelity, Hibernia and Commerce, for the COLLEGE GREEN portico, although these were not his original compositions but are from designs by John Flaxman. On the FOUR COURTS Smyth carried on the trophy compositions which decorate the screens on the river front, and five massive figures on the pediment, Authority, Justice, Moses, Mercy and Wisdom. All the sculptor's internal decorations were damaged when the building was set on fire in 1922. The King's Inns has a Royal Arms above the entrance gateway from Henrietta Street and on the west front of the building are four CARYATIDS and two long frieze panels with complicated figure compositions. These represent on the left a Dionysian harvest festival with the female caryatids, Plenty and Wine, below, and on the right, aspects of Justice with the male caryatids, Security and Law, below. The identity of the central panel over the entranceway is unclear. The only substantial and clearly attributed surviving plasterwork by Smyth is in the King's Inns and the marvellous CHAPEL ROYAL in DUBLIN CASTLE, and these further extend the impression of the force and imaginative scope of his work.

**SOUTH CITY MARKETS**, South Great George's Street, D2. Red-brick Gothic Revival shopping complex occupying an entire city block bounded by Exchequer Street, Fade Street and Drury Street. This was the only large-scale Victorian shopping development in Dublin planned as a single enterprise and its ornamental brick and tile façades form an attractive alternative to the normal Dublin street composed of individual buildings. Designed by Lockwood and Mawson and opened in 1881, it had a great central glazed arcade very much like that in the present-day ST. STEPHEN'S GREEN CENTRE, but the Markets were burnt down in 1892 and were rebuilt with a much more modest interior.

**SPEED, JOHN**, (1542-1629). Cartographer, his 1610 map of Dublin is the earliest surviving map of the city. Although schematic and presented as a bird's eye view without much attempt at differentiation of separate kinds of building, it does give a clear view of the walled enclosure of the still surviving Medieval city and the extent of the suburban development beyond its walls. Some prominent elements of the later city can be seen in embryo on Speed's map – TRINITY COLLEGE already established since 1592, and such important elements of the present-day street layout as the junction of Dame Street and South Great George's Street which appear here as 'Damas Street' and St. George's Lane.

**SPENSER, EDMUND**, (1552-1599). Poet and planter, he came to Dublin in 1580 as secretary to Lord Grey of Wilton, the Lord Deputy. The first three parts of *The Faerie Queen* which he had begun in 1579 were published in 1589. Spenser became one of the undertakers who organised the plantation of Munster, and he lived at Kilcolman Castle, Co. Cork, from 1588 to 1598 when his Castle was burned during an insurrection.

*Rugby at Lansdowne Road.*

**SPORT.** Facilities for an exceptional variety of sports exist in and around Dublin, and all those which require some aspect of the great outdoors are well provided for in the mountains, plains and on the waters of DUBLIN BAY. Associations and organisations for the promotion of most sports can be found in the city with an emphasis on the most popular activities – soccer and football, tennis, golf and athletics. Sports involving animals – dog and horse racing – are also immensely popular, as is anything on which a wager may be laid.

Cospoir, the National Sports Council, tel 734700, is the Irish wing of the Council of Europe's Sport For All programme, and it is the co-ordinating body for all sports activities in the country. Listed below are contact telephone numbers for the various sports. The House of Sport, Long Mile Road, Walkinstown, tel 501633, is the organising centre for many different bodies.

ANGLING. Irish Federation of Sea Anglers, tel 501633. See also separate entry under ANGLING.

ATHLETICS. National Athletics Association, tel 308925.

ARCHERY. Irish Amateur Archery Association, tel 481574.

BADMINTON. Badminton Union of Ireland, tel 505966.

BALLOONING. Dublin Ballooning Club, tel 983989.

BASKETBALL. Irish Basketball Association, tel 733476.

BIRDWATCHING. See IRISH WILDBIRD CONSERVANCY and IRISH WILDLIFE FEDERATION.

BOARDSAILING. Irish Boardsailing Association, tel 426577.

BOWLING (indoor). Dundrum Bowl, tel 980209; Stillorgan Bowl, tel 881656.

BOWLING (outdoor). Blackrock, tel 881933; Clontarf, tel 332669; Dun Laoghaire, tel 801179; Sandymount, tel 691783.

BOXING. Irish Amateur Boxing Association, tel 984275.

CANOEING. Irish Canoe Union, tel 509838.

CRICKET. Irish Cricket Union, tel 893943.

CYCLING. Federation of Irish Cyclists, tel 727524.

FENCING. Irish Amateur Fencing Federation, tel 855810.

FLYING. Irish Aviation Council, tel 874474.

GAELIC GAMES. (Gaelic Football and Hurling) Gaelic Athletic Association, GAA, tel 362222.

GLIDING. Irish Hang Gliding Association, tel 509845.

GOLF. Golfing Union of Ireland, tel 694244. Golf courses, virtually all of which are private, usually grant temporary membership. There are around forty courses in the Dublin area; below is a small selection:
Deerpark, Howth, tel 322624
Dun Laoghaire, tel 801055.
Howth, Sutton, tel 323055.
Royal Dublin, Dollymount, tel
   337153.
Woodbrook, Bray, tel 824799.

GREYHOUND RACING. Harold's Cross, tel 971081; Shelbourne Park, tel 683502.

GYMNASTICS. Irish Amateur Gymnastic Association, tel 501805.

HANDBALL. Handball Association of Ireland, tel 741360.

HANDICAPPED SPORTS. Special Olympics Ireland, tel 501633.

HOCKEY. Irish Hockey Union, tel 858632.

HORSE RACING. Curragh, tel 045-41205; Fairyhouse, tel 256167; Leopardstown, tel 893607; Navan, tel 046-21350; Punchestown, tel 045-97704.

HURLING. GAA, Croke Park, tel 363222.

ICE SKATING. See SKATING RINKS.

JUDO. Irish Judo Association, tel 344742.

MOTOR CYCLING. Motor Cycle Union of Ireland, tel 411891.

MOTOR RACING. RIAC, tel 775141

ORIENTEERING. Irish Orienteering Association, tel 501633.

ROWING. Irish Amateur Rowing Union, tel 501633.

RUGBY. Irish Rugby Football Union, IRFU, tel 684601.

SAILING. See YACHTING and YACHT CLUBS.

SHOOTING. Rifle and Pistol Association of Ireland, tel 804641.

SHOW JUMPING. Equestrian Federation of Ireland, tel 387611.

SOCCER. Football League of Ireland, tel 766864.

SQUASH. Irish Squash Rackets Association, tel 501564.

SWIMMING. See SWIMMING POOLS.

TABLE TENNIS. Irish Table Tennis Association, tel 421679.

TENNIS. Tennis Ireland, tel 681841. Tennis courts are both private and public; below are listed some of the public variety:
Bushy Park, tel 900320.
Herbert Park, tel 684364.
St. Anne's Park, tel 313697.

**SPRING SHOW.** See ROYAL DUBLIN SOCIETY.

**SQUARES.** If the signature of Georgian Dublin is to be found in the uniform terrace of brick-fronted houses, then the square must certainly be its most formal address. The open spaces of the squares allowed Georgian planners to achieve the maximum of convenience and effect, and nothing gives the viewer a more tangible sense of the period than to walk around the tree-lined spacious streets of the squares, with vistas running off at the corners, apparently to infinity. The Dublin square divides into classic set pieces, usually the earliest examples and later variations on the theme, and the form provides one of the happiest solutions for urban living yet to be devised, that of the residential enclave within the heart of the city. Under the category of 'squares' come all manner of geometric shapes, rectangles, triangles, and shapes which fit into no category at all, but the rectangle is by far the most common. In the city centre, FITZWILLIAM, MERRION and ST. STEPHEN'S GREEN form a relevant set of examples of the Georgian square, and for the nineteenth-century version, the suburbs around RATHMINES Road have a wide range of interesting variants on the theme. Of these, Dartmouth, Belgrave, Brighton, Grosvenor, Mount Pleasant and Kenilworth extend all the possibilities of the form as regards style, shape and quality of housing. They form some of the finest residential areas of Dublin and deserve to be appreciated as much as their Georgian predecessors.

**STAINED GLASS.** Over a period of approximately seventy-five years, dating from the beginning of the twentieth century, there has been a remarkable flourishing of stained glass in Ireland, with Dublin studios producing work of international stature. Prior to this period most of the glass in Irish churches was imported from Britain or the Continent. During the eighteenth century a number of excellent stained-glass artists had been trained in Dublin, but most of their work was done abroad. In the nineteenth century studios were established in Dublin, but these had great difficulty in competing with products from Birmingham and Munich which were in great demand during this era of intense church building. The two studios of significance in Dublin which caused the resurgence of the stained-glass movement are AN TÚR GLOINE, founded in 1903, and the HARRY CLARKE Studios, founded by Clarke's father but only reaching its full potential when Harry Clarke took over the design and execution of the windows. The glass produced by Clarke and the artists working at An Túr Gloine – A.E. CHILD, Beatrice Elvery, Wilhelmina Geddes, Michael Healy, EVIE HONE, Hubert McGoldrick, Catherine O'Brien, SARAH PURSER and Ethel Rhind – formed one of the most important bodies of art produced in any sphere of Irish culture during the twentieth century.

**STANFORD, SIR CHARLES VILLIERS,** (1852-1924). Composer, born 2 Herbert Street, D2. His large output of orchestral and operatic compositions established his reputation. Irish melodies form the themes of numerous works and he also set work by Irish poets to music.

**STANYHURST, RICHARD,** (1547-1618). Historian, born in Dublin. His principal work is a contribution on the history of Ireland to Holinshed's *Chronicles*, published in 1577.

**STAPLETON, MICHAEL,** (d 1801). Stuccodore and building developer. His work is in the Adam manner and is represented in numerous Dublin houses most notably POWERSCOURT HOUSE, 1771, the Trinity Examination Hall, 1784, and BELVEDERE HOUSE, 1785.

**STEPHENS, JAMES**, (1880-1950). Writer, born at 5 Thomas Court, D8. Stephens shares with JAMES JOYCE the honour of being one of the few great imaginative writers to come from Dublin. His masterpiece, *The Crock of Gold*, 1912, is an extraordinary amalgam of fantasy, folklore, philosophy, and inspired humour. Like AE and OLIVER ST. JOHN GOGARTY, Stephens became disillusioned with the free Ireland and left in the 1920s to live in London. He was for ten years Registrar of the NATIONAL GALLERY OF IRELAND.

**STEYNE, THE**. Monolith erected by the Vikings to mark the position of their original landfall. It stood at what is now Townsend Street, originally the river bank, from AD 804 to 1726 when it was removed. Rough drawings of the stone appear on some contemporary eighteenth-century maps. A replacement Steyne was erected on the presumed spot in 1984. It is a rough granite obelisk decorated with two faces of Vikings, by Cliodna Cussen.

**STOCK EXCHANGE**, 28 Anglesea Street, D2, tel 778808. The public are admitted to the visitors' gallery to observe the workings of the Exchange. Mon-Fri 9.30-10.30, 2.00-2.45.

**STOKER, BRAM** (ABRAHAM), (1847-1912). Writer, newspaper editor and theatrical manager, born at 15 Marino Crescent, Fairview, D3. Although he published a dozen novels, only *Dracula*, written in 1897, ensures the survival of his name. This tale of vampirism has been a worldwide bestseller in all media from comics to cinema and has suffered countless adaptations.

**STONECARVING**. During the late nineteenth century in Dublin the Medieval revival which produced buildings in the Venetian Gothic, French Gothic and Hiberno Romanesque styles brought back a love of external decoration and elaborate stonecarving. Carvers such as the Harrison firm and the O'SHEA BROTHERS decorated a great number of buildings in the city and their work can be a pleasure to search out and examine. TRINITY MUSEUM, the KILDARE STREET CLUB, NEWMAN UNIVERSITY CHURCH, the church of SAINTS AUGUSTINE AND JOHN, the Corporation Markets, the Ulster Bank on COLLEGE GREEN and a whole group of commercial buildings on Dame Street are some examples. This fashion for rich surface decoration, unknown in the Georgian era but for a few exceptions – the CASINO and NEWCOMEN'S BANK – died out as suddenly as it had begun and by the 1920s was completely obsolete. Human and animal forms abound in the decoration of these buildings, fruit and vegetables, flora and fauna, the real and the mythological, and in Dame Street alone griffins, wyverns, putti, gods and gargoyles can be found.

**STONYBATTER**, D7. An interesting mixture of eighteenth- and nineteenth-century houses gives this street a character unlike any other part of the city, and is suggestive of a prosperous urban village. The name of the street is one of those composite words like Poolbeg that are an amalgam of Irish and English words, in this case 'stony' and '*bóthar*', a street, which doubtless accurately described the quality of the roadway. Bus 37 Middle Abbey Street.

**STRONGBOW, RICHARD LE CLARE, EARL OF PEMBROKE**, (d 1176). One of the leaders of the Norman invasion of Ireland in 1169-70. The Normans had been invited to come to Ireland by Dermot McMurrough, King of Leinster, who had been deposed as High King. Strongbow quickly established his forces on the east coast and captured Dublin from the Hiberno Norse in 1170. He married Aoife, daughter of McMurrough, an event which is commemorated in DANIEL MACLISE'S painting in the NATIONAL GALLERY. After the death of McMurrough, Strongbow succeeded him as King of Leinster. A tomb effigy in CHRIST CHURCH CATHEDRAL known as Strongbow's Tomb is in fact that of another Norman baron, Fitz Osmund, as is indicated by the armorials on the shield.

**SWASTIKA LAUNDRY.** Throughout the Second World War and up to 1990, the swastika emblem of this laundry was a common sight around Dublin, emblazoned on the company's vans and prominently displayed on their premises on Shelbourne Road, Ballsbridge. The use of the swastika was of course devoid of ominous associations in the era prior to the 1930s – for example, Rudyard Kipling used it as an emblem on his books – and it had been used as the laundry's emblem since the early years of the century. Nonetheless there must have been many who were not sorry to see the disappearance of this symbol from Dublin's streets, where it could only be open to misinterpretation.

**SWIFT, JONATHAN,** (1667-1745). Writer and propagandist, he was born in HOEY'S COURT off Werburgh Street. Swift was the dominant intellectual figure of Dublin in the early eighteenth century, and it is curious to think that most of what is now regarded as the epitomy of Georgian Dublin – JAMES GANDON'S buildings and the squares –

*Death mask of Jonathan Swift.*

was not built during his lifetime. Swift's early professional years were spent in England, first as secretary to Sir William Temple, then as a pamphleteer, first for the Whig and then for the Tory cause. He hoped for some clerical appointment in England, or perhaps an Irish bishopric, but all he got was the deanery of ST. PATRICK'S, a position he held from 1713 to his death in 1745. It is as 'the Dean' that he is remembered, and particularly for the series of savage social satires and polemics which he wrote during those years. *The DRAPIER'S LETTERS*, 1724, *Gulliver's Travels*, 1726, and *A MODEST PROPOSAL*, 1729, are all directed towards showing up the follies of human behaviour. Swift celebrated his daily life, friendships and enmities in poetry, prose and letters in which his humour and vigour of language are as vital to readers now as they were when written in the heat of the passion and indignation which so often possessed him. His ambiguous relationships with STELLA and VANESSA have been the source of some of his best poetry and letters and show him as a man of great charm and intensity. A contemporary, Letitia Pilkington, described the Dean in her *Memoirs* as 'a man of fire, a little wild and sufficiently irritable'. In his attitude to himself, Swift is capable of seeing both his vanity as well as his strengths and in 'Verses on the Death of Dr. Swift' lampoons his own failings as fiercely as he did the failings of others. Swift championed the poor and dispossessed and left his money to found a hospital for the mentally ill. He is buried next to Stella in ST. PATRICK'S CATHEDRAL.

> For Poetry, he's past his Prime,
> He takes an Hour to find a Rhime:
> His Fire is out, his Wit decay'd,
> His fancy sunk, his Muse a Jade,
> I'd have him throw away his Pen;
> But there's no talking to some Men.

('Verses on the Death of Dr. Swift', Jonathan Swift.)

**SWORDS**, Co. Dublin. 12.8km (18 miles) from the city centre. There is a fine Medieval castle in Swords and an Early Christian round tower. The castle has a large battlemented walled enclosure with gate tower and subsidiary buildings. The round tower is complete to the cap but the upper level has been reconstructed. Bus 33, 41, 41B Eden Quay.

**SYNGE, JOHN MILLINGTON,** (1871-1909). Playwright, born in Rathfarnham. He is one of the founding dramatists of the Irish Literary Revival and the greatest of the playwrights originally associated with the ABBEY THEATRE. Synge's plays of Wicklow and west of Ireland life form an archetype of the fascination of the poetic and the primitive in Irish rural society. He returned to Ireland in 1898 after some years on the Continent and visited the Aran Islands where he was captivated by the poetic speech of the local people which he used in his otherwise realistic plays. *The Shadow of the Glen*, 1903, *Riders to the Sea*, 1904, *The Well of the Saints*, 1905, and *The Playboy of the Western World*, 1907, were received with controversy as Synge's perception of country people did not correspond to that of the Dublin Nationalist audiences of the Abbey, and he was virulently attacked in the newspapers as a corruptor of public morals. This reaction led to riots during the first production in the Abbey of *The Playboy*. Synge responded:

'To a sister of an enemy of the author's who disapproved of *The Playboy*'

> Lord confound this surly sister,
> Blight her brow with blotch and blister,
> Cramp her larynx, lung and liver,
> In her guts a galling give her.
>
> Let her live to earn her dinners
> In Mountjoy with seedy sinners:
> Lord, this judgment quickly bring,
> And I'm your servant, J.M.Synge

('A Curse', J.M. Synge.)

**T**AILORS' HALL, Back Lane, High Street, D8. Now the headquarters of AN TAISCE, The National Trust, the Tailors' Hall, built in 1706, is the oldest guild hall in Ireland although records of the Guild of Tailors go back to the fifteenth century. Within the building the most interesting features are the hall itself and the fine early oak staircase which has the low balustrade and 'barley sugar' balusters characteristic of the late seventeenth century. The Hall, which is lit by tall windows to the north and south, has a screen on its west wall bearing the names of Masters of the Guild from 1419 to 1841. There is also a fine marble fireplace presented by eighteenth-century guild members and a unusual minstrels' gallery overlooking the Hall. The Tailors' Hall has always had varied usage, being from the beginning used for meetings of the other guilds as well as for religious assemblies, dancing, fencing and even as a school. The most important political meetings held here were the 1792 gatherings which became known as the 'BACK LANE PARLIAMENT', when the Catholic Committee met to petition the actual parliament in London for the repeal of the laws which discriminated against Catholics and Dissenters. Having been for many years the centre of a neglected area of the city, the Tailors' Hall is now, probably for the first time since the mid-eighteenth century, again at the hub of a bustling and developing part of Dublin.

*The Tailors' Hall.*

**TAISCE, AN.** The Tailors' Hall, Back Lane, High Street, D8, tel 541786. The National Trust for Ireland, founded in 1948 as a voluntary body, it is the most important environmental organisation in Ireland. As An Taisce receives no state subsidy and relies entirely on subscriptions from its members, its valuable work is continually hampered by lack of funds. The headquarters of An Taisce is in the TAILORS' HALL, an architecturally important and historic early eighteenth-century guildhall which An Taisce restored and saved from demolition. An Taisce's areas of interest and influence are the environment, architecture, and both urban and rural gardens and landscape. Specialist committees deal with a variety of areas within the mandate of the trust and frequently act in a consultative role to government agencies and public bodies. The Trust owns and cares for a number of properties around the country as well as considerable nature reserves in the Dublin area – BOOTERSTOWN MARSH, IRELAND'S EYE and HOWTH summit and cliff walks. The society has a useful list of environmental publications on specific subjects and areas. Bus 21A, 78, 78A from Fleet Street.

**TALBOT, MATTHEW,** (1856-1925).
Dublin labourer and reformed alcoholic
who after his death acquired an extensive popular following due to the ascetic
manner of his life, which involved mu-
tilation of the flesh through the wearing
of chains around his waist. He is buried
in a shrine in the church of Our Lady of
Lourdes on Seán Mc Dermott Street. A
sculpture of Talbot by Albert Power
stands at the southern side of Talbot
Memorial Bridge and there is a drawing
by Flora Mitchell in the NATIONAL GAL-
LERY of his bedroom, with plank bed and
timber pillow, at 18 Upper Rutland
Street.

**TALLAGHT,** D24. Extensive suburban development, with a population of
80,000, to the south west of the city of
largely local authority housing built in
the 1970s and 1980s, and absorbing the
village of Tallaght. West Tallaght stretches to the foothills of the Dublin Mountains. The Square, Tallaght's town
centre, built twenty years after the housing, is one of the most comprehensive
shopping developments in Dublin.

**TANDY, NAPPER,** (1740-1803). Revolutionary, he was, with WOLFE TONE
and Thomas Russell, a founder of the
UNITED IRISHMEN. Like Tone, he was
suspected of plotting rebellion and had
to leave the country. He eventually made
his way to France from where in 1798 he
returned to Ireland with an invasion
force, but this fled before it engaged in
any action. A man of remarkably lugub-
rious and conspiratorial appearance, it is
difficult to associate him with the dash-
ing Tone. Tandy is commemorated in a
ballad of the period which seems to be
his chief claim to current remembrance.

*Temple Bar and Merchant's Arch.*

**TAPESTRY.** The eighteenth-century
tapestries in the House of Lords of the
Old Parliament House, woven in 1733,
represent a form of interior decoration
common from the Medieval period in
Ireland and which lasted later here than
in other countries where paintings
tended to supersede woven hangings.
Other early hangings are to be seen in the
NATIONAL MUSEUM, but the most impressive are those modern additions to
the genre, now on display in the public
parts of large office buildings and executed by contemporary Irish artists.
Fine examples are in the Bank of Ireland
on Baggot Street by Patrick Scott, and in
the Carrolls Building, Grand Parade, by
Louis Le Broquy.

**TARA BROOCH, THE,** National Museum of Ireland, Kildare Street, D2, tel
765521. One of the chief metalwork
treasures of the NATIONAL MUSEUM, the
Brooch was found in Co. Meath in 1850

but has no known connection with the site of Tara. It consists of an eighth-century AD silver gilt dress ornament minutely decorated with surface patterns, filagree, glass and amber studs. The decoration of the brooch resembles that of the illuminated manuscripts of the period and the ornamentation is as intricate as anything in the Book of Kells. Brooches of this kind were a common form of personal ornament in the eighth and ninth centuries in Ireland, but the standard of decoration on the Tara Brooch indicates that it must have been the possession of a person of great wealth and importance.

**TARBARY, JAMES.** Huguenot wood carver who executed the work in the Chapel of the ROYAL HOSPITAL KILMAINHAM.

**TEMPLE BAR**, D2. Dublin's 'Left Bank', this quarter, only a few minutes' walk from O'CONNELL STREET could hardly be more different, and its narrow streets hold a rich assortment of studios, galleries, recording studios, second-hand clothes shops, pubs and restaurants. The Project Arts Centre, established in the 1960s, runs a theatre and gallery with the emphasis on Avant Garde art and alternative theatre, and this has set the style of all later developments in the area, which now include the Temple Bar Gallery and Studios, the Irish Film Institute, Recording Studios, and the Resource Centre, a communally run vegetarian restaurant and meeting place. The district was until recently under threat of total demolition.

**TENEMENTS.** The appalling tenements for which Dublin was noted in the early years of the twentieth century were some of the worst in any European city,

*A Dublin tenement.*

a cause of high infant mortality and the scene of frequent cholera epidemics. Housed in decaying eighteenth-century mansions, which had a century after the ACT OF UNION deteriorated into the hovels of the destitute, sometimes even the stairs were ripped out to make way for more rooms. The squalor of these living conditions probably only finds a contemporary counterpart in the shanty towns of Third World countries. Four families to a room has been recorded in surveys conducted by the health authorities, and of course sanitary facilities were non-existent. Eighteenth-century houses were built without toilets, high society having an abundance of servants to empty chamber pots and perform other menial tasks. When these houses became tenements, sixty people might have to use a single earth closet in the yard. The stench would have been unbearable, and the drinking water came from a tap in the same polluted yard.

Towards the end of the nineteenth century, a number of agencies, the IVEAGH TRUST and the ARTISANS' DWELLINGS ASSOCIATION, provided the first purpose-built accommodation for the poor of Dublin and from this period onwards the tenements gradually began to disappear. However there are still streets, particularly on the north side of the Liffey, where gaunt brick houses stand with an ever open doorway, each decayed room a separate home.

> And the bare bones of a fanlight
> Over a hungry door.

('Dublin', Louis Mac Neice.)

**TENTER'S FIELDS**, D8. Area to the south of the LIBERTIES developed as Corporation housing during the 1920s. These were the fields of the linen weavers during the eighteenth century.

**THACKERAY, W. M.** (1811-1863). Novelist, he travelled extensively in Ireland in 1842 and published his observations in *The Irish Sketch Book*. Thackeray was an accomplished artist and the *Sketch Book* is illustrated with his own sketches. In Dublin he stayed at the Shelbourne Hotel.

**THEATRES AND THEATRICAL VENUES** (See MAP). The constants in the Dublin theatrical world from the 1920s up to the present have been the ABBEY, GAIETY, GATE and OLYMPIA theatres, and between them they have provided a mixture of classics, new Irish plays, variety and pantomime. Small experimental theatres like the PIKE came and went, for with small seating capacity they were never sufficiently profitable to survive very long. The two-week-long Dublin Theatre Festival, held annually ever autumn, which developed out of the An Tóstal cultural festival of 1953,

*Yeats's 'Cúchulainn Cycle' at the Abbey.*

began and continues to be the single event of greatest importance in Dublin's theatrical year. The Festival brings many new Irish plays to the stage as well as introducing companies and productions from all over the world. This increase in activity has spawned new companies and more recently a number of well equipped new theatres, the Tivoli and Andrew's Lane, have begun to make a valuable contribution to theatrical life in the city. The work of Dublin dramatists of the last two centuries, RICHARD BRINSLEY SHERIDAN, OLIVER GOLDSMITH, DION BOUCICAULT, OSCAR WILDE and GEORGE BERNARD SHAW, are usually to be found on some theatre's programme and Ireland's national theatre, the Abbey, continues the tradition begun by W.B. YEATS, SEÁN O'CASEY, J.M. SYNGE and LADY GREGORY of supporting contemporary Irish drama. The work of established and up-and-coming contemporary writers can be seen in the smaller and experimental theatres and the potential theatre goer is in the happy position of being spoiled for choice. The following list includes occasional venues which often host performances during the Theatre Festival as well as the regular theatres.

ABBEY THEATRE, The National Theatre, Lower Abbey Street, D1, tel 787222. The history of the modern theatre in Dublin and in Ireland generally is inextricably bound up with the Abbey and the writers, actors and producers connected with it, stretching back over a period of almost a century. The Abbey opened with a programme of four one-act plays on 27 December 1904 and this initial presentation can be seen as setting the guidelines which the theatre was subsequently to follow: *Spreading the News* by LADY GREGORY, *On Baile Strand* and *Cathleen Ni Houlihan* by W.B.YEATS, and *In the Shadow of the Glen* by J.M.SYNGE were presented under the auspices of the Irish National Theatre Society. This Society had been set up two years previously, with Yeats as president and MAUDE GONNE, DOUGLAS HYDE and GEORGE RUSSELL (AE) as joint vice presidents. The Society was without premises in which to perform

until the philanthropic Annie F. Horniman agreed to fund the purchase of the old Mechanic's Institute in Abbey Street, and to have it refurbished as a theatre. The reconstruction was designed by Joseph Holloway, now remembered as a diarist of theatrical life in Dublin. The idea of the Theatre Society developed from the Irish Literary Theatre which had been producing plays since 1898, based on the concept of poetic drama, and with subject matter drawn from Irish folk legends, sagas and the life of the country people. Prior to this, theatre in Dublin tended to be a reflection of current fashions on the London stage. However, the dynamic and innovative productions which the new theatre brought before the Dublin public were not always well received. Late Victorian Dublin took offence on numerous occasions at what was perceived as indecency, and when the *Playboy of the Western World* was first performed in 1907 the reaction was a violent one. This play presents a romantic but not highly moral picture of west of Ireland life which failed to accord with the Nationalist viewpoint of the times. The event is commented upon in a few lines by Yeats:

> Once, when midnight smote the air,
> Eunuchs ran through Hell and met
> On every crowded street to stare
> Upon great Juan riding by:
> Even like these to rail and sweat
> Staring upon his sinewy thigh.

In 1926, following the production of Seán O'Casey's *The Plough and the Stars*, the same reaction was experienced, but the cause of offence on this occasion was a scene during which the national flag was carried into a pub frequented by prostitutes. Riots were nothing new in Dublin's theatres and had occurred frequently in the previous two centuries whenever the volatile audiences considered that life as represented on stage failed to accord with their own view. Throughout the 1930s and 1940s the Abbey settled into a period of complacently presenting plays written in the image of the founding fathers, yet lacking the element of controversy. Irish kitchen tragedies and dramas of small-town life became the staple, without much indication being displayed of a desire to confront contemporary Ireland. The fact that significant works like O'Casey's *The Silver Tassie*, DENIS JOHNSTON's *The Old Lady Says 'No'*, and BRENDAN BEHAN's *The Quare Fellow* were all rejected by the Abbey indicates the theatre's shift from leader of the avant garde to that of the conservative establishment. It was said facetiously of the Abbey during this period that for thirty years the sets never needed to be changed, so similar were all the plays! The original Abbey building was burned down in 1951 and the company transferred to the QUEEN'S THEATRE in Pearse Street, returning in 1966 to a new building and new possibilities. The new Abbey, designed in an international minimalist manner by MICHAEL SCOTT has a 638-seat auditorium and below it an experimental theatre, The Peacock, of 157 seats. The company emerged from the doldrums of the previous thirty years and new playwrights began to appear and create a new image for the Abbey. Plays by a new generation of Irish dramatists – Tom Murphy, Brian Friel, Tom Kilroy – began to attract international attention again and despite continuing controversy as to its aims the Abbey has begun to have a major impact on the theatrical world. The Abbey, which in 1925 was the first theatre in the English-speaking world to receive a state subsidy, has developed a unique and personal style of performance and a sense of continuity with the ideas and the principles of the Literary Revival of the 1890s. Controversy continues as to the importance or otherwise of this tradition of 'poetic realism', and everybody in the theatre has their own idea as to what the Abbey *should* be doing. The Abbey now presents a mixture of the starkly contemporary new Irish writers, classics from its own great heritage and plays from the international theatre which make it a vital if controversial force in Dublin's theatrical life. The collection of theatrical portraits in the Abbey's foyer is a who's who of Irish theatre, with many perceptive portraits of the players and playwrights associated with the theatre, most notably portraits by JOHN B. YEATS and CECIL FFRENCH SALKELD.

ANDREW'S LANE STUDIO, 9-11 Andrew's Lane, D2, tel 6795720. Upstairs venue of the theatre of the same name, seating 80.

ANDREW'S LANE THEATRE, 9-11 Andrew's Lane, D2, tel 6795720. A new theatre which opened in 1989, situated a few minutes' walk from Dame Street. The auditorium seats 220, and there are plans to develop the foyer as a lunch venue and exhibition area. Contemporary theatre, music and solo performances.

BÉAL BOCHT, AN, Charlemont Street, D2, tel 755614. Pub venue associated with one-person performances, comedy and cabaret.

CARROLL'S THEATRE, Grand Parade, D6. Occasional venue in the premises of the Carroll Tobacco Company.

CITY CENTRE, THE, Moss Street, D2, tel 770643. Arts centre on the south Liffey quays with two galleries and performance space on two floors.

FOCUS, Pembroke Place, off Pembroke Street, D2, tel 763071. Small studio theatre whose acting tradition derives from the Stanislavsky method. Twentieth-century European and American drama.

GAIETY THEATRE, South King Street, D2, tel 771717. Dublin's oldest theatre, designed by C.J.Phipps, it opened in 1871. The interior is that of a Victorian music hall, all gilt and gingerbread. The Dublin Grand Opera Society (DGOS) hold their twice yearly seasons in the Gaiety and it is otherwise associated with variety and the annual Christmas pantomime for which it is the perfect venue.

GATE THEATRE, Cavendish Row, D1, tel 744045/746042. The Gate is the main venue for contemporary Irish, European and international theatre in Dublin and one can expect lavish, and superbly acted and designed performances. In this way the Gate contrasts radically with the shoestring and 'use the drawing room curtains' design approach of the experimental theatres. The company was founded by Hilton Edwards and Mícheál Mac Liammóir in 1928 as the Dublin Gate Theatre Studio with a performance of PEER GYNT. This was produced in The PEACOCK in Abbey Street and it was not until 1930 that the company moved to the eighteenth-century premises of the old ROTUNDA ASSEMBLY ROOMS, designed by Richard Johnston in 1784, with which the Gate has been associated ever since. The Gate has been the main source of innovation in Dublin theatre for over half a century during which Edwards-Mac Liammóir Productions produced the best of contemporary drama. Both Orson Welles and James Mason acted in the Gate as young unknowns. The theatre was shared with LORD LONGFORD's company for many years, each company touring for six months and giving a Dublin season for the other six months. Modern ideas of lighting, production, and casting were the hallmark of the Gate tradition and this has been maintained today with intellectually stimulating and visually attractive productions of new work as well as revivals of the classics.

INTERNATIONAL BAR, Wicklow Street, D2, tel 779250. Pub venue for the best fringe or alternative comedy in Dublin.

LAMBERT PUPPET THEATRE, Clifton Terrace, Monkstown, Co. Dublin, tel 800974. Directed by the Puppet Master Eugene Lambert, this theatre presents the world of puppetry on an exceptionally imaginative and professional level, with productions geared for audiences from very small children upwards. Facilities at the theatre include a Puppet Museum and the repertoire includes Irish and international classics and the Lambert family's own individual productions. A must for children and the not-so-young.

LOMBARD STREET STUDIOS, off Westland Row, D2, tel 772941. Occasional theatrical venue.

OLYMPIA THEATRE, Dame Street, D2, tel 778962. Dublin's largest theatre, built in 1879, is a nineteenth-century music hall and it still carries on this tradition. Musicals and Gilbert and Sullivan as well as touring hit shows from abroad are the standard repertoire of the Olympia.

PEACOCK THEATRE, Lower Abbey Street, D2, tel 787222. Basement experimental venue of the Abbey. Short-run new plays and lunchtime performances. The venue for the Yeats International Theatre Festival held in August which aims to present all of the poet's neglected dramatic work. The name comes from the peacock decorations of the original Peacock Theatre, destroyed in the fire of 1951.

PLAYERS THEATRE, Trinity College, D2, tel 772941. The Trinity student theatre housed in cramped quarters in the corner of the front quad, regarded as a nursery for major theatrical talents. Lunchtime and evening performances of classics and modern drama.

POINT DEPOT THEATRE, East link Bridge, D1, tel 363633/365720. A new addition to the city's theatre spaces in converted Victorian railway sheds. Visits of ballet companies such as the Bolshoi and international rock performers have established the Point Depot, or Point Theatre as it is also called, as an important venue for large audiences.

PROJECT ARTS CENTRE, Essex Street East, D2, tel 712321. Experimental theatre venue with 120 seats, attached to the oldest arts centre in the city, founded in 1966. New productions by contemporary Irish writers.

RUPERT GUINNESS HALL, Watling Street, off Thomas Street, D8. Part of the Guinness Brewery complex and occasional theatrical venue.

SFX (Saint Francis Xavier Hall), Upper Sherrard Street, D1, tel 788277/788857.

TIVOLI THEATRE, Francis Street, D8, tel 5355998. This new theatre began life in 1936 as the 'Tivo' cinema, a Liberties landmark where the children got into the Saturday matinée for two jam jars or the equivalent. Now the best-equipped and adaptable theatre space in Dublin. Classics and contemporary writers.

**THINGMOTE or THENGMOTE.** A mound at Hoggen or COLLEGE GREEN which had been a meeting place during the Viking era, but which was removed in 1682 to augment the defences of the city during the panic of contemporary political struggles.

**THOLSEL.** Seventeenth-century equivalent of the Royal Exchange which stood in Christ Church Place. It was demolished in 1806, but can be seen in one of JAMES MALTON'S aquatints. The two unattractive statues of Charles II and James II by William de Keysar which decorated the front now languish in the gloom of the crypt of CHRIST CHURCH CATHEDRAL.

**THOMAS STREET.** The straightness and width of Thomas Street suggest one of the great boulevards of the Georgian city, but there is little on it today which remains from that period. The most impressive buildings are ST. CATHERINE'S CHURCH which has the finest eighteenth-century church façade in Dublin, heavily worked in dark granite and the nineteenth-century church of SAINTS AUGUSTINE AND JOHN. Further to the west, as a continuation of Thomas Street in James's Street, is the Guinness complex, occupying land on both sides of the street and to the north extending to the Liffey. On the south side of James's Street are some of the finest Victorian industrial buildings in Dublin and the GUINNESS MUSEUM is contained in one of these, the Hop Store. At the end of James's Street is a Georgian obelisk at the base of which is a rather decayed fountain.

**THREE ROCK MOUNTAIN**, Ticknock, Co. Dublin. Phenomenal rock formation on the summit of the mountain which although a natural formation of the granite outcrop, has acquired all sorts of supernatural explanations for its appearance, associated with druids and fairies. The rocks provide a commanding view over the whole landscape north across DUBLIN BAY to HOWTH, and a bird's eye view of DUN LAOGHAIRE below.

**TITLES.** The representative of the British monarch in Ireland was known as the Lord Deputy up to the Restoration, and subsequently as the Lord Lieutenant or Viceroy. The Chief Secretary was the political representative of the Westminster government, and the Under Secretary was the head of the Irish civil service.

**TOLKA.** Tributary of the Liffey, the mouth of which has been altered through land reclamation over the last two hundred years and now enters directly to DUBLIN BAY at Fairview Park. The Tolka rises in Co. Meath, and flows through Dunboyne, Blanchardstown and Glasnevin before entering the bay. At Glasnevin it runs through the rural landscape of the BOTANIC GARDENS before being totally hemmed in by housing developments.

**TONE, THEOBALD WOLFE,** (1763-1798). Revolutionary, born at number 44 in what is now called Wolfe Tone Street. Tone studied law but did not practise, devoting himself to politics and propaganda on behalf of independence from England. Of all the Irish revolutionaries of his day, Tone believed most firmly in an Ireland in which the different strands of political and religious opinion would be united under common aims. He founded the United Irishmen in 1791, based on the principles of the French Revolution. The BACK LANE PARLIAMENT of 1792 was organised by Tone but failed to achieve the

*Town Design Centre, Pearse Street.*

concessions he had expected from the British government. In 1796 he became involved in the abortive French invasion of Ireland under General Hoche. A longboat or YOLE, captured during this unsuccessful expedition is on display in the IRISH NATIONAL MARITIME MUSEUM. During a second expedition in 1798 Tone was captured and sentenced to death. He attempted to commit suicide but failed, although he did die from the wound some days later. Tone's burial place in Bodenstown, Co. Kildare, has become one of the most emotive shrines of Irish Nationalism, visited annually (and separately) by the various groupings of Irish Nationalist opinion.

**TOURIST OFFICES.** Bord Failte, the Irish Tourist Board, have their principal office at 14 Upper O'Connell Street, D1, tel 747733, which as well as dealing with all sorts of routine tourist enquiries, runs an accommodation service. The Northern Ireland Tourist Board's offices are at 16 Nassau Street, D2, tel freefone 1-800-230-230. See BORD FAILTE.

**TOWER DESIGN CENTRE**, IDA Enterprise Centre, Pearse Street, D2, tel 775655. Overlooking the Grand Canal Basin the seven-storey granite and brick tower rises out of a complex of modern factory buildings and houses the largest craft centre in the city. Within the tower are workshops and studios where craftworkers in wood, ceramics, fabrics and metalwork produce one-off items and small production lines where the emphasis is on craftsmanship. Domestic and decorative pottery, architectural ceramics, jewellery, knitwear, woodcarving, graphics, handmade paper and paper conservation are some of the crafts practised here and they can be seen in the craftworkers' own studios. The tower was built in 1862 as a warehouse and sugar refinery by the theatre architect Alfred Darbyshire in collaboration with the engineer Sir William Fairbairn. The restoration project won a Europa Nostra award in 1983 as well as numerous other commendations from the Royal Institute of Architects in Ireland. In the weeks before Christmas, the tower holds an annual fair. General opening hours, Mon-Fri 9.00-5.30.

**TRAMS**. Horse-drawn trams operated in Dublin from the middle of the nineteenth century but, in 1886, were replaced by electrically powered ones operated by the Dublin United Tramway Company. The most famous tram journey was on the Howth Tram which brought passengers creaking up the slope to Howth Summit. This service lasted until 1959, although the city service had closed down ten years before. A number of Dublin trams are preserved in the TRANSPORT MUSEUM in HOWTH.

**TREATY**. Agreement signed on 6 December 1921 between England and the representatives of the nascent Irish Republic which brought an end to the hostilities of the War of Independence and provided for a British withdrawal from the south of Ireland with the exception of certain designated ports and other naval facilities. The Treaty provided for the establishment of the Irish Free State, as a separate entity from Northern Ireland. Civil War followed the rejection of the Treaty by elements within the Nationalist movement.

**TRESSELL, ROBERT**, (1870-1911). Dublin-born writer whose real name was Robert Noonan. After his death the socialist classic *The Ragged Trousered Philanthropists* was published in 1914 by his daughter. In this work Tressell satirises the behaviour of both the bosses and the workers and their mutual incomprehension in the fictional town of Mugsborough.

**TRINITY COLLEGE**, College Green, D2, tel 772941. Founded by Elizabeth I in 1592, Trinity is the oldest university in Ireland, predating the other colleges by over 250 years. No buildings remain from the Elizabethan period and in fact the earliest part of the university is the residential block, The Rubrics, which date from 1701, although even this building has been given a Victorian facelift. Architecturally, Trinity is an eighteenth-century university, with important Victorian and modern additions. The collegiate atmosphere which is maintained within the precincts of the university is a unique aspect of Dublin's cultural identity, and represents four centuries of continuity and scholarship.

The great library by THOMAS BURGH, 1712, which houses the BOOK OF KELLS, has the finest interior space in Dublin, a combination of the eighteenth-century structure with a Victorian barrel-vaulted

*Front Arch, Trinity College.*

roof by DEANE and WOODWARD, added in the 1860s. RICHARD CASTLE'S earliest Dublin building, the Trinity Printing House, 1734, designed as a Doric temple, is a miniature masterpiece. Castle also designed the Dining Hall during the 1740s which, although recently destroyed by fire, has been splendidly restored. The monumental mid-eighteenth-century west front of the college by Theodore Jacobsen which faces College Green is one of the most important elements of the Georgian streetscape of the city, ending the vista of Dame Street magnificently and balancing the extravagance of the Bank of Ireland. The main arched entrance under the west front brings the viewer into

Front or Parliament Square with matched porticos on either side of buildings by SIR WILLIAM CHAMBERS. These are the Theatre and Chapel, built during the 1780s, and the last major Georgian buildings to be added to Trinity. Prior to their work on the Library, Deane and Woodward had built the new Museum Building, 1852, which was to be vastly influential in the development of architectural taste in the latter half of the nineteenth century. Designed in the Venetian Gothic style with handsome marble interior, the building is richly embellished with stone carvings, all executed with a freedom which emulates the work of Medieval stonecarvers. Nothing of great architectural significance was added to Trinity until the 1970s when the BERKELEY LIBRARY and the Arts Building, 1980s, were designed by Paul Koralek. The Library, with a concrete and granite façade that makes no concessions to Georgian pastiche, successfully fits in with its neighbours, Burgh's Library and Woodward's Museum, which is no mean achievement. The Atrium, 1985, by de Blackam and Meagher, is an altogether delightful addition to the college, an internal timber space off the Dining Hall which has the atmosphere of a Shakespearean theatre-in-the-round. By the same architects is the whimsical architectural joke, the recreation of Adolf Loos's Kärtner Bar designed for Vienna in 1907 which has become the new Fellows' Bar, above the dining hall, an act of architectural homage to one of the founders of the modern movement. Outside the college quadrangles, at the bottom of Grafton Street, is the Provost's House, 1759, a Palladian mansion by John Smyth, and the only one of the great eighteenth-century town houses in Dublin still to be in use as a permanent residence. The exterior is heavily rusticated and severe, but internally it has fine plasterwork and some magnificent spaces, in particular the staircase hall and first floor salon. Trinity has an important art collection, beginning with portraits of early figures associated with the college and developing into contemporary painting and sculpture. Two twentieth-century sculptors whose works are excellently sited within the college grounds are HENRY MOORE in Library Square and ALEXANDER CALDER in Fellows' Square, in front of the new Arts Block. Within the grounds of Trinity is College Park, used as sports and athletic grounds, and an important although gradually shrinking green space within the city centre.

**TROLLOPE, ANTHONY,** (1815-1882). Novelist, he worked as a clerk in the General Post Office in London and was transferred to Ireland in 1841 where he lived for the following eighteen years. He found the subject matter for his early novels in his travels around the country in the course of his post office work. Trollope lived in a large Georgian house at 6 Seaview Terrace, Donnybrook, for five years before leaving Ireland.

**TUOHY, PATRICK,** (1894-1930). Artist born at 15 North Frederick Street. He studied under WILLIAM ORPEN in the Metropolitan School of Art where he subsequently taught. Tuohy was an accomplished portrait and genre painter and he painted many of his contemporaries, amongst them JAMES JOYCE and JAMES STEPHENS. He committed suicide in New York where he had emigrated in 1927. Tuohy's portrait of Stephens is in the NATIONAL GALLERY and 'A Mayo Peasant Boy' is in the HUGH LANE GALLERY.

**TÚR GLOINE, AN.** Co-operative stained-glass studios established in 1903 by SARAH PURSER and Edward Martyn at 24 Upper Pembroke Street, D2. The studios operated on the principle that the entire work of execution on a window should be the product of an individual artist, in design, choice of glass and painting. The studio proved to be one of the most influential forces in the Irish arts and crafts movement, involving a talented group of artists over a period of sixty years and ensuring that whatever tawdry religious statuary and decoration may be expected in Irish churches, the stained glass is usually worth looking at, and so widespread are the products of An Túr Gloine that they may be encountered in any part of the country. In Dublin, windows by artists who worked in the studio are also abundant and can be found under the names of individual artists, A.E. CHILD, BEATRICE ELVERY, MICHAEL HEALY, EVIE HONE, CATHERINE O'BRIEN and Purser.

**TURKISH BATHS,** Lincoln Place, D2. Between the Lincoln Place entrance to Trinity and the corner of Westland Row are the remains of a curious onion-domed turkish baths which opened here in the 1860s. The dome and chimney-minaret are gone now but the turreted wall which fronted the male and female chambers still remains. Furnished in oriental style, the baths were considered to be homeopathic and there was even a separate section for animals!

**TURNER, J.M.W.** (1755-1851). The NATIONAL GALLERY has a collection of Turner's watercolours which are exhibited annually in January under the terms of the H. Vaughan Bequest by which they were presented to the Gallery. Typical Turner subjects – Venice,

Petworth, the English coast and Roman campagna – are well represented in this small but brilliant collection, one of the single finest groups of pictures by an individual artist in the gallery.

**TURNER, RICHARD** (1798-1881). Iron master, who designed the ironwork of the Great Palm Houses at Kew, (which was prefabricated at Turner's Ironworks at Ballsbridge), 1845, and Belfast, 1839, was also responsible for the Curvilinear Range at the Botanic Gardens, GLASNEVIN, 1842. These early examples of iron and glass architecture are among the finest achievements of the Victorian era and deserve much wider appreciation than they receive.

**TUSSAUD, MADAME MARIE**, (1761-1850). The celebrated waxwork artist accompanied by her son Joseph came to Ireland in 1804 and spent until 1808 living in Dublin and travelling around the country where she visited Kilkenny, Waterford, Belfast and Cork with her historical exhibition. Her timing might have been better, as in the wake of the EMMET rebellion of 1803 curfews were commonplace and movement restricted. Foreigners with a pronounced French accent naturally excited suspicion. Madame Tussaud opened her 'Grand European Cabinet of Figures' exhibition at the Shakespeare Gallery in Exchequer Street where she exhibited a tableau 'The late Royal Family of France', as well as figures of Marat, Robespierre, Voltaire, Rousseau and Napoleon. To this she added portraits of prominent Dubliners, among them HENRY GRATTAN. The Dublin public responded enthusiastically to the waxwork exhibition, which is hardly surprising given the fact that all the waxworks were modelled on the heroes and villains of the French Revolution and the exhibition was a tangible link with these recent events. Some of the original figures exhibited in Dublin, such as Marat and Robespierre, are still on view in Madame Tussaud's in London.

**TYRONE HOUSE**, Marlborough Street, D1. Designed by RICHARD CASTLE for Sir Marcus Beresford in 1740. When the house became the headquarters of the Department of Education in 1835, a replica block was built to the north which tends to confuse the identity of the original house. Tyrone House has fine plasterwork by the FRANCINI brothers and the stairhall and principal rooms have heavy dark oak balustrades, panelling and doorcases.

**U***LYSSES*. JAMES JOYCE's mammoth novel, published in 1922, in which he used the Greek Ulysses myth as a basis for a saga of contemporary life. Set in Dublin in 1904, Joyce made use of directories and newspapers of the period in order to establish accurate circumstantial detail. Against this background he wrote an extraordinary work of imaginative fiction in which experimental techniques extend the possibilities of the narrative. LEOPOLD BLOOM, the Ulysses of the title, and Stephen Dedalus, his companion as well as Joyce's alter ego, travel around the city on 16 June 1904, experiencing all that the life of a city has to offer. The Dublin of *Ulysses* is to Joyce the archetypal city, but it is also most particularly itself, and even today, nearly a century after 'Bloomsday', it can be difficult to see Dublin divorced from Joyce's rendering of it, so firmly did he capture its essences.

**UNITED ARTS CLUB**, 3 Upper Fitzwilliam Street, D2, tel 762965. Founded in 1907 by Ellie Duncan who was later to become the first Curator of the Municipal Gallery of Modern Art. Early members included LADY GREGORY, HUGH LANE, William Orpen, COUNTESS MARKIEVICZ, JACK B. YEATS and W. B. YEATS, Estella Solomons and SARAH PURSER. The Club has had a varied history and in its early years organised some very important exhibitions in Dublin, most notably of the POST IMPRESSIONISTS and an exhibition of the theatrical design of Edward Gordon Craig. Today the Club continues to provide a meeting place for artists and to hold exhibitions of members' work, but it has moved a long way from the avant garde position in which it originated.

**UNITED IRISHMEN**. Revolutionary organisation established in Dublin in 1791 by WOLFE TONE and others, which espoused the spirit of the French Revolution and wished to separate Ireland from English domination.

**UNIVERSITIES**. University education in Ireland, as with much else in the country, was for centuries bedevilled by religious differences. Trinity College, (TCD), established in 1592, was regarded as a Protestant university and for long periods Catholics and Dissenters were debarred from taking degrees. Catholics seeking higher education tended to study on the Continent. It was not until 1845 that three non-denominational colleges were established by the government, but due to Catholic opposition, this move was not a success. In 1854 the Catholic University was established in Dublin, but, without the right to grant degrees and without any funds at its disposal, it quickly ran into difficulties. As a compromise measure in 1879, the Royal University of Ireland was set up and this absorbed the Catholic University, becoming University College Dublin (UCD) in 1882. The National University of Ireland came into being in 1908 with UCD as one of its constituent Colleges. There was no further addition to the city's universities until 1989 when the Dublin City University (DCU) was created out of the National Institute for Higher Education in Glasnevin.

**UPPER AND LOWER IN DUBLIN STREET NAMES**. In the naming of Dublin Streets, upper and lower are common designations. Lower is always closer to the mouth of the Liffey.

**USSHER, ARCHBISHOP JAMES**, (1581-1656). Scholar and antiquarian, he was born in Nicholas Street. Ussher amassed over his life an important collection of early books and manuscripts which, following his death and after many vicissitudes, were bought by TRINITY COLLEGE. They now form an important part of the library collection. He had been one of the first graduates of the College, entering it two years after its establishment.

**VAN BEAVER, JOHN.** Huguenot weaver, the two tapestries which have hung since 1733 in the HOUSE OF LORDS of the Old Parliament House in COLLEGE GREEN are his work. They were designed by Johann Van Der Hagen, a Dutch artist then living in Dublin, and woven by Van Beaver at Robert Baillie's tapestry works in Abbey Street. They represent 'The Glorious Battle of the Boyne' and 'The Glorious Defence of Londonderry'. Van Beaver also wove a tapestry in 1738 for the WEAVER'S HALL depicting George II and carrying the inscription, 'The Workmanship of John Vanbeaver Ye Famous Tapestry Weaver'. It is now in the Metropolitan Museum of Art, New York.

**VAN NOST, JOHN,** (1712-1780). Sculptor of Dutch origin who worked in Dublin from the mid-eighteenth century. The two figures of lead – a material commonly used by sculptors at the time – which stand on top of the gates to DUBLIN CASTLE, representing Mars or Fortitude over the west gate and Justice over the eastern main entrance, are by Van Nost, as is a figure of George III in the MANSION HOUSE. These three sculptures are very characteristic of Van Nost's work – Mars and Justice are represented as Roman deities and George III as a Roman Emperor. An equestrian statue of George II by Van Nost stood in the centre of ST. STEPHEN'S GREEN from 1758 until it was blown up in 1937. It can be seen in JAMES MALTON'S famous aquatint of the Green, standing in the middle of what then looked like open parkland.

**VANESSA,** (Esther Vanhomrigh), (1688-1723). One of the two women with whom DEAN SWIFT is associated, although the precise nature of his rela-

tionship with either has been the cause of much speculation. She was the daughter of Bartholomew Vanhomrigh, a successful merchant who had been Lord Mayor of Dublin. Swift met Vanessa in 1708 in London when she was twenty and he was forty-one. They developed a firm friendship which he commented on in the poem 'Cadenus and Vanessa'. However, life in Dublin was complicated for Vanessa by the presence of STELLA (Esther Johnson) who had moved there specifically to be near the Dean, and Vanessa's attentions were unwelcome to Swift. Vanessa lived at Celbridge Abbey, her family home, and in a house in Foster Place off DAME STREET. She died, reputedly of a broken heart, after a quarrel with Swift in which he rebuked her for writing to the 'other woman'. Vanessa is buried in the now-vanished churchyard of St. Andrew's, Suffolk Street.

But what success Vanessa met,

Is to the World a Secret yet:

('Cadenus and Vanessa', Jonathan Swift.)

*VANISHING DUBLIN.* Published in 1966, FLORA MITCHELL'S book of Dublin scenes is an important landmark in the recording of the destruction of Georgian Dublin and also the beginning of a popular movement towards conservation of the city's heritage.

**VERMEER, JAN,** (1632-1675). As part of the SIR ALFRED BEIT Bequest, one of the finest of all Vermeer's paintings, 'The Letter' became part of the collection of the NATIONAL GALLERY. Unfortunately, what the Gallery actually possesses is the empty frame, the painting having been stolen from Russborough House, Co Wicklow, home of the Beits and the Beit Foundation. The Vermeer was stolen together with paintings by Goya, Murillo and others in 1986 and so far has not been retrieved.

**VERNON ESTATE.** The Vernon family of CLONTARF CASTLE was established in the seventeenth century by John Vernon, Quartermaster General of Oliver Cromwell's army. An estate of some hundreds of acres, which comprised most of CLONTARF, surrounded the Castle. Today the estate has been dispersed and the Castle is a hotel.

**VICEREGAL LODGE.** See ÁRAS AN UACHTARÁIN.

**VICEROY.** The office of Viceroy or Lord Deputy, the official representative of the British monarchy in Ireland, was instituted in 1172 and lasted until 1922 when the role was taken over by the Governor General of the Irish Free State. The office was abolished with the declaration of the Irish Republic and the creation of the Presidency. The official residence of the President is the Viceregal Lodge in the PHOENIX PARK. Arms of all the Viceroys are displayed on the gallery of the CHAPEL ROYAL in DUBLIN CASTLE. Important members of the Anglo Norman aristocracy who have occupied the office are the Earls of Kildare and the DUKE OF ORMOND. English appointees include Lord Chesterfield and the Dukes of Grafton and Rutland.

**VICTORIA, QUEEN,** (1819-1901). During her long reign Victoria visited Ireland four times, staying at the Viceregal Lodge while in Dublin. On her first visit in 1849 she appointed her son, the Prince of Wales, Earl of Dublin. Subsequent visits were in 1853 when she opened William Dargan's Dublin Exhibition, in 1858, and lastly in 1900, the year before her death. On this occasion MAUD GONNE organised a party for children of the poor in competition to one given by the Queen on the same day. An obese statue of a sitting Victoria by John Hughes, looking like a Wagnerian Rhinemaiden, and certainly the ugliest monument in the city, was placed in front of LEINSTER HOUSE in 1908, but removed to storage in the ROYAL HOSPITAL in 1948, and recently sold to the city of Victoria in New South Wales. Victoria has left her mark on Dublin in the naming of streets, parks, quays and hospitals and there are many other similar tokens of her visits including the vellum page with her signature which was bound into the BOOK OF KELLS. In this instance was the compliment to the manuscript or to the Queen? No Victorian memorial in Dublin is more singular than the public reaction commemorated in popular songs:

'An' I think ther's a slate,' sez she,
'Off Willy Yeats,' sez she,
'He should be at home,' sez she,
'French polishing a pome,' sez she,
'An' not writin' letters,' sez she,
'About his betters,' sez she,
'Paradin' me crimes,' sez she,
'In the *Irish Times*,' sez she.

('The Queen's After Dinner Speech', Percy French.)

Queen Vic she came to call on us,
   she wanted to meet all of us –
'Tis well she did not fall on us, she's
   eighteen sto-an.

('Monto', Dublin ballad.)

**VICTORIAN ARCHITECTURE.** Victorian Dublin, as evident in its way as the Dublin of the GEORGIAN era, is mainly a city beyond the canals in contrast to the eighteenth-century city which was confined within them. Suburbs and separate townships are the characteristic elements of the nineteenth century in Dublin as the structure of what was to become Greater Dublin began to develop. All the little villages which stood on the periphery of the Georgian city, RATHMINES and RATH-GAR, GLASNEVIN and CLONTARF, became residential centres and the more prosperous graduated into independent boroughs, Rathmines, Ballsbridge and KINGSTOWN/DUN LAOGHAIRE being the most prominent of these. In the early Victorian era the Georgian idiom prevailed but by the mid-century a new aesthetic had taken over, and from then until the First World War the greatest of the Victorian suburbs were built, the last fling of brick building in Dublin until the revival in the 1970s. Ailesbury and Shrewsbury Roads in Ballsbridge represent the apogee of Victorian housing, the Merrion Square of a later era as far as a smart address was concerned. From these broad tree-lined streets with mansions set back in spacious grounds, the same bright red brick can be found spreading through hundreds of more modest streets right down to artisans' cottages. Public buildings too showed a red-brick personality to the world, some of absolutely startling variety. Hospitals, markets and banks led the field in architectural fantasy – the Richmond, Royal City of Dublin, the Royal Victoria Eye and Ear Hospital all have riotous façades of decorative brickwork. Banks and insurance companies needed a somewhat more sober look to impress prospective clients with their seriousness. Stone was considered the right material and particularly on Dame Street these temples to Victorian commerce still impress with their grandeur. Churches too were of stone, a material which churchmen had always favoured. More churches were built in Dublin during the Victorian peri-od than ever before or since, and a small number of them are architecturally distinguished. The eccentric JOHN HUNGER-FORD POLLEN'S University Church is the only exception to this rule of stone, barring Gospel Halls. In Dublin's Victorian public buildings eccentricity seems to be the norm. Unlike the eighteenth century when uniformity was considered a virtue, the Victorian public building had to be different from its neighbours. Again the banks on DAME STREET amply demonstrate this phenomenon. See BANK-ING HALLS.

**VIERPYL, SIMON**, (1725-1810). Sculptor, he was brought to Dublin from Rome in 1756 by the EARL OF CHARLE-MONT to work on various building projects. Vierpyl had already worked for Charlemont for some years in Rome, carving copies of antique busts and statuary. This collection of seventy-eight busts of Roman emperors later decorated the library of CHARLEMONT HOUSE in Parnell Square, and is now in the ROYAL IRISH ACADEMY. Vierpyl's principal project in Dublin was the CASI-NO at MARINO, designed by SIR WILLIAM CHAMBERS. As Chambers never visited Ireland, Vierpyl was also the building overseer. Vierpyl did all the stonecarving on the building with the exception of the gentle lions which are by Joseph Wilton. As the most sumptuously carved Georgian building in Dublin, the Casino is a tribute to Vierpyl's ability and sense of Classical ornamentation and it is no surprise that the greatest Dublin-born sculptor of the eighteenth century to remain in the city, EDWARD SMYTH, should have been his student. The sculptural decoration on the CITY HALL is also by Vierpyl but it is much more restrained than his work on the Casino. His only known funerary monument, that to Lady

*Viking child's boot from Wood Quay.*

Doneraile, *circa* 1761, is in ST. PA-
TRICK'S CATHEDRAL.

**VIKINGS.** Dublin is a Viking city, as
are Cork, Waterford and Wexford although only in Dublin have there been
large-scale excavations of the Viking
period. The Scandinavian raids,
prompted by a population explosion at
home, began with the pillaging of Lambay Island in AD 795 and this process of
armed incursions continued until 841
when a trading settlement was established in Dublin, probably at Islandbridge where Viking burials have been
discovered. This settlement lasted until
902 when the Vikings were driven out
by an alliance of Irish kings to bases in
the north of England. However, the city
was re-established in 917 and this is the
settlement which became the core of the
Dublin of today. The location of a hill to
the south of the Liffey, where CHRIST
CHURCH CATHEDRAL is situated, gave the
Vikings an ideal setting for a citadel,
easily defended and with a harbour or
*'longphort'* for their ships where the
PODDLE RIVER meets the LIFFEY It was
around this citadel that the residential
and trading settlement of the tenth to
twelfth centuries developed. Surrounded by an earthen embankment, and
with a population of five thousand, it
covered about 12 hectares (29.7 acres).
The wealth of the Dublin Vikings was
based on trade in silver, slaves and pir-
acy. The BATTLE OF CLONTARF in 1014
diminished the power of Viking Dublin
and the city was finally taken by the
ANGLO NORMANS in 1170. Christianity
had been introduced into Dublin in the
eleventh century by Sitric Silkbeard.
The Viking inhabitants, or Hiberno
Norse as they had become, were ban-
ished to north of the Liffey where they
established Oxmantown, the 'Eastmantown'. A great deal is now known about
Viking Dublin and it is regarded by archaeologists as probably the best-
preserved Viking city outside
Scandinavia. Excavations carried out by
the NATIONAL MUSEUM and the Board of
Works on the Hill of Dublin have revealed intimate details of the daily lives
of Dublin's inhabitants during the Viking age. Their arts, crafts, agriculture,
fishing, diet, housing, the animals which
they domesticated, the pests which in-
fested their wattle homes, the nature of
their roads and harbour works have all
been revealed in the many thousands of
artifacts and the remains of whole streets
of houses. The light this casts on the
earliest Dubliners shows the Vikings not
just as warlike foreigners but as people
going about their daily lives, with domestic concerns and household utensils
quite similar to those of the Dubliners of
today. Viking culture heavily influenced
the development of the visual arts in
Ireland and the Ringerike style of orna-

CHURCH on High Street, actors bring the Viking age to life in the Irish Life Viking Adventure and here it is indeed possible to see and speak to the first Dubliners.

**VISITORS.** The visit of HANDEL to Dublin in 1742 is well known, as are the visits of other artists, musicians, writers, generals and politicians whose passing has stuck in some corner of popular memory. Shelley, Scott, Thackeray all wrote about their visits to Dublin, others like Oliver Cromwell are remembered for their force of personality or general infamy although they failed to publish their travel experiences. Some who did not intend to stay in Dublin did so by unfortunately dying there, GERARD MANLEY HOPKINS for example, or Wilfred Scawen Blunt who was thrown into KILMAINHAM JAIL as a response to his concern for Ireland. Visitors whose presence has not attracted due attention are legion, and a few are certainly worthy of mention. Benjamin Franklin, at that time acting as envoy in Paris for the American revolutionaries, arrived in Dublin in 1771 and was enthusiastically received by the parliament in COLLEGE GREEN. Naturally, the radical element in the parliament espoused the cause of American independence. Another American, not an inventor and pragmatist but a leader of men and former President, General Ulysses Grant, was presented with the Freedom of the City in 1879. Thomas Carlyle came twice, John Wesley many times during the nineteenth century, Thomas de Quincey in 1800, MADAME TUSSAUD and her waxworks in 1804, William Cobbett in 1834 and JAMES McNEILL WHISTLER in 1900 when his Nocturnes bemused the art lovers of the city. John Berryman and Heinrich Böll, two of the major figures of twentieth-century literature, have

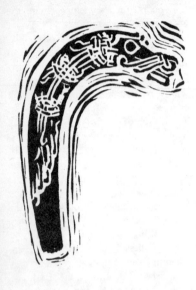

*Viking wood carving, National Museum.*

ment from Scandinavia, with its use of interlace and animal head motifs, was absorbed into Irish Early Christian art and became the basis of the native style. Around Dublin topographical names of Viking origin abound, but these are generally confined to the coastline and Liffey valley: Leixlip – Lox Halop, the salmon leap; Dalkey – Dalk Ey, thorn island; Howth – Hoved, a headland. Family names also betray Scandinavian origins, as in Doyle – Dubh Gall, the dark strangers. The National Museum in Kildare Street now provides the most tangible link between tenth- and twentieth-century Dubliners and while one can't quite converse with Sitric Silkbeard and his subjects, all the objects which passed through their hands are on display. In the crypt of ST. AUDOEN'S written of their very diverse impressions of the city.

**VISUAL ARTS.** As a measure of the success of the visual arts in Dublin, there is now a greater number of ART GALLERIES than cinemas in the city, a situation which would certainly not have been the case twenty years ago. This proliferation of galleries covers every shade of opinion from the ultra avant garde to the avowedly conservative and represents a rapidly developing and vital visual arts community. A beneficial overlapping occurs between public and private institutions in the manner in which they present complimentary exhibitions of Irish and international art. In the public sector the NATIONAL GALLERY, HUGH LANE GALLERY and ROYAL HOSPITAL KILMAINHAM represent the national holding of historic and contemporary art. The private sector is by far the larger grouping in the visual arts and it includes a wealth of private galleries and a number of cooperative organisations such as the PROJECT ARTS CENTRE, the TEMPLE BAR GALLERY, the DOUGLAS HYDE GALLERY and the ROYAL HIBERNIAN ACADEMY. Artists' representative bodies – the ARTISTS ASSOCIATION OF IRELAND and the SCULPTORS SOCIETY – have done much to promote the arts and to interest public bodies in comissioning work.

**VOLTA PICTURE THEATRE.** At 45 Mary Street, Dublin's first cinema opened in 1909 although cinema productions had been seen in Dublin from 1895. The cinema manager was JAMES JOYCE who was attempting to introduce the magic of the silver screen to his fellow citizens. However, the Volta received the same reaction as his writings were to later on and it closed shortly afterwards. Later it became the Lyceum Picture Theatre.

**VOLUNTEERS.** Two separate movements acquired this name, one in the eighteenth and the second in the twentieth century. The original organisation was a militia, begun in the 1780s and staffed by the aristocracy and gentry. It was ostensibly designed to protect the country from possible French invasion, but in reality was an expression of national identity devoted to wringing concessions from Westminster. LORD CHARLEMONT became the Commander-in-Chief in 1780 and the regiments of Volunteers wore distinctive ornamental uniforms. There is a very interesting painting by Francis Wheatley in the NATIONAL GALLERY called 'A View of College Green with a Meeting of the Volunteers' 1779, which shows Volunteer infantry and cavalry at a review with the façades of the Parliament House and TRINITY disappearing in gunsmoke behind them. The Volunteers were eventually disbanded by Charlemont when armed conflict with DUBLIN CASTLE authorities seemed likely in the rising tensions of the 1790s. The later organisation, the IRISH VOLUNTEERS, was founded in Dublin in 1913, and inspired not by their eighteenth-century predecessors but by the recently organised Ulster Volunteer Force. The stated aim was the same as that of the earlier Volunteers – defence of the Realm – but in actuality the force was being trained in preparation for hostilities against the British government. The Nationalist movement had a readymade army, and the Volunteers who formed the core of the forces fought during the 1916 RISING.

WAR MEMORIALS. Dublin is peppered with plaques which commemorate the position of a Republican garrison or the site of an ambush in a narrow street. These memorials generally relate to the gun battles within the city during the hostilities of the early years of the century and are relics of skirmishes rather than total war. The GARDEN OF REMEMBRANCE in PARNELL SQUARE commemorates all those who gave their lives in the cause of Irish freedom, without reference to the victims of any particular period. The imagery of the memorial derives from Irish mythology – the Children of Lir and the Red Branch Knights. In KILMAINHAM PRISON, Arbour Hill and GLASNEVIN CEMETERY the dead of 1916 are remembered or buried, as are the many more who were killed between then and 1922. Memorials to the dead of greater conflicts, the Boer War and the World Wars, commemorate larger numbers and mostly those whose death occurred far from home, in South Africa, Europe and the Middle East. The BOER WAR MEMORIAL, in the form of a miniature triumphal arch, commemorates the dead of the Royal Dublin Fusiliers and was erected in 1907 at the north west corner of ST. STEPHEN'S GREEN. The names of the casualties are inscribed under the vault of the monument. For the 50,000 Irishmen who died in the First World War, the NATIONAL WAR MEMORIAL at Islandbridge is an appropriate point of remembrance. Designed by SIR EDWIN LUTYENS, not in the triumphalist manner of the Boer War memorial, but as a place of quiet and contemplation, it is the finest memorial in Dublin, dignified without being overbearing. Memorials to the dead of the Second World War during which Ireland remained neutral, are more modest and

*German war memorial, Glencree.*

on a less official scale. The numbers of Irish casualties were of course far less than in the previous conflict. The main memorial is in Glasnevin and it is merely a series of inscribed slabs, bearing the names of the dead. In DUN LAOGHAIRE the 'Christ The King' sculpture by Andrew O'Connor at Haig Terrace, among the finest examples of public art in Dublin, was executed in France as a First World War memorial but was not erected for that purpose. Many parish churches around Dublin, and particularly the two CATHEDRALS have memorials to the dead of both world wars and other far-flung conflicts in obscure corners of the Empire, but sentiment relating to Irish involvement in 'England's Wars' has so far prevented the establishment of a national memorial or ceremony to commemorate all those Irish people who died in the wars of the past. Ironically, there is a memorial to the Germans in GLENCREE, Co. Wicklow, which is an altogether different phenomenon as the war dead are actually buried here. In a corner of the road at Glencree below the overhanging rockface small slabs surrounded by heather record the names of the young airmen whose planes crashed on Irish mountainsides or who lost their lives in other ways in this country. This is the most restrained of all the memorials. Dubliners have always had an ambiguous attitude towards those who enlisted in the British Army – as well as to the 'culchies', those from the rest of Ireland.

Now if you go to the fighting line and
there to fight the Boer,
Will you kindly hould the Dublins
back, let the culchies go before.

('Get Me Down My Petticoat', Dublin ballad.)

**WEAVERS.** The LIBERTIES is traditionally associated with the weaving trade, and the WEAVERS' HALL, a guild hall like the surviving TAILORS' HALL, stood on THE COOMBE. Weaving became established in the Liberties during the middle of the seventeenth century, and with the influx of HUGUENOT refugees from France it received further impetus. The trade in silk, woollen, poplin and worsted weaving thrived there until restrictive measures were enacted in Westminster which prohibited the export of Dublin-made fabrics. Between 1730 and 1760 the number of silk looms in the Liberties was reduced from 300 to fifty. This threw the trade into a decline from which it never fully recovered. Various attempts were made to encourage the use of Irish-made fabrics in Ireland and the avoidance of imports in order to encourage the native trade. Towards the end of the eighteenth century weaving revived slightly but not for very long. The Duke of Leinster left money in his will for the mourners to wear Irish linen scarves at his funeral as a measure of encouragement. This created a fashion for linen scarves. JONATHAN SWIFT'S lines on supporting local industry strike a familiar note, two hundred years later:

We'll dress in manufactures made at
home,
Equip our kings and generals at the
Coombe.
We'll rig in Meath Street Egypt's
haughty queen,
And Antony shall court her in rateen.

The corporation of weavers had ceased to exist by 1840 with the decline of local manufacture due to the availability of French and Italian fabrics which were freely imported. However, weaving continued in Dublin until the 1960s when the last of the old-style firms closed. The tradition survives in the form of craft weavers and there is a number of small workshops around the city which produce fine fabrics by the traditional methods.

**WEAVER'S HALL**, the Coombe. Built in 1745 to replace a seventeenth-century guild hall, it was demolished in 1956. The hall, a diminutive Palladian composition by Joseph Jarratt had a decorative niche over the main entrance which contained a statue of George II. This gilded lead figure, by Benjamin Rackstrow collapsed during the 1930s but its head and feet are in the Civic Museum.

**WEAVER'S SQUARE**, off Cork Street, D8. The precursors of the great squares of GEORGIAN DUBLIN are a number of smaller versions, built towards the latter end of the seventeenth century. Smithfield, Newmarket and Weaver's Squares were merely cobbled open spaces surrounded by buildings, designed for utility rather than leisure, without the central park so characteristic of the later residential developments. Brick houses of three storeys with the gable end facing the street surrounded Weaver's Square, and the same house type was to be found in all the adjoining streets. None of these now remains although the square still exists, surrounded by a jumble of unrelated council flats and Victorian buildings. By the mid-nineteenth century the original houses had all become tenements and the last of them was demolished during the 1930s. Bus 50, 50A, 77, 77A from Aston Quay.

**WELLESLEY, ARTHUR, DUKE OF WELLINGTON,** (1769-1852). Military leader and Prime Minister, born at 24 Upper Merrion Street, D2. His father, the Earl of Mornington, was at the time Professor of Music at TRINITY COLLEGE. After military training he entered the Irish parliament in 1790. Rejoining the army after a few years, he saw active service in Europe and India and received rapid promotion. His greatest triumph was as the commander of the British forces which achieved the defeat of Napoleon at Waterloo in 1815. Showered with honours, he became Prime Minister in 1828. It was under his administration that the Catholic Emancipation Act was passed in 1829, although he was not personally in favour of it. Wellington is remembered in Dublin by the gargantuan WELLINGTON TESTIMONIAL in the PHOENIX PARK, an expression of imperial glory on a heroic scale. The man himself may be confronted, face to face, in the NATIONAL GALLERY and in TRINITY LIBRARY, both of which have fine busts of him. The version in the gallery, by Peter Turnerelli, is almost surreal in its detail

and it suggests that the Iron Duke was without earlobes, a factor which would have fascinated Victorian criminologists.

*Wellington Testimonial.*

**WELLINGTON TESTIMONIAL.** Phoenix Park, D7. The DUKE OF WELLINGTON as the victor of Waterloo and a Dubliner, (although he was not too keen on the place of his birth being mentioned), was honoured with the tallest and most massive monument erected in Dublin during the nineteenth century. At 30m, (98ft) it was considerably taller than its only rival, the NELSON COLUMN, and has also outlived that monument which was blown up in 1966. Designed by Sir Robert Smirke, and built between 1817 and 1861, the Testimonial, which is the largest obelisk in Europe, rises from a vast rectangular stepped base on which is a plinth set with bronze plaques and a commemorative inscription. The plaques, cast from cannon captured at Waterloo, depict 'Civil and Religious Liberty' by JOHN HOGAN, 'Waterloo' by THOMAS FARRELL and the 'Indian Wars' by Joseph Kirk. The fulsomeness of the inscription would be hard to equal in any other Dublin monument. Modesty was not one of the Duke's failings it would appear, or at any rate, not a failing of his admirers:

Asia and Europe, saved by thee, proclaim
Invincible in war thy deathless name,
Now round thy brow the civic oak we twine
That every earthly glory may be thine.

An equestrian statue of Wellington was planned to accompany the obelisk but funds ran out and it got no further than the plinth which stood untenanted for many years until it was at length removed. Seen from the south quays, the Testimonial rises over the trees of the Phoenix Park like a granite spaceprobe, prepared for take-off.

**WESLEY, JOHN,** (1703-1791). Preacher and founder of Methodism, he was an indefatigable traveller throughout his life and visited Ireland over twenty times in the course of his evangelising tours. His *Journals* record his impressions of life in Dublin in great detail and combine acute observations on architecture and society with pious aspirations for the salvation of its benighted citizens. The lower down he went among the social orders the more unlikely the prospect of salvation, it seems.

**WEST, ROBERT,** (1790). Stuccodore, his work is characterised by the use of swirling motifs and birds executed in exceptionally high relief. West's own house, 20 Lower Dominick Street, 1755,

has very extravagant plasterwork, as has 86 ST. STEPHEN'S GREEN, 1765. Both these houses are fortunate in being well preserved, unlike the majority of houses decorated by West. The staircase halls and main apartments on the first floor in both houses are particularly magnificent.

**WESTLAND ROW,** D2. Part of the MERRION SQUARE area laid out by JOHN ENSOR in the 1770s. Buildings of importance are No. 36 the ROYAL IRISH ACADEMY OF MUSIC, 1771, and ST. ANDREW'S CHURCH, 1832, both on the east side. Westland Row railway station, now known as Pearse Station, was the city end of Ireland's first railway, the Dublin to Kingstown, which first ran from here in December 1834. The terrace on the west side of the street is a later and more modest treatment of the Georgian idiom. Interestingly the Georgian stucco at street level graduates into Victorian terracotta at cornice level with an elaborate frieze of swags uniting the buildings. All these houses are now departments of TRINITY COLLEGE. OSCAR WILDE was born at No. 21 which is marked by a plaque. The O'Reilly Institute, 1989, the most recent addition to the buildings of Trinity, occupies the northern end of this terrace, a modern steel and glass building by Scott, Talon and Walker. Across Westland Row runs the cast-iron railway bridge, introduced in 1891 to connect the northern and southern railway systems.

**WESTMORELAND STREET,** D2. This street, laid out around 1800, is a typical example of the work of the WIDE STREETS COMMISSIONERS, as its width, regular roofline and ordered façades show. There is a number of fine late nineteenth- and twentieth-century buildings inserted into the fabric of the Georgian street which harmonise well with the overall layout. On the east side, at the corner with D'Olier Street and dominating the approach from O'Connell Street, is the ICS Building by J.J.O'Callaghan, 1895; halfway along on the corner with Fleet Street the EBS offices by Sam Stephenson, 1976, which cleverly incorporates a nineteenth-century façade in its composition, and at the College Street end is the AIB by T.N.DEANE, 1895. On the west side is the reconstructed BALLAST OFFICE on the Aston Quay corner, Beshoff's by W.G. Murray, 1866,, CDL by G.C. Ashlin, 1866, Air Canada, 1867, by W.G. Murray, and JAMES GANDON'S portico for the House of Lords, 1789, facing down COLLEGE STREET.

## WHALEY, RICHARD CHAPELL,

(d 1779). Father of 'BUCK' WHALEY and the builder of 86 ST. STEPHEN'S GREEN, he was known as 'Burn Chapel' Whaley because of his intolerant religious views. He is reputed to have deliberately built his house in a style out of sympathy with its neighbour, Clanwilliam House, to spite the owner. Capricious behaviour seems to have been a characteristic of Dublin's eighteenth-century grandees, and they were prepared to go to great lengths to achieve rather ignoble ends. A typical example of such behaviour is the developer who built Marino Crescent in Clontarf to block LORD CHARLEMONT's view of DUBLIN BAY.

## WHALEY, THOMAS 'BUCK',

(1766-1800). Rake and member of parliament, born at 86 ST. STEPHEN'S GREEN. Having inherited a fortune at an early age he lived a life of dissipation and quickly ran through his money. In 1788 he wagered that he would travel to Jerusalem from Dublin and return within a year. Whaley succeeded, even claiming that he had played handball against the walls of Jerusalem, and returned to Dublin nine months later to claim his winnings of £20,000 – an enormous sum in the eighteenth century and equivalent to the fortune which the EARL OF CHARLEMONT spent on the CASINO at Marino. Buck Whaley did not spend his winnings so wisely.

## WHEATLEY, FRANCIS, (1747-

1801). Artist, he came to Dublin in 1779 to escape financial difficulties in England and while in Ireland painted a number of highly important works. Two of these capture particularly dramatic incidents in the life of late eighteenth-century Dublin. These vivid and colourful paintings are 'A View of College Green with a Meeting of the Volunteers' in the NATIONAL GALLERY and 'The Irish House of Commons'. In the latter HENRY GRATTAN is seen delivering his speech on the repeal of Poynings' Law and the attentive crowd scene contains the portraits of LUKE GARDINER, NAPPER TANDY, and the DUKE OF LEINSTER among many others. Amongst his other works are views of the PHOENIX PARK with military reviews and aristocratic travellers. Wheatley remained in Ireland for only four years, but his impressions of those years are, with the aquatints of JAMES MALTON, the finest of any group of paintings of life in Dublin during the heyday of its parliament. The artist left Dublin for the same reasons he had originally arrived – to flee creditors.

## WHISTLER, JAMES McNEILL,

(1834-1903). Artist, and one of the dominant intellectual figures of the nineteenth-century London and Paris art worlds. His aesthetic theories were embraced by OSCAR WILDE who owed him a great deal in terms of his ideas, flamboyance and epigramatic conversation. In 1884 the Dublin Sketching Club invited Whistler, then the most controversial artist of the day, to exhibit with them in Dublin. The exhibition of the Club was held in the Leinster Hall in MOLESWORTH STREET and it included two of Whistler's most famous paintings, the portrait of Thomas Carlyle and that of the artist's mother, 'Arrangement in Grey and Black', as well as twenty-four other smaller works. Public opinion in Dublin was outraged by the exhibition and a heated correspondence raged in *The Irish Times* and *Freeman's Journal* as to the merits or otherwise of Whistler's work. Even some of the exhibiting members of the Club wished to disassociate themselves from Whistler, but not surprisingly he had the support of JOHN BUTLER YEATS, WALTER OSBORNE and the more enlightened members. Only two of Whistler's paintings sold at the exhibition, 'Nocturne in Grey and Gold, Piccadilly' and 'Yellow and Grey', both of them watercolours. They are now in the NATIONAL GALLERY and are the sole works by the artist in the collection. Whistler did not come to Dublin for the opening of the exhibition but contemplated visiting later to deliver a lecture on his famous aesthetic theories. This plan was preempted by Oscar Wilde who took it upon himself to deliver a lecture on the Aesthetic Movement in the Gaiety Theatre, speaking as an interpreter of Whistler's views. The artist was not amused. Whistler did visit Dublin in 1900 when he rented a house in Sutton and managed to annoy his neighbours by obscuring the windows with brown paper. Controversy was a hobby for Whistler, author of *The Gentle Art of Making Enemies* and he wrote to the organisers of the Dublin exhibition, apropos its stormy reception, 'I like fighting'.

**WHYTE'S ACADEMY**. Eighteenth-century school on Grafton Street, where BEWLEY'S now stands. Among the students were ROBERT EMMET, THOMAS MOORE, RICHARD BRINSLEY SHERIDAN and the DUKE OF WELLINGTON.

**WIDE STREETS COMMISSIONERS**. Established by Act of Parliament in 1757 they exerted a profound influence on the development of the physical fabric of GEORGIAN DUBLIN. They began by creating 'a wide and convenient way from Essex Bridge to the castle of Dublin', now called Parliament Street, in 1762. This improvement was followed by DAME STREET, 1777, Sackville Street extension and Carlisle Bridge 1785. Also responsible for the development of D'Olier Street and Westmoreland Street, which with Sackville Bridge and the extending of Sackville Street united the two areas of expansion of the Georgian city, north and south of the river. These had previously existed as unrelated islands of development. Some of their standard granite shopfronts are to be seen in the city, for instance Nos. 8, 10 and 16 D'Olier Street. The Commissioners were disbanded in 1849.

**WILDE, LADY JANE FRANCESCA**, (1826-1896). Writer and folklorist, she wrote patriotic poems and ballads under the name 'Speranza' which were published in *The Nation*, the newspaper founded by THOMAS DAVIS. Married to the antiquarian and surgeon, WILLIAM WILDE, she was the mother of OSCAR WILDE. The Wildes moved from their house at 21 WESTLAND ROW, where their son Oscar was born, to 1 MERRION

SQUARE, the most fashionable professional address in Dublin at that time, (plaques on both houses). Lady Wilde was a woman of great strength of character and her work expresses a passionate involvement in fighting the injustices of nineteenth-century Ireland.

There's a proud array of soldiers –
what do they round your door?
They guard our master's granaries
from the thin hands of the poor.

('The Famine Year', Lady Wilde.)

## WILDE, OSCAR, (1854-1900).

Playwright, born at 21 WESTLAND ROW, D2. The most brilliant wit and conversationalist to come from Dublin, Wilde was the product of an intellectually stimulating and ambitious background, both his parents being well known leaders of the YOUNG IRELAND generation. Success came early to Wilde when he won the Newdigate Prize for poetry at Oxford in 1878, but despite the notoriety of his American lecture tours and prolific journalism it was not until 1892 when *Lady Windermere's Fan* was performed that he became a successful playwright. By 1895 when *The Importance of being Earnest* was produced he was the unrivalled master of the London stage as well as the most sought after conversationalist in London society. The year of his greatest success also proved to be that of his undoing and he was sentenced to two years' hard labour for homosexual activities. Wilde spent most of his sentence in Reading prison and after his release wrote the harrowing 'The Ballad of Reading Gaol' which deals with the pain and humiliation of his experiences in prison. Broken by his incarceration and the enforced separation from his family and friends, he died in Paris without writing anything else. Wilde is buried in Père Lachaise

under an Assyrian monument by Jacob Epstein, inscribed with a verse from 'The Ballad of Reading Gaol':

And an alien tear will fill for him
Pity's long-broken urn
For his mourners will be outcast men,
And outcasts always mourn.

But such is the emnity with which Wilde is still regarded that nearly a century after his death, his funerary monument continues to be defaced and vandalised. Wilde's epigrams are widely quoted and cover an impressively wide range of subject matter, their wit as vibrant as when first uttered.

As long as war is regarded as wicked,
it will always have its fascination.
When it is looked upon as vulgar, it will
cease to be popular.

(*The Critic as Artist*, Oscar Wilde.)

You should study the Peerage, Gerald.
It is the best thing in fiction the English
have ever done.

(*A Woman of No Importance*, Oscar Wilde.)

## WILDE, SIR WILLIAM, (1815-1876).

Surgeon and antiquarian, husband of the spirited 'Speranza' and father of OSCAR WILDE. He established a highly successful practice in Dublin and specialised in eye and ear surgery, fields in which he made important advances. As a man of wide interests he published travel books, medical reports and treatises, and works dealing with antiquities. His life, while full of professional achievements, was tragic – he lost two of his illegitimate daughters in a fire and later his youngest daughter as well. A libel action by a patient became a celebrated court case in 1864 and his medical practice never fully recovered from the scandal. The plaque on his house in MERRION SQUARE gives a list of Sir William Wilde's achievements as 'aural and ophthalmic surgeon, archaeologist, ethnologist, antiquarian, biographer, statistician, naturalist, topographer and folklorist', which seems quite a lot to cram into a single lifetime.

All her bright golden hair
Tarnished with rust,
She that was young and fair
Fallen to dust.

('Requiescat', Oscar Wilde in memory of his sister.)

**WILDLIFE.** See IRISH WILDLIFE FEDERATION and IRISH WILDBIRD CONSERVANCY.

*Windmill, Guinness Brewery.*

**WINDMILLS.** Commonplace in Dublin during the eighteenth and nineteenth centuries, only one still survives, but even this is without its vanes. It stands within the GUINNESS BREWERY lands on Thomas Street and its oriental silhouette of conical walls and onion dome with St. Patrick on the weather vane is an interesting addition to the skyline of church spires.

**WISHING STONE**, Killiney Hill Park, Killiney. Between the obelisk on the summit of the hill and the cliff face which falls down to the Vico Road is a strange stepped structure known as 'The Wishing Stone' and bearing the date 1852 in Roman numerals. In the form of a stepped pyramid with a flight of smaller steps on the southern face, local lore states that 'one must walk around the seven levels clockwise to the top and overlooking DALKEY ISLAND make a wish'. As a product of the era of follies the ritual is unusual and more like that associated with holy wells and places of pilgrimage. Whatever about its purpose the view from the top is breathtaking. Another artifact for the wishful thinker and one of much greater antiquity is the Lucky Stone in old ST. AUDOEN'S CHURCH.

**WITTGENSTEIN, LUDWIG**, (1889-1951). Austrian philosopher, he lived for two years in Dublin (1947-49), staying at what is now the Ashling Hotel, across the bridge from HEUSTON STATION.

**WOFFINGTON, PEG**, (1714-1760). Actress, born in 7 George's Lane, she graduated from child parts in circus amusements to the stage of the Smock Alley Theatre where she was much admired. The greatest actress to come from Dublin during the eighteenth century, she appeared in London in 1740 and played opposite David Garrick in many roles. Woffington was painted by Hogarth and her life became the subject of a novel by Charles Reade, 1853.

**WONDERS.** In art and architecture, nature and landscape, the exceptional will

*Wishing Stone, Killiney Hill.*

occasionally appear, more rarely that which is phenomenally unusual, and even more rarely the unique. To make a shortlist of the unique or the 'Wonders of the City', does require the chosen candidates to stand up to more than casual scrutiny. They need to be very important on an international scale as well as on a local one, a factor which does considerably limit the area of choice.

ARCHITECTURE: The CASINO at Marino. ROUND TOWERS at CLONDALKIN, LUSK, and SWORDS.

ARCHITECTURE OF THE TWENTIETH CENTURY: The CENTRAL BANK on Dame Street.

ART: The BOOK OF KELLS in Trinity College Library; Korans at the CHESTER BEATTY LIBRARY.

ARTISTS: HARRY CLARKE'S 'The Eve of Saint Agnes' window, HUGH LANE GALLERY.

ENGINEERING: HA'PENNY BRIDGE, GLASS HOUSES, BOTANIC GARDENS.

ENVIRONMENT: BULL ISLAND, a UNESCO Biosphere Nature Reserve.

EVENTS: BLOOMSDAY 16 June.

INTERIORS: The Apollo Room, NEWMAN HOUSE; The Long Room of TRINITY COLLEGE LIBRARY; the Oratory of the Sacred Heart, Dun Laoghaire.

LANDSCAPE: The Hill of HOWTH; SANDYMOUNT STRAND.

LANDSCAPE ARCHITECTURE: The NATIONAL WAR MEMORIAL, Islandbridge.

LITERATURE: The JAMES JOYCE MUSEUM at Sandycove and *ULYSSES.*

MARINE ARCHITECTURE: DUN LAOGHAIRE HARBOUR; THE SOUTH BULL WALL, Poolbeg.

MONUMENTS: The WELLINGTON TESTIMONIAL in the PHOENIX PARK.

MUSEUMS: Celtic gold objects at the NATIONAL MUSEUM.

MUSIC: The first performance of HANDEL'S *Messiah* in Fishamble Street. John Field's Nocturnes. BUSKERS in Grafton Street.

NATURAL HISTORY: The Great Irish Elk, NATURAL HISTORY MUSEUM.

SPORT: The All-Ireland Hurling Final, CROKE PARK.

**WOODCARVING.** The Huguenot woodcarvers, James Tarbary and John Houghton, who worked in Dublin in the early years of the eighteenth century established a tradition of expressive and vigorous work which lasted for over two hundred years. The chapel of the ROYAL HOSPITAL, the House of Lords, ST MICHAN'S, and ST. WERBURGH'S all contain outstanding examples of woodcarving. From the nineteenth century the Chapel Royal in DUBLIN CASTLE is the most interesting example.

**WOODWARD, BENJAMIN,** (1816-1861). Architect. Despite the fact that he designed only a small number of buildings in Dublin, Woodward was the most influential architect to work in the city during the mid-nineteenth century and he is the only Irish architect one can confidently hope to find in books on international architecture. His relevance lies in the fact that with just a few buildings he brought the lingering Georgian era to an emphatic close. By the declaration of a new set of values and by finding his inspiration in the Medieval era, far from the language of Classicism, Woodward set the tone for a new dominant architectural mode which was to last until the end of the century. Woodward, who worked in the firm of SIR THOMAS DEANE in Cork, first came to Dublin with Deane to work on his most important building in the city, the Venetian Gothic TRINITY MUSEUM Building, 1852. The innovation which this building introduced was the use of decorative stone carving on a wide scale. Not since the Medieval period had stone carving been so exhaustively employed in architecture and the museum is probably the most highly decorated building in Dublin. The museum has one of the most distinctive staircase halls in Dublin, and here the carving has not been corroded with grime – the fate of the exterior. Another innovation, inspired by William Ruskin's ideas, was to allow the masons freedom in their choice of decoration and to avoid repetition. Following their success in Trinity, Deane and Woodward made alterations to Thomas Burgh's College Library in 1856 by re-

moving the existing flat ceiling and introducing a timber barrel vault, an imaginative scheme which proved to be another success. The KILDARE STREET CLUB on the corner of Nassau Street was begun in 1858, also in the Venetian manner. It is a brick building decorated with highly original and humorous stone-carving. This also had a fine staircase hall which unfortunately has been removed, but the original Coffee Room is now the exhibition area of the Museum of Heraldry and the carving of the cornice gives some measure of the richness of the lost interiors. Other buildings by Woodward are St. Stephen's School, Northumberland Road, 1856, Dundrum School, 1857, and 28 Fitzwilliam Place, 1854. Woodward's most famous building is not in Dublin but in Oxford, where he designed the University Museum on Parks Road in 1854, a work which is regarded as one of the greatest buildings to come from the Gothic Revival.

**WRITERS.** Dublin has produced so many writers relative to the size of its population that literature might be considered as one of the city's more successful industries. However, unlike its other and more famous export, Guinness, the material produced by the writers of many generations cannot claim the same level of appreciation at home or a commensurate financial return for the authors. Three writers who are identified with the city of their birth, JONATHAN SWIFT, W.B. YEATS and JAMES JOYCE, have in their different generations, dominated the literature of their time, not just in Dublin but throughout the English-speaking world. From the eighteenth century onwards the path of Dublin's writers has been towards acceptance on the wider stage of London, and the number who actually achieved this goal is remarkable. Swift was the first of significance, and after him in rapid succession, William Congreve, Richard Steele, EDMUND BURKE, OLIVER GOLDSMITH and RICHARD BRINSLEY SHERIDAN. Then in the nineteenth century, GEORGE MOORE, SAMUEL LOVER, CHARLES LEVER and DION BOUCICAULT, and in an extraordinary logjam of talent, WILLIAM LECKY, BRAM STOKER, OSCAR WILDE, GEORGE BERNARD SHAW, W.B. YEATS, J.M. SYNGE, SEÁN O'CASEY, JAMES JOYCE and JAMES STEPHENS. Another generation passes and SAMUEL BECKETT is followed by BRENDAN BEHAN. The literary life of the city is sustained as it was in the eighteenth century by the presence of an exciting theatrical world and this perhaps more than any other aspect of Dublin literary life has changed the most in recent years. During the period between the founding of the ABBEY in 1903 and the 1960s, the theatrical world remained relatively static, with the Abbey and the GATE theatres centre stage, so to speak, and the occasional interloper like the PEACOCK and the Focus. Now there is a considerable number of small new well-equipped pocket theatres, and an ever-growing group of new companies staging exclusively contemporary work. PATRICK KAVANAGH's remark about the standing army of Irish poets never falling below the level of ten thousand seems as true today as it was an exaggeration in the 1950s, and little presses as well as the major ones continue to issue slim volumes. Poetry readings have even invaded the streets, bringing about a return of the phenomenon of the street balladeer, a ubiquitous presence in Dublin during previous centuries. Every bookshop in the city has a significant Irish section and some specialise in Irish writing, a fact which is strengthened by the emergence in the past twenty years of a thriving native publishing industry.

**WROUGHT AND CAST IRON.** One of the joys of the Georgian street is the quality of the ironwork railings and street furniture which are trademarks of the period, however a great deal of this has disappeared from those streets which have changed from residential to totally commercial use, such as O'CONNELL STREET. However, scattered oases of ironwork remain and in some quarters like MERRION and FITZWILLIAM SQUARES little has changed since the squares were built. Other streets and buildings can be singled out for mention, Ely House in ELY PLACE; HENRIETTA STREET; IVEAGH HOUSE on ST. STEPHEN'S GREEN; THE MANSION HOUSE; THE PRO CATHEDRAL; TRINITY COLLEGE; THE BANK OF IRELAND and the Ulster Bank in COLLEGE GREEN and North Great George's Street, but in fact as the tradition of ironwork extended into the nineteenth century, fine examples can also be found beyond the canals in the suburbs. Two of the greatest of the Victorian ironmasters were Dubliners Robert Mallet and RICHARD TURNER, and both contributed sections to the railings of TRINITY COLLEGE – one of the most characteristic and best preserved examples of Dublin ironwork.

YACHTS AND YACHT CLUBS. Rowing and yacht clubs which organise competitive racing have been a prominent feature of life on the LIFFEY and in DUBLIN BAY since the eighteenth century. With the establishment of notable yacht clubs early in the nineteenth century, there had been a rapid increase in the number of people sailing for pleasure with, in more recent years, an ever-increasing number of participants. DUN LAOGHAIRE is the centre of sailing in Dublin with a concentration of four of the principal club premises on the harbour, the Royal St. George, Royal Irish, National, and Motor Yacht Club. Other clubs and associations, such as the Dublin Bay Sailing Club and the Irish Yachting Association, are also located in Dun Laoghaire. Closer in to the city there is the Poolbeg Sailing Club at Ringsend. On the north side of the Bay, there are clubs at various intervals along the coast in Clontarf, Kilbarrack and Sutton, with the major club at HOWTH.

**YEATS, JACK B**, (1871-1957). Artist, younger brother of the poet W.B. YEATS, he has long been the most widely popular Irish painter of any period in Ireland. Yeats painted prolifically and his subject matter ranges over every aspect of Irish life, history and mythology. His work developed from an 1890s anecdotal manner into an impassioned expressionism during his later years. A collection of his paintings, spanning various aspects of his career, can be seen in the NATIONAL GALLERY where he is the only artist accorded the singular honour of having a room solely devoted to him. The HUGH LANE GALLERY also has a fine collection of Yeats's work. A distinctive feature of Yeats's painting is his capacity to deal with both mundane and highly imaginative themes in a unified manner, such as 'The Liffey Swim' and 'In memory of Boucicault and Bianconi', both in the National Gallery.

**YEATS, JOHN B**, (1839-1922). Artist, he excelled as a portrait painter and his intimate portraits of the literary and political figures of Dublin in the 1890s, most of whom were his friends, form the finest record of the personalities of the period. John B. Yeats is overshadowed by the fame of his two sons, William and Jack, Ireland's premier poet and painter, but he was in his own right a remarkable artist, writer and conversationalist, and certainly the most stimulating and attractive member of an extraordinary generation. Portraits by Yeats can be seen in the ABBEY THEATRE, HUGH LANE GALLERY and NATIONAL GALLERY, each of which has a substantial collection of his works. In 1908, at the age of sixty-nine, when many would be thinking of retirement, Yeats went to New York and liked it so much that he remained there until he died. In New York he found a new career as conversationalist and writer, and became an influential figure among artists of the 'Ashcan school', John Sloane and Robert Henri, and it was from there that some of his finest letters were written.

> Beautiful lofty things: O'Leary's
>    noble head;
> My father upon the Abbey stage, before him a raging crowd:
> This Land of Saints, and then as the
>    applause died out,
> Of plaster Saints; his beautiful mischievous head thrown back.

('Beautiful Lofty Things', W.B. Yeats.)

**YEATS MEMORIALS.** At ST. STEPHEN'S GREEN in a paved enclosure under mature trees is 'Knife Edge' by

HENRY MOORE, erected in 1966 in memory of W.B. YEATS and in Sandymount Green, close to where Yeats was born, is a vigorous bust of the poet by ALBERT POWER. In 1989 the ABBEY THEATRE instituted the first Yeats International Theatre Festival, designed to bring back to the stage the neglected dramatic works of the poet.

## YEATS, SUSAN MARY, (1866-1949).

She worked with her sister Elizabeth Corbett Yeats at the Dun Emer Guild in Dundrum, an Arts and Crafts Movement workshop jointly founded in 1902 by the Yeats sisters and Evelyn Gleeson for the production of tapestry, carpets, embroidery and printing. A copy of a Medieval tapestry which the Guild completed in 1907 for the NATIONAL MUSEUM can be seen hanging on the main stairs. Later, in 1908, the Cuala Press was set up independently in Churchtown by the Yeats sisters, and they produced hand-made books and broadsheets. Some of these were written and illustrated by their brothers, JACK B. YEATS and W.B. YEATS who was also the editor of the press. Other prominent writers and artists also worked with the press. Reproductions of the broadsheets produced can still be found in print. The Cuala Press printing press is now in the Bunratty Folk Park, Co. Limerick.

## YEATS, WILLIAM BUTLER, (1865-1939).

Poet and dramatist, born at 5 Sandymount Avenue. More than any of his contemporaries, Yeats's life and work are inextricably bound up with the Ireland of his times and he both shaped and was shaped by the events of those years. Throughout his life, in tune with the changing tenor of the intellectual, political and spiritual turmoil which the country was experiencing, Yeats man-

*Yeats Memorial, St. Stephen's Green.*

aged to interpret these movements and transform them into inspired poetry. As one of the founder members of the ABBEY THEATRE, he contributed both to the practical realities of the theatre and as an experimental dramatist furnished it with compelling philosophic plays, derived from a mingling the Celtic and Japanese traditions. The riots in the Abbey, the RISING of 1916, the HUGH LANE GALLERY, CHARLES STEWART PARNELL, LADY GREGORY, J.M. SYNGE – contemporary events and personalities are all absorbed into Yeats's work and have become part of the intellectual fabric of Dublin. Simultaneously the poet and the man of affairs, Yeats was appointed to the Irish Senate, the upper house of the parliament, in 1922, where he made an important liberal contribution to the otherwise conservative debates. The following year he received the NOBEL PRIZE for Literature, the culminating honour of a remarkable life. In 1915 he had re-

*W.B. Yeats,*

jected the offer of a knighthood.

> You that would judge me, do not
> judge alone
> This book or that, come to this hal-
> lowed place
> Where my friends' portraits hang and
> look thereon;
> Ireland's history in their lineaments
> trace;
> Think where man's glory most be-
> gins and ends,
> And say my glory was I had such
> friends.

('The Municipal Gallery Revisited', W.B. Yeats.)

> Earth, receive an honoured guest;
> William Yeats is laid to rest;
> Let the Irish vessel lie
> Emptied of its poetry.

('In memory of W.B. Yeats', W.H. Auden.)

*YOLE*, The National Maritime Museum of Ireland, Haig Terrace, Dun Laoghaire. French longboat captured from the frigate *Résolue* during the 1796 French expedition to Bantry Bay. WOLFE TONE was on board another ship of the fleet, the *Indomitable*. The dimensions of the *Yole* are 11.6m (38ft) long and 2m (6ft 7in) breadth, with accommodation for ten oars and two lugsails. Prior to its presentation to the museum, the *Yole* had been since 1796 in Bantry House, Co. Cork, where up to the beginning of the twentieth century it was sailed annually in the Bantry regatta.

**YOUNG IRELAND MOVEMENT.** Mid-nineteenth-century Nationalist movement led by Thomas Davis and William Smith O'Brien and propagated through the pages of *The Nation* newspaper. More extreme in their views than the supporters of DANIEL O'CONNELL, the Young Irelanders demanded independence, not just HOME RULE. Following an unsuccessful armed rebellion in 1848, the movement disappeared.

**Z**AFFOIRINI, FILIPPO. Eight-eenth-century landscape and mythological artist, he decorated ALDBOROUGH HOUSE, North Circular Road, with a series of wall paintings, but these have now disappeared.

**ZOO, THE**, The Phoenix Park, Dublin 8, tel 771425. One of the oldest public zoos in Europe, Dublin Zoo was founded in 1831 by the Zoological Society of Dublin, which had been established in the previous year, with the grant of 2.2 hectares (5.5 acres) of the PHOENIX PARK by the Lord Lieutenant, the Duke of Northumberland. It became the ROYAL ZOOLOGICAL SOCIETY OF IRELAND in 1838 and gradually increased over the years to cover an area of 12.1 hectares (30 acres) in a setting of remarkable beauty. During the famine of the 1840s, the Zoo was in the impossible ethical position of having to feed animals while people were starving, but this was partly resolved by only using foodstuffs unsuitable for humans. During the 1916 RISING, the more common animals had to be slaughtered in order to provide food for the carnivores. Dublin Zoo is famous for its success in the breeding of animals, particularly lions, one of which went on to fame if not fortune as the roaring lion of the Metro Goldwyn Meyer film studios. Lion-breeding in the Zoo began in 1857 with the birth of the first lion cubs. Over 700 have been bred since then. The layout of the Zoo was designed by the landscape gardener Decimus Burton, and one of the early buildings, the quaint 1833 thatched entrance lodge, is still in use. The most attractive areas of the Zoo are those where the creatures can live as close to their natural habitat as possible. In recent years the accommodation of many of the larger animals has been greatly improved and the Zoo has concentrated on breeding endangered species. Particular successes have been recorded in the breeding of clouded leopards and Siberian tigers and hippopotami. All the animals one would expect to encounter are here, elephants, lions, tigers, orang utang, giraffe, cheetah, monkeys, reptiles, birds, bears and camels. The Zoo is run by a council which has a curious tradition, dating from its early years, of meeting for breakfast, which begins with porridge always eaten while standing. The rest of the meal may be taken sitting down. A miniature tram brings visitors on tours of the Zoo. An early response to the delightful setting of the Zoo, while fanciful in the extreme, is not really too far off the point, and gives an impression which is still to be felt today:

> Look at the grounds, ye that have travelled to London and Paris, and say, could a better spot be selected. As we enter the grounds, can we not fancy ourselves in paradise and see Adam and Eve walking in innocence amongst the creatures while they sported and frisked about them?

(*Dublin Penny Journal*, 1832.)

Zoo facilities include Pets' Corner, a number of restaurants, the Lion's Den coffee shop and the Aviary Restaurant, shops and kiosks. Open seven days a week, year round, except 25 and 26 December. Mon-Sat 9.30-6.00. Sun 11.00-6.00. The Zoo closes at sunset in winter. Admission charge. Bus 10 from city centre.

**'ZOZIMUS'**, (1794-1846). Blind ballad singer, born in Faddle Alley in the LIBERTIES, his actual name was Michael Moran. The nickname comes from one of his recitations, a poem about St. Mary of Egypt in which the Blessed Zozimus is mentioned. Zozimus, habitually dressed in a long cape, performed from a pitch on Carlisle now O'CONNELL BRIDGE, and recited rather than sang his compositions, which he sold on broadsheets to the passersby. Many of Zozimus's ballads have passed into the oral tradition and are still popularly performed. One of the most characteristic definitely attributed to him is 'The Finding of Moses' in which the Biblical story is told in a Middle Eastern location but with a decidedly local ambiance.

On Egypt's banks, contagious to the
  Nile.
The Ould Pharoah's daughter, she
  went to bathe in style.
She took her dip and she came unto
  the land,
And to dry her royal pelt she ran
  along the strand.
A bullrush tripped her whereupon she
  saw
A smiling babby in a wad of straw;
She took him up and says in accents
  mild
Oh taranagers, girls, now which of
  yis owns the child?'

# MAPS

# Historical Sites

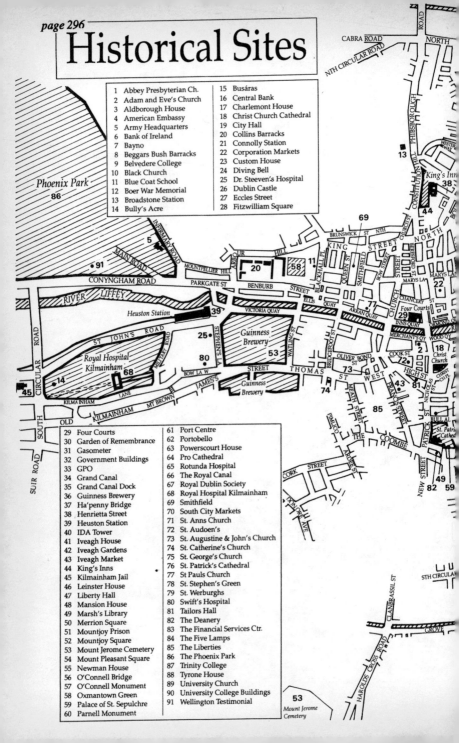

| | | | |
|---|---|---|---|
| 1 | Abbey Presbyterian Ch. | 15 | Busáras |
| 2 | Adam and Eve's Church | 16 | Central Bank |
| 3 | Aldborough House | 17 | Charlemont House |
| 4 | American Embassy | 18 | Christ Church Cathedral |
| 5 | Army Headquarters | 19 | City Hall |
| 6 | Bank of Ireland | 20 | Collins Barracks |
| 7 | Bayno | 21 | Connolly Station |
| 8 | Beggars Bush Barracks | 22 | Corporation Markets |
| 9 | Belvedere College | 23 | Custom House |
| 10 | Black Church | 24 | Diving Bell |
| 11 | Blue Coat School | 25 | Dr. Steeven's Hospital |
| 12 | Boer War Memorial | 26 | Dublin Castle |
| 13 | Broadstone Station | 27 | Eccles Street |
| 14 | Bully's Acre | 28 | Fitzwilliam Square |

| | | | |
|---|---|---|---|
| 29 | Four Courts | 61 | Port Centre |
| 30 | Garden of Remembrance | 62 | Portobello |
| 31 | Gasometer | 63 | Powerscourt House |
| 32 | Government Buildings | 64 | Pro Cathedral |
| 33 | GPO | 65 | Rotunda Hospital |
| 34 | Grand Canal | 66 | The Royal Canal |
| 35 | Grand Canal Dock | 67 | Royal Dublin Society |
| 36 | Guinness Brewery | 68 | Royal Hospital Kilmainham |
| 37 | Ha'penny Bridge | 69 | Smithfield |
| 38 | Henrietta Street | 70 | South City Markets |
| 39 | Heuston Station | 71 | St. Anns Church |
| 40 | IDA Tower | 72 | St. Audoen's |
| 41 | Iveagh House | 73 | St. Augustine & John's Church |
| 42 | Iveagh Gardens | 74 | St. Catherine's Church |
| 43 | Iveagh Market | 75 | St. George's Church |
| 44 | King's Inns | 76 | St. Patrick's Cathedral |
| 45 | Kilmainham Jail | 77 | St Pauls Church |
| 46 | Leinster House | 78 | St. Stephen's Green |
| 47 | Liberty Hall | 79 | St. Werburghs |
| 48 | Mansion House | 80 | Swift's Hospital |
| 49 | Marsh's Library | 81 | Tailors Hall |
| 50 | Merrion Square | 82 | The Deanery |
| 51 | Mountjoy Prison | 83 | The Financial Services Ctr. |
| 52 | Mountjoy Square | 84 | The Five Lamps |
| 53 | Mount Jerome Cemetery | 85 | The Liberties |
| 54 | Mount Pleasant Square | 86 | The Phoenix Park |
| 55 | Newman House | 87 | Trinity College |
| 56 | O'Connell Bridge | 88 | Tyrone House |
| 57 | O'Connell Monument | 89 | University Church |
| 58 | Oxmantown Green | 90 | University College Buildings |
| 59 | Palace of St. Sepulchre | 91 | Wellington Testimonial |
| 60 | Parnell Monument | | |

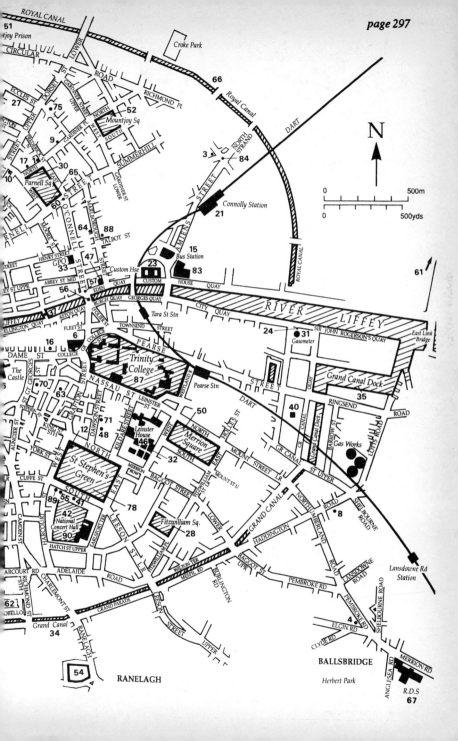

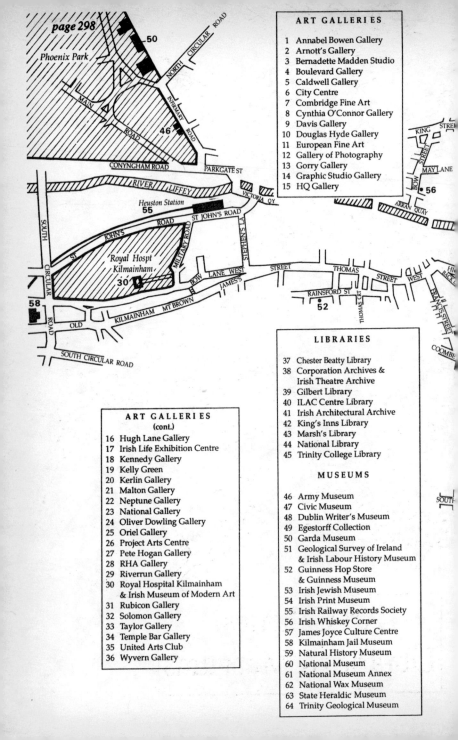

Phoenix Park

NORTH CIRCULAR ROAD

MAIN ROAD

CONYNGHAM ROAD

PARKGATE ST

50

46

RIVER LIFFEY

Heuston Station
55

ST JOHN'S ROAD

VICTORIA QY

ARRAN QUAY

ST JOHN'S ROAD

ROAD

JOHN'S

ST

SOUTH

CIRCULAR

Royal Hospt
Kilmainham
30

MILITARY ROAD

BOW LANE WEST

JAMES'S

STREET

ST JOHN'S

STREET

THOMAS

STREET WEST

58

ROAD

OLD

KILMAINHAM   MT BROWN

RAINSFORD ST

52

THOMAS CRT

FRANCIS STREET

HIGH BACK

SOUTH CIRCULAR ROAD

COOMBE

KING STREET

MAY LANE

BOW

56

SOUTH

## ART GALLERIES

1 Annabel Bowen Gallery
2 Arnott's Gallery
3 Bernadette Madden Studio
4 Boulevard Gallery
5 Caldwell Gallery
6 City Centre
7 Combridge Fine Art
8 Cynthia O'Connor Gallery
9 Davis Gallery
10 Douglas Hyde Gallery
11 European Fine Art
12 Gallery of Photography
13 Gorry Gallery
14 Graphic Studio Gallery
15 HQ Gallery

## LIBRARIES

37 Chester Beatty Library
38 Corporation Archives &
   Irish Theatre Archive
39 Gilbert Library
40 ILAC Centre Library
41 Irish Architectural Archive
42 King's Inns Library
43 Marsh's Library
44 National Library
45 Trinity College Library

## MUSEUMS

46 Army Museum
47 Civic Museum
48 Dublin Writer's Museum
49 Egestorff Collection
50 Garda Museum
51 Geological Survey of Ireland
   & Irish Labour History Museum
52 Guinness Hop Store
   & Guinness Museum
53 Irish Jewish Museum
54 Irish Print Museum
55 Irish Railway Records Society
56 Irish Whiskey Corner
57 James Joyce Culture Centre
58 Kilmainham Jail Museum
59 Natural History Museum
60 National Museum
61 National Museum Annex
62 National Wax Museum
63 State Heraldic Museum
64 Trinity Geological Museum

## ART GALLERIES
(cont.)

16 Hugh Lane Gallery
17 Irish Life Exhibition Centre
18 Kennedy Gallery
19 Kelly Green
20 Kerlin Gallery
21 Malton Gallery
22 Neptune Gallery
23 National Gallery
24 Oliver Dowling Gallery
25 Oriel Gallery
26 Project Arts Centre
27 Pete Hogan Gallery
28 RHA Gallery
29 Riverrun Gallery
30 Royal Hospital Kilmainham
   & Irish Museum of Modern Art
31 Rubicon Gallery
32 Solomon Gallery
33 Taylor Gallery
34 Temple Bar Gallery
35 United Arts Club
36 Wyvern Gallery

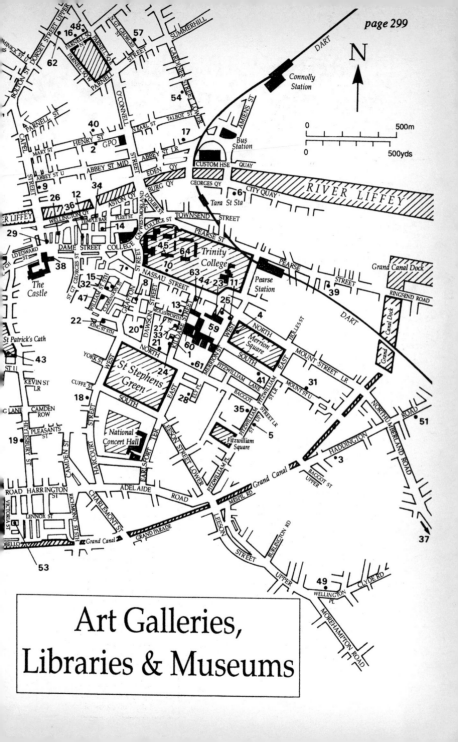

Art Galleries,
Libraries & Museums

# Theatres, Cinemas & Music Venues

**River Liffey**

Heuston Station

Royal Hosp. Kilmainham

ST. JOHN'S ROAD

MILITARY ROAD

STEPHEN'S LA.

BOW LA W

JAMES'S

KILMAINHAM MT BROWN

STREET

THOMAS STREET

USHER'S QUAY

MERCHANT'S Q.

COOK ST.

HIGH ST.

CHRIST CH. "PL"

WINETAVERN

LD EDWARD ST.

WOOD QY

PATRICK ST.

NICHOLAS ST.

FRANCIS STREET

THE COOMBE

BLACK LA.

Kings Inns

KING ST NTH

BOLTON ST.

CAPEL STREET

DORSET ST.

PARK

ABBE

17

13

14

37

48

8

12

30

45

44

54

## ▲ THEATRES

1 Abbey Theatre
2 Andrews Lane Theatre
3 Carrolls Theatre
4 Focus Theatre
5 Gaiety Theatre
6 Gate Theatre
7 Lombard Street Studio
8 Olympia Theatre
9 Peacock Theatre
10 Players Theatre (TCD)
11 Point Depot and Theatre
12 Project Arts Centre
13 Rupert Guinness Hall
14 Tivoli Theatre
15 The Damer Hall
16 The International Bar
17 The Royal Hospt. Kilmainham

## ■ CINEMAS

18 Adelphi Cinema
19 Cameo Cinema
20 Carlton Cinema
21 Savoy Cinema
22 The Lighthouse Cinema
23 The Screen Cinema College St.
24 The Screen Cinema O'Connell Br.
25 Irish Film Centre

DOLPHIN'S BARN

SOUTH CIRCULAR ROAD

Grand Canal

HARRING

LENNOX

PORTO

RATHMINES

LEINSTER ROAD

38

52

## ● MUSIC VENUES

26 Alliance Francaise
27 An Beal Bocht
28 Bad Bobs
29 Bartley Dunnes
30 Clarençe Hotel
31 Goethe Institute
32 House of Lords (Bank of Irel.)
33 Hugh Lane Gallery
34 Jurys Hotel
35 Lansdowne Road Stadium
36 McGonagles
37 Mother Redcaps Tavern
38 National Stadium
39 O'Donoghues
40 RDS
41 RHA Gallery
42 Royal Irish Academy of Music
43 R&R Musical Society
44 SFX
45 Slatterys
46 St. Stephens Church
47 The Baggot Inn
48 The Brazen Head
49 The College of Music
50 The City Centre
51 The Dublin Underground
52 The Lower Deck
53 The National Concert Hall
54 The Pipers Club
55 The Waterfront
56 Comhaltas Ceoltóirí, Monkstown

43

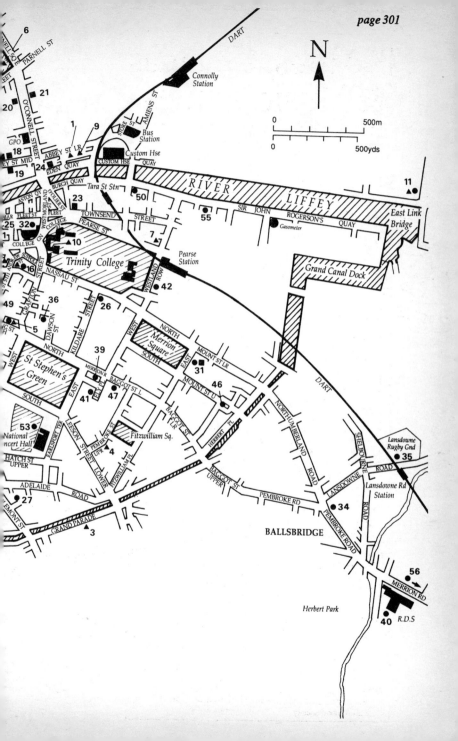

N

0        500m

0        500yds

**6**

PARNELL ST

**21**

**20**

O'CONNELL STREET

GPO

**18**

**19** **24**

ABBEY ST LR

EDEN QUAY

BURGH QUAY

AMIENS ST

STORE ST

Connolly Station

Bus Station

Custom Hse

Custom Hse Quay

**1** **9**

Tara St Stn

**23**

TOWNSEND STREET

PEARSE ST

**50**

**55**

RIVER LIFFEY

SIR JOHN ROGERSON'S QUAY

Gasometer

**11**

East Link Bridge

ASTON QY

FLEET ST

**25** **32**

COLLEGE

COLLEGE ST

**16**

NASSAU ST

**10**

Trinity College

Pearse Station

**7**

**42**

WESTLAND ROW

Grand Canal Dock

**49**

**36**

**5**

DAWSON ST

**26**

KILDARE STREET

WEST

NORTH

Merrion Square

EAST

SOUTH

MOUNT ST LR

**31**

MOUNT ST U

**46**

St Stephen's Green

SOUTH

**39**

MERRION R

BAGGOT ST L

**41** **47**

BAGGOT ST LR

NORTH

EAST

DART

NORTHUMBERLAND ROAD

**53**

National Concert Hall

EARLSFORT TER

LEESON STREET LR

PEMBROKE ST UPR

**4**

Fitzwilliam Sq.

FITZWILLIAM PL

HERBERT PL

BAGGOT ST UPPER

SHELBOURNE ROAD

Lansdowne Rugby Gnd

**35**

HATCH ST UPPER

ADELAIDE ROAD

**27**

MONT ST

GRAND PARADE

**3**

PEMBROKE RD

Lansdowne Rd Station

LANSDOWNE ROAD

**BALLSBRIDGE**

**34**

**56**

MERRION RD

**40** R.D.S

Herbert Park

# City Centre Pubs & Restaurants

## ▲ PUBS

1 Alfie Byrnes
2 Anna Livia
3 Bad Bobs
4 Bowes
5 Doheny & Nesbitts
6 Hartigans
7 Hughes
8 Hunters
9 McGraths
10 Mulligans
11 Mother Redcaps Tavern
12 O'Donoghues
13 O'Dwyers
14 Slatterys
15 The Auld Dubliner
16 The Baggot Inn
17 The Brazen Head
18 The Foggy Dew
19 The Harp
20 The Norseman
21 The Oval
22 The Palace Bar
23 The Parnell
24 The Pembroke
25 The Temple Bar
26 Toners

## ● RESTAURANTS

27 Beshoffs
28 Bewley's (Mary St)
29 Bewley's (Westmor. St)
30 Burdocks
31 Gallaghers Boxty Hse.
32 Kylemore
33 La Vie En Rose
34 Little Lisbon
35 Locks
36 National Gallery Restaurant
37 Nicos
38 Patrick Guilbaud
39 Puerto - Bella
40 Tante Zoes
41 The Bad Ass Café
42 The Elephant & Castle
43 The Grey Door
44 The Old Dublin
45 Well Fed Café
46 Whites of the Green

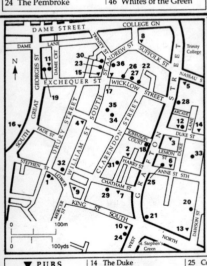

## ▼ PUBS

1 Bartley Dunnes
2 Bruxelles
3 Davy Byrnes
4 Grogans
5 Judge Roy Beans
6 Kehoes
7 Nearys
8 O'Neills
9 Peter's Pub
10 Sinnotts
11 Stag's Head
12 The Bailey
13 The Dawson Lounge
14 The Duke
15 The Old Stand
16 The Long Hall
17 The International Bar

## ● RESTAURANTS

18 Bewley's (Grafton St)
19 Bewley's (Sth Gt George's St)
20 Café Kiara
21 Captain Americas
22 Casper & Giumbini
23 Cedar Tree
24 Chicago Pizza Pie Factory
25 Coffee Inn
26 Cornucopia
27 Imperial Chinese
28 McDonalds
29 Pasta Fresca
30 Quo Vadis
31 Rajdoot Tandoori
32 Shay Beano
33 The Buttery Brasserie
34 The Periwinkle
35 The Salad Bowl
36 Trocadero

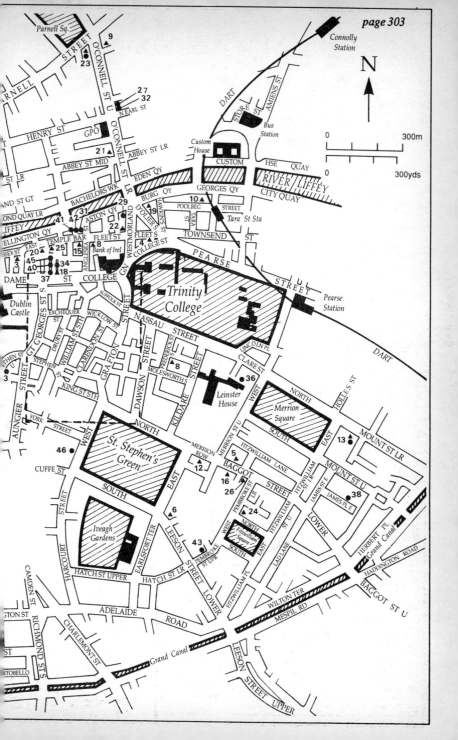

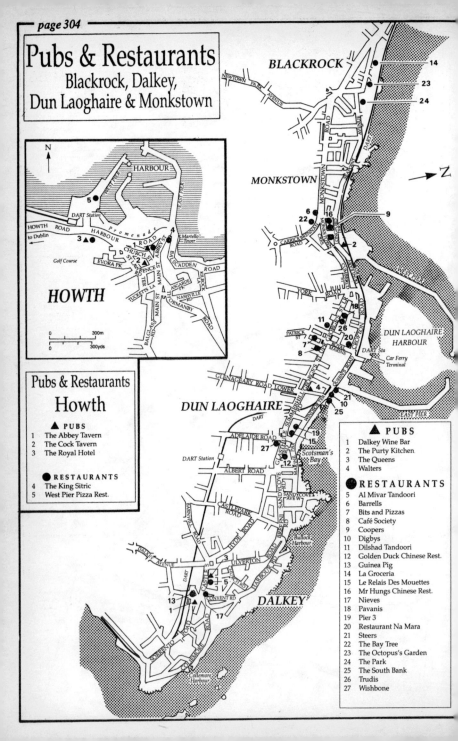

# Pubs & Restaurants
## Blackrock, Dalkey, Dun Laoghaire & Monkstown

**HOWTH**

## Pubs & Restaurants
## Howth

▲ PUBS
1 The Abbey Tavern
2 The Cock Tavern
3 The Royal Hotel

● RESTAURANTS
4 The King Sitric
5 West Pier Pizza Rest.

▲ PUBS
1 Dalkey Wine Bar
2 The Purty Kitchen
3 The Queens
4 Walters

● RESTAURANTS
5 Al Mivar Tandoori
6 Barrells
7 Bits and Pizzas
8 Café Society
9 Coopers
10 Digbys
11 Dilshad Tandoori
12 Golden Duck Chinese Rest.
13 Guinea Pig
14 La Groceria
15 Le Relais Des Mouettes
16 Mr Hungs Chinese Rest.
17 Nieves
18 Pavanis
19 Pier 3
20 Restaurant Na Mara
21 Steers
22 The Bay Tree
23 The Octopus's Garden
24 The Park
25 The South Bank
26 Trudis
27 Wishbone

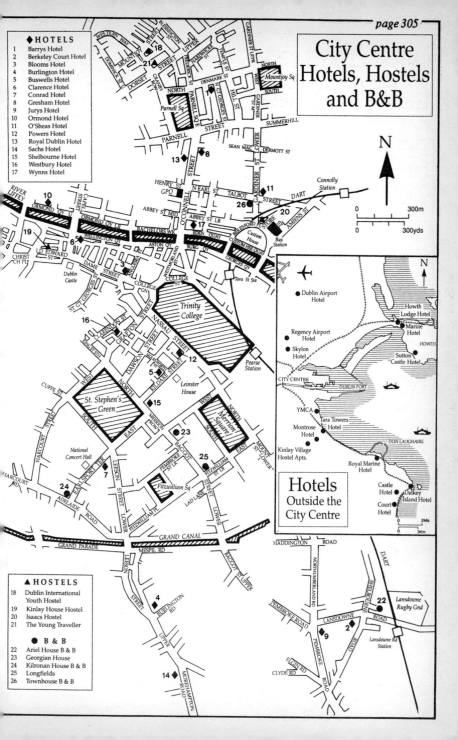

# City Centre Hotels, Hostels and B&B

## ◆ HOTELS

1. Barrys Hotel
2. Berkeley Court Hotel
3. Blooms Hotel
4. Burlington Hotel
5. Buswells Hotel
6. Clarence Hotel
7. Conrad Hotel
8. Gresham Hotel
9. Jurys Hotel
10. Ormond Hotel
11. O'Sheas Hotel
12. Powers Hotel
13. Royal Dublin Hotel
14. Sachs Hotel
15. Shelbourne Hotel
16. Westbury Hotel
17. Wynns Hotel

## ▲ HOSTELS

18. Dublin International Youth Hostel
19. Kinlay House Hostel
20. Isaacs Hostel
21. The Young Traveller

## ● B & B

22. Ariel House B & B
23. Georgian House
24. Kilronan House B & B
25. Longfields
26. Townhouse B & B

## Hotels Outside the City Centre

Dublin Airport Hotel
Regency Airport Hotel
Skylon Hotel
Howth Lodge Hotel
Marine Hotel
Sutton Castle Hotel
YMCA
Tara Towers Hotel
Montrose Hotel
Kinlay Village Hostel Apts.
Royal Marine Hotel
Castle Hotel
Dalkey Island Hotel
Court Hotel

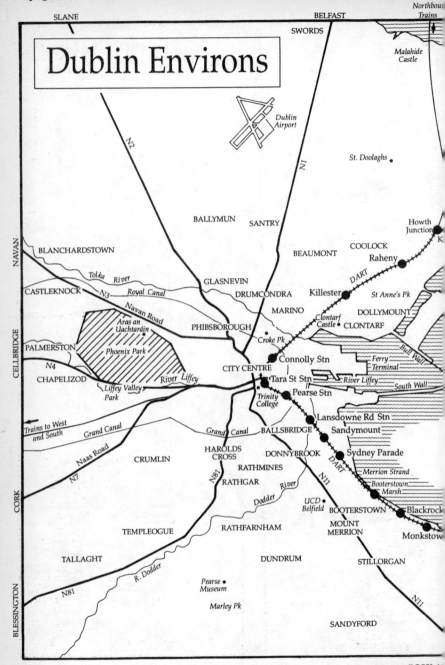

# Dublin Environs

SLANE     BELFAST     *Northbound Trains*

SWORDS

*Malahide Castle*

Dublin Airport

St. Doolaghs

N2

N1

BALLYMUN    SANTRY

Howth Junction

BLANCHARDSTOWN

BEAUMONT    COOLOCK

Raheny

NAVAN

CASTLEKNOCK

*Tolka River*

GLASNEVIN

DART

*Royal Canal*

Killester

St Anne's Pk

N3

*Navan Road*

DRUMCONDRA

PALMERSTON

Aras an Uachtardin

PHIBSBOROUGH

MARINO

DOLLYMOUNT

Clontarf Castle

CLONTARF

N4

*Phoenix Park*

Croke Pk

CELLBRIDGE

CHAPELIZOD

*Liffey Valley Park*

*River Liffey*

CITY CENTRE

Connolly Stn

Tara St Stn

*Ferry Terminal*

*Bull Wall*

*River Liffey*

*South Wall*

Pearse Stn

Trinity College

*Trains to West and South*

*Grand Canal*

Lansdowne Rd Stn

*Grand Canal*

BALLSBRIDGE

Sandymount

*Naas Road*

CRUMLIN

HAROLDS CROSS

DONNYBROOK

Sydney Parade

*Merrion Strand*

N7

N81

RATHMINES

RATHGAR

*Dodder River*

N11

*Booterstown Marsh*

UCD Belfield

BOOTERSTOWN

Blackrock

CORK

TEMPLEOGUE

RATHFARNHAM

MOUNT MERRION

Monkstown

DART

TALLAGHT

*R. Dodder*

DUNDRUM

STILLORGAN

N81

Pearse Museum

N11

BLESSINGTON

*Marley Pk*

SANDYFORD

*Wicklow Mtns.*     ROSSLA

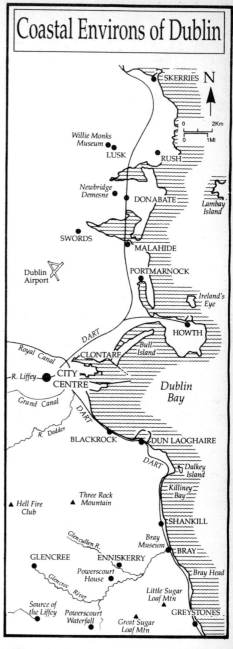

## Coastal Environs of Dublin

# Acknowledgements

I wish to thank the directors and staff of the many public and private institutions who were unfailingly helpful to me in my research for this book, in particular, The Arts Council – An Chomhairle Ealaíon, Allied Irish Bank, Bord Failte, The Board of Works, CAFE, Dublin and East Tourism, Dublin Bus, Dublin Corporation, Dublin Corporation Archives, Dublin Civic Museum, The Electricity Supply Board, The Gilbert Library, The Hugh Lane Municipal Gallery of Modern Art, The Irish Booksellers Association, The Irish Architectural Archive, The Irish Museum of Modern Art, The Astronomical Society of Ireland, The ILAC Centre Library, The Irish Peatland Conservation Council, The Italian Cultural Institute, The James Joyce Cultural Centre, The National College of Art and Design, The National Gallery of Ireland, The National Library of Ireland, The National Museum of Ireland, The Natural History Museum, The Old Dublin Society, The Royal Hospital Kilmainham, Scott, Tallon and Walker, Trinity College Dublin. My thanks are due to the following publishers and copyright holders for permission to use quotations from copyright material: Faber & Faber for Samuel Beckett, W. H. Auden, Louis McNeice and J.M. Synge; Beatrice Behan and Methuen & Co. for Brendan Behan; John Murray (Publishers) Ltd. for John Betjeman; Secker and Warburg for Christy Brown; Dardis Clarke and Wake Forest University Press for Austin Clarke; The Devin-Adair Co. for Oliver St. John Gogarty; The Society of Authors for James Joyce; Oxford University Press for Gerard Manley Hopkins; Eunan O'Halpin for Patrick Kavanagh; Rupert Hart-Davis for Flann O'Brien. Also my thanks are due to Peter Pearson for his careful reading of the text and his perceptive comments, to Sadbh Model for negotiations and to Allegra and Eve Lalor who organised the illustrations, to Frances Power for her diligent and patient editing, to Ide ní Laoghaire, David Sheehan, Peggie Dordan. Lastly, to the many individuals too numerous to mention who helped in different ways, I take this opportunity of extending my thanks.

**A Valley of Kings**
**THE BOYNE**

**Henry Boylan**

An inspired guide to the myths, magic and literature of this beautiful valley with its mysterious 5000-year-old monuments at Newgrange. Illustrated. *Paperback*

**TRADITIONAL IRISH RECIPES**

*George L. Thomson*

Handwritten in beautiful calligraphy, a collection of favourite recipes from the Irish tradition. *Paperback*

**SPLENDID FOOD**

*Guide & Recipes from Irish Country Houses*

**Gillian Berwick**

Mouthwatering recipes from Ireland's beautiful country houses, with detailed information on accommodation, opening times etc. *Paperback.*

**THE BLASKET ISLANDS**

*Next Parish America*

**Joan and Ray Stagles**

The history, characters, social organisation, nature - all aspects of this most fascinating and historical of islands. Illustrated. *Paperback*

## SKELLIG
*Island Outpost of Europe*

### Des Lavelle
Probably Europe's strangest monument from the Early Christian era, this island, several miles out to sea, was the home of an early monastic settlement. Illustrated.
*Paperback*


## DUBLIN — One Thousand Years
### Stephen Conlin
A short history of Dublin with unique full colour reconstruction drawings based on the latest research.
*Hardback & Paperback*

## CELTIC WAY OF LIFE
The social and political life of the Celts of early Ireland. A simple and popular history. Illustrated. *Paperback*

## MARY ROBINSON
*A President with a Purpose*

### Fergus Finlay
Fascinating account of the Robinson campaign. The making of a President as it really happened. *Paperback*

## LAND OF MY CRADLE DAYS
*Recollections from a Country Childhood*

### Martin Morrissey
A touching and informative account of growing up in County Clare during the war years. Sensitive, detailed, moving story of a bygone era. *Paperback*

## Children's Books

**BIKE HUNT**

*A Story of Thieves and Kidnappers*

**Hugh Galt**

An exciting story, set in Dublin and county Wicklow - winner of the Young People's Books medal in the Irish Book Awards. *Paperback*

**CYRIL**

*The Tale of an Orphaned Squirrel*

**Eugene McCabe - illustrated by Al O'Donnell**

A moving story set in nature - winner of the Reading Association Award. *Paperback*

**JIMEEN**

*A Comic Irish Classic*

**Pádraig O Siochfhradha - illustrated by Brian Bourke**

The first English translation of the much-loved antics of this madcap character. *Paperback*

**THE LUCKY BAG**

*Classic Irish Children's Stories*

**Ed. Eilis Dillon, Pat Donlon, Pat Egan and Peter Fallon**

**- illustrated by Martin Gale**

A collection of the best in Irish children's literature. *Paperback*

## THE LOST ISLAND
**Eilis Dillon** - *illustrated by David Rooney*
The mystery and danger of the sea in this gripping adventure story. *Paperback*

## FAERY NIGHTS/ OICHEANTA SÍ
*Micheál Mac Liammóir*
A unique treasury of Celtic stories in dual language texts and illustrated by the author. *Paperback*

## THE LITTLE BLACK SHEEP
*Written and illustrated by Elizabeth Shaw*
A simple, charming book to delight the younger child. *Boards*

## HEROIC TALES from the Ulster Cycle
Classic stories derived from ancient Irish Legends. *Paperback*

## THE COOL MAC COOL
**Gordon Snell - Illustrated by Wendy Shea**
The life and times of legendary Celtic hero Finn MacCool. *Paperback*

## EXPLORING THE BOOK OF KELLS
**George Otto Simms**
**Illustrated by David Rooney & Eoin O'Brien**
A world-renowned authority offers a compact guide to an outstanding national treasure. *Hardback*

## BRENDAN THE NAVIGATOR
*Explorer of the Ancient World*
### George Otto Simms
### Illustrated by David Rooney
One of the great adventures of the world. Made famous by Tim Severin. *Paperback.*

## JANEY MACK ME SHIRT IS BLACK
*Eamonn MacThomáis*
The street rhymes, stories and incidents of bygone Dublin. *Paperback*

## TOMMY -THE THEATRE CAT
*Maureen Potter - illustrated by David Rooney*
A charming tale of backstage theatre life by this well-known entertainer. *Paperback*

## CHRISTMAS WONDER
*Craftwork, Lore, Poems, Songs and Stories*
### Seán C. O'Leary - various illustrations
A lively collection of Irish traditions and lore, with lots of things to make and do. *Paperback*

## *Busy Fingers - Art and Craft Series*
*1 Spring 2 Summer 3 Autumn/Halloween*

*4 Christmas/Winter*
### Seán C. O'Leary
A popular collection of simple and attractive things to make throughout the year. Paperback. Also available as a pack of four books. *Paperbacks*

*O'Brien Junior Biography Library*

**1 WOLFE TONE**
**2 W.B. YEATS**
**3 GRANUAILE**
**4 BOB GELDOF**
**5 JONATHAN SWIFT**
**6 COUNTESS MARKIEVICZ**
**Mary Moriarty and Catherine Sweeney**
Major world figures in simple accessible language. Beautifully illustrated. *Paperbacks*


## CHILDREN'S TAPES
**The Boyne Valley Book and Tape of**
**IRISH LEGENDS**
**Brenda Maguire - illustrated by Peter Haigh**
Favourite legends told by: Gay Byrne, Cyril Cusack, Maureen Potter, Rosaleen Linehan, John B. Keane, Twink.

**TELL ME A STORY, PAT**
*Pat Ingoldsby*
Eight stories, seven poems - over an hour of fantasy, fun and magic.

The above is a short selection from the O'Brien Press list. A full list is available at bookshops throughout Ireland. All our books can be purchased at bookshops countrywide. If you require any information or have difficulty in getting our books, contact us.

**THE O'BRIEN PRESS**
20 Victoria Road, Rathgar, Dublin 6.
Tel. (01) 979598
Fax. (01) 979274